Lift High the Cross

Related titles available from Canterbury Press

Anglican Papalism: A History
Michael Yelton   978 1 85311 861 6

Alfred Hope Patten and the Shrine of Our Lady of Walsingham
Michael Yelton   978 1 85311 753 4

Outposts of the Faith: Anglo-Catholicism in Some Rural Parishes
Michael Yelton   978 1 85311 985 9

The Labour of Obedience: The Benedictines of Nashdom, Pershore and Elmore
Peta Dunstan   978 1 85311 974 3

Merrily on High: An Anglo-Catholic Memoir
Colin Stephenson 978 1 85311 912 5

Walsingham Way
Colin Stephenson 978 1 85311 913 2

www.canterburypress.co.uk

Lift High the Cross

Anglo-Catholics and the Congress Movement

John Gunstone

In association with
The Society of the Faith

© John Gunstone 2010

First published in 2010 by the Canterbury Press Norwich
Editorial office
13–17 Long Lane,
London, EC1A 9PN, UK

Canterbury Press is an imprint of Hymns Ancient and
Modern Ltd (a registered charity)
St Mary's Works, St Mary's Plain,
Norwich, NR3 3BH, UK
www.scm-canterburypress.co.uk

All rights reserved. No part of this publication may be reproduced,
stored in a retrieval system, or transmitted,
in any form or by any means, electronic, mechanical,
photocopying or otherwise, without the prior permission of
the publisher, Canterbury Press.

The Author has asserted his right under the Copyright,
Designs and Patents Act, 1988,
to be identified as the Author of this Work

British Library Cataloguing in Publication data

A catalogue record for this book is available
from the British Library

978 1 85311 817 3

CONTENTS

Introduction	ix
1 Preparations for the First Congress	1
2 England in the 1920s and 1930s	12
3 The Church of England	24
4 The First Congress 1920	38
5 Weston and the Lambeth Conference 1920	54
6 Catholics and the Church Assembly	74
7 The Congress Follow-up and the First Priests' Convention 1921	86
8 The Provincial Congresses	108
9 The Second Congress 1923	122
10 Communities, Societies and the *Church Times*	141
11 The Congress Movement	161
12 Prayer Book Revision	175
13 The Eucharistic Congress 1927	185
14 Reservation and the Birmingham Rebels	199
15 Summer Schools, Strikes and Slums	216
16 Conversions to Rome	232
17 The Fourth Congress 1930	251
18 The Parishes	269
19 The Faithful	281
20 Worship and the Arts	293

21 Preparations for the Centenary and the Second Priests' Convention 1932	305
22 The Centenary Congress 1933	322
Postscript	343
Notes	349
Brief Biographies	361
Bibliography	364
Index of People	369

Lift high the Cross, the love of Christ proclaim
Till all the world adore His Sacred Name.[1]

Lift High the Cross is co-published with
THE SOCIETY OF THE FAITH

The Society of the Faith is a small charity founded in 1905 by two high-churchmen, the Revd Canon J A Douglas, Vicar of St Luke's Camberwell, and his brother, the Revd C E Douglas.

The Douglas brothers were deeply committed to the catholic tradition within the Church of England. The Society they founded was to be 'an Association of Christians in communion with the See of Canterbury for mutual assistance in the work of Christ's Church and for the furtherance of such charitable undertakings as may from time to time be decided upon, more especially for the popularisation of Catholic faith.'

The Society's first work was the printing of Sunday School stamps, which proved immensely popular. This success inspired the foundation of Faith Press, publishing books both scholarly and popular, as well as church music.

In 1916 the Society also founded Faith-Craft to produce high quality vestments and church furnishings. Their biggest single commission was the complete refurbishment of St Mary le Bow in London after the Second World War.

The Douglas brothers lived on into the 1950s. Times (and tastes) were beginning to change, and this eventually led to the closure of both Faith Press and Faith-Craft in 1973. However, the Society of the Faith remains committed to its original objectives, seeking to promote good standards in publishing and church furnishing, and in theological education. Recent co-publications with the Canterbury Press include Michael Yelton's book *Anglican Papalism* (2005) and Paula Gooder's Advent book *The Meaning is in the Waiting* (2008).

Since 1935 the Society has held the lease of Faith House, 7 Tufton Street, Westminster. Faith House is currently home to the church furnishers Watts & Company, and to Students Partnership Worldwide, 'the global leader in supporting young people to address the urgent health, education, and environmental issues which affect their lives, communities, and countries'.

The Society of the Faith – Faith House, 7 Tufton Street, London SW1P 3QB
Registered in England as a Limited Company number 214216
Registered with the Charity Commission number 232821

INTRODUCTION

This is the story of the Anglo-Catholic Congresses and their role in the Church of England during the years between the first and second great wars. They took place at a time of great change in the nation's life, so Chapter 2 introduces the political, economic, and social background to the Church's ministry and mission during these years. Chapter 3 gives a similar account of the situation in the Church of England within which the Congress movement developed alongside other Anglo-Catholic societies. The interaction between the rest of the Church, these societies, and the movement itself forms the main theme of the story.

Printed reports of talks given at meetings such as the Congresses do not usually make interesting reading, except perhaps for those who delivered them. I have, therefore, been selective in summarizing what was said in the Albert Hall and elsewhere. As a general guide I have chosen passages which are, I hope, relevant for what they tell us of Anglo-Catholic attitudes to the affairs and controversies of the time, particularly those which show how far ideas and practices have been developed over the years since. In most cases I have included one or more quotations to illustrate how a speaker presented his or her subject.

In the book I have dropped the clergy's titles and simply referred to priests by their initials and surname. I have, however, retained the custom of calling members of religious orders 'Father' when they are introduced for the first time in a chapter to distinguish them from secular clergy. Lay people are introduced as Mr, Mrs, etc. Readers who lose track of who's who as they read the book can refer to the Brief Biographies section at the end.

I regret that I have not been able to describe in detail events related to the Congresses organized in Scotland, Wales, Northern Ireland, other parts of the Anglican Communion and the USA. To attempt this would have taken the story beyond the limits I set for myself.

The illustrations are reproduced from pictures which appeared in the *Church Times* and in other publications at the time, so they may not have the quality we expect today.

I am grateful to the Society of the Faith for a grant towards the cost of the publication of this book, and to the Anglo-Catholic History Society for publishing two preliminary papers by me on the Congresses. Canon Alan Wilkinson, Dr John Taylor, Mr Michael Yelton, Mr Michael Smith-Bristow and Mr John Rackham kindly sent me material which was extremely useful. Christine Smith and the staff of Canterbury Press have, as usual, assisted me in various ways. I especially thank the Revd Reg Macklin for his help in reading and commenting on drafts of many of the chapters. And, above all, I want to thank my wife Margaret for her prayers and support during my work on this book.

John Gunstone
Holy Cross Day, 2009

I

Preparations for the First Congress

The Anglo-Catholic Congress movement had a modest beginning. Just before the 1914–18 war H. F. B. Mackay, the vicar of All Saints, Margaret Street, and P. H. Leary, vicar of St Augustine, Kilburn, friends since their Oxford days, formed a monthly dining club for incumbents of Catholic parishes in London. Members met in each others' vicarages in turn to read and debate a paper which one of them had prepared. They limited their number to twelve, but when other clergy wanted to join, further clubs were arranged during the next two or three years in different parts of the city. Younger clergy had fun giving the clubs names. Mackay's twelve were called 'The Apostles'; other groups 'The Wise Men from the East', 'The Wild Men of the West', 'The Northern Lights', and so on. It was a member of the Wise Men from the East, C. R. Deakin, the vicar of Christ Church, South Hackney, who suggested that after the war there should be a conference of Catholic priests in London so that they could get to know one another and clarify their aims when peace returned. The suggestion was passed on to Mackay's group. After the armistice it was followed up with a meeting of clergy and laymen at All Saints on 26 May 1919. The meeting agreed that such an event should be organized the following year in Church House, Westminster, and those present offered £1,000 to underwrite the expenses.

The title 'Congress' was chosen as it was understood to mean a gathering which was simply consultative and educational; titles such as 'synod' or 'council' were regarded as more authoritative. Church Congresses had been a familiar feature in the life of the Church of England since they began in the 1870s. These usually took place annually when clergy and laity chosen from the dioceses met for several days to discuss theological, pastoral and national concerns. Different dioceses acted as hosts each year. In October 1920 the Chelmsford diocese was the host, and the Church Congress was held at Southend-on-Sea. Catholics were sometimes invited to speak at the Church Congresses but they felt they had no real opportunity in them to explain their beliefs and practices adequately. Some of those at Mackay's meeting would have remembered that in 1908 the Roman Catholic Church had organized a Eucharistic Congress based at Westminster Cathedral, when a proposed procession of the Blessed Sacrament through the streets of London roused such a controversy that questions were asked in Parliament.

Mackay seemed to be the obvious choice for a chairman of the proposed Congress. As incumbent of one of the most famous Catholic parishes in the London diocese, he was regarded as a leader and known to be trusted by his bishop, Arthur Winnington-Ingram, who had offered him the living in 1908. But Mackay held back. Although in public he was an outstanding preacher and teacher, in private he was shy and reserved, giving the impression of aloofness. He never saw himself as a leader and preferred to encourage others to be at the forefront. So another member of the Apostles, Marcus Atlay, vicar of St Matthew, Westminster, was asked to take the chair. Since St Matthew's clergy house was round the corner from Church House, it would provide a convenient administrative centre for the Congress. The choice of Atlay turned out to be providential. At this stage the group had no idea that what they imagined would be a gathering of a few hundred clergy would snowball into a rally of thousands. But when it did, Atlay had the enthusiasm and organizing ability to cope with it. For years afterwards the 1920 gathering was known as 'Father Atlay's Congress'.

Atlay was the son of a former Bishop of Hereford. An Oxford graduate trained at Cuddesdon, he went as a newly ordained curate to St Matthew's in 1904 to serve under W. B. Trevelyan, who had built the church up into a well-known Catholic centre during a long incumbency. Trevelyan left shortly after Atlay's arrival, and the senior curate, G. Hockley, was appointed the next vicar. When Hockley left in 1914 Atlay, who by then was the senior curate, succeeded him.

St Matthew, Westminster, like other large Catholic parishes in London and elsewhere, had a staff of unmarried clergy. The four curates lived in the clergy house with their vicar. They were looked after by a cook, one or two housemaids and an odd-job man. The church attracted folk from the slums and flats in the parish as well as well-to-do families from the West End. On Sundays the right-hand side of the nave was reserved for men only, as was the custom in many such churches. These varied from high-ranking military officers, Members of Parliament and judges, to the owner of a fish barrow and working men from nearby Old Pye Street and Perkins' Rents. On the left-hand side were women of a similar social mix. On average four hundred people received Communion at the early masses on Sundays and weekdays; this did not include the crowds who attended the Sunday non-communicating high mass.

PREPARATIONS FOR THE FIRST CONGRESS

The list of members of the parochial church council included names such as Sir George Arthur, Major General Carlton Jones and Commander R. U. Davis. Finances were strong. The clergy were paid above the recommended diocesan level, and large sums were spent on social welfare in the neighbourhood. Again like many such parishes, St Matthew's sponsored guilds and clubs for children, young people, men and women. Trevelyan Hall, built near the church in Atlay's time, was the focus of these activities. Nuns of the All Saints' community supervised the pastoral work among the women and children and looked after the Good Shepherd Mission in Strutton Ground. There was also a church primary school. St Matthew's had close connections with the Universities' Mission to Central Africa (UMCA), whose offices were nearby. Some of its clergy went on to serve in Africa, including Frank Weston, one of Trevelyan's curates, who became Bishop of Zanzibar. It was because of this strong parochial base that Atlay was able to respond to the increasing demands when the proposed Congress grew into something bigger. He could enlist the assistance of able and reliable men and women from the congregation to help him – and appeal to them for finance.

He was fortunate in having a competent assistant in one of his curates, H. A. Wilson. In his book *Received with Thanks* Wilson wrote an account of working with Atlay. He described his vicar as a tall man with considerable personal authority, who could sometimes upset people with his forthright manner and brisk chairmanship but then charm them with his gentle kindness and generous hospitality. Wilson judged him to be a capable teacher rather than an inspiring preacher.

Although he was strict with his staff in matters of punctuality and dress outside as well as inside the church, Atlay treated them as equals rather than as subordinates – a collaborative style of ministry. Wilson's book was written in 1940 when he was a parish priest in the East End, facing the prospect of the Blitz, so perhaps it was coloured by memories of busy and happy curacy days. But there is no reason to doubt him when he wrote of Atlay: 'In public he was often, as he had need to be, stern, vehement, austere, severe. At the altar and in the ministration of any of the other sacraments he was nothing but a reverent priest; who – like all such who entertain a lively sense of their vocation and profession – "seeks both to draw aside the veil that conceals God from his people, and to hide himself in its folds". But we, who lived with him and were acquainted with not a little of his private life, knew that side by side with all this his boyhood never wholly left him; and this was not the very least of the reasons why we loved him as we did.'[1]

On the day in 1919 when he returned from the meeting in Margaret Street, Atlay went to Wilson's room and announced to his curate, 'Next year there's going to be an Anglo-Catholic Congress.' 'Oh,' Wilson said, 'and what on earth is that?' 'I'm not at all sure yet,' Atlay replied; 'but you're the secretary, and I'm the chairman.'[2]

The first task was to form an executive committee. Invitations were sent to incumbents of other Catholic churches, including A. Montford of the Ascension, Lavender Hill, E. A. Morgan of St Andrew, Willesden, H. Ross of St Alban, Holborn, and a number of laymen. To encourage support from outside London, diocesan groups of the Federation of Catholic Priests (FCP) were invited to send representatives. Among those who joined from the provinces were F. Underhill of St Alban the Martyr, Birmingham, G. H. Clayton, vicar of St Mary-the-Less, Cambridge, and Dr Darwell Stone, Principal of Pusey House, Oxford.

The organizers realized the importance of gaining the support of the English Church Union (ECU) – the oldest and largest of the Catholic societies in the Church of England – so they also invited on to the executive Sir Robert Newman, MP, the president, A Pinchard, the newly appointed general secretary, and Mr H. W. Hill, the former general secretary. Lord Halifax, the previous president (he had just retired from that office) was almost certainly invited but his name did not appear on the executive's list. His wife had recently died and he was ill at this time, so he may have felt he could not give any practical help (he was over eighty). Or perhaps he was initially suspicious of the organizers' intentions. If so, he changed his mind later and was the main speaker at a Congress anniversary rally in the Albert Hall in 1925. The Bishop of London may have turned down an invitation to be president of the Congress for the same reason, although he sent a letter of commendation to the executive – and, as we shall see, turned up at the last meeting.

The hall in Church House which seated 1,500 was booked for a week in May 1920. Letters about the proposed Congress were sent round the country to eight hundred incumbents who might be interested. Then came an unexpected change of plan. When news of the proposal spread, numerous laity asked why attendance at the Congress was restricted to clergy. They wanted to come as well. Protests came from so many quarters that the executive decided they must accede to the request. On 23 January that year Wilson inserted a letter in the *Church Times* asking those who hoped to be present to send him a postcard. To his astonishment two thousand cards arrived in the post within a few days.

Realizing Church House could not accommodate such numbers, he and Atlay searched for larger premises. They approached Westminster

PREPARATIONS FOR THE FIRST CONGRESS

Central Hall, but the Methodists were unco-operative. The *Church Times* noted wryly on 7 May: 'Methodists appear to be greatly exercised over what their journal describes as "the misuse of our premises in Westminster". The Central Hall has not, we think, been let for a prize-fight: but it has been let recently for a meeting of the National Socialist Party [*sic*], at which "disorderly scenes and free fights were frequent". In fact, it seems to be available for all and sundry except the Anglo-Catholic Congress, which has the proud distinction of having been refused the use of the hall.'

Instead Atlay and Wilson booked the Queen's Hall in Langham Place, venue of Sir Henry Wood's Promenade concerts (it was destroyed in the Blitz). Then, as more applications came in, they approached the Royal Albert Hall in Kensington. It happened to be available from 29 June to 1 July, so the executive agreed to alter the dates and make the Albert Hall the main venue for the Congress.

The change of date had an important consequence. Since this particular week was just before the opening of the 1920 Lambeth Conference, bishops from dioceses overseas were able to arrive early to attend the Congress before going on to Lambeth. These bishops from different parts of what was still known as 'the Empire' and from the USA contributed enormously to the success of the event. Indeed, it is not an exaggeration to say that had they not been there, the Congress would not have had the impact on the Church of England that it did. But the change was not welcomed by everybody. When the alteration of the dates was announced, Catholic parishes and organizations in the north of England objected. A local branch of the Confraternity of the Blessed Sacrament (CBS) wrote to point out that support would be reduced because that week clashed with the traditional holiday season for Lancashire businesses. Atlay replied, explaining apologetically why the change was necessary and hinting that another Congress might be held in the north the following year. This suggests he was already thinking that it might not be a one-off event.

A hospitality committee was set up for clergy who needed beds in London during the Congress. Stone headed the subjects committee charged with the task of choosing the speakers. Arrangements were made for advertisements in the church press, in parish churches and on the London underground. The parish room in St Matthew's clergy house became the Congress office, though eventually a bedroom had to be commandeered to handle requests for hospitality in London, and the one and only bathroom to deal with making arrangements for the stewards. A Miss Gilder was employed as a shorthand typist. An account was opened at the London Joint City and Midland Bank. It was agreed that Catholic missionary and other societies would be allowed to set up their stalls in the Albert Hall.

On 23 January 1920 the *Church Times* published a full-page advertisement announcing the Congress and listing over 150 clergy and 120 laity who had agreed to form the general committee. They included priests from London and different parts of the country and prominent Catholic laity such as the Duke of Argyll, Viscount Gort, the Duke of Newcastle, the Earl of Shaftesbury, Edward Wood M P (Lord Halifax's son, a future Foreign Secretary in Neville Chamberlain's government in the 1930s, and ambassador in Washington during the second world war), Sir Samuel Hoare M P (another future Cabinet minister), together with a handful of titled ladies. Members of Atlay's congregation were recruited as officers: Commander Rotherwell as treasurer, Lady Beryl Oliver as chairwoman of the hospitality committee, and Major General Carlton Jones as supervisor of the 140 stewards, many of whom also came from St Matthew's. It is not known if this general committee ever met. Maybe the list of names was intended to demonstrate that the executive's intentions were honourable. The Catholic movement had a notable following among the aristocracy, and the executive made use of this in drawing up lists of supporters. In those days titles still counted for something – especially among the bishops.

The executive soon had to cope with widespread suspicions and misunderstandings. St Paul's Cathedral was approached to see if the Congress could open there with a procession, sermon and *Te Deum*. Dean W. R. Inge, who regarded the Catholic movement as one of the worst things that could have happened to the Church of England, refused. Atlay was incensed. He wanted to expose the Dean's prejudices by publishing their correspondence, but the executive restrained him. Southwark Cathedral was more accommodating. Permission was given for the final service of the Congress to be held there in the evening of Friday, 2 July. But others like the Methodists at the Central Hall and the dean of St Paul's, distrusted the project. Before Wilson's full-page advertisement appeared rumours were already spreading about the intentions of the executive. It was a campaign to make the service of benediction legal. It was a subtle bid by Catholics to take control of the Church of England. It was a Catholic demonstration in force designed to frighten the bishops at the forthcoming Lambeth Conference. It was a dark and underhand conspiracy to submit the Church of England to the tyranny of Rome.

In a long letter, which appeared in the same issue of the *Church Times*, Atlay vigorously refuted these rumours. He began by explaining that many Catholics felt it was time for them to come out into the open and declare what they believed. They wanted, he said, 'to make it plain and evident that the Catholic position in the English Church is the true mind of the Church of England; to proclaim to the world that we will no longer submit merely to toleration, that we will no longer accept the position that we are just regarded as a handful of cranks who have got hold of a particular theory of Catholic doctrine and practice which, in the eyes of the multitude, will inevitably land us at the feet of Peter'.

'It is the aim of the Congress', he continued, 'to put before the English-speaking world what English Catholics really hold with regard to such great questions as modern philosophy, modern criticism, the Roman Church, Non-Conformity, and social and industrial problems. And further, we desire above all things to publish plainly and distinctly the good things of the Catholic Faith and the Christian religion. The Congress is designed to be evangelical, but we also have to make clear to the world where we stand and where we are meant to stand, that we are not going in any direction save in the direction of our Lord through His grace given to us in the Sacraments of the Catholic Church in England.'

Far from wanting to frighten the bishops (such a suggestion was 'impertinent and presumptive in the extreme') he hoped the Congress would inform them. 'It has, of course, been in our minds that when the Lambeth Conference did meet in July it would be useful for that Conference to have before it a clear and definite statement of what the Catholic party in the English Church does stand for, for believe me there is no body really more ignorant of our aims than the bishops taken as a whole.' In short, he hoped the project would strengthen the faithful, extend the knowledge of the faith, and make plain what the Catholics' position was on various matters. 'This is necessary,' he concluded, 'for not only had chaplains coming back from the war complained how ignorant of the faith thousands of ordinary men were, but it was true to a very large extent of the educated classes.'

There was talk of following up the Congress with a national evangelistic mission, but in the early months the executive could think of little beyond satisfying the huge demand their initiative had created. There was plenty to do. Stone's subjects committee invited speakers to follow a sequence of themes such as Atlay had summarized in his letter. The first addresses would discuss the effect of contemporary criticism and speculation on the faith and on the proclamation the Gospel of the Kingdom in the modern world. Next would be talks on authority and discipline, the limits of toleration and the ideal to be kept in view. Under the theme of Christian unity there would be papers on the Roman Catholic Church, the Orthodox Church and other Christian bodies, followed by an address on the distinctive witness of the English Church. Different aspects of the faith would be explained: the sacrifice of the altar, the reserved sacrament, the faithful departed, and our Lady, saints and angels. Under the heading of personal religion there would be talks on prayer and Communion, meditation and mysticism, retreats and the religious life. At the last meeting the Church's relation to the social and industrial problems of the day would be discussed.

In the introduction to the report of the Congress, published by SPCK later in the year, the principal of Pusey House said that speakers were asked to introduce their topics clearly and simply so as to help listeners understand the foundation of their faith as the basis for their Christian lives. Their aim must be not to engage in detailed controversy but – as Stone put it – 'to increase knowledge, to strengthen faith, to preserve hope and to deepen love'. Finally Stone explained, 'The papers are an outcome of a common faith. They express what the writers believe to be the truth which God has revealed and has made to be the indestructible heritage of the Catholic Church. As Catholics the writers have desired to be a mouthpiece through which may be declared what they have learnt from the Church, their Mother. In consequence the papers represent a great agreement in belief and aim.' But then he added, conscious that Catholics are not always of one mind: 'It does not follow that on every detail not part of the faith, the writers think or have spoken exactly alike. Possibly in every paper there maybe some sentence which some other reader would have wished different. So far as this is the case, it may serve to illustrate the fact that there are many questions round about the faith concerning which there is not the same obligation as in regard to the faith itself.'[3]

The *Church Times* gave the coming Congress full coverage. With a circulation of over 60,000, it provided the committee with a valuable means of communication throughout the Church of England as plans for the Congress unfolded. Many of its issues in the first half of 1920 contained articles, letters and items of news about it. On 19 March the paper published another letter from Atlay for those who feared they would not hear in the vastness of the Albert Hall; he assured them that a large shell was being hired to act as a sounding-board to amplify the speakers' voices. On 9 April Wilson wrote to say he had dispatched 1,500 posters to parish priests round the country. He invited all Catholics to observe the period between Ascension Day and Whitsunday as a novena of prayer and asked priests to say mass for the Congress. On 14 May the paper reported that 6,000 tickets had been sold and applications were being received at the rate of between 150 and 200 a day. Clergy who wanted

PREPARATIONS FOR THE FIRST CONGRESS

to say their own daily mass in London during the Congress should write immediately to Montford who would make arrangements for them. On 4 June a letter appeared from Major General Carlton Jones appealing for more men to act as stewards. The official guide to the Congress was published that month. The guide contained details of the programme and a special collect:

V. Her foundations are upon the holy hills.
R. And the gates of Hell shall not prevail against her.

Lord of all power and might, send thy blessing, we pray thee, upon the Anglo-Catholic Congress and grant that thy Holy Spirit may inspire the minds of those who speak, and open the hearts of those who hear; that all may learn to see and know thy Son our Lord Jesus Christ: who with thee and the same Spirit liveth and reigneth, one God, world without end. Amen.

Meanwhile, the rumblings of discontent continued. Inge, in a much publicized talk, said that the Anglo-Catholic party was breaking up into petty factions and would not survive more than a few more years. 'It is very kind of the Dean to write our epitaph,' said the *Church Times* editorial on 7 May, 'but we have no intention of dying yet.' The other church paper, the *Guardian*, aimed at middle-of-the-road Anglicans, gave less space to the Congress.

By Tuesday, 29 June, the first day, 13,000 tickets had been sold at 5/- and 2/6 each (25p and 12½p in today's currency). Three thousand more were sold at the doors on the following two days. The Congress opened with twelve hundred clergy processing along Holborn for a high mass at St Alban's. The clergy, marshalled in fours and led by a large crucifix from Atlay's church, made up the body of the procession. They were followed by 22 bishops from overseas dioceses of the Anglican Communion.

A souvenir booklet of the procession was published a few days later. The photographs show the crowds on the pavement watching curiously, with passengers looking down from the open top decks of buses and the driver of a stationery horse-drawn van with an advert for Bournville cocoa on its side gazing at the procession in astonishment. The clergy, as instructed by the organizers, were vested in cassocks, cottas or short surplices and birettas; some were swinging thuribles. 'There was', noted the *Church Times* reporter on 2 July, 'a surprising absence of the clerical oddity which is often to be observed, and made fun of, in clerical gatherings. Instead, as one of the newspapers remarked, there was the impress of asceticism upon the whole.' The bishops in mitres of varying shapes were each escorted by two priests, one wearing a dalmatic, the other a tunicle. At the rear, representing the Orthodox Church, was the Archbishop of Cyprus with five attendant Anglican priests. Atlay and Wilson stood on a street corner watching the procession go by. It was an exhilarating moment for them.

In St Alban's the celebrant of the mass was H. Ross, the vicar; his deacon was the aged G. W. C. Russell who had been at the church since Mackonochie's days. There was criticism afterwards about the music: the elaborate setting, it was said, glorified the choir but reduced the congregation to the role of an audience. The preacher was Bishop F. E. Ridgeway of Salisbury. It was an unexpected choice, for Ridgeway was an Evangelical. But as he was the only English bishop except M. B. Furse of St Albans to accept the invitation sent to all diocesans to attend the Congress, the committee felt they ought to invite him to preach.

He did not disappoint them. In his sermon he said he had accepted the invitation for two reasons. First, he knew the Congress was to be an important event in the life of the Church of England and he felt it was his duty as a bishop to be there (perhaps an implied criticism of his absent episcopal colleagues?). Second, he understood its aim was to present Jesus Christ to the nation, and that was a purpose which was close to his heart. He trusted the Spirit of Christ would infuse all that was said and done at their meetings. There were murmurs of 'hear, hear', from the congregation as he spoke and at the end of his sermon a round of applause. When he appeared on the platform of the Albert Hall later that day, he was introduced as 'the bravest bishop in the Church of England' and given a tremendous ovation.

There were masses in other London churches that morning. In St Paul, Knightsbridge, the Bishop of Milwaukee called on the congregation to thank God for all the Catholic movement had achieved, though not without much cost to individuals. He added that he had visited some war cemeteries in northern France the previous week and, as he remembered the wooden crosses over the graves of young men who had given their lives for their country, he wondered if the members of his audience were willing to give their lives to bear the cross of Christ. In St Augustine, Kilburn, Archdeacon Holmes of London took as his text 'Christ loved the Church', from Ephesians 5.25, and declared that he loved the Christ's Church in England, too – the Church which St Gregory had established ('I don't care very much about any other kind of establishment!'). There were also crowded congregations in All Saints, Margaret Street, St Mary

Magdalene, Munster Square, St Peter, Vauxhall, St Stephen, Gloucester Road, and St Michael, Shoreditch. So many turned up at St Matthew, Westminster, to hear Weston preach, that an estimated five hundred had to be turned away from the door. That afternoon they descended on the Albert Hall in their thousands.

2

England in the 1920s and 1930s

With the signing of the armistice on 11 November 1918, British people expected that their daily lives would return to what they had been before August 1914. Back to peacetime normality was their dream. But society was never the same again. The Great War – as it was known before 1939–45 – had resulted in far-reaching changes. It was against this background that the first Congress was launched.

One painful gap in the social scene was the loss of a large proportion of a whole generation of men. In a population of 35 million, British casualties had numbered two and a half million, of whom over 700,000 had been killed. Families in all classes of society had experienced the loss or disablement of its young and early middle aged males – fathers, sons, uncles, nephews, cousins and friends. Ernest Barnes, a future Bishop of Birmingham, noted sadly that half the undergraduates he had taught as director of mathematical studies at Trinity College, Cambridge, had been killed. Women, too, had been among the casualties – about one thousand five hundred nurses and others died in field hospitals near the front line or drowned when ships were torpedoed; many more were killed in accidents at munitions factories. Percy Dearmer, author of *The Parson's Handbook* and editor of *The English Hymnal,* lost one of his two sons, Christopher, at Gallipoli in 1915, and in the same year his first wife, Mabel, died of a fever while nursing wounded soldiers in a Serbian hospital.

National grief found expression in the erection of the Cenotaph in London, in the burial of the Unknown Soldier in Westminster Abbey, and in the institution of Armistice Day. Locally it was expressed in the thousands of war memorials in churches, churchyards and town squares, in parades and the two minutes' silence on 11 November each year, and in raising funds for social amenities like public halls, swimming-baths and gardens dedicated to the memory of those who never returned. These ceremonies provided bishops and clergy with opportunities to demonstrate that the established Church had a role on such national occasions.

Then, to add to these wartime losses, at the beginning of 1919 the country was stricken with an epidemic of Spanish flu in which over 150,000 died in England and Wales, more than 15,000 of them in London. Again, Anglican clergy carried out the majority of the funerals. It revealed the truth of what Anglo-Catholic priests had been saying for years, that the provisions of the Prayer Book for the Communion of the sick and the burial of the dead were inadequate. The campaign for the permanent reservation of the sacrament and for the revival of requiem masses and prayers for the dead became more relevant. In many Anglo-Catholic churches a requiem chapel was furnished as a war memorial. Even some Evangelicals were willing to support prayers commemorating the departed provided the phrasing of them did not imply a belief in purgatory.

Immediately after the armistice, Parliament was dissolved and fresh elections held. The popularity of Lloyd George, with his promise of 'a land fit for heroes to live in', resulted in a return to power of nearly the same administration as that over which he had presided during the last years of the war. The Conservative Unionists formed a coalition with those Liberals who were willing to support Lloyd George. Other Liberals who were not willing to trust the wily Welshman became a breakaway group. The 'khaki vote' secured fifty seats for Labour, the largest number they had held since their first members entered the House of Commons in 1906. Christian socialists, including Anglo-Catholics who supported the Labour Party, hoped that it might be a first glimmer of a new dawn for the country.

But they were disappointed. The new government had to struggle with complex economic and social problems never encountered before. During the war the state had taken over the nation's major industries and services. With the coming of peace some of these were returned to private ownership; government control was retained over others. The powers of existing Boards, such as Education and Trade, were strengthened and they were renamed Ministries. New Ministries of Labour, Pensions, Health and of Transport were established. Other public bodies appeared and the number of civil servants grew. This led to a slow but subtle change in the attitudes of ordinary folk. In the past they had looked to the churches, voluntary societies and benevolent charities for help in time of need. Now they began to expect the government to provide it for them. As one contemporary commentator put it, the state slowly was becoming everyone's nurse, doctor, chemist, benefactor, guide, philosopher and friend. The Churches generally, and the Church of England in particular, had to adjust their changing role to this creeping state control over people's ordinary lives. It was a sign of increasing secularization in society and in popular attitudes. Some opposed it as a work of the devil. Others wanted to work within it as a means of forwarding the purposes of the Kingdom of God.

'Reconstruction' was the buzz word. It was adopted by Bishop Charles Gore for his book surveying Christian faith and practice, *The Reconstruction of Belief* (1926). There was much talk of tackling persistent social and industrial problems. But the cost of the war, particularly the huge debt owed to the USA for armaments and supplies, left an economic legacy which blighted national life and international trade for the next decade and beyond.

Believing they could save the nation, labour leaders began organizing themselves to win the right to govern. The creation of the Trades Union Congress (TUC) drew together the political arm in the party and its representatives from the workers in industries. This offered the workers an opportunity to exercise their democratic power and to curb the influence of extremists. If we exclude the armed struggles for Irish independence, it helped to save Britain from the political upheavals experienced by other European countries in the postwar years.

Throughout the period two severe problems haunted the country and were of particular concern to the Churches: unemployment and the housing shortage. The five million men and women employed in industry during the war were now joined by the millions demobilized from the armed forces. The closing down of many industries and the gradual decline in Britain's status as the workshop of the world deprived the country of the means of creating wealth. By 1921 over two million were out of work, about one in fifteen of the entire population. In Manchester, where the cotton mills could no longer find markets for their products, the number of unemployed increased from 23,000 to 33,000 between 1921 and 1922.

Those who worked in the coal mines and the steel and shipbuilding industries were particularly affected. Under government control during the war, workers in these industries had enjoyed subsidized wages. This ended when the industries went back into private ownership. Miners' pay was reduced to a half of what it had been. Shipbuilding yards on the Clyde and the Tyne were shut down. The railways, which before the war had been owned by different companies, were reorganized into the famous four – LMS, LNER, GWR and SR – and once again were subject to the profits of shareholders. Protest meetings, marches and strikes became common occurrences. The government was forced to introduce legislation which led eventually to the payment of benefit to those in certain categories who were out of work. The phrase, 'on the dole', became all too familiar. In these conditions socialism flourished, while alongside it emerged a small but active communist party. Many clergy were well aware of these deprivations, especially those in the working class areas round London and the big cities, south Wales and industrial Scotland.

ENGLAND IN THE 1920S AND 1930S

Fear of Communism swept through the nation as news reached this country of deportations, pogroms and executions in Russia, including the assassination of the Tsar and his family. The church press carried reports of Orthodox churches being sacked and of bishops and priests being imprisoned and shot. Refugee Orthodox clergy and laity were welcomed to this country. Among the trade unionists were militant groups whose impassioned speeches against capitalism, the monarchy and the landed classes raised alarm throughout the nation. In a few places Communists were strong enough in local government to turn town halls into 'little Moscows'. All this was a gift to the Conservatives and Liberals, who played on the fear of Bolshevism to warn their constituents what they could expect if they voted for Labour.

The living conditions of the poor in the inner cities persisted in all their degrading squalor. Present-day TV historical documentaries remind us how awful they were. There were various attempts by the national and local government bodies as well as private firms and housing associations to tackle the problem by building new houses on out-of-town sites. People began moving out of the centres of cities. The great Becontree estate between Barking and Dagenham was launched by London County Council for families from the East End. Similar projects were started elsewhere. They were part of a general movement of population to the suburbs. Metroland beckoned seductively. The building of Welwyn Garden City began in 1920. Young marrieds from middle-class families went to live in the new estates like those round Wanstead and Beckenham. So, too, did the more ambitious of the young from the working classes; they 'bettered themselves', it was said. When Wilson left St Matthew's he was moved by the numbers of young men and women, former members of the congregation and its guilds, who came in from their suburban homes all round London to his farewell mass and party.

But money for local authority housing soon ran out as building costs soared. It was not until the thirties that further government aid initiated a housing boom. It was then that Manchester began building the Wythenshaw estate south of the city. This was the age of the ubiquitous semi for those who could rent one (seven shillings or so a week) or afford to buy their own (around £400). In 1930 over one thousand people were leaving inner London for the suburbs every week. By 1939 four and a half million new homes had been built in the country, though without solving the housing problem completely – at least a million more were needed. All Christian denominations found themselves having to negotiate for sites on which to build new churches and to raise the funds for them.

Besides unemployment and the lack of housing, the war had left other problems, less easy to quantify. Family life had been disrupted. Wives had been separated from husbands for years. Children had grown up hardly knowing their fathers. Men returning home expected to resume life where they had left it when they joined the forces. But the demobilized soldier often seemed very different from the man who had volunteered or been conscripted a few years before. The horrors of trenches and the terrors of the sea meant that for long afterwards many were afflicted with what we now call post traumatic shock syndrome. Sadly few understood the causes for this condition. Relationships suffered. Divorce, which had been rare before 1914 and limited largely to the wealthy, became more common in all levels of society. Since practically all the Churches refused to marry divorcees, the number of weddings in registry offices grew.

The divisions of class were also being eroded. Men and women forgot social distinctions in the face of common dangers and bereavements. The war had brought unexpected wealth to entrepreneurs but impoverished many of those who had been rich. Some social orderings were turned upside-down. J. B. Priestley, the novelist and playwright, who was an undergraduate in Cambridge in 1919, recalled how ex-servicemen used to have rowdy arguments and parties in their rooms until dawn so that college porters, who had until recently been serving as other ranks in the army, found themselves having to reprimand their former officers. After the war the *Church Times* continued to print one or more pages of advertisements for 'Christian young women from respectable families' to act as housekeepers and maids. But by the end of our period such advertisements were disappearing. Young women, Christian or not, no longer wanted that kind of job.

Yet life began to offer improvements and opportunities for many such as had not been known before. Children benefited from more educational openings. The school leaving age was raised to fourteen (attempts to raise it to fifteen did not succeed until after the Butler Act of 1944). Secondary schools developed alongside older grammar schools, and brighter pupils obtained scholarships for the new universities and technical colleges as well as Oxbridge. The period also saw a great increase in the number of children's and young persons' clubs, many of them run by the Churches. Britain was evolving from an aristocratic into a mediocratic society. For younger generations, names, titles and family background were becoming less important; what mattered were your qualifications, your career and your income.

Most significant of all was the change in the role of women. Many who formerly would never have considered working after marriage had been drawn into war work of all kinds. Among the working classes it had been common for wives, mothers and daughters to work in the mills and factories of the Midlands and the North; but now a growing number of middle-class women no longer felt they should be expected to give up careers for home and family as former generations had done. The development of contraceptives liberated them from unwanted childbearing. The first family planning clinic was opened in London in 1921. Politically, too, women became an influence to be reckoned with in the constituencies. The pre-war campaigns of the suffragettes finally triumphed. Immediately after the armistice, legislation was passed allowing women over thirty into the polling booths; the age limit was reduced to twenty-one a few years later. Nancy Astor became the first woman to take her seat in the House of Commons. The old universities also bowed to the feminist pressure. Dorothy L. Sayers, a future distinguished writer, was one of the first women to be awarded Oxford degrees. Another was Maude Royden, who pioneered new roles for women in the Church; she became a well-known preacher and campaigner for women's ordination.

As the twenties evolved, technical and scientific skills were needed in the new industries producing a greater variety of consumer goods in response to the challenge of imports from the USA. Advances in medicine and the growth of other caring services opened up careers for women as well as men who could take advantage of the new educational opportunities. Numbers of white collar and blue collar workers increased.

After the war, a blanket of what Lloyd George called 'national amnesia' descended in people's minds. Those not immediately affected by its consequences wanted to forget the war. Other things were distracting them. Leisure activities were more diverse than ever. There was plenty of money about among those who could take advantage of them. For the bright young things who had been children during hostilities, it was the age of abandonment of restraint, of cheerful adventure and experiment. The music of the period (revived today on CDs) evokes this atmosphere. Jazz became popular; the charleston and the tango invaded dance floors and night clubs. Parties were all the rage. Youth wanted to get the best out of life while they could. The 'weekend' became more significant as leisure time than Sundays for church-going.

Fleet Street had been the primary source of news and comment. The cheap popular papers of the Beaverbrook and Rothermere domains were in the ascendant. But two new forms of information and entertainment were becoming available without costing more than all but the poorest could afford. One was the 'wireless', the other the cinema. The BBC was formed in 1922. Its manager, J. C. W. Reith, later Lord Reith, became director general when the company was made a public corporation in 1927. An earnest Presbyterian, he remained in his position at the BBC until 1938, and his ethical standards continued to influence the Corporation for years afterwards. The wireless was soon to be found in most homes, though the churches were slow to realize its potential. The first broadcast service, led by the vicar H. R. W. ('Dick') Sheppard, was from St Martin-in-the-Fields in 1927. The following year the BBC began transmitting the Daily Morning Service as a result of a petition from five thousand listeners organized by a Miss Kathleen Cordeux.

Films were beginning what was to be their golden age. At first there were only silent films with subtitles and music provided by a resident pianist. Full-length talking pictures arrived in 1928. From then on, since Hollywood dominated this industry, American culture and language began to seep into British life. Everybody picked up new words, such as 'cornflakes', 'chewing-gum', 'the movies' and 'dames'. 'Going to pictures' became a major leisure activity, with a high proportion of the population visiting the local Odeon or Plaza twice a week. Use of slides and films for educational purposes in church were being tried by the more adventurous clergy. Someone at one of the later Congresses asked whether the outdoor processions could be filmed.

The use of the telephone was spreading into offices and better-off homes. The English Church Union found it an invaluable means of instant communication in arranging meetings, and it began to be installed in the vicarages. But the less technically minded priests were wary of it. Mackay, much to the amusement of his curates, preferred to walk out and deliver notes through doors rather than ring parishioners up.

Opportunities for travel increased. Motorized public transport replaced horse-drawn carriages, and buses and tramcars appeared in cities and towns in increasing numbers. Charabancs gave urban dwellers days out to sports activities and other events. Holiday camps and camping grounds made it possible for poorer families to enjoy a week by the seaside. The London underground was extended into the suburbs. Bicycles were produced in hundreds of thousands and cycling clubs were formed. By 1930 there were over a million private cars. The railways gradually recovered from the strains of wartime to offer more efficient services. Hiring special trains became a common means of taking supporters to national events such as the Congresses, and Sunday school children and their teachers for a day at the seaside.

Ferries opened up the continent to tourists. New ocean liners offered cruises in the Mediterranean as well as regular services to North America, the countries of the Commonwealth and other parts of the world. When Weston was invited to the 1923 Congress, the committee sent him £50 to cover the cost of half his fare from Africa. Air transport was only just beginning. Regular flights to Paris and other continental capitals began in the twenties. Imperial Airways, operating from Croydon, was formed to open up air routes to other parts of the world in the thirties. An Australian bishop used the newly instituted air mail facilities to book his places at the 1930 Anglo-Catholic Congress and the Lambeth Conference which followed it.

But to return to the political scene. The coalition government fell in 1922 and in the ensuing election the Conservatives won a substantial majority. A new cabinet was formed with Arthur Bonar Law as prime minister. It was in this administration that Neville Chamberlain as minister of health introduced a housing act which made available modest subsidies for houses built by local authorities and housing associations founded by the churches. But by 1924 the economic situation had deteriorated again. That year Stanley Baldwin, who had succeeded Bonar Law, called a snap election. Although the Conservatives were returned with a majority, the Liberals supported Labour under Ramsay MacDonald and so the first Labour government came into being. Henry H. Slesser, a lawyer who acted for the party and the trade unions, and who was a leading figure in the Congress movement, was made Solicitor General. He was not an MP at the time, though he won the Leeds South East seat at the next election.

It could have been a glorious moment for Labour but, as the party held only a minority of seats in the Commons, they could do little to promote their policies without Liberal consent. Unemployment benefits were raised and state scholarships to universities established. Subsidies for housing were increased. But fears among the general public that Labour was dominated by crypto-communists seemed to be confirmed when the government signed a trade treaty with Russia. Other disagreements resulted in the Liberals' withdrawal of support, and the government fell after a few months in office. The election, held at the height of the 'red scare', resulted in another Conservative administration under Baldwin. This was the House of Commons which rejected the Revised Prayer Book in 1927 and 1928.

That government was no more successful than its predecessors in dealing with the post-war depression. When the Chancellor of the Exchequer, Winston Churchill, announced a return to the gold standard and the lifting of trade barriers, British exports became more expensive and foreign imports cheaper, aggravating a worsening situation. The owners of the collieries tried to impose lower wages and longer hours, but the miners resisted with the slogan, 'Not a minute on the day, not a penny off the pay'; 800,000 were locked out. The Trade Union Congress called for a general strike in support of the miners and on 4 May 1926 one and three-quarter million workers walked out.

The general strike might have been much worse. Through the nine days that it lasted, the strike was generally peaceful. Riots broke out in London and some other cities, and the government had to send in troops to break the strikers' blockade of the East London docks. But there was nothing like the armed uprising which occurred in parts of Europe in the post-war years. Months before, plans had made for such an emergency and the shutdown of essential services was avoided. Stories of the volunteers who manned buses and delivery vehicles have passed into the folklore of history. After long negotiations the TUC called the strike off on 12 May. It was accused of turning traitor and letting the miners down; the latter remained out until the end of the year. However, the strike jogged the government into taking action. Chamberlain introduced a contributory benefits scheme for widows, orphans and pensioners, and Churchill attempted to redistribute the burdens of taxation to aid industry and reduce unemployment. But growing dissatisfaction led to another general election in 1929. This time Labour won the largest number of seats in the House of Commons but not an overall majority.

This second Labour government was able to raise unemployment benefits, to bring some reforms to the coal industry, and to set in motion plans for slum clearance and subsidies for new housing. But astonishingly the House of Lords blocked a proposal to raise the school-leaving age to fifteen. Then came the New York stock market crash on 29 October 1929, and the effect on the British economy was drastic. Within a year unemployment reached two and a quarter million. By 1931 the government had lost the goodwill it had enjoyed when it came to office and, after another election, a National Government was formed with MacDonald as prime minister and a cabinet made up of a handful of Labour and Liberal members and a majority of Conservatives led by Stanley Baldwin. Many Labour members, including Clement Atlee, a future prime minister, refused to serve on it. Oswald Mosley left the Conservative Party and formed the British Union of Fascists. Left-wing groups reacted by coming together in the Popular Front against Fascism.

It was the workers in the heavy industries who suffered most. Not all parts of the national economy were weakened. When the gold standard was abandoned, there was considerable growth in the production of goods for the domestic market and jobs in the service industries and leisure activities. Generally speaking, it was the middle classes who prospered, especially in the south east, as living standards improved. The rest of the country only benefited when the government, alarmed by military developments in Germany and Italy, began to rearm in 1935.

During these years there were considerable changes in the countryside, too. Farming had prospered during the war when it was subsidized to increase food production to counter the effects of the blockade by German submarines. But then agriculture went into a decline from which it never recovered until the second world war (when once again home production was essential for the same reason as before). Farm labourers deserted their tied cottages and sought work in cities and towns. In many parishes the Church of England and its clergy was hated among those farmers who were compelled to pay tithes to it. When a farmer didn't pay, bailiffs were liable to be sent in. In 1932 there were 16,000 cases of non-payment. The Tithe Act of 1936 modified the system, though injustices remained for years afterwards.

The rural population changed. It gradually became home for commuters and retired professionals. These 'comers-in' replaced many of the landowners in the local hierarchy. They treated the countryside as a holiday resort and a place for retirement. Wealthy residents of big houses invited their friends down from the city for weekend parties. Car and motorbike ownership became more common, and village greens and lanes were crowded and noisy at weekends and during bank holidays. Some who lived in the cities and towns purchased cottages as second homes. But at the same time increasing numbers of country churches lost their incumbents as the number of clergy declined and the abolition of tithes made it difficult to maintain a parson for every parish.

The government faced plenty of other problems abroad as well as at home. Ireland remained a running sore. Following the 1917 rebellion, the first general election after the war demonstrated the strength of support for Irish independence when over seventy Sinn Fein candidates won seats outside Ulster. These candidates, being unwilling to take the oath of loyalty to the monarch, did not attend the House of Commons; instead they set up their own representative assembly, the Dial, in Dublin and began to act as if the Westminster Parliament did not exist. The Dial wanted to negotiate a peaceful transference of power but the Irish Republican Army, aiming to unite the whole island, resorted to violence in 1920. Hostilities continued until a truce was called and the division of Ireland reluctantly accepted. Memories of those years, and particularly the execution of the Irish leaders and the brutality of the Black and Tans, added to the legacy of hatred of the British from earlier centuries. The Irish Free

State eventually came into being in 1932 when De Valera became prime minister and all remaining links with Britain were severed. The name of the Irish independence party became well known. One speaker at a Congress said the Church of England should not be Sein Fein ('on our own') as it was part of the Catholic Church.

At the beginning of the century much of the former British Empire was being transformed with the granting of dominion status to Canada, South Africa, Australia and New Zealand. Offers of cheap sea passages encouraged individuals and families to immigrate to these countries. Empire Day was celebrated with processions, meetings and special events in schools, although people were learning to drop the title of Empire and to use instead the phrase the British Commonwealth of Nations. India began its struggle for independence led by Gandhi with his policy of peaceful resistance. Edward Wood (Lord Irwin), was Viceroy in the early thirties. He only accepted the difficult posting after visiting his father and going to mass with him on the Halifax family estate at Hickleton to pray for God's guidance.

After the armistice the vexed questions of reparations from Germany and the future of that country's African colonies were finally settled at the Treaty of Versailles (part of German East Africa had been in Weston's diocese). But many felt the reparations were too harsh. They were imposed at the insistence of France for all that country had suffered in the war, and Gore was among the more foresighted in the Church who were critical of them. The treaty also resulted in radical changes to the political and geographical map of Europe. Old empires collapsed under the pressure of nationalism, leading to the formation of Austria, Czechoslovakia, Hungary, Poland and Yugoslavia. The Ottoman Empire was divided up into mandates allotted to Britain (including Palestine) and France.

The formation of the League of Nations, initiated by Woodrow Wilson, the US president, was greeted with high hopes. Surely this would ensure that the last war was indeed the war to end all wars? 'Never Again' became the fervent watchword. The League of Nations Union was one of the most popular organizations in Britain, its membership reaching a peak of over 400,000 in the early thirties. Many of these were Anglicans and other Christians. The 1930 Lambeth Conference urged support for it. But the appalling economic situation in Germany and unrest in other parts of Europe created political instability. Mussolini was elected in 1922 and gradually assumed dictatorial powers. Hitler became German chancellor in 1933.

The Labour Party strongly opposed any plans for rearmament. Remembering what happened in the years before 1914, they argued that rearmament would only make another war inevitable, and that the nation would be left in peace if it did not pose any threat to another European power. The famous resolution of the Oxford Union that its members would not fight for king and country was symbolic of this conviction. But hopes in the League of Nations died when it failed to act when Hitler's army marched into the Rhineland and when Mussolini's annexed Abyssina (Ethiopia) The significance of these events was only beginning to be realized when MacDonald retired and Stanley Baldwin succeeded him as prime minister in 1935. A fresh election enabled the National Government to continue, but this time its members hesitantly realized they must prepare for possible future hostilities. The outbreak of the Spanish civil war in 1936 was a foreshadowing of things to come.

King George V was a titular focus of national life. Ascending the throne in 1910, he was regarded with distant respect rather than affection, though a serious illness in the early thirties and his first Christmas Day broadcast in 1932 brought him closer to people than before. Edward, the Prince of Wales, was popular. He travelled throughout the country and the Commonwealth, supporting public events and showing concern about miners' strikes and slum conditions, though unable to do much about either problem. His accession to the throne on the death of his father in 1936 was greeted with enthusiasm, but that quickly waned when he abdicated in a few months to marry Mrs Wallis Simpson, a divorcee. His shy brother, Bertie, the Duke of York, came to the throne as George VI. Married to Lady Elizabeth Bowes-Lyon and the father of two daughters, Elizabeth and Margaret, he had remained out of the public eye. All that was known about him was that he hosted a joint camp for boys from public schools and working class families each summer and led them in singing and performing actions to the chorus, 'Underneath the spreading chestnut tree'. There was little indication of the quiet courage he would show when with his queen he saw his country through another war.

During these years most English citizens, from the farm labourer and working man to the monarch and members of Parliament, looked to the Church of England as representing the Christian legacy of the nation. The great majority, most of whom rarely attended its services, regarded it as 'our Church'. Its clergy were generally treated with respect, even by those who had little personal contact with them. To the outsiders, only the Anglo-Catholics seemed to be disturbers of that status quo.

3

The Church of England

There were thirty-eight dioceses in the Church of England when the first Congress was being planned after the war. Five more were founded in the next few years: Blackburn and Leicester in 1926; Derby, Guildford and Portsmouth in 1927. Within these dioceses there were about 14,500 parishes and about 20,000 clergy. The majority of the parish priests were in the south of England, a high proportion of them in rural areas. They were more thinly scattered in the industrial conurbations of the north. In 1931 the diocese of Liverpool calculated that 4.40 per cent of the population of England lived within its boundaries, the fourth highest in the country, but only 1.73 per cent of the incumbents, whereas the Hereford diocese had only 0.57 per cent of the population and 2.36 per cent of the incumbents. These percentages for Liverpool and Hereford had not changed much when the *Paul Report* was published in 1964.

The majority of the clergy were middle class, through education rather than family lineage. Twenty out of thirty-eight diocesan bishops went to public schools (six to Eton); all but two of the rest went to grammar schools. The exceptions were Herbert H. Henson of Durham, who was privately educated, and J. E. Watts Ditchfield of Chelmsford, who was brought up a Methodist and became an Anglican in later years. All but two of the bishops were Oxbridge graduates, the exceptions being Watts Ditchfield, a non-graduate, and H. R. Wakefield of Birmingham, who studied in Paris and Bonn.

Like the bishops, most of the clergy had also attended public or grammar schools, and about half of them were graduates of Oxbridge. Some had upper-class connections through birth or marriage; a few had inherited titles, like Lord Vincent Seymour, Vicar of St Stephen's, Gloucester Row; he was President of the Confraternity of the Blessed Sacrament until he retired in 1929. Theological colleges had been established from the middle of the previous century onwards, but attendance at them was not compulsory until 1917. Some of the older clergy, including fourteen of the diocesan bishops, had never attended one. Those who were fellows of Oxbridge colleges were entitled to be ordained without any formal preparation. Others did some reading privately under the direction of the bishop's examining chaplain. Consequently some bishops and senior clergy were ill-equipped to appreciate the historical and theological reasons why the better-trained among Anglo-Catholic clergy believed and practised what they did.

To improve this situation the Central Advisory Council of Training for the Ministry (CACTM) was set up in 1912 to coordinate the selection, funding and training of ordinands. Theological college principals, jealous of their independence, regarded it with suspicion and even hostility. B. K. Cunningham at Westcott House in Cambridge was said to see his task as turning out 'English gentlemen in holy orders', while at Ripon Hall in Oxford Henry Major, 'the high priest of Modernism', wanted his students to be capable of relating their faith to contemporary thought and culture. Evangelical colleges aimed at training preachers and pastors who would not be hassled by scriptural criticism or Modernist speculations. Other courses were provided by local institutions like the Leeds Clergy School and the temporary college, set up in Knutsford in a disused prison after the war, for ex-servicemen who were accepted for ordination. Finance was a common problem for would-be ordinands. A limited number of grants for students from less affluent homes were available from some dioceses; others from various sources, though qualifying for these often depended on personal connections and/or churchmanship. The Evangelical Churchmen's Ordination Council coordinated the funds of twelve smaller agencies 'for helping Evangelical candidates for the Ministry'. Even so, graduates were only required to attend a theological college for one year until well into the 1940s.

Colleges which were regarded by Anglo-Catholics as suitable for training priests were, with varying reservations, Chichester, Ely, Mirfield, Kelham, Lincoln, Salisbury and Wells, as well as those in the universities, Westcott in Cambridge, Cuddesdon and St Stephen's House in Oxford, St Chad's in Durham, and King's in London. The colleges sponsored by the communities at Kelham and Mirfield opened the route to ordination for young men from poorer families by providing their students with free tuition and accommodation. Even so, some bishops exercised their own judgment about whom they should ordain. Bishop A. C. Headlam of Gloucester preferred to ordain men who had studied either at King's in London, at the theological faculty he had founded, or who had undertaken a reading course set by him. William Temple, it was rumoured, would lay hands on anyone who convinced him he had a vocation. The war hastened the decline in the number of ordinations. In 1919 only 161 were made deacon compared with 610 in 1914. The numbers rose in the next few years but never achieved the higher figure again. One result was the gradual amalgamation of parishes, beginning in rural areas.

Nearly all those who lived in parishes expected the parson to minister the rites of passage. Nine out of ten babies were baptized in Anglican fonts. Most marriages took place in the local parish church. A small but increasing number of more liberal-minded clergy were prepared to re-marry a couple, one or both of whose previous spouses were still living; others went to registry offices. Most of the dead were buried with the rites of the Prayer Book, cremation only just becoming acceptable to a minority.

Homes still cherished big family bibles, even if they were opened only to record details of births, marriages and deaths on special pages provided for the purpose. On the walls of the sitting room there might be a copy of Holman Hunt's painting of Christ knocking at a door and, if the family had suffered bereavement during the war, perhaps another of James Clark's 'The Great Sacrifice' which depicted a dead soldier lying at the foot of Christ on the cross.[1]

A quarter of all children in the country were educated in Church of England schools, where there were regular acts of worship and weekly Scripture classes, often given by the vicar or a curate. One of my aunts, who attended a church school in Derbyshire in the first years of the century, could answer the questions of the catechism and recite the Prayer Book collects word-perfect even when she was in her eighties. Whatever present-day educationalists might think of such methods, she had been taught 'to bear no malice or hatred in my heart, and my tongue from evil speaking, lying, and slandering . . . to keep my body in temperance, soberness and chastity', and so carried in her memory a treasury of Christian doctrine, ethics and devotion which served her well throughout her long life.

The majority of Church of England congregations were broadly middle class, especially in towns and cities. At the beginning of the century 34.5 per cent of the population of South Kensington worshipped regularly in an Anglican church but only 1.6 per cent in Somers Town.[2] Going to church on Sundays was regarded as a decent thing to do and a good example to the children and the servants. The public schools reinforced a family's religious practices with compulsory chapel and more or less compulsory confirmation. Those who could not afford public school fees paid a few guineas a term to send their children – particularly their sons – to a local grammar school. Some grammar schools had Anglican chaplains. County secondary schools were more secular in ethos, though a daily assembly for worship was normal in most of them.

About two million children went to Church of England Sunday schools, including many in working-class areas. Attendance was encouraged by annual prizes, summer outings and Christmas parties. Even in poorer parishes households took pride in the new suits worn by their sons and the white dresses worn by their daughters for confirmation services. In northern towns Sunday school children and youth organizations paraded in the 'Whit walks'.

If fewer people went to church in working class areas, the parish church and its clergy were widely respected, especially if priests stayed for many years. With their helpers – some of whom were people from better-off homes outside the parish – the clergy organized a variety of social and educational events. Priests in these areas, conscious of the social gap between themselves and their parishioners, made special efforts to encourage vocations to ordination among the congregation. Desmond Morse Boycott, assistant priest of St Mary, Somers Town, helped young lads to prepare for matriculation (to qualify for university entrance) at evening classes after they had finished work, and then raised funds for them when they went to college. These kinds of projects contributed to a greater social mix among the clergy. In the thirties Ivor Bulmer Thomas, an Anglo-Catholic lawyer, prophesied, 'Perhaps some Hoxton lad will yet find his way to the chair of St Augustine.'[3]

Two and a quarter million people received Communion at Easter, one in fifteen of the population. Many others felt it was their duty to attend church on special occasions. In towns and suburbs as well as in villages the parish hall and the church school were the focus of activities to which people came who hardly ever went inside a church building. In the early 1920s the average number of confirmations was 220,000, but by the end of that decade it was 190,000 (in both cases about 40 per cent were male and 60 per cent female). The falling off of the number of children attending Sunday school was more dramatic; by 1939 it had more than halved. Children from non-church homes were engaging in sports and other leisure activities on Sundays instead. In the diocese of London, between 1927 and 1928 attendance at Sunday school dropped from 174,406 to 148,724.

Among the 1,900 clergy returning to their parishes after chaplaincies in the armed forces, there was a widespread conviction that the Church was out of touch with working-class people. Living with men in the trenches and other theatres of war, they realized that much of what their contemporaries were saying and doing back in England was irrelevant to the mindset and needs of those among whom they had served. Their attitude reflected that found among most of the troops who fought in the war:

'they' at home have no ideas what 'we' are going though. Radical views were thrust forward – equalization of clerical stipends, the establishment of a body of roving missioners, clergy working in industry. A more measured response is revealed in a letter the chaplains of the army's seventh division wrote to Temple when they heard of his involvement in the Life and Liberty movement: 'No matter what type or party we belonged to of old, we are now all haunted by the fear that the Home Church cannot see, and will not rise up to meet, the needs which have shocked each one of us on entering, as ministers of Christ, this huge intermingling of all sorts and conditions of our countrymen.'[4] Their complaints gave impetus to a cautious reform of the Church's government, described in a later chapter.

A key figure in the Church until his retirement in 1928 was Randall Davidson, the Archbishop of Canterbury. Davidson was appointed in 1902 and with tactful wisdom and a gracious manner exercised considerable influence among the powers-that-be. Even cabinet ministers and educationalists sought his advice. He was a firm believer in the establishment of the Church and convinced it was essential for the good of the nation. He also believed in the comprehensiveness of the Church so that it included the various parties within it. This attitude antagonized those Anglo-Catholics who felt what they stood for was not on the edge of the Church but at its centre. But they recognized that the Archbishop tried to be fair and respected him for his sincerity and courtesy.

When he retired in 1928 Davidson was succeeded by the Archbishop of York, Cosmo Gordon Lang, another former Scots Presbyterian. A complex character, Lang differed from Davidson in many ways, particularly in being more concerned for his role as a Church leader than as a national figure. He believed in the Catholicity of the Church of England but felt Anglo-Catholics harmed their cause by promoting it too forcefully. In his message to the 1930 Congress he said that while he welcomed it he knew things would be said with which he disagreed. He was a bachelor who liked to have people round him. At York the chaplain's family lived in Bishopsthorpe. He reflected the social attitudes of his age by advising Mrs Temple, when her husband succeeded him at York, that it was not fitting for an archbishop's wife to be seen entering local shops.

The year 1920 saw the resumption of the ten-yearly Lambeth Conferences of the Anglican Communion. The last one had been in 1908. The presence of so many bishops from overseas dioceses was a reminder that Canterbury and York were two provinces in a worldwide Communion. For people who were taught to be proud of the achievements of the British Empire, it was not difficult to transfer that pride to this fellowship of

Anglican provinces planted mainly in lands which were, or had been, part of the Empire. But Anglicans from overseas, especially those from the self-supporting and increasingly wealthy Episcopal Church of the USA, could easily resent what they took to be the patronizing attitudes of their English brethren. Those from the West Indies, Africa, and other former colonies, however, had stronger ties with the mother country, and still depended on the support of the missionary societies based in London.

Many members of the Church of England saw themselves as being within a certain stream or tradition of teaching and worship. The usual name for this stream or tradition was 'party'. Although the name was disliked by those who deplored a 'party spirit', it is a convenient word to use for discussing the distinctive features of the various groupings.

More than half of the clergy – and the laity – did not regard themselves as belonging to any party. This meant that they did not belong to any of the organizations which promoted certain party lines. If pressed they would reluctantly identify themselves as 'just Church of England', 'Broad Church', 'Middle-of-the-Road', or 'Prayer Book churchmen'. This meant that they were generally content with the teaching and practice of the Church based on the Prayer Book and the Thirty-Nine Articles 'as by law established'. Among them there was a suspicion of, if not hostility towards, the other parties. The more informed, however, understood the theological and historical reasons behind the rise of the Modernist, Evangelical and Anglo-Catholic parties and to some extent were influenced by them. But they were cautious about change and only accepted it when they were assured that many of their like-minded contemporaries accepted it, too.

It was this latter group, especially those with the right family and personal connections, who were earmarked for appointment to the posts of archdeacon, canon, provost, dean and bishop. As firm believers in the establishment, they regarded it as their duty – perhaps their vocation under God – to uphold the intellectually respectable and tolerant character of the Church of England. They felt dogmatic enthusiasm was alien to the spirit of Anglicanism. They identified themselves comfortably with the culture of the society within which they lived and worked. Davidson was this kind of Anglican, which is probably why he had so much influence among members of Parliament as well as in the Church. He personified what most people expected a Church of England parson to be. The rest of these clergy worked within the parochial customs which had been handed down to them. They regarded the geographical area of the parish as their personal patch and, according to their initiative and temperament, were known and generally respected by those who lived within it. It would be wrong to dismiss them all as diffident or ineffective pastors. Among them were those whose scriptural teaching and pastoral care earned the gratitude of their congregations.

The newest party in the Church of England was the Modernists. The term 'modernism' came into use at the beginning of the twentieth century to describe theologians in different denominations who were attempting to relate the Christian faith not only to contemporary biblical scholarship, but also to studies in comparative religion, scientific research and philosophical debates. H. Major was the best-known propagandist of the movement. An able scholar, he launched the *Modern Churchman* magazine in 1911 and organized the Union's first conference the following year. In 1918 Ripon Hall, the college for those wanting to be ordained which he had started in Yorkshire, moved to Oxford where, with Major as its principal, it acquired a reputation for being a Modernist hotbed. It was there, according to Weston, that 'ordinands are taught by "superior" dons to criticize the Christ as boldly as the best of his critics'.

Although Oxford University was regarded as the academic bulwark of Anglo-Catholicism, others among its scholars had modernist leanings, including J. M. Thompson, Dean of Magdalene College, and B. H. Streeter, of Queen's College. Thompson wrote a book trying to rationalize Christ's miracles, and Streeter stirred up controversy by questioning the traditional doctrine of the incarnation in his essay 'The Historic Christ' in *Foundations* (1912). Modernists generally were in favour of remarriage after divorce, birth control, the ordination of women and reunion with Nonconformists. Bishops Barnes of Birmingham and Henson of Durham were regarded as Modernists for they both spoke at Major's conferences, though Henson was wary of extremists and too independent to have a party label attached to him.

The aftermath of the war favoured the Modernists, as many in Britain and in Europe saw the conflict as a dreadful warning that the traditional Christianity preached by the Churches had collapsed under the tide of evil, and that fresh ways of presenting the Gospel of Jesus Christ had to be found to make it appealing to men and women of the new scientific age. It seemed a thoroughly civilized form of the Christian faith for the twentieth century. This was one of the reasons why the Modernist creed, in all its diversity, was attractive to thoughtful Christians of all denominations.

The movement created problems for Anglo-Catholic scholars. Since the time when Gore, then principal of Pusey House, addressed the matter of biblical criticism in *Lux Mundi* (1889), many of them realized that the next task for theologians was to relate the Christian faith to modern intellectual and moral problems. But in doing so they risked alienating their friends if they appeared to go too far. Younger Anglo-Catholic scholars admired the teachings of the Roman Catholic Modernist, George Tyrrell, in his attempts to integrate new knowledge and new values into the faith which was once delivered to the saints. Tyrrell argued that this kind of integration is what had been done in the past, and that contemporary Christians ought to be willing to do it again. In spite of his condemnation by the Vatican in 1907 (an act which made his teaching even more interesting to Anglicans), Tyrrell's books continued to be reprinted. The fact that Baron von Hugel, the distinguished Roman Catholic, was known to be sympathetic towards him, if not underwriting all his views, strengthened Tyrrell's influence. That influence can be traced among the talks given at the Congresses.

The adjective 'liberal' came to be applied to Catholics who were willing to take into account some of the things the Modernists were saying, but the qualification must be understood in the terms of the day. Liberal Catholics had no intention of questioning the fundamentals of the Christian faith as enshrined, for example, in the creeds. Rather, they realized the importance of the historical and critical study of the Scriptures and its relevance to teaching the Gospel in their own times. It was only later in the century that the adjective 'liberal' came to be applied to those who criticized these fundamentals and became known as 'radical Catholics'. In 1934 Alec Vidler wrote: 'The newer type of theology, in which it is now expressing itself, may be held to support the suggestion that what the Roman modernists, in various ways but entirely unsuccessfully aspired after is likely to be realized, in part at least, in Anglicanism, by a development of the historic Catholic religion whose theology will take account of the progress of human knowledge.'[5]

What made it a sensitive issue was that the word Modernist was associated with heresy – an association reinforced by sensational reports in the popular press of what certain clergy were supposed to have said. It was regarded as an intellectual enemy by older Anglo-Catholics and Evangelicals alike. Modernists, however, did not have access to the levers of control in the Church, and so they depended on interested lay patrons or the patronage of certain colleges for parish appointments and preferment.

Although Evangelicals' influence in the Church had peaked in the nineteenth century, they were still a party to be reckoned with. They preached a straightforward biblical faith, stressing the substitutionary doctrine of the atonement and the need for a new birth through personal commitment to Jesus Christ as Lord and Saviour. They regarded themselves as the true heirs of the Protestant Reformation, and they interpreted the Prayer Book and the Thirty-Nine Articles in this light, opposing any who, in their view, challenged it.

Their strength was in the parishes. For many years wealthy adherents had inherited or purchased parochial avowsons (the right of patrons to nominate incumbents), some of which they donated to Evangelical organizations. By 1930 the Church Association, the Church Pastoral Aid Society, the Martyrs' Memorial Patronage Trust and the Simeon Trustees between them were patrons of about 380 parishes. It was calculated that these trusts, together with other supportive patrons, controlled the appointments of up to two thousand benefices. Among them were notable churches such as Bath Abbey, Beverley Minster and Bridlington Priory, and the parish churches of Birkenhead, Clapham, Cheltenham, Hampstead, Macclesfield, Southport, Tonbridge and Walthamstow.

Within this network Evangelical incumbents and curates could work without having much contact with other Anglicans – a church within the Church. This suited them, for they were wary of parties who embraced biblical criticism or who seemed to be pushing the Church of England towards Rome. Among the bishops their leaders included E. A. Knox of Manchester (1903–21), father of the Knox brothers, and J. E. Watts-Ditchfield of Chelmsford (1914–23). They also had friends in Parliament, like Thomas Inskip (later Lord Caldecott) and Sir William Joynson-Hicks (Home Secretary 1924–29, later Lord Brentford). The annual Islington conference, which from 1920 met in Church House, was their main rallying point. Their church paper was the *Record*.

St Aidan's College, Birkenhead, Ridley Hall, Cambridge, and Wycliffe Hall, Oxford, were regarded as safe for Evangelical ordinands. Three new colleges were founded in the 1920s and 1930s: the Bible Churchman's College, Bristol, Clifton Theological College, Bristol, and Oak Hill College, Southgate, London. Children and young people of Evangelical families were encouraged to join the Crusaders or the Christian Union while they were at school, and the Inter-Varsity Fellowship (founded in 1928) at university. Parents who could afford it sent their children to public schools established by Evangelicals, the most famous of which was Monckton Combe near Bath. The Keswick Convention, started in 1875, was an important rallying point, with the result that Evangelicals often felt a greater affinity with Evangelicals in Nonconformist Churches than with many of their fellow Anglicans.

The shock of the war increased Evangelicals' tendency to withdraw behind their parish boundaries. A few individual Evangelicals saw the importance of social and political involvement and appreciated Anglo-

Catholic arguments for this, but the majority concentrated on nurturing their congregations and engaging in evangelism. They strongly supported foreign missions through various societies, the largest of which was the Church Missionary Society (CMS) founded by the Clapham Sect in 1799. Consequently they imparted an Evangelical character to those Anglican dioceses which emerged from their missions in Africa, South America, India and Burma.

However, the supporters CMS were divided by a controversy which began with the appearance of Modernism. Early in the century the Anglican Evangelical Group Movement was formed. One of its primary aims was 'to apprehend by means of study the findings of modern scholarship in relation to the Bible and Christian doctrine'. A struggle began within the CMS on how it should respond to this development and, eventually, after discussions which lasted several years, a majority opted for a certain liberty of opinion in the interpretation of Scripture. A minority refused to accept this decision, and in 1922 they separated themselves to form the Bible Churchmen's Missionary Society (BCMS). Evangelical parishes were divided as to which society they should support. The different theological emphases were reflected in the teaching of the Bristol theological colleges, Tyndale being pro-BCMS and Clifton pro-CMS, until they eventually merged in Trinity College in 1971. Liberal Evangelicals only became a majority after 1945, when they began to overtake the Anglo-Catholics in numbers and influence.

Anglo-Catholic clergy were usually divided into two types: those who drew their inspiration from contemporary Roman Catholicism, and those who aimed to recall the Church of England to its pre-Reformation Catholic heritage. It was a convenient categorization but an over-simplified one. The real picture was much more complex (as it was for Modernists, and to a lesser extent for Evangelicals). Clergy were inclined to pick 'n mix, limited only by what their congregations would accept and what their bishops would tolerate or prefer not to notice.

To explore this complexity a little further I will attempt to distinguish between Anglo-Catholic varieties by listing them under the seven colours of the rainbow (remembered from school days by the dictum, 'Richard Of York Gave Battle In Vain') to try and sketch different types of Catholic priests. I shall use the spectrum rather like those political cartoonists who draw a few lines which enable readers to recognize a politician by well-known characteristics (facial features, hair style, physical stance, etc). Since the types were often revealed in the way these clergy ordered the liturgy as well as what they wore, my verbal sketches focus on the worship in their churches and their clothes. I should add that there is no hidden significance in attaching certain colours to particular types, except that the red vesture of Roman cardinals seems appropriate for Anglican papalists.[6]

Red. Saw himself as a priest of the Western Church, temporarily out of Communion with the Pope through a tragic accident of history. Haunted by doubts about the validity of his orders after the condemnation of them in the papal letter *Apostolicae curae* (1896). Used the Roman missal and breviary in Latin, though read audible parts of the mass in English in church services. On Sundays: early low mass(es) for those wishing to receive Communion; a later non-communicating high or sung mass. Benediction on Sunday evenings, perhaps after solemn vespers, for which he vested in a cotta, stole and cope (abhorred the hood and scarf as 'Geneva rags'). Considered baroque the ideal setting for the liturgy. Full Western ceremonial. Reservation in a tabernacle. Confession to a priest and fasting before Communion taught as matters of obligation. Wore a soutane and biretta out-of-doors as well as in church (dispised the Sarum cassock). Regarded celibacy as mandatory for Anglican clergy. Expected to be addressed as 'Father'. Disliked the custom of older Catholics like Stone and Halifax who persisted in addressing priests as 'Mister'.

Orange. Very similar to Red, except that on Sundays he used the words of the Book of Common Prayer (BCP) Communion service, saying the Roman canon silently. BCP evensong before benediction. Daily mass and BCP offices. Wore a black suit rather than a soutane outside church. Was usually married, though this made him feel a second-class priest when compared with his celibate brethren.

Yellow. Saw himself as a priest of the Western Church but was glad to belong to the Anglican 'branch'. Didn't doubt the validity of his orders. Regarded the Roman Church to be in error, especially since the 1870 decree on papal infallibility. Used BCP Communion service with those additions from the Western rite which he felt were permissible in the absence of any other provision. Reserved the Sacrament in an aumbry in a Lady chapel. Devotions only on weekday evenings for the local branch of the Confraternity of the Blessed Sacrament. Daily mass and offices. Regarded baroque as 'un-English'. Confessions advertised. Preferred a Sarum cassock, never wore a biretta. Valued the freedom of Anglican clergy to marry.

Green. Very similar to Yellow. Saw himself as a priest of the Anglican Communion and liked to call himself a 'Prayer Book Catholic'. Followed the English Use of the Alcuin Club: altar with cross, two candles and riddell posts. Incense used only at festivals. Preferred the 1549 or the 'interim' rite (i.e., BCP prayer of oblation added to the prayer of consecration, etc). Sung mass on Sundays with Communion if communicants fasting; solemn evensong on festivals. Mass on saints' days and one or two weekdays. Reserved the sacrament for the sick. Saw the value of private prayers before the aumbry, but not corporate devotions. Confession taught in confirmation classes. Wore a suit of clerical grey.

Blue. Saw himself as a priest of the Church of England within the Anglican Communion. BCP Eucharist (did not use the term 'mass' in public) on Sunday mornings at 8 or 9 o'clock or thereabouts with general Communion. Choral matins later. Wore vestments at all Eucharists, and surplice, hood and scarf for matins and evensong. Preached that fasting was desirable but wasn't strict on this. Regarded a non-communicating mass as contrary to Anglican teaching and practice. Confessions advertised discreetly. Described himself as 'High Church'. Did not belong to any Anglo-Catholic organization.

Indigo. Saw himself as a priest in the established Church; opposed talk of disestablishment. Early Communion service on Sunday mornings; Sung Eucharist and sung matins on alternate Sundays. Never used incense. One weekday Eucharist. Fasting occasionally mentioned in sermons. Confession only advised privately in cases of pastoral need. Wore surplice and stole for all services in church, though hoped to introduce Eucharistic vestments one day. Liked to called 'Rector', 'Vicar', or – if he had been a chaplain during the war – 'Padre'.

Violet. Saw himself as a pastor of the established Church. Early Communion service (he rarely used the word 'Eucharist' and never 'mass') on Sunday mornings and sung matins later; Communion rite added to matins once a month for those who wished to 'stay on'. Said he would like to have a sung Communion every Sunday but 'the congregation isn't ready for it'. Reserved the sacrament temporarily if it was not possible to arrange for a Communion service in the home of the sick. Never mentioned confession, but in parish notices invited people to let him know if they wanted a private talk with him. Admitted he was 'a bit high' and went to some Anglo-Catholic meetings and services, but never joined any Anglo-Catholic society.

This is, as I have said, very much a cartoon categorization. But there were further complications. While Red and Orange were regarded by others as papalists, they in their turn did not consider Indigo and Violet (and perhaps one or two others further up the spectrum) to be Catholics at all (they called them '*only* High Church', using the label in a derogatory manner).

Then the colours tended to spill over their pots and mix with others. For example, it was quite possible for a Violet priest to be as firm on the need to receive Communion fasting as a Red, and for an Orange priest to be as averse to a non-communicating high mass as a Blue.

Occasions arose when alliances were formed across the whole spectrum. In a local Congress the different colours often joined together in organizing it; and if a Yellow priest was subject to episcopal discipline over, say, introducing reservation in his parish, the rest of the spectrum would support him. On the other hand, if a Red or an Orange disobeyed their bishop's instruction to stop having benediction the others, especially Indigo and Violet, would be unsympathetic. When new problems arose – over matters such as divorce, birth control, reunion schemes, Prayer Book revision, Modernism – the picture was confused even more. Those at the Red end of the spectrum might find themselves joining up with Evangelicals in opposition to those at the Violet end, while Indigo might be more accepting of certain Modernist ideas than Orange.

Over the years individual priests moved up and down the spectrum as personal convictions, parochial circumstances and ecclesiastical appointments changed. As they learned things from other parties which attracted them, some from the Red end moved a colour or two towards the Violet end, and vice versa. Parish customs and prejudices could also have their effect on new incumbents. A curate brought up under an Orange or Yellow vicar might adapt to an Indigo surplice-and-stole parish if he was getting married and needed a sole charge.

Acceptance of non-partisan, non-parochial posts also caused priests to modify earlier convictions. Anglo-Catholics who were appointed bishops or to other posts in the diocesan hierarchy found themselves having to work with clergy and laity of all traditions, and in the process they began to appreciate viewpoints and customs which they had ignored before. This is one of the reasons why Anglo-Catholic bishops were a disappointment to some in the party. When Fr W. Frere CR became Bishop of Truro, he was careful to treat all his clergy fairly, to the disappointment of certain Catholics in Cornwall and beyond. A. Blunt's appointment as Bishop of Bradford was hailed as a sign of great hope for Catholics in the diocese, but within a few years he was disgusted by the extremists among them and became less supportive. Then, long before the first Congress, there were a few bishops and others in the diocesan hierarchy who were generally Catholic by conviction but who for pastoral reasons preferred not to be so closely identified with that party's activities.

I must stress again that these categories are only cartoons. They would certainly give the wrong impression if they are regarded as comic characters. Clergy and their foibles could be the subject of jokes. It is part of the Anglo-Catholic culture to laugh at one another. But those in all categories believed that the Catholic faith could save their country from the after-effects of the war, and that God was calling them to persuade the rest of the Church of England of the truth of this. They also believed that the way worship was presented, especially in the mass, could be a powerful symbol of what the Catholic faith taught about the Church's sacraments, its priesthood, its Scriptures and its mission. Catholics more than any of their contemporaries appreciated the relationship between beliefs and the symbols which expressed those beliefs. That is why they fought for the right to use them – and, forty or so years before our period, had been willing to go to prison for them.

Because of their diversities, especially those at the Indigo and Violet end of the spectrum, it is not easy to calculate their numbers. Some guidance is provided by the membership of the various Anglo-Catholic societies. At this time the English Church Union (ECU) had about 4,000 clergy among its 20,000 members. The Federation of Catholic Priests (FCP) had about 1,500, the majority of whom would also be in the ECU. Bearing in mind that the ECU's records of membership were not fully up-to-date, and that not all priests belonged to either the ECU or the FCP, 4,000 seems a reasonable estimate of their number. Accepting that figure suggests that just over one in five of all the clergy in the Church came within our Red to Blue categories. But if we add the Indigo to Violet clergy the ratio probably increases to one in two.

However, they were not all vicars, rectors and priests-in-charge. A considerable number were curates: big Anglo-Catholic parishes usually had three or four. Many others were on staffs of schools, universities and cathedrals. Some were working for missionary and other extra-parochial bodies. A number were retired. Nevertheless, they constituted a considerable movement within the Church of England (and in the Catholic dioceses of the Anglican Communion), and the Congresses were one of the principal means of demonstrating that, beginning in the Albert Hall in the summer of 1920.

4

The First Congress 1920

The first session of the Congress opened on Tuesday afternoon, 29 June. The Albert Hall was nearly full when Weston took the president's chair. On either side of him were Marcus Atlay and Bishop Roscow Shedden of Nassau. A large crucifix was suspended behind them. In his opening remarks Weston refuted the rumours about the intentions of the Congress, as Atlay had done in his letter to the *Church Times*. They were meeting as members of Christ's Church, he said. They were conscious that they were losing the allegiance of men and women in the world who wanted to put themselves at the feet of Jesus to ask, 'Lord, what wilt thou have me to do?'

The order of proceedings was:

Hymn
Opening Prayer
First Paper
Hymn
Second Paper
Interval
Third Paper
Hymn
Fourth Paper
Hymn
Blessing

Like many conference programmes, it was over-optimistic about what could be done in the space of two and a half hours. Speakers over-ran their time and the lengths of their texts in the published report shows why. Not all of them may have stuck closely to the scripts they submitted later for publication, though the accounts in the *Church Times* of what they said suggest most of them delivered their papers more or less as they were printed. One exception was Weston, who did not write a script but later in the week spoke spontaneously on the ministry of a bishop in his diocese.

The first paper on Tuesday afternoon was by C. H. Turner, a distinguished lay theologian and ecclesiastical historian. He had been briefed to address those whose faith had been disturbed by stories in the press that Modernists were claiming the Bible was no longer historically reliable. He set out to demonstrate that, on the contrary, a critical study of the New Testament made the incarnation and resurrection of the Lord more credible. Unfortunately his scholarly exposition, with references to Erasmus, Zahn, Lightfoot, Harnack and Schweitzer, would have been more suitable for the Oxford lecture rooms where Turner usually taught. His talk was so long and his voice was so weak that, in spite of the sounding-board set up behind the speakers' rostrum, he was not heard by those in the upper balconies. When Weston thanked the speaker, he tartly remarked that the clergy present (presumably in the front rows of seats) might have got more out of it if they had been less fidgety.

Another lay Anglican, A. E. Taylor, the professor of moral theology at St Andrew's University, was due to give the next talk on 'The Faith and Modern Speculation'. But Weston sensed that the audience needed something less academic, so he changed the order of the speakers and invited W. L. Vyvyan to give his paper on 'The Faith and the Evangelization of the World'. Vyvyan spoke with the authority of one who had worked in Zululand for twenty years, seventeen as Bishop. He began by describing what was involved in converting adherents of primitive religions to the Catholic Faith in his part of Africa:

'Against the magic of the witch doctors we set the joyful, loving mysteries of the Sacraments; for the self-inflicted tortures we substitute the pain of self-denial, of penitence and self-discipline; against the sacrifices to dead idols and ancestors we lift up the adorable Sacrifice of the Eucharist. In contrast to the principles of fetish and taboo we bring the Commandments of God and the sanction of Holy Scripture . . . As a foil to the songs of lasciviousness we chant the noble Psalter and Christian hymns. We show the Christian life lived for the service of others as a proof of the value of the faith for the uplifting of mankind. Above every name that is named we exalt the beloved name of Jesus.'[1]

In his diocese, he said, they had great freedom to practise Catholic worship and discipline without hindrance from the State, and to loud applause he congratulated the Church in Wales for getting itself disestablished (the bill for this had been passed by Parliament and given the royal assent that year). He went on to comment that the Church at home seemed more concerned with its own maintenance than with mission overseas, and ended by challenging the Congress to demonstrate its support by having a collection.

'There are those who can give large sums, others smaller sums,' he said. 'There are those who can pour out jewels of value into the treasury of God's cause. Is this an extravagant appeal? If so, even so let it be successful; some reckless giving to the missions of the Church will be a refreshing novelty. It can be done if the will is there.'[2]

When the bishop sat down there was long applause. Atlay hurriedly consulted other members of the executive on how they should respond to the bishop's challenge. Mackay thought they should appeal for £10,000; Weston said they should go for £50,000. With the committee's agreement, Atlay went onto the platform after the interval and announced in his booming voice that the Congress would respond to the bishop's challenge with a target of £50,000. That, he said, would show the forthcoming Lambeth Conference that Anglo-Catholics were not indifferent to the needs of foreign missions. 'You may make your cheques payable to me,' he called out. 'Atlay is my name. One initial will suffice, M: M for Mug.'

It was a bold gesture. In present-day values he was asking for about half a million pounds. But the audience was carried along on a wave of enthusiasm. Donations poured in. Before each session on the following days Atlay announced the total received up to that time, and read out letters from donors. A retired priest had given his life's savings. Another with an income of £45 a year had sent the money he was saving for his holiday. If some people could spend £1,000 on a new car, Atlay asked, could they not give the same amount for the collection? The next day a £800 cheque was donated. One woman gave three rings from her fingers; another gave her mother's engagement ring. Gold watches and chains, bracelets, wristlets, brooches, war bonds and savings certificates were handed in. The organizers had to hire two policemen to sit with the collection each night in a small room in the Albert Hall until the money and the valuables could be banked next morning.

After Atlay's announcement, Taylor was due to give his paper, but as he was ill it was read for him by the Bishop of Nassau, who had a strong voice. Taylor warned his hearers that, unless they could present the Christian faith in ways that answered the questions raised by contemporary atheistic philosophies, the retreat from Christianity in British society would continue in the years to come. Catholics had to realize that there was more at stake than contending for minor doctrines or devotional practices. The Christian faith itself was being attacked by philosophers and teachers who were being listened to by many of the present generation. Previously philosophers like John Stuart Mill and T. H. Huxley, though rejecting traditional Christian beliefs, had been generally in sympathy with Christian ideals of personal conduct. Their optimistic view of the inevitability of human progress had brought them unwittingly close to the Christian hope that the Holy Spirit is guiding God's people towards the Kingdom of God. But the war had shattered that view. Nobody talked of human progress in those terms any more.

He went on: 'Now it was being said (to young people and others) that there is no intelligent plan or purpose in the universe, that there is no wisdom or goodness higher than our own, that since at death all a man's thoughts perish, the whole spiritual history of the human race is only the tale of an adventure foredoomed to end in nothing. They are told, too, by pervasive voices, sometimes that there is not even any real distinction between good and bad, only the irrational prejudices of individuals, sometimes that there is indeed a distinction, but that the law of Christ has drawn it up in the wrong way, and that the future must set itself to affirm a "transvaluation of all values". Humility, meekness, gentleness, all that Christians affirm to be "the fruits of the spirit", are symptoms of weakness and disease; pride, self-will, preferring himself in honour before others, these are the tempers of the "strong" man, these are the real virtues.'[3]

Although Taylor did not name names, it is likely that he had Bertrand Russell and his followers in mind. Russell was at the height of his influence among staffs and students in universities, and he was well known for his dictum, 'You should set out to work to doubt things and retain only what you cannot doubt because of its clearness and distinctness.'

How, asked Taylor, were Christians to respond? It would be a failure of Christian charity to ignore such arguments, and to present the faith in a take-it-or-leave-it attitude (a critique of simplistically dogmatic Catholic preachers?). Because Christ claims to be the whole truth, his Church must always be seeking a reason for the faith she proclaims – *fides quaerens intellectum*. She must demonstrate that the affirmations of Christianity are not contradictions of what reasoned science and philosophy present but a fulfilment of what people are seeking. The knowledge of and love of God is the only possible basis for human peace and development. To do this it is necessary for the Christian apologist not only to be convinced of the truth of the doctrines he is defending, but also to know how to meet his antagonists on their own ground. And more, he must be able to convince his opponents that he is not out to defeat their arguments but to demonstrate his love for them as persons.

'To be a really great Christian philosopher a man must also be a great lover of souls . . . and . . . a man of great faith, in the sense that his faith is the expression of an intensely lived Christian personal life. When he speaks of the things which are unseen and eternal, he must be felt to be speaking not merely of something which he honestly *believes* to be real, but of things the sense of which is always about him in his daily life.'[4]

Taylor acknowledged that the Christian apologist may find allies in those who have a deep respect for Jesus Christ but who for various reasons do not identify themselves with the Church. But in contrast a Christian philosopher will be 'an active member of the historic community of Christians, profiting in his inner life to the full by the organized Sacraments and devotions and living traditions of the great brotherhood of the Christian life'.[5] Finally, Taylor reminded his audience of the centrality of the Cross. For any philosophy to be adequate for Christians the 'word of the Cross' must be paramount within it. 'It is only a religion in which the Cross is central which is entitled to claim the titles, often so mistakenly divorced, of Catholic and Evangelical.'[6]

Shedden did not finish reading Taylor's paper until fifteen minutes before five o'clock when the session was due to end. The result was that the last speaker that afternoon, Fr Lionel Thornton, CR, delivered a lengthy lecture on 'The Kingdom of God' to an audience which gradually dwindled as everyone left in order to get a meal before coming back for the evening meeting.

The Church, Thornton said, was 'the primary embodiment of the Kingdom'. From this he insisted that, if a Catholic is to work for the fulfilment of the principles of the Kingdom, the social consequences of his or her own obedience to the Lord cannot be ignored. The incarnation of God meant that the world itself was to experience Christ's redeeming work through those who renounced their own concerns and who through baptism submitted to the Cross and the gift of Pentecost. He rejected the view, current among certain socialists, that human society could become more Kingdom-like through political, social and psychological processes without reference to the whole purpose of God. Even though some of these groups seem to have Kingdom-like objectives, he said, and that should be welcomed by Catholics, nevertheless the Church's witness is to a Kingdom which is coming out of heaven as a divine gift, and which at the end of time will finally be manifested in its perfection beyond this world-order by the mighty power of God. For the Christian, the Cross is always a reminder that self-renunciation must be the motive for living.

In spite of its attractions, he also rejected the dream of those Christian thinkers who longed for a return to Christendom as a visible theocracy. With recent events in Russia and the spread of Communism in mind, he said the Church must be more like a revolutionary body, infiltrating society with Kingdom principles and demonstrating what society could be like with the grace of God.

'If God is really to reign over His world, the powers of the Kingdom must move out to consecrate not only human souls, but everything by which souls live – the whole bodily life of men, all their use of material goods, the whole nexus of social arrangements, economic and political, all intellectual activity and artistic expression. Into all these things the leaven of the Kingdom must come, if the world is to be saved.'[7]

Like many of the Mirfield fathers, Thornton was a supporter of the Labour Party, and he warned his listeners not to be seduced by the contemporary idols which were the modern equivalent of that ancient paganism which opposed the early Church.

'Catholicism at its best always stands for a common social life, whereas the whole structure of our modern world spells irresponsible individualism. Catholicism stands for the redemption of the whole life of man under Christian ideals, whereas the modern world took its rise from the revival of the semi-pagan ideals of the Renaissance. With that inspiration it has carved out a purely secular career for itself, being greatly aided in this false emancipation by the Protestant principle that religion consists solely in person piety, with no real concern with either criticizing or consecrating the organization of our common life.'[8]

He was articulating the widespread resentment of a capitalist system through which industrialists had made fortunes in the manufacture of munitions. Although by no means all who attended the Congress would agree with what Thornton said – they included wealthy people who were deeply suspicious of the Labour Party – nevertheless Thornton signalled the alliance which had grown up, and would continue to grow, between many Catholics and socialists in the years ahead.

Taylor's and Thornton's papers were the most important delivered at the Congress that week. They had a prophetic quality which we can appreciate now. Together they pointed to changes in society – philosophical, social and political – which were to be very relevant to the Church's teaching and mission as the century unfolded. Taylor became professor of philosophy at Edinburgh and wrote *The Faith of a Moralist*, which included material from this address. Thornton was later to make his reputation through his contribution on 'The Christian Conception of God' in *Essays Catholic and Critical* (1926) and his pioneering work of process theology *The Incarnate Lord* (1927). In some places his Congress address looked forward to his best-known book, *The Common Life in the Body of Christ* (1942). In later years he became more absorbed in biblical typology.

Weston spoke on his ideal of a bishop, drawing on his experience in Zanzibar. Such a bishop, he said, would be the father of his flock and accessible to all. He would be a constitutional governor ruling with his synod of priests and in consultation with the laity. As a member of the universal Church's episcopate – perhaps one day meeting in a constitutional general council presided over by a constitutional pope – he would represent the universal Church to his diocese. The ideal diocese would be manifesting the love of God in its common life, and acting as a missionary agency by helping its members in their witness in the world. There would be no distinction based on colour, caste, class or wealth. His audience was left in no doubt that he thought the way the episcopal office was exercised in the Church of England was far from his ideal.

During the week there were addresses on Modernism, authority and discipline, the limits of comprehensiveness, the Eucharistic sacrifice, reservation, prayers for the departed, personal faith and practice. Most of these topics will be discussed in later chapters. Two others, however, had an immediate relevance in 1920, spiritualism and Christian Unity: the former because of its growing popularity, the latter because it was to be one of the major items on the agenda of the Lambeth Conference a few weeks later.

The considerable growth of interest in spiritualism among those who had lost loved ones in the war disturbed Catholics and other Christians. The practice was given publicity by Arthur Conan Doyle, who devoted the later years of his life and much of his fortune to promoting it, and Sir Oliver Lodge, whose book, *Raymond* (1916), recounted conversations he claimed to have had with his dead son via a medium and sold in thousands. Lodge, a distinguished scientist who pioneered work in radio transmission, saw no conflict between spiritualism and Christianity.

A. Pinchard, the secretary of the ECU, was given the task of explaining why this practice was unacceptable to Christians. He began his talk with a lengthy description of what he had learned of the Beatific Vision and the cleansing of Purgatory from Thomas Aquinas and Roman Catholicism. Then, turning to spiritualism, he pointed out that no one instructed in the Catholic faith could believe that the spirits of those who are in God's care could be 'at the beck and call of a sentimental and often unholy curiosity through means of communication that are as ludicrously undignified in character as they are unsatisfactory in result'. The so-called 'messages' are 'drivel and meaningless'.[9] But there were other dangers. The evidence of what happens in spiritualist séances seems to suggest that there are either wandering spirits or, more likely, evil spirits which take advantage of human folly and credulity to lure men and women away from God and gain ascendancy over them with disastrous results. Catholics must beware of these dangers and rest content with what Jesus has taught about life after death and wait until more is revealed to them in his good time.

Many Catholics were wary of using the word purgatory, conscious they had assented to number XXII of the Articles of Religion which declares that the 'Romish Doctrine concerning Purgatory . . . is a fond thing vainly invented, and grounded upon no warranty of Scripture, but rather repugnant to the Word of God'. Darwell Stone summed up their reservations when he said that, while the weight of tradition supported the value of prayers for the dead and the offering of the holy sacrifice on their behalf, it 'does not support the dogmatic assertion of much detail as to the state of the dead'. Others preferred to commemorate the departed rather than pray for them. A few years later formularies were incorporated into the Revised Prayer Book commemorating All Souls in its liturgical calendar (2 November) with collects and Scripture readings for a Eucharist which, the accompanying rubric said, could be used on any other suitable day. By then many Catholic parishes had begun celebrating a high mass of requiem with a catafalque in the nave on the Sunday nearest Armistice Day. Pinchard's forthright denunciation of spiritualism was warmly received, as was his claim that spiritualism would not have been so popular if the Church had given its people clear teaching on life after death.

In spite of the cool relationships between Roman Catholics and the Church of England, Anglo-Catholics were hopeful that things would improve in the years to come. E. M. Milner-White, Fellow and Dean of King's College, Cambridge, expressed this in his talk when he said that in spite of their divisions Anglicans and Romans were united in their Catholicity:

> There have been many developments since [the Reformation] both in Rome and England, but each has maintained its atmosphere and principle – two genuine Western traditions, one Cis-Alpine and one Trans-Alpine . . . Rome is still an army with banners, and boldly prefers a strict uniformity to freedom. That is her strength in these days of confusion, and her weakness in days when masses of new knowledge have to be related to ancient truths. From the Infallible Church, if Rome be that, the world has received no help in a succession of desperate bewilderments; none in the guidance of our social upheavals; none in the co-ordinating of new knowledge to the one truth of God; none in the political relations for the State system . . . Canterbury, bolder still, prefers freedom to think and seek truth above strict uniformity. That again is both our strength, which even Rome envies us, and our plain weakness, which

nobody envies. One day, and perhaps not long hence, the two principles will discover that they are not opposed but complementary. They influence one another for good even now, when outwardly at war; what will they now do when they discover the terms of peace! Catholicism would then be both united and free, both authoritative and reasonable, both ancient and modern, both full and being filled; would persuade and embrace the world.[10]

The policy of Anglo-Catholics, he suggested, should not be to try to copy Rome but to help all Anglicans to appreciate that their Church was truly Catholic and work towards restoring that historical truth in their doctrine and worship. Then Rome would begin to realize Anglicans were not Protestants but members of the one true Church with them.

'That is our contribution to unity with Rome – to establish here, in the United States, and in the Dominions, and perhaps more widely still – a true and deep Catholicism, deliberately chosen by a thinking and educated people as the most reasonable and loving form of Christ's religion; a *tolerant* Catholicism, ready and eager and fit to marry again in the Church of St Peter, when Rome is convinced by the Holy Spirit that the authority of love and reason is not only possible, but true.'[11]

All Roman Catholics and most Anglicans assumed that the only way in which reunion was likely to take place would be by Anglicans submitting to the Pope. Milner White, however, envisaged the two Churches existing side-by-side in full Communion with one another. In it Anglicans would be united but not absorbed – a scheme which was to emerge from the Malines conversations a few years later.

A. C. Headlam, Regius Professor of Divinity at Oxford, had recently published his Bampton lectures, *The Doctrine of the Church and Christian Reunion,* in which he suggested a number of practical steps to bring Anglicans and Nonconformists together. They included items which would attract the support of Catholics with ecumenical sympathies – regulating the celebration of the sacraments of Baptism and the Eucharist, the Nicene Creed as a doctrinal basis for unity, episcopacy as a basis for Church order, and respect for the varieties of liturgical and pastoral traditions. But his proposals that Nonconformist ministers should be recognized as validly ordained without the laying on of hands by a bishop, and that the rule of apostolic succession was not a divine ordinance, roused their opposition.

Headlam had intended his book to be a talking-point at the forthcoming Lambeth Conference – his publishers had arranged for all the bishops to be given a copy – but it had attracted so much publicity that G. H.

Clayton felt he had to answer it at the Congress as he had been given the subject of 'Other Christian Bodies'. He began with what was for some Catholics present an over-generous appreciation of Nonconformists:

> The primary reason (to work and pray for reunion with Nonconformists)', he said, 'is this: That we believe that they and we have received the Holy Spirit; that that Holy Spirit is one; that where there is one Spirit, there should be one Body; and that where the Body of Christ is rent and torn, there the work of the Spirit of Christ is hindered; the Spirit has not free course. In the conversion of the sinner, in the building up of the Christian life, the work of the Holy Spirit is manifest in Nonconformist bodies in this country. It is equally manifest in the mission field. And it is the task of Christian wisdom to search for a way in which, for the good of all of us, and in accordance with the mind of our Lord expressed in His High-Priestly prayer, the unity of the Spirit may find expression in the unity of the Body. This must ultimately involve corporate reunion.[12]

He next turned to Headlam's book and acknowledged there was much of value in it. He welcomed Headlam's emphasis that every step in a scheme towards reunion should be done in an orderly manner with the agreement of all concerned, and that it would be hindered rather than helped by impatient actions, like an unauthorized exchange of pulpits or casual intercommunion. But then Clayton said Catholic doctrine and practice had developed from New Testament times and within the course of that development the Holy Spirit had guided the Church to discern that the apostolic succession of bishops was God's way of preserving order within the Christian community, and that ordination to the diaconate and the priesthood were only valid through the episcopal laying on of hands. These must be preserved in any scheme of reunion.

Clayton recognized that the truth these teachings preserved had been obscured by the way the Church had developed in the course of its history. This was particularly so in the Church of England because of its established status. Anglicans should be willing if necessary to get rid of that in the cause of reunion. He became rhetorical about this:

> If many [Nonconformists] object to the establishment, as many say they do, then let it go! Let everything go that belongs to this earth – position, wealth, privilege – if any wound in Christ's body may thereby be healed. We long for reunion with our fellow-Christians, and we know that they have much to give us. We do not stand – Heaven forbid! – for prelacy,

episcopal palaces, or indeed episcopal autocracy. We have much to learn about the rights of presbyters. We have much to learn about the rights of individual congregations, about the functions of the laity. Nothing would gratify us more than the recognition of societies with a large degree of freedom within the Church. All this would be pure gain. We lament sincerely that we are made so often to appear as obstructionists. We have no desire to be so. We most fully and gladly recognize the experience and work of others. We ask our [Nonconformist] brethren on their side that we too are justified in guarding . . . doctrines which are essential to our own religious lives and the usefulness of our ministry to others. It is in the interests of that ministry and in loyalty to our Master, whose mind we believe to be expressed in the faith and order of the Catholic Church, that we take our stand.'[13]

One of the other speakers on the subject of Christian unity was Fr W. H. Frere, Superior of the Community of the Resurrection, Mirfield. He had visited the Orthodox Church in Russia before the war and spoke warmly of what he called 'the rock from whence we were hewn'. He pointed out that the Eastern fathers of the early centuries had made a great contribution to the development of Christian doctrine, and that for centuries several Orthodox Churches had been subject to Muslim rule. He contrasted the Eastern and Western traditions: 'The unity of the Church in the Eastern mind is an organic unity of freely operating cells, organs and limbs; in the West it becomes a governmental unity under a terrestrial autocracy.'[14] Both traditions could learn much from each other.

The Russian Church was subject to persecution under the Communists, but the Orthodox were 'throwing off the nightmare of Mohammadan domination' in Greece and among the Yugoslavs; he hoped the same would soon happen in Syria and Turkey (as a result of the peace treaty which broke up the old Ottoman empire). Increasing numbers of Orthodox believers were coming to live in Britain; Anglicans should be aware of this and befriend them. 'For many of us Anglo-Catholics there is a great deal still to be learnt; and it must be learnt not merely as part of our Western heritage, but also (and by some of us perhaps more easily) through growing in friendship with the Eastern Orthodox Church.'[15] In other words, Anglo-Catholics should rely more on the Orthodox for the truth than Rome.

From ecumenical relationships the Congress turned to the Church of England's own party differences – its internal ecumenical task. F. Underhill said Catholics and Evangelicals were united in believing in the fundamentals of the Christian faith – 'our common faith in the Holy Trinity, the Incarnation, the Atonement, the Second Coming of our Lord, and . . . our common devotion to the historic English Church which we all desire to serve' – and they should come together to learn from one another rather than continue in suspicion and controversy. He realized that his openness towards Evangelicals would cause some of his friends to warn him that he was showing a dangerous tendency towards surrender, and that he did not realize what the consequences would be if he allowed himself to get on to the slippery slope of accommodation. But he thought such an attitude ignored the fact that there was already a good deal of interaction between the two parties.

'I would answer,' he said, 'that the Catholicism of the future will be a very much bigger thing than the Catholicism of yesterday or today; that altered circumstances are calling us in no uncertain terms to modifications in various directions; that we must be prepared to act constructively in such matters as obviously call for reform; that we discover in ourselves and disclose to others things valuable for the life of the whole Church. The fundamentals must always remain; but their implications are always developing, and their manifestations often changing. It is in this sense that we have many profitable lessons to learn from our brethren about the extension of the kingdom of God.'[16]

Underhill was secretary of the FCP, and his openness towards Evangelicals was not typical of many of its members. But he was one of a growing number of Catholics who, as Taylor had pointed out, recognized that the real enemy was atheism, which was undermining the Christian basis of society. They were coming to realize that their own country was the new mission field and that the Church would only be effective for the Gospel if all Christians worked together.

The demand for the evening sessions was so great that overflow meetings were held in the Queen's Hall on the Wednesday and Thursday, when some of the speakers went to Langham Place to repeat their talks. At the final rally in the Albert Hall people began arriving to queue for three hours before the doors opened and, besides the thousands who packed the Hall to its full capacity, many were turned away. Stone and the subjects committee had decided that the last session of the Congress should be on current social and industrial problems and that it would be appropriate to invite two laymen as well as two clergy to be the speakers.

One was a Mr A. Moore, introduced as the President of the Silvertown Branch of the Rubberworkers' Union. He began his brief talk by apologising for being unable to speak properly as he had just had all his teeth extracted. He said he met many men in the trade unions who would become faithful Catholics if only they met the right kind of priest to instruct them. He was thankful for what the Church in the East End had done to support the trade unions, especially during a recent dock strike (it had occurred earlier that year when Ernest Bevin was leader of the Dockers' Union). 'If we mean business,' he concluded, 'this Congress will bring much nearer the day when the Catholic Church of England can perform her duties and teach the Sacraments in the way the Master commanded.'[17]

The other layman was the journalist, essayist and poet, G. K. Chesterton. He had become well known for his championing of Christian orthodoxy before the war and his name on any list of speakers was a great attraction. But unfortunately he had – characteristically – misunderstood the kind of meeting he had been invited to address. He thought he was going to an informal gathering of Christians to talk about the Labour Party. When he entered the hall and saw the size of his audience, he tried unsuccessfully to persuade Wilson to cancel his appearance.

He had a small, high-pitched voice, of which he was well aware and found painfully embarrassing in a vast auditorium. So when he began with a long-winded explanation of why he had not expected to speak on such an occasion, there were cat-calls and shouts from parts of the hall that people couldn't hear. He struggled to expound his favourite theme – that because the Church was so influential in the middle ages, commerce and industry were conducted then in a much fairer and just way.

'The modern world began when the Middle Ages broke down, and ... since then a certain non-Christian and anti-Christian spirit has been more and more the constructive and creative powering our institutions; in other words, whatever you call it, scepticism, rationalism, worldliness, had run its own way, and done practically what it liked in an increasing degree for a considerable time. And it has made a most ghastly mess of it.'[18]

Christians should respond by upholding the ethics of the Gospel in their own lives and using all the influence they had to encourage society to return to that ethic. At the end he returned to his claim about the middle ages with a typical GK paradox. He described a Protestant picture which had been drawn of Queen Victoria presenting a Bible to an Indian or Afghan chief with the words: 'The Secret of England's greatness', and then went on:

'I think we've got seriously to consider whether the whole of our civilization has not been sufficiently on the decline for it to be possible sometime soon for people to be looking not for the explanation of our greatness, but for the explanation of our weakness; and I hope that in some future ages there will not be shown another kind of picture, showing the ruins of

THE FIRST CONGRESS 1920

Bolton Abbey or the desecrated shrine, the empty shrine of Glastonbury, with the title, "The Secret of England's failure".[19]

He sat down to the evident relief of the audience as well as himself.

Bishop Gore, the third speaker, had no difficulty in making himself heard. Like most of the clergy, he was used to preaching in large churches without modern public address systems. He said the most effective way the early Church witnessed to Jesus Christ was in the ethical standards of its own communities. It was a sort of communism, but without legal compulsion: a brotherhood which was the main instrument in converting the world.

Two other characteristics of that brotherhood, he said, deeply impressed outsiders during the years in which the Church was persecuted: the witness of self-control in sexual matters, and the courage in the face of death. He briefly outlined the changes which came within the Church during succeeding centuries and deplored the increase in the number of divorces and the practice of birth control. He then invited those in the audience who were willing to maintain moral purity and the sanctity of marriage to stand as an act of public witness. The editor of the report noted that everyone did so and there was lengthy applause.

He went on to say the rise of Labour represented a revolt not only by 'working people' – an expression he disliked – but by many men and women who were unhappy at the condition the country was in. English people were in a state of moral confusion and needed the Church's witness now more than ever. This was a task in which all denominations could work together. 'It is the return to our origin, it is the will of God, and I am persuaded that it is on this field that all Christians can at once, without any danger to our principles, begin to think and act together.'[20]

The last speaker was Fr E. K. Talbot CR who followed Frere as Superior at Mirfield when the latter was made Bishop of Truro in 1922. Talbot's was a very brief address on the Church's task of reclaiming the secular order of society for the Kingdom of God. 'Without such an intention,' he said, 'the Catholic faith will become the hobby of a small coterie, instead of a force for laying hands on the whole world, so that it will not be a perpetual contradiction to the eternal laws of God's being.'[21]

He had just finished when the Bishop of London appeared in a purple cassock making his way down a gangway. Enthusiastic applause greeted Winnington-Ingram as he mounted the platform. 'Uncle Arthur' was a popular figure in the diocese – except among extreme Catholics when he tried half-heartedly to discipline them. With the chairman's permission to address the audience, he said he had not come to give a lecture but to congratulate the organizers of the Congress on its success. Then he pronounced a blessing. Afterwards there was an uncomfortable silence. People wondered if the last hymn was to be sung. It wasn't. The records do not reveal if the bishop's appearance had been planned. It seems more likely he had decided on the spur of the moment that, as the Congress turned out to be more popular than he imagined, he had better identify himself with it. But his action meant the audience left the Hall with a feeling of anticlimax. His benediction had been like a splash of icy water on Catholic enthusiasm.

On Friday a private meeting of priests was held in Church House at which it was agreed the executive should be asked to organize a second Congress in two or three years' time. That evening thanksgiving services were held in St Alban, Holborn, St Augustine, Kilburn, and in All Saints, Margaret Street. All these churches reported full congregations. But the most memorable service was in Southwark cathedral. By half-past six a large queue was forming outside the main door and by eight o'clock, when the service was due to begin, it overflowed from the churchyard across London Bridge to the Monument. They sang songs such as 'Hail Mary, Hail Mary, Hail Mary, full of grace'. Atlay commented in his parish magazine afterwards that it was the first time since the Reformation that London Bridge had heard the Mother of the Lord invoked on it. It demonstrated the determation of many Catholics to restore prayers to the Blesed Virgin and the Saints to Anglican worship. Hundreds could not gain admission to the cathedral, so the Bishop of Nassau held an impromptu service outside, preached a brief sermon, and led them in singing further hymns. They roared 'Ye who own the faith of Jesus' so loudly that the congregation inside the building could hardly hear the cathedral choir singing a delicate polyphonic Gregorian setting of the *Te Deum*.

The preacher in the cathedral was Bishop M. B. Furse of St Albans. He had just returned home after seventeen years in South Africa, thirteen of them as Bishop of Pretoria. The experience of the Congress convinced him, he said, that the Church should give a high priority to evangelism, increase the number of bishops so that they related more closely to their clergy, and strive for Christian unity.

'I come back to serve once again in the homeland a thousand times more convinced than I was when I left England in 1903, that the only hope for the world is Christianity, and the only hope for Christianity is the reunion of Christendom... And in spite of its obviously partial and inadequate expression as we see it today in England, the Catholic view of faith and order which has been handed down to us in the Anglican Communion is nearer the mind of Christ than any other view I have ever come across.'[22]

So ended the first Anglo-Catholic Congress. Its success was greater than anything which Atlay, Wilson, Mackay and the others could have imagined when they first discussed it over a year before. Two results were immediate. One was that Weston was acclaimed as the leading Catholic bishop in the episcopate of the Anglican Communion. The other was that, when the jewellery had been sold and the promised donations had come in, a total of £44,000 was received – only £6,000 short of the target. After making gifts to overseas dioceses, the executive had enough money to sponsor future Congresses and other teaching and evangelistic initiatives. What came to be known as the Anglo-Congress movement had begun.

5

Weston and the Lambeth Conference 1920

When Weston received the invitation to attend the Lambeth Conference he wondered if he should boycott it. He was conscious that over the years his various letters of protest about persons and events in the Church had made him such a nuisance to the Archbishop of Canterbury that his presence might not be welcomed. Sidney Dark remarked that Zanzibar must have been one of the most troublesome bishops Davidson ever had to deal with. Yet in his own diocese Weston was hugely popular. He lived closely to his people and got to know them intimately. When he died one of his African clergy wrote, 'I think there was no European who knew black people better than he did, their characters and customs, their hardships and their longings. I think there was no European who did more to range himself on the side of the black people, and who was so desirous that they should advance.'[1]

He attempted to run his diocese on the model he described in the Albert Hall. During the war he was hampered in doing this as the mainland part of it was a German colony and he was only able to visit it with difficulty. Among the things he saw there which troubled him was the practice of sending men away into forced labour camps to work on roads and railways. When under the terms of the Versailles peace treaty the former German colony became a British protectorate, he was angry that this practice was not immediately abolished. He protested about it in a pamphlet entitled *The Serfs of Great Britain* (1919), saying it was immoral because it ignored the right of men to be paid for their labour, it broke up families and communities by separating men from their wives and their tribes for long periods, and it involved cruelty because the living and working conditions were intolerable (overseers often used the lash). Furthermore, men were being forcibly recruited by the colonial administrators not only for government purposes but also for commercial businessmen who sometimes used bribes to achieve their aims.

Behind his concern was Weston's deep conviction that black people are just as much children of God as white people and that they should be treated equally – an attitude by no means common among the colonial administrators of his day. He believed Africans should be helped to develop within their own tribes and culture. Without wanting to withhold from them the benefits of modern medicine and education, he argued these should be introduced in a manner sensitive to African abilities and customs, not as a means of exploiting black people for the profits of British colonists. He was not alone in these convictions. Arthur Chandler, who was Bishop of Bloemfontein from 1902 to 1921, had made himself unpopular among the whites by initiating education schemes for African children and ordaining the first black priests in his diocese. The priest-poet Arthur Shearly Cripps had spent most of his life in Southern Rhodesia (now Zimbabwe) fighting for justice for Africans, especially over land-rights. But Weston took the initiative in publicizing these evils and planned to go to England after the war to petition the government to forbid the practice.

In the meantime he had become more and more disillusioned with the news of the Church he received while he was in Africa and with what he discovered on his visits to this country. The rise of Modernism alarmed him, and he issued warnings of its effect in the mission field where Islam was strong. Preaching in St John Church, Red Lion Square, in 1911 he said, 'Save our converts in Africa from reading in books by Christians at home all those things which are calculated to make them doubt whether there be a God at all, and such a thing as a Catholic revelation.' To drive the point home he went on, 'Imagine a Mohammedan speaking: "We have always maintained that your Scriptures are corrupt and interpolated, and lo! Now your learned men tell you we are right. The Prophet told us that Jesus did not really die on the cross and rose again, and your learned men agree that He only rose again in the imaginations of His disciples. We have been taught that Jesus was a Prophet and not God, and your learned men say the same."'[2]

He was conscious, too, that he had the reputation of causing the Kikuyu controversy. In 1913 a missionary conference was held in what was then British East Africa between Anglicans, Presbyterians and other Protestants under the leadership of Bishops W. G. Peel of Mombasa and J. J. Willis of Uganda. At this conference it was proposed that the churches should work together for the spread of the Gospel in a loose federation within which, it was rumoured, members would be free to practice intercommunion. The conference ended with a Communion service at which the Bishops gave the sacrament to all who were present. When Weston heard of this he protested to Davidson that the proposed federation denied important aspects of the Catholic faith, including the acceptance of episcopacy in the divine ordering of the Church. Many in the Church of

England, including some Catholics like Halifax, thought Weston overreacted. It is possible that he read more into the proposals than was intended. In response the Archbishop with his usual sagacity explained that within the federation Nonconformists might receive Communion from Anglicans but that Anglicans should not seek Communion from Nonconformist ministers. Weston was still not satisfied, but publicity about the controversy faded with the outbreak of war and left the general impression that Weston was fiercely opposed to all things ecumenical.

Weston in Africa made another protest when Lloyd George nominated H. H. Henson for appointment to the see of Hereford in 1917. The prime minister, as a Welsh Nonconformist, had been impressed when he heard Henson wanted union between the Church of England and Nonconformists and nominated Henson, then Dean of Durham, for the see. The appointment caused a minor uproar. The English Church Union, the *Church Times*, Evangelicals and many others also joined in protesting. What upset them was Henson's questioning of the virgin birth and the resurrection, and the Archbishop was petitioned not to accept the nomination. In the end Davidson only agreed to proceed with the consecration after he and Henson issued a joint statement in which the latter seemed to modify his earlier views. In his book *The Christ and His Critics* (1919) attacking Modernism, Weston branded Henson as a heretic.

It was for these reasons that Weston came to England feeling depressed and wondering if he should boycott Lambeth. However, his gloom was swept away by the success of the Congress. He was overwhelmed by the huge Albert Hall gatherings and the packed churches. He was moved by the tremendous reception he received personally. What he saw and heard convinced him that God could revive the Church of England in the Catholic faith and that he might, after all, have a role in this. A man of swings of moods, he suddenly took heart.

During the Congress his hopes were buoyed up further by meeting a group of overseas bishops who would be going to Lambeth with him. Up to then he had thought of himself as a lone Catholic voice among a hostile episcopate. Now he realized he would be joining a company of like-minded bishops. Having been out of England, except for occasional visits, since he went to Zanzibar, Weston did not fully realize the changes which had taken place in the Church, especially since the war. Catholics were no longer feeling besieged as they had been in the days when he had been a curate at St Matthew, Westminster. He found a new confidence among them. He met a rising generation of able Catholic scholars like Turner, Taylor, Williams and Thornton. He discovered he would be at Lambeth with some Evangelical bishops who were discovering that there were Catholics who, like themselves, had the cause of the Kingdom at heart. These included Ridgeway of Salisbury who had preached at the opening Congress sermon; Watts Ditchfield of Chelmsford who had written to say he would have liked to have attended the Congress for one day but was unable to fit it into his diary; and Theodore Woods of Peterborough, who was in sympathy with much that Catholics stood for and who would be one of the episcopal secretaries at Lambeth.

There would also be English bishops who could be relied on to support Catholics provided the latter were not extremists and showed tolerance for others: Lang of York, Winnington-Ingram of London, Furse of St Albans, E. S. Talbot of Winchester, C. F. Garbett of Southwark, E. Hoskins of Southwell, and Bishop Montgomery of SPG, the other episcopal secretary. Then there would be supportive bishops from overseas, besides those who had attended the Congress, from the West Indies, South Africa, North America and the Far East. Three of these were black. On their side, these bishops had heard stories of Weston's pioneering ministry in East Africa and of his campaign against forced labour, and they admired him even if some of them questioned his theology. All of them were intrigued to see how Weston and Henson would react to one another.

Preparations for the Conference had been particularly trying for Davidson. Although he had the experience of presiding over the two previous Lambeths, he was conscious that this one was the first gathering of the bishops after the war, and that among the items on an accumulated agenda were highly contentious issues – questions concerning marriage and divorce, racism and the ministry of women, challenges thrown up by the growth of Modernism and the popularity of spiritualism, and problems facing the Communion in the post-war world. He was especially anxious about the Conference's reactions to the movements for Christian unity. The bishops had not had an opportunity of voicing their corporate mind on the reports of the World Missionary Conference held in Edinburgh ten years' previously and the International Missionary Council which had been set up afterwards. Headlam's *The Doctrine of the Church and Christian Reunion* had resulted in warnings being sent to him from Catholic groups, that any attempt to compromise the Church of England's doctrine and discipline in schemes for reunion with non-episcopal bodies would be resisted by them. And he was apprehensive that clashes between Henson and Weston would disrupt the Conference. Although the Archbishop found Weston troublesome, yet he admired the Bishop of Zanzibar for his work and was touched by his friendliness.

The 252 bishops met throughout July in the Great Hall of Lambeth Palace on chairs specially made for the occasion (and which the bishops were invited to purchase at the end of the proceedings for fifteen shillings each). In the first week they met in full session, and for the next two in committees to prepare reports on the various subjects on the agenda. These reports were to be presented at a full session during the fourth and final week. In the hall it was noticed that Weston and Henson were stiffly polite to one another; they were sitting in the fourth row opposite the Archbishop, who presided from a small rostrum. Davidson therefore had the two antagonists immediately in front of him.

During the first week Weston got up and spoke several times. In a debate about the League of Nations he forcefully pointed out the grave wrongs being inflicted on Africans in mandated territories. On another day, just as a resolution about marriage and divorce was about to be put, he strode to the rostrum and said menacingly he would not like to determine his relation to the Conference if it voted on such a resolution (a hint that he would walk out). When foreign missions were discussed he claimed episcopacy had failed in England and elsewhere because it did not faithfully represent the Fatherhood of God to the diocese. He went on to declare he would like to scrap the agenda of the Conference so they could take time in learning how to reconcile the episcopate with truly paternal government. Each diocese, he said, should be a family, and dioceses together should constitute a real unity round its bishop. It was virtually a re-run of what he had said in the Albert Hall.

In his diary Henson wrote: 'The speeches of the Bishop of Zanzibar were somewhat perplexing. He speaks contemptuously of the Conference and all its ways, tells the Bishops to live among the poor in the slums and ask them to dinner, describes the episcopal character very grotesquely, and is generally treated as a "chartered libertine". He is elaborately polite to me. I doubt whether he is taken quite seriously by anybody, though he is universally popular.'[3]

Yet Weston became one of the stars at the Conference. Those who had not met him previously expected a bigoted firebrand. Instead they encountered a charismatic charmer who overwhelmed them by his friendly openness. They may have disagreed with him, or they may have been uncomfortable as they recognized the truth of his criticisms; but they felt they were in the presence of a man devoted to his Lord and to justice for his African people. Moreover, his vision of the Church as a Communion of communities gathered round their bishop inspired the younger among them. They wanted to be the kind of bishop he described, but they were restricted by the administrative and social situations in which they found themselves. In their big dioceses most people saw them as distant gaited figures belonging to the ruling classes who had to be addressed as 'my lord'. No one would have dreamt of following the present-day custom of calling a diocesan like Henson 'Bishop Herbert'!

The bishops' reactions to meeting Weston for the first time are reflected in a letter Weston's biographer received from Bishop E. H. Pearce of Worcester: 'I had expected a physique worn and shriveled and racked with the ravages of an insidious climate and with the effects of prolonged apostolic labour, but instead I found a well set-up Apollo – if you can conceive the god in a purple cassock, and wearing a considerable pectoral cross. I had expected an expression of some petulance, with signs of one who had little experience of bearing the yoke in his youth; but the face, tanned indeed, but almost ruddy in its apparent heath, had upon it a certain majesty of large-mindedness, which seemed to belie the possibility of his having railed against Kikuyu and all that Kikuyu implied.'[4]

In the second and third weeks Weston found himself with Henson in the committee on reunion. Davidson had asked the Archbishop of York to chair this committee as he knew Lang to be particularly interested in the subject. Although as a young man Lang had left the Church of Scotland to become an Anglican, he still looked back on the Church of his baptism with affection, and often discussed ways of bringing the Kirk and the Church of England together without compromising his Catholic principles. But having accepted the Archbishop's invitation, he did not look forward to the task. 'It seems humanly impossible', he wrote to his mother, 'to get a crowd of Bishops representing every possible point of view, and already disclosing great cleavages of principle, to unite in any proposals short of mere platitudes.'[5] He was dismayed that the committee was so large: seventy, a third of the Conference, had applied to be on it. When they came together most did not expect it would be possible to do anything more than reaffirm the terms of the Lambeth Quadrilateral, first published in 1888, as conditions for uniting with any non-episcopal Church. The Catholics, it was rumoured, would not accept anything less.

The opening meetings were, as Lang feared, depressingly unproductive. Headlam, already a *persona non grata* among Catholics for his book, had produced a memorandum on Anglican relations with other Episcopal bodies and this was distributed to the committee members. Headlam had written that there had been no sign of any progress in relations with the Roman Catholic Church. Some of the more enlightened bishops and clergy of the Eastern Orthodox Churches, who had taken part in recent conferences at Oxford and London, revealed a more accommodating spirit, though the great body of Orthodox remained conservative.

An encyclical letter from the Patriarch of Constantinople to Christian Churches throughout the world, issued in January 1920, had suggested the acceptance of a uniform calendar and joint consultations on pastoral matters such as mixed marriages. The Scandinavian Churches were becoming increasingly friendly. They were episcopal in constitution and Lutheran in doctrine, though only the Swedish Lutheran Church claimed to possess the apostolic succession.

Discussion of the report occupied two or three days. Davidson's chaplain (and later biographer), G. K. A. Bell, was kept busy as the committee's secretary. It was noticeable that the Catholics were interested in what Headlam had reported about the Orthodox and the Roman Church but became uneasy when reunion with the Nonconformists was mooted. They grew restless, too, when Henson proposed that Presbyterian orders like those in the Church of Scotland should be recognized by Anglicans, and when Bishop Whitehead of Madras spoke enthusiastically about a scheme for a united Church in South India, proposed by a conference at Tranquabar the previous year. Only Lang's firm chairmanship saved the committee from being lost in irreconcilable wrangling.

But it was noticed Weston did not always join other Catholics in voicing objections. The bishops were surprised he seemed ready to acknowledge the possibility that non-episcopal bodies might be brought within the framework of a united Church. With an emotional outburst typical of him he told Bishop Samuel Azariah of Dornakal, 'If you are one of the Bishops of the South India United Church, I shall be entirely satisfied.' Perhaps what moved Weston was Azariah's devotion and sincerity. He was the first Indian to be consecrated a bishop, and he was as eager to develop an indigenous ministry as Weston was an African one.

Then Lang had an inspiration which brought the committee together in a remarkable way. He proposed that they should compose a letter inviting non-Anglicans to consider what the possibilities were for reunion. He wanted the letter to be addressed to all Christians rather than to their Churches, as he guessed it would be more likely to attract attention than putting forward a scheme of reunion. It would also avoid giving the impression that Lambeth's idea of unity was that everyone else should become like the Anglicans. His proposal was accepted, and a small sub-committee was elected to set about the task of discussing what should go in the letter and compose drafts. Weston and Henson were both on it.

Weston was one of the most enthusiastic members of the sub-committee. He eagerly discussed the proposed letter's contents with different groups of bishops, sometimes in the evening after the conference had officially adjourned. In doing so he revealed openness to matters of Church order which surprised those who heard him. What they did not know was that he had years of experience in discussing united prayer and action with Nonconformists. In the follow-up to the Kikuyu controversy he met with other denominations to consider the possibility of co-operation between episcopal and non-episcopal missions in East Africa. These discussions were suspended by the outbreak of war, but in 1918 he returned to the subject in an article published in UMCA's magazine, *Central Africa*, outlining proposals for reunion. The contents of this article go some way towards explaining why Weston was so co-operative in drafting the letter.

In the article he began by saying it was essential all Christians seeking reunion should acknowledge the existence of the Catholic Church of Christ as a universal brotherhood. Some saw this in terms of a sacramental incorporation into the Body of Christ, and others saw it as a fellowship drawn together in the Holy Spirit; but whatever their view, they must agree that it was Christ's will that all his faithful are to be united. 'I submit,' he wrote, 'that on an agreement such as this it is not impossible to unite in one society.' It was necessary too that all should accept episcopacy as the only form of oversight which can be historically justified – a ministry which is from above as well as below, and which has extended down the ages. 'Once episcopacy is accepted, each "communion" can be free to reconcile its existing organization with its newly acquired bishops. We do not want, for example, to abolish Presbyterial forms of Church government. We want to perfect them.' He proposed that the ministers of uniting 'communions' should be willing to accept from one another the laying on of hands: 'My desire, in God's sight, whose ordained minister I believe myself to be, is to be in a position to minister everywhere. Therefore I am willing to accept at the hands of each community that will unite with me, whatever it thinks it can add to me, provided that it will also receive from my community what we think we have to offer.'[6]

The Holy Scriptures and the Catholic Creeds must be the common doctrinal basis accepted by all. He confessed he did not see clearly how different interpretations of the Bible were to be handled, but he did not think this would be an insuperable difficulty. All, too, should agree that God uses sacramental means of grace, though he was open to different understandings of it. 'For myself, I do not want to know how men define the sacraments, unless they desire to teach under my authority. But I do desire to know that they have sufficient belief in sacramental grace to make them value Baptism, with the laying on of hands, and the Holy Communion of our Lord's Body and Blood; and to cause them at least to acquiesce in other people's use of the rest of the sacraments.' These other sacraments included the ministry of absolution, though in exercising it there would be 'forbearance in all questions of method and detail'. Finally he wanted the uniting communities to agree to use certain fixed liturgical formulas for the central prayers at Baptisms, the Eucharist, and other sacramental acts. 'Otherwise there can be no common participation [in them]. But for the rest of these sacramental rites no uniformity is necessary. Much less do we need uniform rites in non-sacramental services. I advocate complete freedom. Let the various communities uniting follow each its own mind.' At the end came a tweak of the Establishment tail: 'And let English Church congregations receive permission to share the liberty of their less enslaved brethren.'[7]

His vision of Christian unity in the article was developed from his book *The Fullness of Christ* (1916) where he traced the emergence of the Catholic Church from the atoning work of Christ and the Christian community's evolution through the centuries. The order of bishops continued the ministry of the apostolate in teaching the Gospel and administering the sacraments, and what was needed was to restore this biblical foundation out of the disunity in which Christians now found themselves. Weston's ideas were inspired by the way individual provinces in the Anglican Communion were beginning to develop their own rites and customs based on the Prayer Book (in Zanzibar he used a form of the 1549 rite translated into Swahili), and by the example Rome had set by being in communion with the Uniat Churches with their own liturgy and married clergy.

Towards the end of the book he wrote: 'The word Church has only two meanings that can claim divine authority. It means either, the whole Mystical Body, the one, holy, catholic, and apostolic Church; or one local section of that Church, whose union within it is expressed by, and secured in, the presence within it of the office and order of the catholic Episcopate . . . Thus English Catholics may indeed take heart, for their position within the Catholic Church is assured to them, in spite of all that Papists or Protestants may say against them. There is . . . no Anglican Church; just as there is no Roman and no Eastern Church. There is the Catholic Church, and there are several thousand local Churches within the unity of the Catholic Church.'[8]

Weston had forgotten the aversion most Nonconformists in Britain had to any suggestion of adopting episcopacy. In Africa bishops like Weston exercised their ministry in such a personal way among their clergy and people that missionaries of other denominations would not have considered them as being much different from their own senior pastors. For them episcopacy had a caring as well as authoritative face. But in Britain there were still long memories of how Anglican bishops in the past had opposed and tried to suppress the dissenters, while at the same time guarding their privileges in Parliament, in the universities, in church schools, and in society generally.

The article reveals how Weston attempted to apply Catholic order to a practical scheme of reunion from his African experiences. He urged his readers to trust that in the process the Holy Spirit would lead those involved to a common mind over their theological and other differences. Christians would find unity in Christ, not by becoming Roman Catholics or Eastern Orthodox – or even Anglicans – but by discovering afresh what it means to become the Body of Christ united in fellowship and mission. It is notable that Weston was willing to accept for himself a mutual laying on of hands in any future scheme of reunion. Most of his Anglo-Catholic contemporaries refused to consider such a condition, saying it seemed to deny the validity of their orders, and to imply Nonconformist ministers had graces for ordination which they as Anglican priests lacked.

So the Lambeth letter began by acknowledging that all who are baptized in the name of the Holy Trinity are members of the universal Church, and that all share in the sin of disunity. Then it continued: 'The times call us to a new outlook and new measures. The Faith cannot be adequately apprehended and the battle of the Kingdom cannot be worthily fought while the body is divided, and is thus unable to grow up into the fullness of the life of Christ... The vision that arises before us is that of a Church genuinely Catholic, loyal to all Truth, and gathering into its fellowship all who profess and call themselves Christians, within whose visible unity all the treasures of faith and order, bequeathed as a heritage by the past to the present, shall be possessed in common and made serviceable to the whole Body of Christ.' Such a unity must rest upon a 'whole-hearted acceptance' of the Holy Scriptures, the Creeds, the Sacraments of Baptism and Holy Communion, and a Ministry 'acknowledged by every part of the Church as possessing not only the inward call of the Spirit but also the commission of Christ and the authority of the whole body'.

The bishops realized that the subject of the episcopacy must be introduced sensitively so they said that, while they thankfully recognized the work of the Holy Spirit in the ministers of non-episcopal Churches, they nevertheless urged that the episcopacy 'is now and will prove to be in the future the best instrument for maintaining the unity and continuity of the Church... It is not that we call in question for a moment the spiritual reality of the ministries of those Communions which do not possess the episcopate. On the contrary we thankfully acknowledge that these ministries have been manifestly blessed and owned by the Holy Spirit as effective means of grace. But we submit that consideration alike of history and of present experience justify the claim which we make on behalf of the episcopate. Moreover, we would urge that it is now and will prove to be in the future the best instrument for maintaining the unity and continuity of the Church.'

At this point the letter echoed what Weston had said at the Congress about a bishop's ministry: 'We greatly desire that the office of a Bishop should be everywhere exercised in a representative and constitutional manner and more truly express all that ought to be involved for the life of the Christian Family, in the title of Father-in-God. Nay more, we eagerly look forward to the day when through its acceptance in a united Church we may all share in that grace which is pledged to the members of the whole body in the apostolic rite of the laying-on-of-hands, and in the joy and fellowship of a Eucharist in which as one Family we may together, without any doubtfulness of mind, offer to the one Lord our worship and service.'

The letter then made a significant proposal. If the terms of union with another denomination had been satisfactorily agreed, Anglican bishops and clergy would be willing to accept 'a form of commission or recognition which would commend our ministry to their congregations, as having its place in the one family . . . It is our hope that the same motive would lead ministers who have not received it to accept a commission through episcopal ordination, as obtaining for them a ministry through the whole fellowship'. Nothing, they said, should be done which could possibly be taken as repudiating anyone's past ministry. They added: 'We do not ask that any one Communion should consent to be absorbed in another. We ask that all should unite in a new and great endeavour to recover and to manifest to the world the unity of the Body of Christ for which He prayed.'[9] What this implied was that, if non-episcopal ministers accepted episcopal ordination then Church of England bishops and priests would accept the laying-on-of-hands as 'a form of commission or recognition' as well.

A number of resolutions were attached to the letter. One declared that, in situations where Christians were working towards unity, a bishop would be justified in giving permission for non-episcopally ordained ministers to preach in churches within his diocese, and for clergy of the diocese to preach in the churches of such ministers. Another resolution said that where a scheme for reunion was being planned, a bishop should not be questioned by other bishops if he gave permission for baptized but not confirmed members of non-episcopal congregations involved in the scheme to receive Communion. However, there was to be no general intercommunion until reunion had been effected, though priests were reminded that they had no authority to refuse Communion to any baptized person unless that person had been excommunicated or been a cause of scandal, and that cases of doubt should be referred to the bishop.

During the course of composing the text the members of the unity committee saw Weston and Henson spending time together when they were asked to work on the final drafting of the letter. Bishop Knox of Manchester wrote:

'Popular anticipation had figured Frank Weston, the Bishop of Zanzibar, on one side, and Bishop Hensley Henson on the other, as the two irreconcilables. Had the public been admitted to our sessions, they would, again and again, have seen these two protagonists literally putting their heads together in search of some formula of agreement. The generous spirit of Christian charity, which characterized the report as a whole, won for it, and still wins for it, wide approval.'[10]

The Appeal

The finished version of the letter was finally scrutinized by a small group which included the two English archbishops. They worked under a tree in Lambeth Palace garden on the Sunday afternoon before the text was presented to the whole Conference the following morning. Davidson wisely allocated a whole day to a discussion of it. Lang gave what those present thought was the best speech in the Conference, urging the bishops to support the document. The most vigorous proposal to reject it came from Bishop Hall of Vermont, a noted Catholic scholar. Weston made a passionate plea for everyone to accept it; so did the Bishop of Nassau. Their speeches brought practically all the Catholics onto their side. When it was passed by a large majority with only three opposing and one abstaining, the Conference stood and sang the *Te Deum*. Later many of those present said they experienced what they called a 'wind of the Holy Spirit' in the hall. So was born what became known as 'The Lambeth Appeal to All Christian People'.

Other resolutions of ecumenical significance were also passed, some of which were to influence Catholic opinion. The bishops accepted Headlam's report on the Swedish Church and agreed that Swedish Christians were to be received at Holy Communion. Following the Conference Henson and Woods went to Uppsala to join in the consecration of a Swedish bishop. Greetings and thanks were sent to the Ecumenical patriarch for his encyclical letter. (Two years later he wrote to say that the Holy Synod accepted the validity of Anglican orders.) The government was urged to do all it could to prevent the further persecution of Russian, Armenian, Assyrian and Jacobite Christians, and prayers were called for them. Relations with the Old Catholic Church on the continent were to be explored. Invitations to receive Communion in Orthodox Churches were to be accepted when the opportunity arose. Anglicans were to encourage the formation of local councils of churches.

On 13 August, after the end of Lambeth, the *Church Times* welcomed the Appeal, and the following week Weston contributed an article to the paper in which he argued that it demonstrated a Catholic spirit that was far removed from the stiffness and self-complacency of Anglicanism and presented the ideal of unity in diversity:

'The visibility of the one organism would be due to an undivided College of Bishops, Orthodox, Roman and Anglican, with bishops from the Presbyterian and Free Church communions. Each communion so represented in the undivided College of Bishops would remain an individual group within the one visible body. It would retain its own customs, methods, and ways of worship, as far as is compatible with life in a universal fellowship that possesses one faith, possesses one Episcopal ministry, and uses sacraments common to all. Between these groups there would be intercommunion and all such acts of mutual fellowship.' But he was realistic enough to expect opposition to the Appeal from some of his supporters, and he ended with a sharp warning: 'If Anglo-Catholics spend their time picking holes in the language of the Appeal, rather than in thanking God for what He has done for us, they will be, indeed, blind leaders of the blind. They will further betray a singular unconsciousness of the dangers from which they have been preserved.'[11]

Atlay arranged for Weston and Shedden to address a special meeting of the Federation of Catholic Priests to discuss the Appeal, and so many turned up that it had to be transferred from St Matthew's to the Great Hall in Church House. Weston's tone was conciliatory: he took the line that the Appeal had come out of a spirit of penitence for the failings of the Anglican Communion since it had broken away from the Roman Church. But many were not convinced. Gore was appreciative but hesitant; he had been at a preliminary meeting of the World Conference on Faith and Order in Geneva that summer and doubted whether German and Scandinavian Protestants would ever accept Catholic doctrines of the sacraments and ministerial order. Stone and N. P. Williams pointed out that Nonconformist Churches did not become Catholic simply by putting forward their ministers for the apostolic laying-on of hands, important though that was. To become true Catholics they had to affirm their faith in the Church, not just as a social organization, but as a spiritual reality of which the apostolic laying-on of hands and the other sacraments are outward and visible signs. In other words, did Nonconformists believe in the One, Holy, Catholic and Apostolic Church in the deepest and ultimate sense of those words? Or were they just accepting episcopacy as a gesture of reconciliation with Anglicans? The meeting ended without any resolution being passed.

There were other Catholics, however, who were enthusiastic. One was Halifax, who wrote to Davidson that few things in his life had given him more pleasure. Another was T. A. Lacey, a canon of Worcester, who had taken part in an ecumenical conference at Mansfield College and signed a manifesto which indicated its signatories were willing to recognize each other's ministries, to exchange pulpits and to offer eucharistic hospitality. F. Underhill was equally keen; it was in harmony with his own ideas of how ecumenical relationships could be developed. The *Church Times* was approving: 'It [the Appeal] is perfectly definite. It does not suggest the possibility of a reunion built on friendliness and fraternity alone. The Church, it recognizes, must hold one faith, and there can be no visible unity without its wholehearted acceptance ... The idea of the Church simply as a body for philanthropic work, ready to admit everyone of good-will who is ready to join in the work, is excluded. It is made quite clear that the Church is a religious society with a creed and a body of dogmatic theology. There must be a minimum of belief.'[12] The paper spoke for a majority of Anglicans.

Weston's return to his diocese was delayed because he had heard Parliament was going to debate the problem of forced labour in Africa, so he took the opportunity of going on a speaking tour explaining the significance of the Appeal. He joined Bishops M. Linton Smith of Hereford and Woods of Peterborough in writing a pamphlet, *Lambeth and Reunion*. When he returned to Zanzibar at the end of 1920, he was disappointed to find that the white clergy in UMCA were cool towards the Appeal.

The reactions of those Catholics who were suspicious of the Appeal came from their conviction that Nonconformists, no matter how worthy as devout Christians, were essentially schismatics who had broken away from the Church and whose ministers therefore were unauthorized to take part in any Anglican service. Years before Lambeth they had become alarmed at the growing custom – which increased during the war – of the exchange of pulpits by Anglicans and Nonconformists.

An example of their strength of feeling about this was demonstrated two years previously when Bishop George Nickson of Bristol, hearing that the signing of an armistice was imminent, made plans for a service of thanksgiving in his cathedral on 10 November 1918, and invited a prominent Congregational minister in the city, Dr Arnold Thomas, to share in the prayers. It was a very successful service with crowds standing in the aisles. However, 33 Catholic clergy in his diocese were criticized for boycotting the service, so they sent a letter to the *Times* explaining their reasons. They were as anxious as any to work for the unity of the Church, they said, but 'to allow ministers of religious bodies separated from the Church to take part publicly in her services, though they deny her authority, reject her priesthood, and repudiate some of her service, is to condone schism, and make it of no account'.

Nickson, who was generally sympathetic towards Catholics, sent a dignified reply to the *Times*. He said he was not advocating participation by Nonconformists in normal Anglican services, but he believed there were special occasions in national life when Christians of all denominations should join in united prayers of thanksgiving. The stress and suffering of war had drawn Christians together and now they were united in a deep sense of gratitude to God that it was over.

'Nothing, I think, helped more to emphasize this unity in thankfulness and this recognition of national unity than the participation of Dr Thomas in our prayers, and had the [Roman Catholic] Bishop of Clifton seen his way to accept the invitation which was sent to him (and which he so kindly acknowledged), the emphasis would have been even more marked. I venture to believe that the conscience of the City, as evidenced by the thousands of its citizens who sought admission to the service, demands just such an expression of our fellowship in Christ, a fellowship which, believe me, transcends any question of formal status in this or that religious body.'[13]

The chaplains to the Forces, he concluded, reported that many men dismissed the relevance of Christianity because they saw the Church as exclusive and the cause of divisions in society rather than unity.

The ECU referred the Appeal to its Theological and Liturgical Committee. Under Stone's chairmanship it submitted a report on 24 November. It wanted the document to be revised so that it contained references to the Nicene as well as the Apostles' Creed, belief in the doctrine of the Sacraments (confirmation and absolution as well as baptism and Holy Communion, with acceptance of infant baptism) and ordination as a sacramental means of conferring the grace of orders and not merely as a means of appointment to a ministerial position. On the proposals for union with non-episcopal bodies the Committee wanted to strengthen the intention of maintaining Catholic faith and order, to allow only ordination candidates to preach, and to ensure baptism is followed by confirmation. They also wanted to make it clear that women are not admitted to synods, and that deaconesses are not in deacons' orders and therefore are not allowed to take services.

The American Church Union was even more critical – no doubt prompted by Bishop Bell who had been one of the three dissidents at Lambeth. It complained that the Lambeth Quadrilateral had been so rephrased and reworded that it could admit such diversity as it amounted to nothing. The treatment of the sacraments was so vague that it could accommodate any sacramental theology. 'Even Zwinglianism could find a happy home in this description.' Finally the Union declared the omission of the phrase 'the historical episcopate' opened the door to the possible abandonment of any traditional, apostolic ministry.

The follow-up to the Appeal continued in England after Weston had returned to his diocese. During the next few months Woods addressed the national assemblies of the Methodists, the Baptists, and the Congregationalists, and spoke at meetings in Scotland. Lang also toured the country for similar occasions. In 1921 Gore and Frere joined the archbishops and half-a-dozen other bishops in conversations with representatives of the Nonconformists. The latter conceded that, after reunion, all ministers should be episcopally ordained, but they were unable to agree on the re-ordination of their own ministers. If, they said, the Appeal acknowledges 'our ministries have been manifestly blessed and owned by the Holy Spirit as effective means of grace', why should they be required to receive the laying on of hands from a bishop? As Gore and others had foreseen, episcopacy was the stumbling block because the Nonconformists did not believe it was a God-given sign of unity and continuity in the Church. Discussions continued intermittently until 1925 and then faded out, though all was not lost for precedents had been set for similar conversations in the future.

Reactions to the Appeal revealed growing differences among Catholics on ecumenical matters. A dividing line was appearing between those who would not consider reunion with any other denomination except under the conditions specified by the ECU, and those who, while acknowledging the importance of the ECU's conditions, were prepared to tolerate some flexible, interim arrangements during the process of uniting episcopal and non-episcopal ministries. These differences were later distinguished in terms of those who regarded episcopacy as being of the *esse* (essential being) or of the *bene esse* (well-being) of the Church. The difference was accentuated because Catholics in the *bene esse* camp – to their embarrassment – found themselves being joined by Evangelicals and others whose concept of the episcopal order was not much different from that of the Nonconformists.

The Lambeth Conference, and particularly the work on the text of the Appeal, affected a reconciliation between Weston and Henson. Before he became Bishop of Hereford, Henson had been a Catholic in his days as vicar of Barking and as chaplain of the Ilford Hospital (almshouses with a chapel). Fr Puller of Cowley had been his father confessor for years, and at one time he had wondered whether he should join the Society of the Divine Compassion at Plaistow. But then he changed. Owen Chadwick suggests that in 1896 the death of his father, a stern puritan and fervid Protestant, caused Henson to wonder if his Catholic stance had been a youthful rebellion against his parent, so when he left Ilford he gradually become more liberal in his theology. While a canon at Westminster his sermons attracted large congregations and he enjoyed the reputation of becoming a popular preacher. It could be, therefore, that beneath his cryptic summing up of his impressions of Weston was a half-acknowledged admiration for the man who personified what Henson once hoped he might have been himself. This is reflected in his final comment about the Bishop of Zanzibar, in spite of his use of the words 'fanatic' and 'bigotry':

'He was, in my belief, a very good unselfish Christian, with all a fanatic's sincerity and all a fanatic's injustice, but by nature entirely lovable. It was impossible not to feel his charm even when one execrated his bigotry. On the whole that represents my deliberate verdict. Something should be added about his practical sagacity, which I think was quite conspicuously great whenever his fanaticism did not influence his judgment: and something more should be said about his passionate love of souls, which lifted him above his fanatical obsessions and carried him into the company of the greater Saints. It was a cause of genuine sorrow to me that I never had an opportunity of getting past his ecclesiastical prejudices, and finding agreement with him in deeper things.'[14]

On his side Weston seems to have discovered that the Bishop of Durham was someone he could work with and respect. At any rate, there is no record of his attacking Henson again. Besides, Henson's letters, published after his death (*Letters of Herbert Hensley Henson*, 2 volumes, 1950 and 1954) reveal a friendly and compassionate nature which is not so obvious in his diary (*Retrospect of an Unimportant Life*). It could be that the emotional Weston responded to this side of Henson's character and sensed Henson was not as unsympathetic towards the Catholic position as Weston had assumed him to be.

Lambeth was also the occasion for another reconciliation. Weston had met Bishops W. G. Peel of Mombasa and J. J. Willis of Uganda during the war and realized that he had misjudged them over the Kikuyu affair. The consequences were noted warily by Davidson in his comment on Weston:

'He and Henson became personal friends, and Uganda and Mombasa were constantly by his side, and he and they desired that I should be photographed with them as a group. This was done. Whether his strange temperament will show itself by some outbreak of another kind now that the Conference is over, I cannot tell. I feel a little uneasy at times. I hope this is not faithless.'[15]

Weston's visit to England – the campaign against African slave labour – was also fruitful. Weston and his supporters had collected names from members of both Houses of Parliament and church leaders for their petition which was presented by a delegation headed by the Archbishop of Canterbury to Lord Milner, the Colonial Secretary. Milner accepted it but did nothing. When Winston Churchill succeeded Milner in 1921, he consulted the Governors of Uganda and Kenya for advice. When he received their replies, he issued an order that Africans could be conscripted and paid to work on government projects for not more than six days in any quarter of a year, but that colonial officials were not to recruit them for private employers. Weston, who had gone back to Africa by then, was very satisfied with this result.

Malines

The Lambeth Appeal, as we have seen, was particularly welcomed by Halifax. He had never ceased to pray for reunion, even after the failure of his attempt in 1896 to get Rome to recognize the validity of Anglican orders. After Lambeth, Frere suggested to Halifax that the Appeal presented an opportunity to open up discussions between Anglicanism and Rome on their differences. Halifax eagerly got in touch with his ally in the earlier negotiations, Abbe Portal. It agreed that a group should meet in Malines under the joint chairmanship of Halifax and Cardinal D. J. Mercier, the Archbishop of Malines, whom Portal knew would be supportive. Pope Pius XI and the Archbishop of Canterbury were informed of what was planned.

The group met five times between 1921 and 1925. The Anglican delegation consisted of Halifax, Frere, and J. Armitage Robinson, the Dean of Wells; on the Roman side were Mercier, Portal, and Mgr Van Roey, the Vicar General to Mercier. Bishop Gore and B. J. Kidd, Warden of Keble College, were added to the Anglican delegation for the third set of conversations in 1923, and Mgrs P. Batiffol and L. Duchesne to the Rome group. But when news of the meetings became public in 1923 their informal nature was misunderstood and criticism rose on both sides. The

Roman Catholic bishops in England complained to the Vatican, while Davidson had to defend himself against Evangelicals and others who accused him of wanting to reverse the blessings of the Reformation. After the final meeting there were arguments and delays about publishing the reports of the conversations.

In spite of these difficulties the Malines conversations have been recognized as a significant event in the development of Anglican–Roman Catholic relations. They showed that at least some Anglicans were willing to recognize how in the course of centuries the Bishop of Rome had become a *primus inter pares* among the Western episcopate, though not with a divine gift of infallibility (except to the enthusiastic Halifax who, to the embarrassment of his companions, was willing to concede even that). The most significant achievement was the way the Roman Catholics came to accept the idea that the Church of England could only be united if, with the Anglican Communion, it retained its corporate identity. 'United but not absorbed' was its watchword. That was, in fact, a suggestion which some Anglo-Catholic theologians had already made. Lacey had envisaged it as a way in which Methodists could be reunited with the Church of England. At the 1920 Congress it was argued that the Uniat Churches offered a model for bringing Rome and Canterbury together.

But by this time authorities on both sides had become alarmed. Davidson indicated that after 1925 he was not willing to commend further meetings and, following the deaths of Mercier and Portal, the Pope ordered the conversations to cease. Two years later Pius XI, prompted not only by the Malines conversations but also the Faith and Order Conference of 1927, issued the encyclical *Mortalium Animos* in which he described ecumenical enthusiasm as 'indifferentism' and accused the Faith and Order organizers of indiscriminately inviting 'infidels and apostate Christians' to their conference. The only true road to unity, he said, was for all to admit their errors and return to Rome – an attitude shared by the English Catholic bishops of the time.

Years later, we have come to recognize that the Malines conversations were an important chapter in the story of the ecumenical movement. Barnard Barlow suggests that they indicated a new methodology for future discussions between two different Churches. At Malines the participants set out to discover both those values held in common within each other's beliefs and expressions of worship, and those areas of divergence which cause separation. Halifax, Mercier, Portal and the others never imagined they could bring the two Churches together; they simply sought to clear the ground so that at some future date authorized and more competent theologians might explore the possibilities of reunion. In the course of their discussions they introduced the concept of searching for 'unity by convergence' which, Barlow points out, was taken up by the Anglican–Roman Catholic International Commission's meetings after Vatican Two.

The other important element which emerged out of the conversations was the notion of achieving unity without necessarily demanding uniformity. Armitage Robinson had introduced the idea early in the conversations, but it was not until later that the Roman Catholic participants came to consider its feasibility. ARCIC accepted the Congress's vision of a Uniat status for the Churches of the Anglican Communion as a possible way forward. This was strengthened by the realization that Anglicans and Roman Catholics shared much common ground in Christian beliefs. But the latter's insistence that papal infallibility was an essential article of faith remained an insurmountable hurdle.[16]

6

Catholics and the Church Assembly

A few weeks before the 1920 Congress the National Assembly of the Church of England – later known as 'the Church Assembly' – met for the first time. Its institution was the result of demands by the Church to have more control over its own affairs. Improvements in communications – especially in rail travel – had made it easier to arrange joint clergy–laity meetings in deaneries and dioceses, and these led to the formation of a national Representative Church Council (RCC). This Council, meeting for the first time in 1903, consisted of the four Houses of Convocation and a House of Laity. The experience of those who attended the meetings made them aware of how much the Church was subject to the State, for none of the resolutions they passed had any legislative authority.

The situation was aggravated because pressure on Parliamentary time had made it difficult to get ecclesiastical matters through the House of Commons. In 1913 a bill to establish two new dioceses – Sheffield and Chelmsford – was only passed as a result of political gerrymandering by a group of Anglican MPs. Afterwards Halifax consulted widely and then wrote to Davidson protesting that the situation was becoming intolerable, and that the Church of England ought to have authority to deal with its own affairs without having recourse to Parliament. The Archbishop was sympathetic but cautious. He believed the Church–State relationship was good for the nation as well as the Church, and he foresaw many difficulties if her members, laity as well as clergy, had more power. J. Balfour, a former prime minister, voiced one of these in a letter to him: 'Will the parson consent to allowing his parishioners, or even the communicants in his parish, to determine the question of vestments and other matters on which the High Church Party feel so strongly?'[1]

The bill to disestablish the Church in Wales was voted through by Parliament in 1913 (though not put into effect until 1920), in spite of opposition by the bishops in the House of Lords, and this prompted the RCC to pass a resolution requesting the archbishops to appoint a committee 'to inquire what changes are advisable in order to secure in the relations of the Church and State a fuller expression of the spiritual independence of the Church as well as of the national recognition of religion'.[2] The Committee was duly set up with Lord Selborne, an experienced politician and a churchman, as its chairman. Its report was published in 1916.

The Committee proposed that statutory authority should be given to the existing Representative Church Council. Its constitution would be like a pyramid. At its base would be an electoral roll in each parish. The members of this roll (aged 21 and over) would be entitled to meet each year and elect members to a ruridecanal conference and to a parochial council, the former being also members of the latter. The ruridecanal conference would elect members to a diocesan conference, who would in turn elect members to a national assembly (the peak of the pyramid). The Upper and Lower Houses of the Convocations of Canterbury and York would be members of the Assembly, as they had been of the RCC. Certain safeguards were proposed. Electors had to be either communicants, or baptized and confirmed. The new Assembly was to define the powers of parochial church councils, ruridecanal and diocesan conferences. Measures to be sent to Parliament had to be passed by all the Houses of the Assembly. An Ecclesiastical Committee of the Privy Council was to be set up to advise Parliament on these measures which, if they went unchallenged in both Houses for 40 days, could be presented for the Royal Assent. Special provisions protected the powers of the bishops in respect of questions of doctrine.

To promote the report an official Church Self-Government Association was formed of which Gore and Athelstan Riley, a leading Anglo-Catholic layman, were members. But some felt this Association dragged its feet, and the Life and Liberty Movement was launched by a group of enthusiasts led by William Temple and Dick Sheppard with the object of urging the Church to press forward with reform. Temple gave up his incumbency of St James, Piccadilly, to devote his time to the Movement. In spite of wartime conditions, it held large and enthusiastic meetings in London and other parts of the country.

As expected, the Representative Church Council accepted the Selborne report in February 1919, but with an important amendment: the franchise was altered from those who were confirmed to those who had been baptized and who declared they were members of the Church of England and not of any other religious body not in communion with the C of E. At that time many felt that, since three-quarters of the population were baptized in parish churches, they had a right to be involved in Church affairs, even if a majority only attended worship for christenings, marriages and funerals. The amendment was opposed unsuccessfully by Catholics. They regarded baptized non-attendees as lapsed and disqualified from voting. The franchise, they said, should be restricted to faithful communicants. Gore, who had been considering retirement for some months, used his opposition to the amendment as an opportunity to announce his resignation from the Oxford bishopric (he was aged 66). The report was passed by Parliament in December 1919 in the Enabling Act, and the Church Assembly met for the first time in June 1920, just before the first Congress.

The English Church Union followed these developments with a mixture of interest and suspicion. Underhill belonged to the Life and Liberty movement and urged the executive to back its objectives. He pointed out that support for the Selborne report was growing among church people, including members of the Union, and that the RCC would probably accept it. So the executive appointed a committee to study the Selborne proposals and to advise the Union on their response to them. The committee presented their report to the Council on 26 November 1919. While generally welcoming Selborne's aims to free the Church from Parliamentary control, the committee questioned whether it was wise to allow laymen to make decisions for the Church at a national level, and whether the Church of England really had power to make all its own laws (without reference, that is, to the wider Church). The committee protested against the assumption that 'the Church is a democracy'. Some also objected to the proposal that women should be admitted to councils with equal voting rights with men. Although most Catholics, including Gore, had supported the bill of 1919 allowing women to vote in Parliamentary elections, many reacted against the custom of allowing them to preach in church. In 1918, when Maude Royden preached on Palm Sunday in the Temple Church and led a Good Friday Three Hours' devotion in St Botolph's, Bishopsgate, the Union wrote to the Bishop of London in protest.

After long discussions on their committee' report, the ECU executive decided to recommend its members to work with the new constitution but to press for further changes: that only those who were confirmed and regular communicants should be admitted to parochial electoral rolls; that the laity should be subject to appropriate discipline, like the clergy; that the ecclesiastical courts should be reformed; and that provision should be made for appeals from clergy who had been unjustly treated by bishops.

When the first elections were held, there was a good deal of confusion in the parishes as to the extent of the Assembly's statutory authority. The Union began to receive letters with anxious enquiries. Would the Modernists be able to alter the doctrine of the Church of England if they achieved a workable majority? Would a congregation through its PCC be able to say what they would accept or not accept in worship? One letter from a parish in the West Country asked if the new Assembly could help them get rid of their vicar. It was not easy to convince all members to follow the Union's recommendations. Some priests resented being compelled to form parochial church councils. As Balfour predicted, they feared that their authority would be weakened. Their vision of Church reform was not an assembly in which they sat with the laity, but a restoration of the traditional synods in which decisions were made by bishops in consultation with their priests. Letters of complaint filled the church press. Among them were a few from ordinary church members who doubted whether they should be in a position to tell their clergy what to do.

Underhill and Williams wrote to the *Church Times* to persuade readers to accept the Union's recommendations. Underhill agreed that the Enabling Act did not give Catholics all that they hoped for, but it did provide opportunities for putting forward urgently needed reforming legislation. 'It should give the Church as a whole a *locus standi* before Parliament such as she has never been allowed to have,' he wrote, 'and it would get rid of the pestilent idea that Parliament or the House of Commons represents the laity, or is a true House of Laymen.' He believed the Act would enable the laity, women as well as men, to have a voice in the affairs of the Church, as they seem to have had in the very early centuries. 'I do not feel able to say anything about the precise limits which should be set to their powers today; that ... must be settled by more learned persons than myself; but I am entirely convinced that there are many departments of the Church's life, parochial and general, in which, without infringing any Catholic principle, the laity should make themselves heard, and in which they have as much right to speak as the clergy ... For myself, I cannot but believe that while we adhere faithfully to the Faith we may also feel sure that the Holy Spirit is leading us to developments which are according to His Will, and which are not contrary to the essence of what we call Catholicism, but consistent as evolutions from it.'[3]

Williams was more confrontational. When he had been an undergraduate a tutor commented that his essays were 'fireworky'. That characteristic sparks through his *Church Times* letters. A priest named Watts had written to say he was going to ignore the requirements of the Enabling Act as a 'signal of resistance' for the whole Anglo-Catholic movement in the country to follow him in opposition to it. Next week Williams replied:

'Without implying the slightest disrespect for Mr Watts, I must need think that he somewhat over-estimated his powers in this regard. It is a fact that all the well-known centres of Catholic life with which I am personally acquainted have accepted the scheme, and are now engaged in compiling their electoral rolls and taking steps towards getting their parish councils into working order. He will not, therefore, convert the whole Catholic party. But even supposing he could, he would not thereby have succeeded in paralysing the Enabling Act. The Moderate and Evangelical sections of the Church, which together constitute two thirds of the *de facto* Church of England, would proceed to elect the National Assembly, and would have things all their own way in it. This point is so important that I must be pardoned for driving it home – even if the passive resistance movement were to extend to the whole of the Catholic party, the National Assembly would none the less come into existence, and it is expressly provided in the Act that "no proceedings of the Church Assembly shall be invalidated by any vacancy in the membership of the Church Assembly or in the defect in the qualification or election of any member thereof".'

To strengthen his point Williams reminded his readers what had happened after the Church in Ireland was disestablished in 1870. In revising the Prayer Book that Church had banned all ceremonial, even candles and crosses on altars. That could happen in England if Catholics failed to support the constitutional innovations:

'It does not require much imagination', he went on, 'to predict what an Assembly in which the Catholic party was entirely unrepresented would do. It would enact a Revised Prayer Book, more or less resembling the Irish Prayer Book of 1870, and designed to make the observance of many Catholic customs, including Reservation, practically impossible; it would arm the Ecclesiastical Courts with power ruthlessly to enforce uniformity on these lines, using the weapon of deprivation wherever necessary; it might well embody in the Revised Prayer Book rubrics allowing token preachers, interchange of pulpits, intercommunion with Nonconformists, and everything else against which we have been fighting for so long. Can anyone who sees facts as they really are and does not labour under the delusion that the Catholic party is coterminous with the Church of England, doubt that this would be the inevitable result of a widespread Catholic abstention from taking part in the scheme?'[4]

But other correspondents saw practical advantages in the new Assembly. For years proposals for the revision of the Prayer Book had been debated, and some Catholics hoped the new Assembly would speed up this process and give legitimacy to the ritual developments of the past sixty years, especially reservation. They agreed with Underhill in recognizing that it offered a means of dealing with various aspects of ecclesiastical administration and finance which were long overdue for reform. Many like

Temple and Sheppard hoped the Assembly would inspire a fresh wave of spiritual renewal and missionary outreach to those outside the Church.

As Williams had pointed out, numerous Catholic parishes throughout the country were already putting the provisions of the Enabling Act into effect. Those that had informal church meetings created electoral rolls and applied the new constitution to their existing arrangements.

According to the All Saints Margaret Street's parish magazine of 1 November 1921, the parochial church council was by then meeting regularly. Its membership of thirty included two churchwardens, two deputy churchwardens, and nine women. The social background of the members is reflected in some of the titles: the Duke of Newcastle (one of the churchwardens), Lord Frederic Hamilton (vice-chairman), Lady Powell, Dame S. Browne, and the Hon. Mary Trefusis. Among the women was Mackay's sister, who kept house for him. The clergy were represented by the vicar as chairman and the senior curate, Geoffrey Heald. There was a parish office which was open daily.

Away from London St Matthew, Northampton, accepted the new constitution without any apparent hitch. The vicar, J. R. Hussey, had been vicar since 1893 and had been responsible for a congregation from the time when they met in a school room until the present church was built. He was Rural Dean of Northampton and very familiar with the provisions of the Act. A new church room had been built at the end of the war, and it was there on 15 April 1920 that the first parochial church meeting was held. At the beginning of the year Hussey had written in the parish magazine encouraging the congregation to collect forms of application to the electoral roll and to hand them to him by the end of March. In spite of the official ruling that anyone who was baptized could be on the electoral roll, he said candidates had to be communicants and over twenty-one. The meeting elected two representatives to the ruridecanal conference and twenty to the parochial church council.

It was decided to hold the PCC meetings once a month, and at the May meeting the finances were reviewed. A budget was agreed and the salary of the organist, Charles King, a distinguished musician, was increased to £40. At the next meeting a finance committee consisting of the vicar, the churchwardens and officers of the PCC was set up.

'The work of the PCC', wrote Mona Harrison, a local historian, 'gave its members a much wider view of their Church life, looking out at the Deanery, the Diocese and the Church in general; such matters were soon to appear on future agendas. It also lightened the load of decision for the Vicar and the Churchwardens and made delegation easier. Certainly the enthusiasm shown by the laity was strong and encouraging.'[5]

In contrast, at St John, Torquay, the elderly B. R. Airey (known as 'High and Airy' behind his back) would have nothing to do with parochial church councils. When he was appointed in 1886 he had caused opposition by dropping what he regarded as Romish practices and closing the two mission churches in the parish. He was temperamentally a shy but autocratic man, who focused all his attention on the worship and spiritual direction (he heard confessions in the vestry with the door locked!). He would not allow any parochial organizations to exist except the Confraternity of the Blessed Sacrament and the St Barnabas Guild for Nurses. He was very elderly when he retired in 1924, so his lack of enthusiasm for the Enabling Act is understandable. It was left to Airey's successor, R. J. E. Boggas, to establish an electoral roll and a PCC.

Similar developments took place in parishes, rural deaneries and dioceses up and down the country. The smooth emergence of the Church Assembly was largely due to the fact that, from the Representative Church Council downwards, meetings like these had already been in existence in some places since pre-war days. In the Winchester diocese, for example, by the time the Act received the royal assent, there were already 142 parochial church councils among its 430 parishes, and gatherings such as ruridecanal and diocesan conferences had been organized on a voluntary basis. What the Enabling Act did was to give Parliamentary approval to a structure which was already up and running in some places, and provide a process whereby its decisions as measures could be submitted to Parliament for legislative authority.

During its first session the Church Assembly set up a provisional standing committee to make recommendations on ordering its affairs, particularly in laying down rules for the working of parochial church councils and ruridecanal conferences. The Hon. Hugh Cecil, a High Churchman, advised on the formation of this committee and saw that the Bishops of York, London and Peterborough (two Catholics and one sympathetic Evangelical respectively) were elected to it. On it, too, were Catholic laymen – the Duke of Northumberland, Viscount Woolmer MP, and Sir Philip Baker. Lord Phillimore (a vice-president of the ECU) was on the committee which drew up the Parochial Church Council (Powers) Measure, and Bishops Furse and Frere were on the committee overseeing the revision of the Prayer Book. All these were on the list of sponsors of the first Anglo-Catholic Congress.

Much time was also spent on the Parochial Church Council (Powers) Measure. Catholic voices were strident among those who defended the authority of the parish priest. Cecil and Athelstan Riley wanted the Lower Houses of Convocation reformed so that they were more representative of the parochial clergy. In debates about the appointment of new incumbents, Phillimore said parochial church councils should be allowed to make representations to patrons during a vacancy but not to name names, and prospective new incumbents should not be compelled to say what changes they proposed to make if appointed. These aims were eventually incorporated into measures and accepted by Parliament.

Hill, representing the Southwark diocese, made a maiden speech which was characteristically brusque. Following the ECU's recommendations, he pressed for the reform of both Convocation and of the ecclesiastical courts, and he argued for a restoration of synodical government. His experience of writing letters of protest to the press about the re-marriage of divorced persons in church led him to foresee difficulties arising in the Church's relationship with the State if the proposals for alterations to the marriage law then going before Parliament became law. 'When there is a collision between the Church and the State on such a matter,' he declared ominously, 'it often happens that the bishops are not to be trusted.'[6] A Mrs Carruthers from the Chichester diocese was worried that the powers of the parochial church councils would 'endanger the prerogatives of his [the vicar's] sacred office as an ordained and consecrated priest of the Catholic and Apostolic Church'.[7] She was clearly a Catholic. Frere said he supported giving parochial church councils some powers but thought it would be disastrous if the Church discouraged the initiatives which specially belong to the parish priest.

The inauguration of the Church Assembly gave the ECU new responsibilities. The executive set up a special committee to monitor the Assembly' proceedings and ensure Catholic interests were not threatened. Phillimore reported to this committee after the first meeting of the Assembly. He said it had commissioned a group to plan pensions for elderly and disabled clergyman and he thought that was worthy of the Union's support. The revision of the Prayer Book was high on the agenda, and the executive decided to set up a special Prayer Book committee to monitor the progress of the revision and publicize the Union's ideas about it. Another of the committee's tasks was to make sure the Union members in the parishes used their votes for the ruridecanal conference and the Assembly to make certain Catholics were well represented on them. Pinchard made this his main theme during visits to local branches.

Clergy had to be convinced they must take the compilation of parochial church rolls seriously. Formerly such rolls as there were had been drawn up informally or, as in St John, Torquay, they did not exist at all. In a review of the situation presented to the ECU executive on 21 November 1921 Hill pointed out that, as things stood, the diocese of London would have only half the number of Catholic representatives on the Assembly compared with the diocese of Manchester, in spite of the fact that proportionately Manchester had fewer Catholic parishes than London. It was no use, he said, saying that there ought not to be a House of Laity; they had got the Enabling Act and they should make the best use of it. He added he deplored the way some younger clergy tended to sneer at older laymen. Another member of the executive said he knew of one parish where there were 1,400 regular Sunday worshippers but only 220 of them were registered on the roll. The executive agreed to prepare a leaflet for the guidance of Catholics on parochial church councils about these and other matters.

Pinchard now realized that Catholics in the parishes needed politicizing. Some were averse to having anything to do with an election. To them it seemed an unspiritual method of deciding holy things. Others, including some women as well as many men, did not believe women should have an equal voice with men in Church affairs. Few had any understanding of how the single transferable vote of proportional representation worked. Confusing, too, was the system whereby the elections to the House of Laity took place every five years where as those to the House of Clergy had to be held whenever there was an election to the House of Commons.[8]

As a first step Pinchard set about reorganizing the Union's own national network so that it was in a better position to support Catholic candidates at forthcoming elections. When it was formed from an amalgamation of local groups, the Union had adopted the county boundaries for its organization in England and Wales. Pinchard now proposed that these should be abolished and new ones drawn up based on deanery and diocesan boundaries so that its branches and districts could more effectively organize election campaigns within them. The proposal was not popular. Members had formed inter-parochial friendships within county boundaries, and they did not see why these relationships should be broken up by the Union's bureaucrats in London. So it was only after much argument and persuasion that the new arrangement was adopted in 1923.

With these constitutional changes the executive took the opportunity to broaden the Union's rules on membership to increase the number of those who might vote for Catholic candidates in the elections. To the original categories of Members and Associates was added a third, Adherents. Members (annual sub 10s. [50p]) received the *Church Union Gazette* and could vote in the Union's national elections; Associates (2s. 6p) did not receive the *Gazette* and could vote only in local elections;

Adherents (1s.) received notice of meetings but were not allow to vote on Union matters. The executive also agreed that women could now be elected to its committees.

A year before the 1925 elections the Union discussed a proposal that they should devise a list of test questions which branch members could put at hustings to candidates for election to the Assembly. But warning voices were raised. Opposition to the changes in the Union's network showed that local branches did not take kindly to interference from London. Instead the executive agreed that the officers of the diocesan and other branches should be invited to the Union's annual conference in London in June that year, when the subject of the talks would be on 'how to increase the general efficiency of the branch, district and diocesan officers in the ECU in view of the changed conditions in the Church of England'. The finance committee agreed to pay the fares of delegates coming to London to ensure a good attendance.

To help Pinchard with this extra work W. J. B. Crouch was appointed as a full-time Organization and Efficiency Secretary on a salary of £400. In 1926 he was able to report that there were Union secretaries in every diocese. Since his appointment he had addressed 65 meetings and delivered 13 sermons, and he had been present at Anglo-Catholic Congresses in Northampton and Middlesborough. In the last four years 60 new branches had been formed, and 15 more were in process of coming together. Most of the old district unions had been dissolved and their responsibilities shifted to the new diocesan committees. The reorganization was nearly complete.

The planning of the 1920 Congress had brought together societies like the Confraternity of the Blessed Sacrament and the Federation of Catholic Priests. Pinchard followed this up by calling together a Central Council of Catholic Societies to coordinate their aims at elections and their voting in the Assembly. It met only occasionally but was a useful network when decisions had to be made which affected all Catholics.

At a conference of diocesan and branch secretaries of the Union in 1929, E. D. Merritt, vicar of St Michael, Camden Town, a rural dean and a proctor in Convocation, said that in their reactions to the provisions of the Enabling Act, priests divided into three categories:

'First, there have been men who said: "We won't have anything to do with it; we won't have any Electoral Rolls; we won't have any Parochial Church Councils; we will take no notice of the whole business." One well-known Proctor in Convocation consistently adopted this attitude by refusing to take his seat in the Assembly. I am quite convinced that this policy was a mistake, and I am glad to notice that those who uphold it have been getting steadily fewer in number. There are still, however, some people who take this line.

'Second, a large number were indifferent or apathetic. They said: "I suppose we must have an Electoral Roll", but they took no trouble to persuade their people to sign it. They said: "I suppose we must elect somebody to the Ruridecanal or Diocesan Conference", but they never bothered to see that the right people were thus elected. I'm afraid there are still a large number of people whose general attitude towards the machinery set up by the Enabling Act can be described in this way.

'Third, there were others who said: "We never asked for this new machinery, and we didn't want it. We don't like it now, but for better or worse it exists, and our duty is to make the best of it." They therefore did all they could to get their *bona-fide* Church people to sign the Rolls. (I hold no brief for those who tried to get every inhabitant to sign, irrespective of Churchmanship.) They took immense trouble to get Catholics elected to the Ruridecanal and Diocesan Conferences and to the Church Assembly. If they themselves were elected to any of these bodies they did all they could to advance Catholic interests, and to prevent the Church Assembly from doing even worse things than it has.'

He advised that while candidates for election should be Catholics, it would be an added advantage if some of them were well known in the diocese in other connections. It could be that such a candidate would attract votes from those who did not regard themselves as Catholic supporters but who nevertheless appreciated his or her work in these other connections. In election addresses candidates should avoid giving the impression that all they were interested in were party matters. For this reason it was better for each candidate to send out an individual election letter rather than a joint one from the Catholic candidates as a group. Although it was more expensive, it helped voters to see that candidates were not ganging up on party lines. Catholics should also be alert when there was a by-election and to study lists of candidates carefully.

He warned officials of the Union never to attempt to influence individual electors on how they should vote. Neither, he said, should they assume a well-known candidate will get in and give their first vote to someone else. They should always give their preferred candidate their first vote; if it is not needed, it will be transferred to their second choice. He had known certain distinguished candidates to be unseated in proctorial elections through the over-confidence of some of their supporters.

The way the proportional voting system worked must be carefully explained, Merritt said. He recounted how in the early campaigns many voters put an 'X' on the ballot paper instead of numbering their preferences. Other misunderstandings occurred. 'I know of two cases where men being at the top of the poll whose names began with the letter A received an unexpected number of first votes. With all respect to those two very excellent men, I suspect this was not entirely due to their excellence, but to the fact that many voters did not understand how to give their preferences. I know it was so in one case, for I saw the voting papers. They are printed in alphabetical order, and a number of voters gave their preferences from the top! Other things being equal, it might then be worth your while to put up an Aaron rather than a Zedekiah.'[9]

The Church Assembly was a disappointment for those who were expecting it to inspire a fresh wave of spiritual renewal and missionary outreach. They had yet to learn that such movements are rarely initiated by bodies elected by a diverse franchise and faced with the enormous task of reforming the Church's administration and finance. They overlooked what the Assembly did achieve in these years. With its 347 lay members, 323 clergy members and 43 bishops, it got through Parliament forty of the forty-four measures it presented (two of the failures being those for the revision of the Prayer Book). These measures authorized a number of important reforms. They defined the powers of parochial church councils, ruridecanal conferences and diocesan conferences. They established the new dioceses of Guildford, Portsmouth, Derby, Leicester and Blackburn. They initiated schemes to bring in a minimum salary for parochial curates as well as incumbents; to provide retirement pensions; to pay for the maintenance of parsonages; to abolish the sale of avowsons; to create united parishes and to limit pluralities. By 1930 4 million names were on parochial electoral rolls out of a population of 24 million.

Adrian Hastings pointed out that during the years between the wars the Church Assembly was dominated by a group of laymen, including 20 Tory MPs (known to their fellow MPs as 'the Church Lads Brigade') who worked in alliance with the bishops. These included members of the High Church Cecil family who were in both the Lords and the Commons. They were sympathetic towards Catholics' aspirations, but they deflected attempts towards extremism of any kind.[10] Hastings might have added that the ECU, benefiting from the enthusiasm spawned by the Congresses, achieved a strong Catholic representation on the Assembly and its committees, so that for long afterwards a complaint of Evangelicals and others was that 'the black-suited gentlemen' constituted the best organized party in the chamber. The confidence and enthusiasm generated among Catholics by the Congresses contributed to that.

7

The Congress Follow-up and the First Priests' Convention 1921

Atlay, Wilson and the executive followed up the first Congress with a number of initiatives. First, they invited a group of English bishops to a consultation at Cuddesdon on 7–8 September. Six came, representing different traditions: F. E. Ridgeway of Salisbury and M. B. Furse of St Albans, preachers at the Congress; H. M. Burge of Oxford, supportive; F. T. Woods of Peterborough and J. E. Watts Ditchfield of Chelmsford, interested Evangelicals. The sixth was Henson, who was just about to move from Hereford to Durham. Perhaps Ridgeway had advised the committee on the choice of names after meeting the Archbishop of Canterbury. The Bishop of Salisbury had reported to the Archbishop about the Congress and told him, 'We are in for a new Reformation.' To which the Archbishop had replied, 'If it is to be a new Reformation, younger men must tackle it. I am too old for that.' Feeling depressed Davidson added, 'I feel very Protestant today.'[1] Ten members of the executive went to Cuddesdon led by Atlay.

The only official record that seems to have been kept was a memorandum written up by Wilson a few days later while he was on holiday in the Scilly Isles. There appears to have been some straight talking. F. Underhill, acting as spokesman, complained that Catholic priests were regarded by bishops as destructive, disloyal and unfit for higher office, while what they are most concerned with was the salvation of souls. The majority of Catholic parishes were faithful to the Prayer Book, yet the bishops seemed to distrust them and hindered what they were trying to do. What Catholics wanted was: permission for some degree of liturgical experiment; a book of offices; diocesan and provincial synods (meetings of bishops with their clergy), and a better means of consulting with the laity. At this stage it was not clear how the House of Laity in the newly formed Church Assembly would fulfil this role.

The bishops replied by pointing out that certain Catholic priests ignored their authority by introducing liturgical and devotional practices into their churches in a haphazard way, sometimes without reference to their congregations. As an example, they cited a recent case at Taunton, where the Bishop of Bath and Wells had begun proceeding against the Revd R. Wynter, Vicar of St John the Evangelist, because he had persisted in using the service of benediction when instructed not to do so. Although the consultation did not solve all problems between individual Catholic priests and their diocesans, the bishops who attended had a clearer idea of the objectives of the Congress, and misunderstandings were allayed.

Next, the executive spent two days, 30 September to 1 October, at the Grand Hotel, Broadstairs, to make plans for the future. They read the many letters they had received and took advice on applying for the Anglo-Catholic Congress to become a charitable organization. An office at 32 George St, Hanover Square, was rented and Wilson was appointed general secretary with a salary of £350 a year. He remained an honorary curate of St Matthew's. It was also agreed to organize a priests' convention in Oxford the following year. The dates Tuesday 19 July – Friday 22 July 1921 were settled; Bishop Burge agreed to be president and B. J. Kidd, the Warden of Keble College, to be chairman. Wilson once again found himself involved in administration: beds and meals for members in colleges and people's homes; altars for nearly two hundred priests who wanted to say their daily mass; letters to parishes suggesting they helped to pay their clergy's fees; ceremonial at the convention masses, including the suggestion that the peace should be given, not just to the sanctuary party but to everyone present.

'Conversion' was suggested as the theme of the convention, later changed to 'Priestly Efficiency'. 'Efficiency' expressed the Catholic ideal of the ordained ministry as a company of men who were equipped to lead and teach the Church, conscious of the authority and powers of their office. 'It is not enough that a Priest shall be cultured, though culture is infinitely desirable – even not enough that he shall be humble and self-sacrificing and eagerly industrious,' wrote Underhill and C. S. Gillett, the editors in their introduction to the published report. 'There is always the primary need that he shall know his business. There is a craft called Priestcraft, and he must diligently set himself to learn it.'[2]

The idea of a national evangelistic campaign was still being discussed in the executive and it was not resolved until just before the convention began. At a meeting on 4 July it was decided more preparation was needed. It was agreed therefore that the Convention should lead up to another Congress in 1922 or 1923 and that the evangelistic campaign should be launched after that. It was pointed out that in any case a continuing Congress organization needed a mandate and that the gathering of so many clergy at Oxford was a fitting opportunity for obtaining this. So it was settled that at the final meeting of the Convention the following proposals would be put forward:

(1) That the Convention pledges itself to seek the conversion of all men, women and children to the person of Our Lord;
(2) That the outcome of the Convention should be a period of preparation of the clergy for 'a great evangelistic movement' after a second Anglo-Catholic Congress which would encourage the laity to support the movement by prayer and alms;
(3) That the Federation of Catholic Priests be asked to undertake all the preparation and training of the clergy for that movement through retreats, local conventions, a deepening of their spiritual life in all dioceses;
(4) That the Convention mandates the committee to collect money, to organize a second national Congress and to formulate a policy for the evangelistic movement.[3]

In asking the Federation of Catholic Priests to organize diocesan groups for training purposes the committee was taking a risk. W. Dudley Dixon, vicar of Glossop, who had succeeded Underhill as general secretary of the FCP, had objected because after the Congress some clergy, with the agreement of the executive, had formed the Fellowship of the Servants of Christ with the intention of keeping the Congress spirit alive. What Dixon disliked was the vagueness of the new Fellowship's conditions of membership. Did their published statement about 'Believing in the Catholic Faith and practicing the Catholic Religion' include attendance at mass on Sundays, fasting before Communion and going to confession? he asked. He pointed out that the FCP had done much to raise support for the Congress, but if the less strict conditions of membership publicized by the Fellowship were to be the basis for future Congresses, the executive might not be able to rely on the FCP's co-operation. The veiled threat succeeded. The executive put pressure on the Fellowship and in the next few months it was quietly wound up, its two hundred or so members being invited to join one of the other Catholic societies.

However, the executive knew there were priests who might be unwilling the come to anything organized by the FCP, so a note was added to the second proposal: 'Whereas it is of the greatest importance that all priests who teach and practise the Catholic Faith should take part, both in the preparation for such a movement, and in the movement itself; and whereas there are some who find themselves unable at present to become members of the FCP: it is resolved that the aforesaid Federation be asked to form diocesan committees, which shall include, if possible, priests who are not members of the said Federation.'4 The executive was relieved that Dixon did not object to that.

The First Anglo-Catholic Priests' Convention

The first Anglo-Catholic Priests' Convention met during one of the hottest weeks of that summer. In all, 1,194 priests registered for it, and on the opening day most of them arrived by train. Mackay, recently made an honorary prebend of St Paul's, later described the scene at Oxford station in his parish magazine:

> Train after train was disgorging Priests upon the Oxford platform. If it be true, as tradition says, that the learning of my brethren is 'stupor mundi", there can be no doubt that their habiliments are. Long before the Reformation the English clergy showed an independence of mind about their walking costume which was the despair of precians. The hot weather on this occasion extended the range of their choice. There were beautiful young clergymen in delicate grey suits, grey Homburgs with black ribbons, and pale wash-leather gloves: but they were in a minority. Several others wore the white linen of the tropics. Elderly men with beards and figures which showed the march of time, tended to saucy Panama hats set at a jaunty angle. There were Religious – a good many – in various habits; some Priests wore the full Anglican vesture of cassock, cap, and gown; others wore the dress of the Italian secular clergy. Truly noble first-rate men like Father Atlay wore frock coats; less noble second-rate men, like me, wore short coats. No wonder a French lady visitor to Oxford asked whether we had assembled for 'un grand enterrement', at which a young spike near me ejaculated, 'Yes, ma'am, for the funeral of the Protestant religion.'5

They came, as one of the speakers put it, as those who longed to be 'unhyphenated Catholics', but reluctantly accepting the need to distinguish themselves from the Church of Rome.

After a high mass in St Barnabas Church, the clergy met in St Mary's at noon to hear a sermon by the Bishop Burge of Oxford who insisted on staying in the vestry while the congregation said the *Angelus* so as not to appear to be joining in. But he entered the church for a bidding prayer:

Ye shall praise God for all those that are departed this life in the true faith of Christ, and were the chosen vessels of his grace and the lights of the world in their several generations; such as were John Henry Cardinal Newman, sometime vicar of this church, John Keble, Edward Bouverie Pusey; and pray unto God that He would grant unto them His light and everlasting peace, and unto us, grace to follow their holy conversation that this life ended we may be made with them partakers of the glorious resurrection, in the life everlasting.

When he got into the pulpit, Burge began by saying he believed the previous year's Congress had been a work of the Holy Spirit, but confessed he had shuddered at first when he saw the theme of the Convention. 'Efficiency' sounded too worldly. But as he read the programme he realized the organizers wanted the clergy 'to be thorough, to get rid of superficiality and contentment with superficiality, to be deeper, to be more real'. After quoting in Greek Paul's exhortation in 2 Corinthians 4 ('since it is by God's mercy that we are engaged in this ministry'), he said the Church could never be regarded as an organization to be managed more efficiently. It was the mystical Body of Christ into which people were drawn through grace and baptism and in which they exercised their ministries through the call of Christ and the work of the Holy Spirit. The busyness of priests' ministry, he cautioned, can lead to formalism and superficiality, so that they fail to commend the Gospel to a world which is increasingly disinterested in it. Yet as Anglicans they had unique opportunities. The constitution of the Church of England reflected the ideals of justice, freedom and democracy which had been developed by the British nation over the centuries and therefore could appeal to all its inhabitants. He referred to an incident before the war when he was headmaster of Winchester school.

'I do not apologize', he said, 'for that system of corporate loyalty which has made our public schools and our colleges and universities institutions that are quite unique in the educational history of the world. A German school-master once stayed with me at Winchester and as he bade me farewell he said: "If only the Kaiser had an institution like this, it would be worth all his Dreadnoughts." He did not mean the curriculum, he did not mean the class-rooms, the organization, the system of discipline, but he meant the *ethos* of it, what it stood for in our corporate life. It was that *morale*, I take it, that gave us the victory in that war. I am not going to apologize for that.'[6]

During the war many former pupils of schools like Winchester went into the commissioned ranks which suffered a high proportion of casualties on the Western Front. What he said about the victory was perhaps his way of trying to make the tragedy bearable. He ended by urging the conference to respect the discipline of the Church of England and to be loyal to their fellow-clergy, bishops as well as priests, whether they were Catholic in outlook or not.

The main sessions were held in the Town Hall which was filled with sweating participants. Besides the teaching they contain, the lectures reveal what was expected of Catholic clergy as the various speakers shared their ideas and experiences with the Convention. They give us snapshots of how these successors of the Tractarians envisaged their role in the Church and in society in the twenties and the thirties.

The first topic on the programme was theology – doctrinal, scriptural and moral. N. P. Williams, Fellow of Exeter College, Oxford, criticized the training of Anglican ordinands for being inadequate when compared with that in the Roman Church and in the Church of Scotland. He said that until recently a man might be ordained on the basis of a scrappy knowledge of a few books of the Bible, the Prayer Book, the Thirty-Nine Articles, and Hooker, hastily crammed up from cheap textbooks. Yet teaching was one of a priest's most important tasks, and to be an efficient teacher a priest needed to know more about the faith than he is ever likely to be called upon to explain. He must be able to detect error and know how to distinguish pious opinions, however edifying, from that which is *de fide*.

Williams warned against an uncritical reliance on Roman Catholic publications. 'For the Anglo-Catholic Priest, whose whole *raison d'etre* as a teacher is to recall men to the faith of the Undivided Church, it is of special importance that, if he has to make use of the dogmatic textbooks of our nearest ecclesiastical neighbours, he should be able to distinguish what of them is specifically Latin and what is truly Catholic.'[7] A priest ought to be equipped to answer the questions raised by intelligent people whose religious ideas were being affected by the rise of Modernism. He should guide them to appreciate that, although the Catholic faith is rooted in the unchanging Gospel, it also develops as the Church's apprehension of the Gospel grows and deepens from generation to generation under the guidance of the Holy Spirit.

'I cannot help thinking that it has been a weakness of the Catholic movement that we have made so little effort to evangelize the intellect of the country. God forbid that I should ever disparage the importance of the work for the poor, the ignorant, and the outcast; but, in a fully developed Catholicism, the spirit of St Francis, who spent himself in the service of the poor and degraded, needs to be complemented by the spirit of St Dominic, who made his appeal to the learned and cultured . . . I do not of course mean that every priest, without exception, ought to endeavour to qualify himself for holding a Regius Professorship; I am merely deprecating the attitude of a Catholic incumbent who once announced, apparently on a basis of little or no study of the subject, "There *is* no Synoptic Problem!"'[8]

In the past, he said, much Anglican theology had been done in vicarages as well as in universities. This was good because the Church must be prepared for the days when the development of universal education means the laity in the parishes will be as well trained as the clergy. He believed that in 50 years' time it would be even more necessary for priests to be theologically competent because 'every working man (in England) will possess his own library of historical, scientific, or philosophical literature'. Finally, Williams said, the study of theology should be a means towards the priest's own sanctification. 'At the most solemn moment of our lives, we promised to "be diligent in the reading of the holy Scriptures, and in such studies as help to the knowledge of the same"; and faithfulness in the observance of this promise will enrich our meditations, our sermons, and our whole lives.'[9]

In his lecture H. L. Goudge, Professor of New Testament Interpretation of King's College, London, warned the clergy of the danger of neglecting their Bibles. He regretted that Catholics had contributed little to the advance in biblical studies in recent years, or become acquainted with the work of scriptural scholars of other traditions.

'If we leave the Scriptures to the Liberal Protestant,' he said, 'we leave our inheritance to the stranger . . . We must study the Gospels with all the help that modern knowledge places at out command. Certainly we must look to the Holy Spirit, whose work is to reveal our Lord to us. But it is not the work of the Holy Spirit to supply us with information which we ought to have obtained, or to compensate for its absence. Intellectual study and devotional study, rightly understood, are inseparable. In divine things the intellect is dull without the spirit of prayer, while to neglect the light, which God has placed within our reach, is to be indevout towards him'[10]

Knowledge of the Scriptures, he said, guards a priest's teaching about the sacraments from distortion or error. Catholics rightly stress the importance of Baptism, the Eucharist and Absolution because teaching on them has been neglected by many or has been insufficient. But often such teaching was given without reference to the New Testament. All teaching must be set within its scriptural context for that is where it is revealed to us. The sacred writings are addressed to the Christian community, not just to the individual. But what, he asked, does such study do for Catholics themselves? It presents them with an authentic picture of our Lord, and so of God, whom he reveals; it enables them to see Jesus as he really is, not as they might wish him to be. He warned that devotion to Jesus in the Blessed Sacrament can become sentimental and self-serving unless it is informed by the Bible.

Equally important, he went on, is that scriptural doctrine must be set beside personal conduct. 'No one who reads his Bible will ever suppose either that morality will enable us to do without religion, or that faith and worship will be accepted without practical obedience to the law of love... Scripture will not only teach and correct us, it will profoundly strengthen our hold on those great truths for which we especially stand, and will enable us, as never before, to commend them to our English people.'[11]

Goudge was concerned about the tendency among Catholic clergy to preach on such topics as personal discipline, worship, and the lives of the saints with only superficial references to the Scriptures.

W. J. Sparrow Simpson, chaplain of St Mary's Hospital, Ilford (old almshouses), spoke on the doctrines of the Incarnation and the Holy Trinity. He was asked to tackle this difficult subject because he was well known for his gift of expounding the faith in ways accessible to ordinary people. Admirers came from all parts of London-over-the-Border to hear his sermons in the hospital's chapel. He was a little man whose head appeared – bird-like – over the top of the pulpit. In his talk he aimed to challenge the teaching of the Unitarians and Modernists. Two quotations give a taste of his expositions. The first is from what he said on the Incarnation:

> For modern thought the ultimate interpretations of Christ are only two. Either he is originally God, or else he is originally Man. In one case he pre-existed eternally, in the other he did not: or at best only ideally in God's mind, which may, of course, be said of any other man. The former is Incarnation of the Divine; the latter is the adoption of a human person. Between these two Christologies the difference is immense. The idea of Incarnation is so glorious that words can hardly exaggerate its magnificence. But Christ, regarded as no more than a richly-gifted man, however unique, belongs to a different level of religious ideas. The humanitarian conception can never be equivalent to the Religion of the Incarnation.[12]

The second quotation from Simpson is on the Trinity, where he argued that personality finds it completion in fellowship with others and that love cannot exist in isolation. It was an exposition of the doctrine of the Trinity which attracted much attention among theologians since it expressed the mutuality or reciprocity of indwelling whereby the love which is God passes and repasses between the Father, Son and Holy Spirit. It was claimed to be the nearest approach to the mystery of God that the human mind is capable of attaining:

God is not only personal; God is Love. That is the deepest thing we can say about him. But if we attempt to analyse the essential nature of Love, all Love demands an object. What is the object of the love of God? The Unitarian can discover no object for God's love except the human race. But how can the creature be an adequate object for the love which is uncreated? Now the dogma of an essential Trinity firmly establishes the fact that God is Love; because it declares that love is eternally given and returned and shared within the inner life of the Deity; that there is in God the Lover and the Beloved and the Love that unites them, and that the Love which unites them is not abstract but personal. And it is surely no accident that the revelation that God is love coincides with the revelation that God has a Son. God conceived as a solitary Person tends always to fade away into a mere abstraction. It is the Trinitarian dogma which maintains the profoundest conception of Divine personality and of Love.[13]

L. A. Phillips, Principal of Lichfield Theological College, spoke on moral theology, describing it as 'the theological science which deals with the moral values of human actions'. He was glad, he said, to see that since 1914 it was now on the curriculum of theological colleges. In that year the principal of a college had asked him what moral theology was all about. The subject created more controversy than dogmatic theology, he went on, because it was directly concerned with how people behaved, and the moral theologian had to deal with cases which lay on the boundary between right and wrong. It was a pity casuistry had become a dirty word, for it was important that priests should understand the basic principles for guidance in individual cases. He quoted P. T. Forsyth, a much-admired Congregational pastor and theologian: 'Casuistry is inevitable, the only question is whether it shall be based on principles or rule of thumb.'

Unless a priest has clear guidelines, Phillips continued, he is ill-equipped to help those with moral problems. He regretted that Anglicans had to resort to Roman Catholic books on morals because of differences between the two Churches in their approach to the subject. For example, Roman Catholic teaching on works of supererogation, based on the idea that there is a certain minimum of conduct which is obligatory (precepts) and other actions which though not obligatory are required for a perfect life (counsels), was decisively rejected by Article XIV ('Voluntary works besides over, and above, God's commandments, which they call works of supererogation, cannot be taught without arrogance and impiety . . .') 'It is indeed a reproach to the English Church,' he concluded, 'that, while there is a science of everything else, the Church of England has not yet produced a single attempt to consider in a detailed and systematic manner what it means to live as a Christian.'[14] He noted, however, that F. Belton's *Manual for Confessors* and K. E. Kirk's *Some Principles of Moral Theology*, published the previous year, were hopeful signs that a distinctly Anglican moral theology was emerging.

Clement F. Rogers, Professor of Pastoral Theology, King's College, London, did what very few professional theologians have done before or since: he preached regularly on an open-air platform in Hyde Park. He told the Convention that since 1915 he had done this every Sunday afternoon except when prevented by the weather and vacations. Each month he gave a series of talks on a theme – the nature of belief, the moral teaching of Jesus, the divinity of Christ, the reliability of the New Testament, comparative religion, etc – and repeated them each year.

His audience varied from a dozen or so on a cold day to over a hundred when the sun shone. Most, he reckoned, were thoughtful men (there were few women in such gatherings) who were seriously interested in what he had to say. Only a minority asked questions, but what they asked revealed the confusion which existed in the minds of many about the Church and its teaching. By far the most frequent question was, Why did God allow the war? The next most frequent was, What has Christianity done? Common, too, were questions about the supposed conflict of religion and science, bishops' incomes, disestablishment, religious persecution and non-biblical references to Christ.

His audiences wanted straight and simple answers. Was the Bible true or not? If it's wrong to hate, how can God hate sin? Why was the Bible revised (the Revised Version was published in 1881–85, followed by an American version in 1901)? How do we know that Christ existed? A few attempted to be more academic. If the story of Genesis is not literal history, then surely man isn't fallen and there was no need for Christ to redeem us? How could the speaker claim that the Incene [sic], who had fought with Boadicea against Julius Caesar, could have drawn up the 'Incene Creed' [sic]? Hardly anybody showed an interest in the things that absorbed Anglo-Catholics' energies and concerns, though he was once asked if it was right to put images in church. But over the years he had noticed that what really hindered men from coming to Christ were the moral rather than the intellectual questions – about sex and marriage, about duty and honesty at work, about personal character.

He made it a rule never to attack fellow Christians. Indeed, he felt that a united Christian witness was essential in such a situation. For himself, he found that only Catholic Christianity was able to stand the test of such cross-questioning. When queries were raised involving denominational differences, he gave as fairly as he could the views of the Roman Catholic Church, the Nonconformists and the Anglicans:

> I can afford to praise their views and point out where they are better than we are (it is an enormous help not to be obliged to make yourself out to be infallible) as in the devotion of Roman Catholics, or the active service of the laity in the Evangelical bodies. I can warn my audience that I am probably biased in what I say about my own Church, for it must be obvious that if I think the others are good I must think my own better or else I would not belong to it. I do not minimize the differences between us or underrate their seriousness, but I always insist on the far greater area of agreement.[15]

Rogers questioned claims by many Catholics that their form of worship could lead the kind of people he met to the Lord. 'Frankly, I do not see these men and women who are accustomed to the freedom and open air unconventionality of the parks going to our churches as they are now. The ceremonial in many would simply distract them. More than that, the stiffness, the constraint, the long rows of pews, the fussing churchwardens, the high-pitched drawling music, and the inaudible reading, the number of little things that lead to a feeling of unreality, would at once choke them off.'[16]

Some of the clergy who were listening would have disagreed with him, convinced as they were of 'the converting power of the mass' and the awesome appeal of benediction. But those who were doubtful of the wisdom of importing elaborate ceremonial – Roman or medieval – into churches would have nodded their heads.

There followed a series of talks on the Anglo-Catholic model of the life and work of a parish priest. Crowning that ideal, for some, was clerical celibacy. Clergy differed in their reasons for undertaking the vow. If reunion with Rome was ever to be a possibility, some celibates said, Anglican priests should act like Roman priests as much as possible and not get married. Others accepted celibacy, believing it was a means of sharing in the sacrifice of Christ for service in his Church, responding to Jesus' saying about those who chose to be eunuchs for the sake of the kingdom of heaven (Matthew 19.12). They felt it was a fitting sign of the sacramental character of the priesthood. Others argued that medieval discipline about clerical celibacy still applied in the Church of England.

J. F. Briscoe, rector of West Bagborough, Somerset, belonged to this last group. When speaking about this he quoted F. E. Brightman's contention that by the third century the rule was established that no bishop, priest or deacon should marry after ordination – a rule that was repeated for many centuries afterwards by councils and popes.[17] If Catholics appeal to the undivided Church, Briscoe said, why should they give greater authority to Article XXIII permitting the marriage of clergy? Briscoe was a campaigner for clerical celibacy. It was rumoured – though it was only a rumour – that he once persuaded a clergyman and his wife to separate on the strength of this argument. But he did not always have the last word on the subject. At a local Congress in Norwich Briscoe brought the subject into his talk. When he sat down the next speaker said that, while he respected Fr Briscoe's views, he personally was extremely glad that after the meeting his wife was coming in their car to take him home.

Celibate priests were much respected by the laity, particularly those who continued the tradition of devoting their lives to ministries in slum parishes and overseas missions. UMCA would only appoint celibates for its work in East Africa. But the exaltation of the discipline had the effect of causing the less charitable among them to regard their colleagues who had wives as second-rate. A married priest who had expressed his views at a meeting of the FCP was angered to overhear afterwards two of his single brethren say to one another, 'Don't take any notice of him: he's married!' The bias against married clergy showed itself in other ways. Certain parishes had a policy of never inviting a married priest to preach at their services; and when vacancies occurred in such parishes, churchwardens warned bishops and patrons they would only accept an unmarried man as their new vicar.

There were other priests who remained single without taking any vows. Young curates were not expected to marry until they were offered livings. C. N. Long, warden of the Birmingham Diocesan House at Coleshill, in his talk complained it seemed it had become the normal aim of many young priests to get married as soon as possible. He feared an early marriage could seriously hamper a priest's efficiency, though he admitted it might be right for some provided they chose the right woman. Until then they should beware of their relationship with the opposite sex as it might result in an easy drifting into marriage. He went on to warn priests to beware of other kinds of relationships. 'Caution is necessary with regard to undue intimacy with boys,' he said. 'If the Cross weighs heavily upon some of us in these respects, let us pray for grace to be generous in bearing it.'[18] Homosexual acts were still an offence under English law, and toleration of them was to be found mostly among certain academic, theatrical and artistic circles. Ronald Knox's friendship with Guy Lawrence was described by Knox's niece as 'deeply emotional though in no way sensual', and that was probably true of many such friendships at the time.[19]

However, there were indications of misogyny among some Catholic clergy. The denunciations against women taking any role in church services seem to have venom in them that soured genuine concern for Catholic order. The well-publicized sermons given by Maude Royden roused indignation in many priests. 'I will never consent to sharing my pulpit with a woman!' one clergyman exclaimed at an ECU meeting. When Wilson was at Ely theological college, he learned a little doggerel, attributed to a former principal: 'Fear no man and do the right, fear all women and never write.'[20] It is to the credit of the Congress subjects committee that they included two women speakers (Evelyn Underhill and Sheila Kaye-Smith) in the programme for the Albert Hall in 1923. Leaders of the Anglo-Catholic Women's Auxiliary also spoke at local Congresses.

The existence of clergy wives was practically ignored. In obituary notices no mention was made of them. That for T. A. Lacey in the *Church Times* in 1934, for instance, gave no hint that he was married with five children (one of his sons served all his life in the UMCA). It is not surprising, therefore, that nothing was said at the Convention about a priest's wife and his family. Although many wives played a role in the pastoral ministry with their husbands, little acknowledgement was made of their value in Catholic circles. They taught in the Sunday school, or ran the girls' catechism class, or organized one or other of the guilds in the parish. Some were used to being summoned urgently to church by their husbands early on a weekday morning to form a congregation when no one had turned up for a daily mass. They struggled to bring up children on their husbands' low incomes, relying on cash gifts from parents and clothes passed on by understanding members of the congregation. There are many untold stories of heroic and faithful clergy wives who spent years supporting their husbands in difficult parishes. And, there were also women who devoted themselves to keeping house for single priests, sometimes an unmarried sister who looked after her ordained brother.

C. H. How, a Fellow of St John's College, Cambridge, and one of the founder members of the Oratory of the Good Shepherd, spoke on the ordained priesthood, a subject on which most of his audience had cherished beliefs. From the days of J. H. Newman's first Tract (1833) on the priesthood, some Catholics had developed an exalted view of their ministry; they regarded 'my priesthood' as a very special gift and authority which separated them from the laity. How may have had such clergy in mind when he reminded the Convention that Christ was the only true High

Priest and, quoting 1 Peter 2.5 ('you are a holy priesthood'), that his Body derives its priestly nature from him. That was a truth which could easily be obscured in emphasizing the sacredness of the ordained ministry.

'We in no way enhance the dignity of the specific orders of the ministry in the Church by slurring over the priestly function of the whole Body of Christ. Precisely because it is a body, the Church needs official representatives in its priestly work. The High Priest, in his wisdom, made provision that there might be in his Body of redeemed humanity, and taken from among them, representatives to discharge the sacred functions of the priestly body; representatives of God, towards man, both within and without the body; and representatives of the body in its corporate relation to God.'[21]

This representative nature of the ordained ministry, How said, meant that the priest should be striving with the grace of God to represent in his lifestyle how Christ would be living within the society and times in which he was exercising his ministry. Although the grace of the sacraments does not depend on the personal worthiness of the priest, yet the way in which he administers them will help or hinder those he serves in receiving the divine grace which the sacraments offer. This was particularly true in the ministry of absolution. A priest may be an expert in moral theology, and he may have the authority to absolve, but he will only attract penitents who trust his guidance if he is known for the Christ-like quality of his life.

How pointed out that a priest is a representative of the High Priest not only in the Church but also in the world which Christ came to save. Therefore the priest ought to seek holiness not only in personal devotion but also by service among men and women in society at large. He needs to be familiar with the world in which individuals and families in the congregation live and work. He should move among them as a fellow human being, but as a redeemed human being – one who is 'in Christ' – lives and works. The inspiration for such a life is faith in a God who loves and who died on the cross and rose again for all.

'At the altar,' he said, 'the priest day by day will stand, as the representative of God and Man in Christ, offering the One Perfect Sacrifice for himself and for the world of men. But not *instead* either of himself or of the community he serves. His ministry for and amongst men – in instruction, exhortation, intercession, administration of sacraments, or personal intercourse – is all towards one end, the preparation of humanity by sanctification of the Holy Ghost for the offering of *itself* in union with the offering of Christ.'[22]

All at the Convention believed a priest's daily mass was of the highest importance. Do you have a daily mass? was a test question (along with, Do you hear confessions?) to check if a priest was 'a real Catholic'. It was taken for granted the clergy would say matins and evensong – if possible in church after a bell had been tolled. Priests who were oblates of one of the religious communities recited one or more of the lesser hours as well. How's talk was a reminder that the vocation of a priest did not end when he left the church. He was to be out and about doing good as Christ had done.

It was customary at clergy conferences to invite a member of one of the religious orders to give a talk on prayer, and at the Convention Fr Jenks of Kelham fulfilled this role. He spoke of the connection between the priest meeting Jesus Christ in the sacrament at the altar and meeting him spiritually in the times he set aside for meditation (at least two hours a week). It should not, he said, be used as an opportunity to prepare a sermon. The aim of a meditation is to come to the point where the one who prays learns to listen to God rather than to form his ideas on what he should preach about. As priests gained experience in the practice, the form of their meditation may well develop until they spend less time on trying to listen to God and more on loving contemplation 'when God speaks to him without words'.

Long, in the session already mentioned, spoke on the practicalities of a rule of life. Every priest should go to confession, he said, otherwise he would be ill-equipped to hear the confessions of others. His rule should include a short act of self-examination each day, times for study (at least an hour a day besides what was spent in sermon preparation), pastoral work and recreation. It should also cover items like punctuality, fasting and abstinence, the spending of money (a tithe was suggested) and an annual retreat. Long thought the daily mass is too often regarded as a means of receiving Communion whereas it is also an opportunity to offer the great sacrifice for the living and the dead.

The Conference programme then led into the themes of worship, preaching and spiritual direction. S. R. P. Moulsdale, Principal of St Chad's College, Durham, complained that, as one who during university vacations said mass in various parishes, he never found two churches where the celebration was the same. 'We have the most extraordinary examples of self-willed and arbitrary eclecticism,' he said. Recalling the way in which mass had been celebrated at the Congress the previous year, he believed it was a good example of how one could be faithful to the Prayer Book but at the same time enrich it with suitable elements from the Western rite. He recommended teaching adults and children how to participate in the Eucharist by having a priest standing among the congregation and acting as a commentator to guide them through the service – a practice which was spreading in parishes.

Mackay stressed the importance of body language when a priest was saying mass. If the celebrant was hesitant or gave the impression he wasn't sure what to do next, he said, it could be distracting for worshippers. 'Many priests at the altar give me the impression that they are nervously afraid someone is going to shoot them in the back!' The way to build up a Sunday congregation was for the priest to say mass daily and invite communicants to attend at least once during the week. Boys can be encouraged to become servers and given breakfast afterwards: 'toast and marmalade can be in truth the pain benit'. Mass should be celebrated at different times on different days according to people's working hours. Mackay was probably aware that one of the most common complaints from laypersons was that priests at the altar said the rite so quickly and softly that they could not be heard by the congregation. He advised priests at mass to cultivate an attitude of recollection and intention, but if they spoke in a soft voice it must be clear enough for everyone to hear.

For those planning to introduce a daily mass in their parishes he recommended simplicity. All that was needed was an altar with a crucifix and two candles; two frontals, one for everyday and one for festivals; plain vestments, clean altar cloths, corporals, palls, purificators, and vessels; fresh wafers, clear and pure wine. The altar should be prepared the night before; the church opened half an hour before the service. The priest must be punctual and the mass should normally not take longer than twenty-five minutes, thirty if there are a number of communicants. It was desirable to keep silence before mass and not to break it until everyone has finished their personal thanksgiving. The priest should be seen kneeling for his private devotions before and after mass as an example to his people. Children can be encouraged to come on their birthdays, young men and women on the morning after they have become engaged, and families when faced with anxiety or sorrow.

Most important of all, said Mackay, is to instill in parishioners a sense of obligation to attend mass on Sundays and holy days. But the way the Sunday mass was celebrated in many churches should be re-considered. He probably surprised his hearers, who knew him as the vicar of a church famous for its faultless ritual, when he seemed to support Rogers' earlier comment by adding: 'A great many will never find utterance for their souls in an intelligent following of the detail of a High Mass. To a great many, the simplest service will always be the most spiritual.'[23]

He was echoing the feelings of some Catholic clergy as they got older. By then they were weary of being pressurized by sacristans and masters of ceremonies brought up on Fortesque or *Ritual Notes*, and by musical directors determined nothing common or Protestant would be sung by their choir. Mackay's curates had recently introduced a said mass with hymns at which Communion was given on Sunday mornings before the high mass, and he was pleased with the way it was developing. Although he had no intention of replacing All Saints' well-attended non-communicating high mass, he knew that a Eucharist at which the congregation received Communion was more faithful to the Prayer Book. It was another decade or so before the phrase 'the parish communion' became familiar, but already it was appearing in services such as this.

By this time the practice of making one's confession to a priest was no longer a matter of public controversy as it had been fifty or sixty years before. Although Evangelicals rejected any notion of an absolution being a sacramental act, it was generally recognized that the traumas and breakdown in relationships caused by the war required all kinds of pastoral care, and that for some a confession of personal sins might be helpful. In his address, therefore, G. Rawlinson felt no need to be apologetic about the practice in the advice he gave on hearing confessions to the Convention.

For most of his ministry Rawlinson (not to be confused with A. E. J. Rawlinson, the speaker at later Congresses) was a curate at St Barnabas, Pimlico. A cripple in poor health, his obvious piety made him a much-sought-after spiritual director. For him the confessional was the chief means by which a priest fulfilled his duty as a curer of souls. He realized that a parish priest was inevitably caught up in running organizations and chairing committees, but he was anxious that such activities should not crowd out the spiritual care of individuals. He had a clinical view of a father confessor's ministry:

> Amateurism in the confessional is unpardonable and as disastrous as amateurism in the doctor's consulting room ... Our people have a right to expect that, like good general practitioners in medicine, we should know how to deal with all the ordinary cases, and know, moreover, where our knowledge ends and where it is necessary to seek the advice of a specialist. But it is just here that we so often fail.[24]

The main concern for a confessor should not be to help a penitent overcome his sins, Rawlinson said, but encourage him to develop what is good so as to build up his immunization from spiritual diseases. To do this, the penitent should be advised to review regularly how he spent time to pray, to meditate, to examine his conscience, and to practice the presence of God. It is not necessary to wait for the penitent to show signs of overcoming besetting sins before doing this. What is good will drive out what is bad. 'The longer I live the more convinced I am that sins are not conquered; they are crowded out. The energies are directed into a fresh channel. The disappearance of sin and the growth of the interior life are not successive but parallel movements.'[25]

Rawlinson was not, like some of his contemporaries, suspicious of the growing interest in psychology. He realized it had things to teach which could be valuable for spiritual directors. He gave an example of how priests, whose spiritual directors in earlier years had advised them to fight against their temptations, were troubled to find the same temptations they had repressed years before recurring with renewed force in middle age. Psychologists could have warned such spiritual directors, he said, that advice to repress temptations can be unwise. Instead such penitents needed gentle counselling. They should not be reproved but encouraged to rely on the Lord who has sought them out and who loves them, and entrust themselves once more to his grace. The art of guiding souls, Rawlinson concluded, is to help them to come to the place where they need less direction because they are more in touch with God through the maturing of their spiritual life.

There were three short talks on the priest as teacher. A. H. Baverstock, vicar of Hinton Martel in Dorset, spoke on the instruction of children. He was regarded as something of an expert in this field because of his work with children's homes. He said the spiritual development of children could begin as soon as they showed interest in their environment. The mother was the child's first pastor and confessor. The earliest teaching of the faith should be accompanied by introducing children to the worship of God and the love of Jesus, so that morning and evening prayers become a normal part of daily life – growing beyond what one three-year-old said: 'Please God make everybody happy, Mother and Father and Auntie and Cook and the cat.' Children should be admitted to Communion around the age of seven. Even if the bishop will not confirm them first, the parish priest has authority to give them the sacrament because the Prayer Book allows Communion for those who are 'ready and desirous' to be confirmed.

It was the era when the Faith Press published stamps with pictures illustrating the Sunday scripture readings, to be stuck into little books as a reward for coming to mass. The blank spaces of non-attendance were marks of shame. Advances in printing enabled many booklets for children to be produced. The one with sketches of the Holy Catholic Railway was very popular. In this the engine (the soul – a sort of spiritual Thomas the Tank Engine) pulled the coach (the body) along a track with stations representing the sacraments, past a dark siding signifying the sin of being shunted away from God, and into a tunnel (death) at which the coach was jettisoned and the engine steamed into glorious sunlight beyond where Jesus was waiting. After he left St Matthew's Wilson wrote a series of instructions for Sunday schools based on the Catechism which were used for years after the second world war.

On the teaching of young adults Underhill regretted that little or nothing was done in public or church schools to teach young people the importance and practice of prayer. And were Sunday schools and Catechism classes any better? he asked. 'Many tragedies in young lives would be averted, and many dark clouds lifted by regular Confession and Absolution . . . All thinking men and women who have grown up in [Sunday schools and Catechism classes] thank God for the culture of their minds at school . . . Yet, if that could be completed by the scientific teaching of Prayer . . . how much more all these other great ideas would mean.'[26]

He quoted from *The Essentials of Mysticism*, written by his cousin, Evelyn Underhill: 'The object of education is to bring out the best and highest powers of the things educated. Do we, in our education, even attempt to bring out the highest and best powers of the things of the spirit, as we seek to develop those of the body and the mind?' Parish priests could encourage the spiritual development of young people by making friends with them (though aware of the possible dangers in that) and by having a disciplined life of personal prayer themselves. 'I know that there are innumerable middle-aged men and women today who are true to the Church and the Sacraments because they received the education of the spirit from some Priest who loved them. Without that affection they would, humanly speaking, have been lost to the Church.'[27] Underhill had been a curate at St Thomas, Oxford, where his work among the youth was remembered long after he had moved to Birmingham. Shortly after the Convention he was appointed Warden of Liddon House, where he gave addresses to students and others on Christian living which were later published.

J. J. G. Stockley, rector of Wolverhampton, said everyone acknowledged that education was a life-long process, and in the Church continuing education was just as necessary for adults as for children and adolescents. The task was urgent because 'we are perpetually being told . . . that our day is past, that intelligent people are now transferring their allegiance wholesale from the Church of their fathers, and are taking as their guides the up-to-date writers of world history, the "critics" or the "experts", the new men and the newer women, the preaching journalists and the journalistic preachers, the professors of quasi-scientific cults, or the bright or gloomy expounders of the very latest type of Malthusian "morality" '.[28]

Stockley repeated Williams' warning about the effect of the increasing publicity being given to unorthodox and anti-Christian views in the popular press. Newspapers were being read by a greater cross section of the population than before, so the ideas of modernists, agnostics, campaigners for women's ordination, birth control advocates, spiritualists and others were widely discussed. Although he did not mention names, in referring to 'up-to-date writers of world history' he was probably thinking of H. A. L. Fisher, the current minister of education and a historian, who denied there was any trace of divine guidance or intervention in world events of the past.

The Church's answer, Stockley continued, was the full Catholic faith: 'Let us have done, once and for all, with what Mr Wells calls the "muffled Christianity" of Anglicanism . . . For, with all our heart and mind, we believe that Jesus Christ is the same yesterday, to-day and for ever: that the Holy Spirit is Lord and Giver of Life, is the potential energy of his Church to-day as he was at Pentecost, and that the Catholic Faith once delivered to the Saints is the one Gospel needed to supply the wants of men and women in the twentieth century as in every age.'[29] He was critical of what he called 'Anglican Untramontanism' since the Church of England stood for a 'non-coercive Catholicism', and he believed that 'extreme Modernism' would remain only an intellectual interest for the educated, not the inspiration for a living faith for all.

Then, he went on, the consequences of the Gospel for the ordering of society must also be worked out. Catholics must never accept the popular assumption (quoting from R. H. Tawney's recently published *The Acquisitive Society*) 'that the acquisition of riches is the main end of man, and confine ourselves to preaching such personal virtues as do not conflict with its achievement . . . So let our teaching of adult men and women – however and whenever given – be intensely personal, fervently and sanely Catholic, and courageously social.' Repeating Newman's famous dictum ('In the higher world it is otherwise, but here below, to live is to change, and to be perfect is to have changed often') he closed his talk saying, 'And let us never be ashamed of correcting, at least in detail and balance, the matter as well as the method, of what we teach, as the Holy Spirit guides us and as experience suggests.'[30]

On the last day of the Convention, A. Montford, vicar of the Church of the Ascension, Lavender Hill, speaking on ways of evangelizing in contemporary society, criticized clergy who tried to copy others without having the necessary ability. Professor Rogers, Montford said, had a special gift for his ministry in Hyde Park, but he put open-air preaching in the same category as playing games in public. If a priest could not hold his own he had much better not attempt it. He was also scornful of well-meaning attempts to popularize Christianity. 'The fetish of "Services for Men only"', he said, 'has been, to a large extent, dethroned. For many men they had become their sole religious observance. Of course they were, at first, well attended. The hour was comfortable; not infrequently there was an orchestra of ladies; and the address which, in accordance with the advertisements, was short and breezy, would have been equally suitable in a Unitarian meeting-house or a Turkish mosque. Nobody was made to feel uncomfortable. It is true that, for a time, this Sunday afternoon venture brought a large number of men to church. But did it bring them to the Cross?'[31]

To forward the Church's mission Montford thought it was better for the priest to be involved in the community, to attend committees, to be businesslike in dealings, to make use of opportunities in schools, and above all to visit people in their homes. 'There is not much good sitting in church in a biretta, waiting for a Nicodemus who never dreams of coming.' Once people begin to come to church, then is the time to offer them further instruction, perhaps with confirmation classes for adults after the evening service on Sundays. 'We are ministers of the word, as well as of the Sacraments; and the number to which we minister the Sacraments will depend largely upon the courage, the simplicity, and the fullness with which we minister the word.' He was in favour of simple mission services on Sunday evenings, and warned his hearers of being so concerned about ceremonial that they neglected the realities which the ceremonies symbolized.

The long-standing divergence between Catholics who wanted to be loyal to the Prayer Book and those who favoured Roman rites came out in one of the public discussions. V. S. S. Coles, an elderly and much respected priest, urged the clergy to consider the promise they had given to obey the Prayer Book. He said he was not only referring to the use of the services but also to practices which had developed which were not permissible. He felt that the sick should always be given Communion in both kinds and that, although he valued the daily mass, he deplored the practice of celebrating private masses without a congregation. His remarks were met with murmurs of disagreement. R. Langford-Jones, rector of Thruxton, Hampshire, and a noted Papalist, challenged Coles by saying the Western Church still had authority in England which was not nullified by promises to follow the Prayer Book. But then Lacey stood up and to a roar of laughter said that if Langford-Jones regarded the

Western Church as having greater authority than the Prayer Book, then he – Langford-Jones – had no authority to say mass at all.

At the final meeting the five proposals drawn up by the committee were put to the vote and, after a lengthy discussion, accepted. The committee received the mandate it asked for to organize a second Anglo-Catholic Congress in London and to encourage local Congress gatherings in the provinces. After the usual expressions of thanks – particularly to Atlay and Wilson – the Convention closed.

The clergy left Oxford more hopeful that the Church's mission could be resumed now the horrors of war were over. They looked forwards to future developments from the Congresses. The *Church Times* summed up that confidence when its reporter wrote: 'To see these thousand priests leaving Oxford bent on the quixotic enterprise of the conversion of England will, perhaps, evoke derisory laughter in some. But the happy thing about the Convention was that it broke up with this quixotic enterprise in mind. A vision? Yes. The same vision as that of the Congress dawned again at the end of this Convention, but accompanied by certain definite ideas how the campaign is to be fought. We are out to do battle unashamedly for the Catholic Faith.'[32]

8

The Provincial Congresses

At their meeting on 3 November 1921 the Anglo-Catholic Congress executive decided to follow up the proposal to organize local Congresses which had been welcomed by the clergy at the Convention in Oxford that summer. The intention was that these Congresses should be held in different parts of the country, using venues like town halls to which Catholics could invite their non-church-going friends to hear the faith explained. The executive wrote to priests they knew asking if they would be willing to organize this kind of event in their area. The response was encouraging. When the executive met the next month Wilson told them that ten areas had taken up the suggestion and were making plans for Congresses in the following year: Birmingham, Liverpool and Leeds in June; the Potteries in September; Manchester, Newcastle, Cardiff and Brighton in October; and Plymouth and Norwich at dates which were to be fixed.

Then the executive began to have qualms. What if local committees in their enthusiasm lost sight of the evangelistic purpose of the meetings? Or what if through careless publicity they gave the impression the Congresses were trying to push the Church of England towards Rome? They remembered the rumours which had accompanied the run-up to the first Congress and they were anxious to avoid anything like them again. So they drew up a statement and urged local committees to adhere to it in their local publicity without further elaboration:

> The purpose and aims of the Congress is to extend the knowledge of Catholic Faith and Practice at home and abroad, and by these means to bring men and women to a true realization of the Lord Jesus Christ as their personal Saviour.

The genius of this statement is in bringing together the words, 'Catholic Faith and Practice' with the phrase used by Evangelicals, 'the Lord Jesus Christ as their personal Saviour'. The executive's minutes recorded the hope that 'these local Congresses would be used as a means whereby might be promoted meetings between ourselves and clergy of other schools of thought'. They suggested that bishops should be invited to act as presidents of the local Congresses, and they formed a sub-committee to advise area organizers in choosing speakers.[1]

The Congress which took place in Manchester on 2, 3 and 4 October 1922 was fairly typical of those held in large cities. The city was chosen as a convenient venue for the North West. The Evangelical Bishop Knox had retired the year before and William Temple had taken his place. The new appointment gave Manchester Catholics fresh hope. Although Temple was not a party man, they knew he would be far more supportive of the Catholic movement than Knox ever was.

The initiative for the Congress was taken by two Catholic priests in the diocese, W. Edelman Kemp, vicar of St Benedict, Ardwick, and E. T. Kerby, vicar of St Marks, Heyside, Oldham. The organization was modelled on that of the London Congress. The committee was made up of representatives from the dioceses of Manchester and Chester as well as that part of the Lichfield diocese which was to become the new diocese of Derby in 1927. A general council was formed with 330 members from the dioceses, two-thirds of whom were priests. The aim was to have a catchment area which spread from Blackpool and Preston in the north to Macclesfield and Crewe in the south. A network of train services converged on Manchester and made travel comparatively straightforward. Subcommittees were appointed for different tasks: the choice of subjects and speakers, administration, finance, church services and the production of a handbook. St Benedict's provided an office and a bookshop. Temple agreed to be President of the Congress; in a letter he said he was honoured to be invited, but could not be present because of earlier engagements. Bishop H. L. Paget of Chester and the Suffragan Bishop of Derby, C. T. Abraham, agreed to be vice-presidents.

The main sessions were in Manchester's Albert Hall, a Methodist building opposite the Free Trade Hall in Peter Street. The Milton Hall, belonging to the Congregationalists and round the corner in Deansgate, was the Congress centre. Stalls were set up by the Society of SS Peter and Paul, the Universities Mission to Central Africa, the Association for Promoting Retreats, the Society for the Propagation of the Gospel, the Church of England Missionary Council, and the Industrial Christian Fellowship. There were also catering facilities where lunches and high teas could be purchased for two shillings (10p).

The Congress opened on the Monday with a reception for the general council in the Town Hall at 5.00 p.m. hosted by the Lord Mayor, who delighted everyone by appearing on the stage to make a speech of welcome at the first session in the Albert Hall and staying for the whole morning. At 6.30 there was a further reception in the Milton Hall for all the members of the Congress, attended by the Bishops of Chester and Derby. Then at 8.00 evensong was sung in the cathedral and an address given by Bishop Paget. Clergy who attended were asked to wear cassocks and surplices (no mention of cottas). The London Congress had not been allowed to use St Paul's Cathedral for their opening service, but there was no such problem in Manchester. The chapter minutes in the cathedral archives merely state that permission was given. It might have been interesting if they had recorded the discussion which took place.

The programme for the two days followed a similar pattern. At 10.30 each morning high masses were celebrated at two different churches around the city with a galaxy of preachers including some from the London Congress and the Priests' convention: F. Underhill, A. H. Baverstock, H. L. Goudge and L. A. Phillips. From 7.30 to 9.30 each evening there was a rally ending a short evangelistic challenge delivered by Fr Vernon of the Society of the Divine Compassion (SDC). Participants were asked to wear large circular badges with their names and churches on them. Besides these main events there were recitals, talks on church music for organists, and a celebration of solemn evensong each day in Sacred Trinity Church, Salford, just over the river Irwell from the cathedral.

The handbook was an impressive affair. Pocket-sized in hard covers, it was sent to those who paid three shillings (15p) to become members of the Congress. It contained the full programme, short biographies of the speakers with photographs, a pullout map showing the locations of the venues, details of tram routes, and train timetables. There were several pages of advertisements. At the beginning was a statement of purpose of the Congress:

> We believe that the Catholic way – the way of Prayer, of Penance, of Communion, of offering the Holy Sacrifice, of a living fellowship with the Saints and all the blessed dead – is the one assured and perfect way whereby the redeemed may find union with their Redeemer. To bring men, women and children of our country, through the full faith of Catholic Christendom, to the love and service of the Incarnate Son of God; the aim of our movement is nothing less than that.

The subcommittee responsible for producing the handbook showed a Mancunian independence by composing their own draft statement rather that copy the one put out by the London executive. Also printed were the collects, readings and hymns for the various services, and the text of the Prayer Book Holy Communion Service complete with the proper

THE PROVINCIAL CONGRESSES

preface of the Holy Spirit. The collect was the one used at the London Congress.

Temple and T. Dilworth Harrison, vicar of Ringley, Manchester, contributed introductory essays. Temple began by saying that the Anglo-Catholic movement is 'one of the channels through which the Holy Spirit is manifestly breathing life into the Church of England', together with the Evangelical movement and the Christian Social movement:

> These three have interacted on each other, and there are signs of actual coalescence. Every true Evangelical knows that his personal faith, rooted in the Gospel, binds him with other believers in the unity of the Body which is sustained by a sacramental life; every true Catholic knows that Catholicism rests upon the Gospel, and that apart from the Word there could be neither Church nor Sacrament; the social reformer knows that what the world needs is not mere reorganization but redemption, which Catholics and Evangelicals alike realize, with responsibility for applying the principles of Christ to the structure of society. Each of these movements gives proof of its origin as it leads to a deeper understanding of the one Lord (for it is the Holy Spirit who glorifies the Lord Jesus, taking what is His and shewing it to us), and as it leads also to a deeper fellowship both within its own ranks and in its relation to the other movements.

He went on that it is impossible that 'any one person, or group of like-minded persons, should exhaust the "unsearchable riches of Christ"'. Different aspects of the Christian experience are appropriated by the different types of human nature. Our need is that all should bear witness to those aspects which are most real to themselves without any depreciation of others, and that we should all seek to learn from one another. He concluded, 'The Anglo-Catholic movement does this in relation to the doctrine and practice which have been the possession of the Church from the beginning and are a priceless part of our heritage today. I heartily welcome it to Manchester, and pray for the blessing of God upon its work.'

This statement was typical of Temple's understanding of Anglicanism, and of the differences between the denominations. It was the basis for his work as a teacher, a bishop and an ecumenist. But Temple's understanding did not satisfy those who believed that Catholicism was the faith of the Church of England and should not to be regarded as merely one stream within it to be set alongside other streams. For them Catholicity already embraced what Evangelicals and social reformers stood for – and much more. Dilworth Harrison was one. He had probably read Temple's forward in manuscript before he composed his own piece and wanted to draw out what he saw as a weakness in the bishop's position without referring directly to it.

'We are convinced', he wrote, 'that the Church of England has failed from an inherent tendency to compromise the truth she holds, thinking, in a mistaken charity, that by tolerating wide divergences from her own Catholic standards, she might "by any means save some" who otherwise would be lost to the Fold. We believe, however, that this method has been weighed in the balance, and found wanting. Our boasted "comprehensiveness" has lost its supposed glory when we realize the multitudes who refuse, even so, to be comprehended. It is plain moreover that the teaching of our religion cannot be both optional and essential. The lowest common denominator of Anglicanism cannot convert tempted men and women to the service of the King of the Universe. The genius of the Catholic Church has ever been to enable each several member of her fold to express his spiritual life in such a manner that Christ's Redemption becomes the overwhelming fact of his existence.'[2]

The Methodist Albert Hall had been chosen because of its good acoustic qualities. The audience was disappointed that the large crucifix which had been used at the London Congress and brought up to Manchester was not set up in the hall. Kemp had to explain that the Methodist trustees had made the hall available on condition the crucifix was kept out of the building. 'Although we cannot have the crucifix,' he announced at the first session, 'we must try to have the Lord uplifted in our hearts all the more.' He might have pointed out that, in spite of their scruples about the crucifix, the Manchester Methodists had shown themselves more accommodating than those in London had been.

In choosing the contributors the Manchester organizers tried to keep in view the evangelistic purpose of the Congress, and that note was struck in the sermon at the opening service by the Bishop of Chester. Paget, a supporter of the Catholic movement, had been a missioner in East London and vicar of St Pancras. He said he believed that in the aftermath of the war people were expecting a religious revival, but that would not happen if they heard the faith presented in a simplistic and sentimental way. Teaching must be grounded on sound doctrine expounded in a manner an intelligent person could understand. 'Mere credulity and sloppy, incoherent talk was not good enough,' he said, 'nor had they ever been.'[3]

The revision of the Prayer Book had reached the stage where texts were being published, and the wording of the prayer of consecration in the Holy Communion Service was causing controversy (as indeed it did for the next fifty years). What concerned Catholics was that there should be explicit recognition of the sacrificial nature of the mass. This was explained in Goudge's address. It was quite true, he said, that the sacrifice of Christ was completed on Calvary but, though finished, its effect continued. We do not just look back on something that happened two thousand years ago. We celebrate it at every Eucharist. 'Today we sing, "My faith looks *up* to Thee", not, "my faith looks *back* to Thee".' He drew an illustration from a local feature. The Manchester Ship Canal had been finished years ago, but ships still come up it. It was finished, but it lasted. So, too, does Christ's sacrifice.

P. T. Browning, vicar of All Saints Hook Memorial Church in Leeds and one of the organizers of the Congress in that city earlier in the year, tackled the suspicions many had of the 'new psychology' of Freud. Like G. Rawlinson at the Priests' Convention, he said that those who were experienced in spiritual direction realized how useful psychoanalysis could be in bringing peace to troubled souls. Psychology threw a new light on what was happening when a penitent made his or her confession to a priest. To share the burden of a guilty conscience with a discreet counsellor was a healing experience in itself, and that was what happened when confessions were sincerely made. It is not clear whether Browning made a distinction between the human benefit brought by psychology and the divine grace of the sacramental act, or whether he saw the human benefit as the 'outward sign' of the 'inward grace' of absolution.

Several speakers surveyed the Catholic movement and discerned within it the work of the Holy Spirit. S. L. Ollard, rector of Bainton, Lincolnshire, saw the hand of God in the labours of the Tractarians and the spread of their teaching among Anglicans, a theme he developed in his books. Carpenter Garnier, a Librarian of Pusey House, believed the Congresses were the Holy Spirit's agents for strengthening the Catholic position. He urged three pairs of qualities in teaching the faith – fearlessness coupled with sympathy, simplicity coupled with reasonableness, and confidence coupled with humility. Above all, and the queen of all, was charity.

J. K. Mozley, principal of Leeds Clergy School, declared that Christian belief both in the Holy Spirit as well as in the apostolic Church was a vital clause in the creed, and that harm was done when one or the other was overlooked. He went on to criticize Catholics for not recognizing that the Spirit was urging them to address the social and industrial problems they were confronted with at that time. The slums, unemployment, industrial unrest in the mines, the shipyards and the railways – these urgently demanded the Church's attention.

The *Church Times*' report on the Manchester Congress occupied two pages. Its correspondent began with a criticism which was often repeated about other Congresses. At the opening service of evensong in the cathedral, the office hymn, 'O Blest Creator of the Light', had been sung to plainchant. 'I wonder', he wrote in exasperation, 'when our Congress Councils will realize the importance of choosing well-known and simple tunes for Congress services; or will ascertain that the tunes to be sung have been adequately rehearsed beforehand. The difference between singing the office hymn and the hymn which followed, "When God of old came down from Heaven", was striking. The one was tantalizing; the other was exhilaration.' But that was his only complaint. For everything else he was full of praise: 'It was a bold and brave thing to bring the Anglo-Catholic Congress to Manchester' (he had earlier commented on the strength of Protestantism in the area). 'Boldness has, however, been completely justified, and I should not be at all surprised if the Catholic cause in this country benefits more from this Congress in this wonderful Cottonopolis than from any other in the provinces. When Manchester takes a thing in hand, it takes it in hand thoroughly. It has done so with the Anglo-Catholic Congress.'[4]

The Congresses in Birmingham, Liverpool and Leeds also received extensive coverage in that paper. Their organization was similar to that in Manchester, and they each produced pocket-sized handbooks. Bishop Wakefield of Birmingham, Gore's successor, willingly accepted an invitation to preside; he had always been relaxed about Catholic practices in his diocese. After the opening high mass in the cathedral, when the preacher was Atlay, there was an outdoor procession of over a thousand including 250 clergy. It went with banners, candles and incense to the town hall where the sessions were held. In his opening address the Bishop said, 'What I am sure the whole of Anglicanism would like to see tested to the full is the usefulness of a fully expressed Catholic Churchmanship in the evangelization of the country.'[5]

In the final session Gore, greeted with clapping and cheers, spoke on the Church's responsibility for understanding social, economic and international affairs. He told his audience that when considering the situation of industrial workers, the Church should not be content with sponsoring charity; she should be thundering against the strongholds of tyranny. He wanted the Church to support trade union policies for the nationalization of major industries, a minimum wage, unemployment benefit, and radical action on slum clearance. He also urged Britain to back the League of Nations so that it could become an international enforcer of peace and goodwill in the world. He described the critical economic state of Germany caused by the heavy reparations and the equally devastating effects of the Bolshevik revolution in Russia. According to the *Church*

Times, 'He asked [his audience] to consider Europe at the present time, and of God as taking account of things as they were. If Europe allowed the millions in Russia to starve because it hated the Bolsheviks, what an awful judgement that would be by God on Europe!'[6]

Gore did not hesitate to reveal his socialist convictions. Other bishops were equally concerned about these problems, but were not so willing to openly support the Labour Party, and they were alarmed at the growing power of the trade unions. Gore's many speeches in different parts of the country and his writings gradually changed that. Alan Wilkinson thinks that Gore was a key figure in awakening the Church of England to its social responsibilities, and that seminal figures like R. H. Tawney, Temple and Bell, derived much of their understanding of the Church's role in society from him.[7]

The Modernism conference at Girton College had taken place just after the Priests' Convention and been given much publicity in the secular as well as the religious press. As the Roman Catholic editor of *The Tablet* wrote: 'Our very separated brethren, the Anglicans, have been holding a feast of infidelity in Cambridge.' This subject was taken up in Birmingham by A. E. J. Rawlinson, Student (Fellow) of Christ Church, Oxford. Rawlinson was a leading Catholic theologian and willing to speak at Congress meetings although he declared himself to be a non-party man. He realized Modernists were attempting to reconcile the Christian faith with contemporary thought, and in his talk 'Catholicism and Freedom' he ridiculed, 'the obscurantism of devout intellectual backwoodsmen'. Because of recent developments in biblical scholarship, religious philosophy, and historical and psychological research, he said, Catholics, 'ought to be committed, not indeed to this or that particular brand of Modernism, but to the recognition of the need for a Modernism of some kind or another'.[8]

Unfortunately his qualified use of the word Modernism was missed. There were shouts of 'No! No!' and disturbances in some parts of the hall. That, of course, was the very opposite of what Rawlinson intended – though using the phrase 'devout intellectual backwoodsmen' was hardly tactful. Like certain other dons who have become bishops (Rawlinson was appointed Bishop of Derby in 1936), he did not realize that when addressing a large and varied audience, he would be wise not to treat them as if he was lecturing theological students.

The Leeds Congress also had an opening high mass followed by an outdoor procession half-a-mile long, wafted on its way to the town hall in clouds of incense. Among those taking part were a large number of religious from Mirfield, Horbury and other communities, and four bishops in copes and mitres. At one point a demonstrator stepped in front of the bishops to 'protest as a member of the Church of England at this humbug and mummery which is nothing but a conversion to Rome'.

Opposition to the Leeds Congress seems to have been particularly vociferous. The protests began with a letter in the *Yorkshire Post* on 25 May from P. W. Weston, vicar of Siddal, Halifax. 'Why an Anglo-Catholic is permitted to remain in a Protestant Church and yet consciously undermine its teaching passes the wit of man,' he wrote. 'They smash laws and dishonour vows – in fact, they are the gunmen of the Church. Clad in Popish vestments with an insane infatuation and mimicry of everything Popish, they yet have not the manhood to go to Rome, where their heart is, but remain in a Protestant Church.' That evoked a succession of letters which the paper printed throughout June and July.

During the Congress the Church Association arranged protest meetings and on the final day had a counter-demonstration outside the Town Hall while the final session was being held inside. As usual in such cases, publicized opposition roused much interest and of the 3,000 Congress tickets which were sold some went to clergy and individuals who were curious rather than supportive. The *Yorkshire Post* responded to this interest by printing full accounts of the addresses. In his final column the editor commented that there had been much of value in what had been said. But he doubted the wisdom of using vestments, candles and incense in an out-of-door procession, and of advertising a private meeting for priests on the confessional: such things roused anti-Catholic feelings unnecessarily, he said.[9]

One of the speakers in Leeds was the lawyer, H. Slesser. Speaking on social righteousness, he said the Christian view of the spiritual equality of all people before God was the only sure foundation for the working of any democracy. Once that was lost, as in Russia, the result was tyranny. His presence at that Congress may have won him votes among the Catholics when he stood for Parliament and won a Leeds constituency for Labour in 1923.

Of all the speeches given at Leeds, that which stirred the greatest enthusiasm was delivered by J. J. G. Stockley. The *Church Times* report of what the rector of Wolverhampton said catches the Congress spirit well:

> Good Anglicans should be good Catholics, and good Catholics should be good Anglicans. The Ecclesia Anglicana has been led and guided through extraordinary experiences for some great purpose of God. Here is Penance, here is the Mass – (*loud cheers*) – here is a noble translation of Holy Scriptures (the *Revised Version*), and here is liberty, too much perhaps, but far better than too little. (*Cheers.*) We ought to have the

widest sympathy for those who are struggling for unity among Christians. But before we can contemplate corporate unity between the East and West, or home reunion with Nonconformist bodies, we must have far more union within our own borders. (*Cheers.*) Cannot these Anglo-Catholic Congresses make for better understanding with the other schools of thought? Catholics must cease to be merely traditionalists. Cannot our Evangelical friends give up suspecting us of trying to enslave men and women? We wholeheartedly admire their splendid missionary efforts. (*Loud cheers.*) Can we never forgive and forget? He thought the signs of such reconciliation were everywhere manifest. But the lives of the Church's members must be much more holy if the Church is to convert the world.[10]

The sharp divide between Roman Catholicism and Protestantism in Liverpool made the organization of a Congress there a delicate matter. Only a few years previously a visiting Anglican bishop had been booed at a public meeting simply because he had been wearing a pectoral cross. The organizers went about their preparations more cautiously than their friends in Leeds. R. T. Brockman, vicar of St John the Baptist, Tuebrook, chairman of the local Congress committee, informed the diocesan, F. Chavasse, of the plans and invited him to be an honorary president. But Chavasse, an Evangelical, refused. Years before, he had put Brockman under a ban for introducing reservation into his church, and he was in no mood to accept such an invitation.

Other negotiations went on behind the scenes. A meeting of Evangelical clergy, called to discuss their reaction to the planned Congress, resolved they would do nothing to express their opposition to it, and the city's Orange Order agreed to make no public demonstration against the Congress on condition there was no outdoor procession. During the event it was noticed that some of the white name-and-parish disks worn by participants revealed there were several from Evangelical churches present and evidently appreciating the experience.

As happened in London, the response was greater than expected and the committee, having hired St George's Hall, had to transfer the meetings to the larger Philharmonic Hall to accommodate the numbers who booked to attend them. Among the speakers were two of the London priests who had planned the 1920 Congress – Leary, of St Augustine's, Kilburn (who had once been parish priest in Liverpool), and Atlay. A local reporter wrote that some of the talks had been too academic for many in the audience, though that did not discourage attendances. Atlay, who spoke at the final meeting, received a standing ovation.

Provincial Congresses continued to be organized in different parts of the country for several years. A highly successful one was held in Bristol a few days before the general election on 6 December 1923. Stanley Baldwin, the Conservative prime minister, spoke at an election rally in the Colston Hall on the same evening as the opening service of the Congress, but in spite of that the cathedral was packed to the doors. Bishop Nickson preached, and during the service he installed M. P. Gillson, the vicar of the Catholic parish of All Saints, Clifton, as an honorary canon – a sign of episcopal approval. As in the cities already mentioned, attendance was over 3,000.

Speakers included K. E. Kirk, Fellow of Trinity College, Oxford, on the incarnation, Fr Vernon SDC on going to confession, Fr Andrew of the same community on the mass as the inspiration for social action, Fr Bull SSJE on vocations, Peter Green of St Philip's, Salford, on suffering, Mary Scharlieb, a former missionary doctor, on the sanctity of marriage, Carpenter-Garnier on prayer, G. G. Elliott, the Vicar of St Bartholomew's, Brighton, on Our Lady and the Saints, Gore on authority in the Church, and Moulsdale on worship. Slesser was due to speak on the world of work, but he had to send his apologies as he was busy canvassing in his Leeds constituency.

The president at Bristol was Lord St Audries, a former Conservative Party Chief Whip in the House of Commons, and the chairman at one of the evening sessions was Sir Dennis F. Boles, CBE, also a former MP, who was Master of the West Somerset Fox Hounds and of the Quantock Stag Hounds. Their names are a further reminder that Catholics in the provinces were supported by some in the upper classes (those older generations called 'the quality').

There were Congresses in other cities and towns in the twenties. Besides those already noted for 1922, they were organized at Nottingham in 1923; Burton-on-Trent in 1924; Torquay, Southampton, Northampton and Middlesborough in 1925; Norwich, Southend, Aldershot, Carlisle, Cambridge, and a second in Manchester in 1926; seconds in Leeds and Norwich in 1928; Bournemouth, Ipswich and seconds in Brighton and Plymouth in 1929.

The theme of the Plymouth Congress was 'Christ the King', no doubt inspired by the feast instituted by Pope Pius XI in 1925. P. E. T. Widdrington, rector of Great Easton in Essex and a leading Christian socialist, forestalled the liberation theologians by saying that to proclaim the Gospel of the Kingdom was to proclaim the Gospel for the poor. The Catholic Church is a Church for the poor, he said, and care for the poor and distressed is the first concern for Catholics. Another speaker, Miss

Ruth Kenyon, secretary of the Anglo-Catholic School of Sociology, made an impassioned plea for the Church to campaign for the provision of more houses. A million new homes had been built since the war, she said, but the rents of many of them were far too high for the low-paid and unemployed; at least a million more with low rents were needed. In Bournemouth the talks focussed on Church affairs, worship, the ordained ministry and reunion.

Not all Congresses were on such a grand scale as those in the cities. A Congress in Kettering in 1927, for example, had meetings in surrounding villages as well as in the town, while a group of villages round Melbourne in Derbyshire organized one in churches and school halls. Other smaller Congresses took place up and down the country. Hope Patten arranged one in Walsingham. Attendances were encouraging: even at Burton-on-Trent there were 1,000.

One of the last provincial Congresses was at Bradford in 1934. A. Blunt, who had been vicar of St Werbergh, Derby, was appointed Bishop of Bradford in 1931. He had a reputation of being a Catholic and his arrival in the diocese was welcomed by those priests who had been cold-shouldered by his predecessor, A. W. Perowne, who had been translated to Worcester. It was reported on the diocesan grapevine that the new bishop wore vestments at mass and reserved the Blessed Sacrament in his private chapel.

Blunt attended the Oxford Movement Centenary in Oxford in 1933, and when he got home he agreed when a group of Catholics suggested the diocese should have its own Congress the following year. Much to their surprise, Blunt headed the organizing committee – becoming the first diocesan in England to do so – and choose the speakers and the theme, 'The Holiness of God'. The Congress took place in the middle of June. Blunt was the celebrant at the opening high mass, present at all the other services, and chaired most of the public sessions. In a report on the events the *Green Quarterly* said, 'Dr Blunt could almost have undertaken the whole of the Congress himself, so masterly and lucid were the remarks with which he introduced and summed up the papers, and connected them into a continuous exposition of the faith. There was never any doubt what he meant; it was always very positive.'[11]

These provincial Congresses did much to strengthen the Catholic cause throughout the country. They demonstrated that what they had to offer was not only for London churches. They enabled large numbers of clergy and laity in the country to share in the Congress experience. It was particularly significant for those who attended the opening high masses and services that they were often celebrated in their own cathedral in the presence of their diocesan bishop. It made them feel the Congress movement was now accepted. Added to this groups from local parishes had opportunities of hearing the faith taught by leading Catholic scholars, religious, overseas missioners and parish priests. Some of the things that were said may have gone over the heads of many, but at least they were left with the assurance that what they were taught was intellectually sound in spite of what skeptics might say. Nowadays, when we are so used to seeing well-known figures on our TV screens, it is difficult to appreciate the thrill it gave Catholics in Nottingham to have the famous Bishop of Zanzibar among them, or those in Bristol to hear the great Bishop Gore. They went home with the heart-warming conviction that the Lord was doing great things among Catholics in those dreary postwar days.

In the provinces, as in London, the Congress experience was kept alive by anniversary celebrations each year. These usually took the form of a high mass and meetings in a large church. In Birmingham they included social events because G. D. Rosenthal, vicar of St Agatha, Sparkbrook, and a leader of the local Congress committee, believed Catholics should be seen to enjoy themselves.

The practice of inviting bishops to preside at Congresses paid off. Some, of course, were already supportive. When Bishop Edwyn Hoskyns of Southwell, as chairman of one of the Congress meetings in Nottingham, welcomed Weston as a speaker, Weston opened his address by remarking that it was the first time he had ever heard an English diocesan refer to Anglo-Catholics as 'we'. Others who had been wary of Anglo-Catholicism began to appreciate the theological scholarship and pastoral wisdom reflected in the addresses, and said so when they spoke at the gatherings. Some of them were surprised to find the Prayer Book used at Congress services, even if the accompanying ceremonial was not always so familiar. They were impressed by the large numbers who turned up, and mildly surprised to realize the majority of the Catholics in their dioceses were trying to be faithful Anglicans, more interested in mission and social concerns than niceties of ritual.

Evangelicals who attended the provincial Congresses began to see that Catholics might be partners in the Gospel rather than enemies in the camp. Bishop Woods of Peterborough wrote to the *Times* declaring that he would join in the 1923 Congress procession in London, not because he agreed with them in everything, but because they stood for '(Christ's) message and His way of life'. Two years later, as Bishop of Winchester, he accepted an invitation to be president of the Southampton Congress and preached at the closing Eucharist in Winchester cathedral, at which he wore a cope and mitre.[12] In his sermon he said he objected to some items in the Congress handbook describing practices such as the use of holy water and the recitation of the Hail Mary; they were, he remarked, 'a string of red rags'. But he immediately added that he felt he could be frank because he was among friends. The *Church Times* commented, 'His lordship has shown, this week and before it, that he is ready to be a sympathetic Father-in-God to Anglo-Catholics, if they will let him.'[13]

The success of the provincial Congresses led to the setting up of a network which made possible various initiatives by Catholics across the country. These will be described in a later chapter.

9

The Second Congress 1923

The proposal for a second national Congress had been so enthusiastically endorsed at the Priest's Convention that the executive had no hesitations in following it up. It had been their intention that the first Congress would have been a launch-pad for a nationwide evangelistic campaign, but that had been postponed on the advice of a committee set up to plan it. Now the plan was revived. Fr Paul Bull SSJE was invited to lead a new committee to discuss it. Months later he reported that once again they had decided it would be inopportune to attempt such a major project at that time. Not enough trained missioners were available, he said, so it would be better to use the congress as an opportunity to infuse Catholics with an evangelistic spirit to bring others to the faith through personal contacts and local meetings. A nationwide campaign might be considered later. Bull added that he hoped Catholics would support any evangelistic initiative in their own area, even if the promoters were not themselves Catholics. 'Our movement is within the Church, and while we are planning our own special witness and work, we shall gain, rather than lose, by active support of such corporate efforts as may arise within our neighbourhoods.'[1] It is likely he was referring to joint initiatives with Anglicans rather than ecumenical groups.

In June 1922 Atlay suddenly announced that he was going to marry and resign as vicar of St Matthew's. The executive was shocked and alarmed. The first Congress owed much to Atlay's leadership and it was assumed he would lead the second. But some on the executive felt it was inappropriate for the chairman of the Congress executive to have a wife ('at the present at any rate,' Wilson tactfully recorded in the minutes of 22 June), and they asked him to step down. Atlay seems to have expected this. He continued as a member of the executive until he was appointed a canon of Gloucester Cathedral the following year. There he exercised a much appreciated ministry of teaching and spiritual direction, and his wife, Violet, a war widow, eventually became diocesan president of the Mothers' Union. He dropped out of the Congresses until one future occasion, which we shall notice later. A. Montford of the Ascension, Lavender Hill, took his place as chairman and C. R. Deakin, who had first put forward the idea of a Congress after the war, was elected vice-chairman.

Preparations went forward much as three years previously. One hundred and twenty London churches committed themselves to taking part in a scheme for days of intercession before the event. The Albert Hall was booked for 10–13 July, and the Queen's Hall and the Great Hall in Church House for overflow meetings. Weston was invited to be the Congress chairman. This time the Bishop of London agreed to be a patron of the Congress, and in a surprising turnaround the dean and chapter of St Paul's gave permission for the opening Eucharist to be celebrated in the cathedral. That may have been because Dean Inge had revised his opinion of Anglo-Catholicism since he had forecast its fragmentation in 1920. In the London *Evening Standard* he wrote, 'This party enlists more zeal and enthusiasm than any other school of thought in the Church of England . . . Though it is chiefly supported by women of limited intelligence, it has won over a few gifted men whose conversion to its tenets seems to be sincere. Purged and purified, it may suffer a sea-change, and resuming its proper place in the Church as a legitimate expression of one side of the national religion . . . No one who has witnessed the admirable work of the clergy of this school would wish to see it decay.' However, the 'Gloomy Dean' could not resist the temptation to end with a note of doom: 'But seeds of decay are nevertheless present in it.'[2]

By the beginning of 1923 everything was well in hand. Daily masses with the intention of invoking God's grace on the Congress were said in churches during the month before it opened. Local meetings were held in a number of venues, including a three-day convention for a hundred priests in Chester Cathedral. Fifty-two Congress booklets of 20–30 pages were published. Edited by Leonard Prestige, many of them were written by well-known scholars and parish clergy, covering aspects of Catholic teaching on Scripture, doctrine and morals. A quarter of a million were sold by the end of the Congress and they were later published in three pocket-sized volumes.[3]

In March an unwelcome complication occurred. Canon T. B. A. Saunders of Carlisle wrote to P. T. Browning, the organizer of the Leeds Congress, to ask if fasting Communion and going to confession were part of the Congress movement's 'propaganda'. He wanted to put a notice in the diocesan gazette but thought the bishop would refuse to publish it if these two disciplines were mentioned in it. Browning sent the letter on to Wilson, who wrote to Saunders on 20 April:

> All around us there are thousands of men and women who have lost their way to God. Some are indeed dead in trespasses and sins; some

are sunk in materialism and indifference; some are vaguely interested in spiritual things, but have forgotten or never known Our Lord; some have been deluded by the teaching of heresy or of false religions. All such we long to make faithful Christians. We believe that the Catholic way – the way of prayer, of penance, of communion, of the offering of the holy sacrifice, of a living fellowship with the saints and all the blessed death – is the assured and tested way whereby the redeemed may find union with their Redeemer.

Saunders put the advertisement into the diocesan gazette quoting part of the letter but, misinterpreting what Wilson had written, added his own words: 'The enterprise will fail in much the same way as the Oxford Movement has failed to effect the normal parish in a vital way, because it did not put sacramental faith and practice in front in a sufficiently broad way.'

He then sent a copy of the proof of the gazette with the notice in it to Wilson. When Wilson read the proof he was dismayed and immediately sent a telegram to the gazette's printer instructing him to take the notice out. Unfortunately he was too late. The gazette had been printed. Wilson then wrote to Saunders complaining that things he had said in his private letter had been published without his permission. Saunders apologized and said he would put a correction in the next issue. But he added that many Catholic priests told him in private that it was difficult to commend sacramental practice if they insisted on fasting Communion and going to confession, except in a few places.[4] The incident illustrates the problems the Congress executive had in co-operating with those who had to adopt a more relaxed attitude to disciplines such as fasting Communion and going to confession. But it had the effect of making the executive decide on what their attitude should be in these cases, and after a long discussion they issued this statement:

> The purpose of our movement is to bring the English people, or as many individuals among them as possible, by the way which we conceive to be the best way, that is, the way of Catholic Faith and Practice, into more intimate fellowship with Our Lord. We believe that Fasting Communion and Private Confession are elements in Catholic Practice which cannot ultimately be omitted without grave loss. And we do not think that a Catholicism which omits these things can be in any sense complete. Naturally we do not think that non-fasting communion is a sin in cases where, in all good faith, the duty of fasting is not apprehended. But we consider that it is important that men and women should come to regard as sin the ignoring of the traditional disciplinary practice of the Catholic Church on this and on other points; and we believe that a religion in

which the whole Catholic system is practiced except its penitential side is profoundly dangerous. For similar reasons we recognize that confession not in the presence of a priest may bring full forgiveness; but we believe that as men learn to take a fuller view of the Christian Church they will come to recognize the necessity of sacramental confession in cases of serious sin, and to seek for themselves the benefit of absolution.[5]

To borrow a distinction from another controversy, the committee was saying that the two disciplines may not always be of the *esse* of the Christian life but they are certainly of the *bene esse*. Its position was defended at the Congress in a talk by T. A. Lacey in which he explained how the ancient discipline of penance, a 'second baptism', for the forgiveness of mortal sins had developed in the early middle ages to include private confession to a priest as a means of dealing with everyday, venial sins. Going to confession therefore, he said, while only essential for the absolution of moral sins, could only be highly recommended for the absolution of venial sins as a sacramental means of growing in grace.[6] In saying this he was commending the Anglican advice about confession to a priest, 'Some should, all may, none must.' Judging by the notices announcing the times when confessions were heard in churches like All Saints, Margaret Street, and St Augustine, Kilburn, the number of penitents before greater festivals in such places must have been considerable, but occasional references in letters in the *Church Times* and elsewhere suggest that in many Catholic parishes only a minority went regularly to confession.

The organizers in London were kept busy. The hospitality committee was overwhelmed by requests for bed-and-breakfasts and had to call a halt to any more. Wealthier parishes were asked to sponsor parties from poorer ones. Cheap tickets were arranged for those travelling to London by train. Parking arrangements were made for 'private omnibuses'. The Church Assembly was meeting the same week as the Congress, so cars were assigned to ferry Assembly members from Westminster to the Albert Hall and back again.

A specially written play on the Church's year called *Annus Domini*, a dramatic series of sketches on the liturgical seasons, was performed two weeks before the Congress opened. A series of stills was prepared on the sacrament of confirmation to demonstrate how a 'cinematograph' could be used for instructional purposes. There were murmurs that it was disrespectful for these to be used in church, but after a preview of the pictures Mackay said it was one of the best things he had seen and he would certainly be using them in All Saints. That was equivalent to an *imprimatur* for most Catholics. Martin Travers, the artist, designed posters for notice boards and the Underground and sketches for the official Report in his distinctive neo-baroque style.

Tickets sold well. Wilson arranged for them to be obtained in shops, agencies and churches in different parts of the country. On 6 July 1923 the *Church Times* printed the list showing the numbers purchased in counties, with the highest at the top:

Surrey 571	Worcestershire 87
Sussex 523	Leicestershire 85
Yorkshire 408	Gloucestershire 83
Kent 346	Wiltshire 76
Devon 322	Dorset 74
Lancashire 285	Cornwall 72
Hampshire 284	Nottinghamshire 70
Essex 246	Northumberland 67
Oxfordshire 231	Cambridgeshire 66
Hertfordshire 169	Derbyshire 66
Somerset 168	Bedfordshire 47
Berkshire 168	Northamptonshire 46
Warwickshire 147	Lincolnshire 46
Norfolk 116	Durham 38
Suffolk 110	Shropshire 33
Buckinghamshire 109	Herefordshire 25
Cheshire 108	Cumberland 18
Staffordshire 106	Channel Islands 17

No numbers for London were given, but in other cities they were:

Birmingham 88	Leicester 32
Leeds 80	Newcastle 29
Liverpool 79	Plymouth 24
Manchester 71	Hull 17
Croydon 69	Nottingham 17
Bristol 37	Southampton 11
Bradford 36	

It is not clear whether the numbers for Leeds and Bradford were included in the Yorkshire total of 408; there were numerous Catholic parishes in that county so it is possible they were additional to those coming from the two cities. Understandably numbers were high from areas round the metropolis – Surrey, Sussex, Kent and Essex. Yet it is remarkable that two or three hundred were sold in those as distant as Devon and Lancashire while only three or four dozen in nearer Bedfordshire and Hertfordshire. In Wales 164 tickets were purchased, 55 in Scotland and 12 in Ireland.

Sales abroad were: 72 in the United States, 19 in Canada and 16 in South Africa. The 22 purchased in Italy and 13 in France presumably went to English people living on the Continent who were coming home for the summer. Other countries listed (using contemporary names) where one or two tickets were sold were Australia, Belgium, Borneo, British East Africa, Bulgaria, Brazil, Calcutta, Ceylon, Cyprus, Egypt, British West Indies, Germany, Gold Coast, Guinea, Holland, Honduras, Malta, New Zealand, Portuguese East Africa, Rangoon and Switzerland.

During the week before the Congress opened Margaret Merryweather, the first full-time woman reporter on the staff of the *Church Times*, toured some of the London churches to see how the days of intercession were being observed. St George, Bloomsbury, had a scattering of prayers, the silence only broken by murmurs from a confessional at the side of the nave. 'Shall we', she wondered, 'some day see St George's filled with curators and others of the British Museum, which stands so conveniently near, before they die in their musty air?' At St Mary-the-Virgin, Primrose Hill, Dearmer's former parish, she found only two people keeping the vigil, kneeling as far apart from each other as possible. In St Augustine, Kilburn, she met three children, 'dusty with pavement games', entering the church at six o'clock. 'Prayers were chalked for them on blackboards in the nave. I thought the choice a little stereotyped, not quite real and spontaneous enough for these three smutty little Catholics. But the church looked quite lovely with its blaze of candles, and the details of its delicate Gothic work so carefully tended.' On another day she saw thirty or forty watchers in St Matthew, Westminster.[7]

The following Sunday various Congress personalities were preaching at masses and solemn evensongs in churches in and around London. Then on Tuesday morning, 11 July, at 11.30 the opening Eucharist was celebrated in St Paul's Cathedral.

During the night there was a thunderstorm which was so bad that the Strand was flooded and traffic had to be diverted. But the Congress members were queuing on the cathedral steps an hour beforehand and, when the cathedral's morning prayer ended at a quarter to eleven, the doors were opened, the bells rang out, and a stream of men, women, monks, nuns and priests flowed in. About a thousand vested clergy filled the east end of the choir and the seats under the dome while nuns occupied the north transept. A procession of two English and a dozen overseas bishops with their attendant chaplains came in at 11.30, followed by the Metropolitan Eulogie, Bishop of all the Russians in Western Europe, and the Greek Archimandrite Pagonis. The Bishop of London was absent: he was at the Church Assembly. So was Dean Inge: he was in Edinburgh receiving an honorary degree and probably glad to be away.

The Prayer Book Communion Service was followed, including the ten commandments. Four nuns were detailed to fast and receive the sacrament to avoid the accusation that a non-communicating mass was being celebrated. Palestrina's *Aeterna Christi Munera* setting was used, much to the disappointment of those who felt Merbecke would have been more congregational. But the *Church Times'* reporter thought otherwise. 'Gounod is reported to have said that the high celebration at St Paul's was the most beautiful high mass in Europe,' he wrote ecstatically. 'He would not have had cause to qualify that judgment this morning.'[8]

During his sermon A. Montfort said, 'We have been accused of striving for a sectional victory. May I say, most emphatically, that this charge is unkind and untrue . . . Our life here is too short, and our work too important, to let us waste our time on anything so unchristian and so second-rate . . . We love the Faith which we hold, and we believe ourselves to be bound by the discipline which we try to practise; not because we think that they are ends in themselves, but because we are convinced that they are the best means of drawing men to their Saviour.'[9]

The fact that this opening Eucharist was celebrated in the most famous of all Anglican cathedrals was highly significant. Those who attended had a sense that at last the Anglo-Catholic movement had come home. By using the Prayer Book the organizers demonstrated both their loyalty to the Church of England and their contention that it was a worthy Catholic rite. St Paul's was one of the first English cathedrals to be influenced by the ritual movement under former canons, Richard William Church, historian of the Oxford Movement, Henry Parry Liddon, biographer of Dr Pusey, and Henry Scott Holland, so there was no problem in lighting candles and wearing vestments. But the dean and chapter would not permit incense to be used.

The opening session of the Congress began at 2.30 the same afternoon in a packed Albert Hall. As on the previous occasion, a huge crucifix hung above the platform but now with the addition of a scroll suspended from the organ pipes which read:

THE SECOND CONGRESS 1923

Blessed and Praised
for evermore be
Jesus Christ
on His
Throne of Glory
and in the most
Holy Sacrament
of the Altar.

Applause greeted the platform party – the Bishop of London, two English suffragans, the overseas bishops, the executive committee and other leading clergy and laity. There was a loud cheer for Weston as he took the chair.

Winnington-Ingram gave the opening address. He said the things he knew his audience expected him to say: the Anglo-Catholic movement stands for the truth, for beauty in worship, for the Church of England as part of the Catholic Church, and for Christian unity. On this last point he suggested that if the Methodists were willing to accept the essentials of Anglicanism – episcopal ordination and confirmation – their churches could become missionary centres throughout the land. But he warned his audience that the primacy of the Roman See could not be separated from its sovereignty; accepting one meant accepting the other. He ended by quoting Lightfoot: 'By the Church which shall be found to have the historic orders in one hand and the open Bible in the other, will Christendom one day be united.'[10]

The Bishop had requested that two hymns to the Virgin Mary printed in the handbook should not be used. He had privately told the executive he had no objection to them personally, but he had received complaints about them and felt he ought to make the request. As he was leaving to return to the Church Assembly, Weston asked him to give a message to the English bishops assuring them that 'Anglo-Catholics can invoke no saint without remembering that every saint is within the heart of the Lord Jesus Christ; that all prayer to them is prayed to them in Him.' Weston then called on the audience to stand and pray for the Russian Patriarch Tiknon of Moscow, who had been imprisoned the previous year for his public protests against the Communist government and its policy of nationalizing church property. (Tiknon was released shortly afterwards but died in 1925.)

Montfort read out a letter from the Bishop of Chelmsford. Since his consecration as the first bishop of the newly created diocese in 1914, J. E. Watts-Ditchfield had changed his opinion about Catholics. He had been impressed by Weston when he met him at the 1920 Lambeth Conference, and he had learned more about what Catholics stood for at the Cuddesdon consultation a few weeks later. That summer the bishop was seriously ill, but well enough to dictate a letter saying he was sorry he was not able to be with them as he had intended to be.

'I am a convinced Evangelical,' he said, 'but on my sick bed I am striving to look at you (may I say it without presumption?) as my Blessed Lord is looking at you, and to view you with His Mind and in His Spirit . . . With all my heart I send, with loving affection, a real "God bless you".'[11] He died a few days later.

When it was announced that messages of greeting were being sent from the Congress to the King, the Archbishop of Canterbury and the Patriarch of Constantinople, Weston suddenly stood up and suggested one should also be sent to the Pope. He proposed it should read: '16,000 Anglo-Catholics assembled in Congress offer respectful greetings to the Holy Father, humbly praying that the day of peace may quickly break'. There were calls of agreement from parts of the hall but it was noticeable that not everyone was enthusiastic. Next day the national papers appeared with headlines such as: 'The Anglo-Catholic Congress sends a message to the Pope.' Many Congress members were uneasy at the publicity.

Two days later Frere, who had not been present when Weston made his proposal, told the audience at the end of his paper that he regretted what they had done: 'Messages of this sort do more harm than good, because they are bound to be misunderstood both here and there' (his words were printed in the *Church Times* but omitted from his text in the report). There were a few cries of 'No!' but applause from others. When Frere sat down, Weston rose and said he was solely responsible for the message to the Pope. He had not consulted anyone beforehand and he regretted that his intention had been so misunderstood. Frere belonged to the small group headed by Halifax which during that summer was in the midst of delicate negotiations with the Archbishop of Canterbury on the future of the Malines conversations. Publicity which linked the Congress with the Papacy was the last thing they wanted.

The controversy caused by the telegram went on for some months. Clergy in Liverpool complained that those in the south had little idea of the damage it had done to the Catholic movement in the North West. Roman Catholicism was strong in their cities and towns and most Anglicans, whose churchmanship was dubbed 'Lancashire Low', were opposed to anything being introduced in their churches' worship which looked remotely popish. Weston subsequently explained that since messages were being sent from the Congress to the Archbishops of Canterbury and York and the Orthodox Patriarchs it seemed to him courteous to send one to the Bishop of Rome as well.

On Wednesday crowds arrived in the Albert Hall with the temperature edging up into the nineties. Weston invited them to look at the great crucifix suspended behind the platform and led them in a meditation on Jesus in his manhood and on the cross. He read a greetings telegram to the Congress from the Archbishop of Canterbury. Mackay announced that an Anglo-Catholic pilgrimage was being arranged to the Holy Land the following year at a cost of £75. It was the first of several in the years that followed. The business over, the audience settle down to hear the papers by K. E. Kirk and J. K. Mozley.

Kirk spoke on the mystery of the divine and human natures in Christ and ended by answering the question, 'How can that Incarnate life of so long ago avail for us as well as for the first followers of Christ?': 'In the Church and in her Sacraments the work of the Incarnation is continued; the royal priesthood of Christ has been handed on to that royal priesthood which is his Body. There are those who doubt whether the Church on earth, a community of frail and sinful men, can be the vehicle and means by which the life of God, the Holy Spirit, is poured into men's souls. But if so, they doubt the very truth of which . . . the Incarnation itself makes us secure – the truth namely that God is capable of working through human nature, and that human nature can manifest and transmit the divine. For the Incarnation is the greatest of all the sacraments, a visible sign of grace invisible, and on that sacrament the Church and all her Sacraments depend.'[12]

Mozley described the sacrifice of the cross as the means through which God dealt with moral evil in the world. In creation God acted on the world from without; in redemption he acts upon it from within. There was a finished work of God which was greater and more complete when Christ died on Calvary than when God rested on the seventh day from all the works he had created. Mozley stressed there was a penal as well as a victorious understanding of the atonement: 'Christ on the Cross accepts God's judgement upon man, and expresses God's judgement on sin.'[13]

The afternoon topics were regeneration, forgiveness and sacramental confession. E. Selwyn, rector of Redhill, Havant, and editor of *Theology*, spoke of baptism as the means whereby a Christian entered into a new relationship with God, established by the finished work of Christ and renewed by the Holy Spirit. But the gift had to be received with faith, and hence a great responsibility fell on those who were godparents (he did not mention parents). He concluded with an appeal to the Church to adopt a stricter baptismal policy. 'We speak of fencing the altar: do we not need to fence the font?'[14] His words were greeted with cheers. It was an early indication that some Catholics were beginning to respond to Roland Allen's campaign for baptismal reform in the years before the war.

By 1923 the social consequences of the war and its aftermath were obvious to everyone and were the subject of much public debate. Gore used his topic, 'The God of the Prophets', to show how the prophets' message of holiness and justice found its ultimate expression in the teaching of Christ. Christians, he said, had a social responsibility as well as a personal calling. Redemption was corporate as well as individual, and the Church needed to proclaim that truth more boldly. He was, as he had been for years, critical of the effects of unchecked capitalism, and he made no attempt to hide his feelings.

'Our industrial and social system [has] been largely built up on the repudiation of the Christian principles of justice, spiritual equality and brotherhood . . . and the current maxims of our commerce, our current attitude towards wealth, our current toleration of selfishness as the normal ideal for the individual, the family and the nation, are direct repudiations of the principles of the prophets and of Christ. At the same time there is a very deep and widespread feeling in the best of men, inside and outside the Church, that the Christian life is rooted in the truth and that there is no alternative to it. And I cannot but acknowledge that it is very largely from outside the Church that we have been, of recent years, relearning the moral meaning of Christ.'[15]

Those last words, 'from outside the Church', reflect what Christian socialists were coming to acknowledge: that in spite of the terrible news about Communist atrocities in Russia, Karl Marx could still teach the Church something of justice and equality in society, and of how capitalism prevented men and women from achieving them.

Mr John Lee, an economics adviser working for the government, followed Gore in developing the same criticism of uncontrolled capitalism. The Church, he said, must preach a Catholic faith which embraces the whole of life: 'In Mr Tawney's words, we cannot believe that religion should abdicate "one whole department of life, that of social and political conduct, as the sphere of the powers of this world and of them alone".' He went on to outline R. H. Tawney's thesis that in the centuries before the industrial revolution, economic and social life had been surrounded by religious sanctions which were regarded as having divine authority. Whatever their faults, he said, these sanctions served to foster charitable giving for the poor and checked the extremes of self-interest. But the emergence of capitalism as the driving force of economic progress saw social righteousness decline, and the Churches on both sides at the Reformation lost their influence over these developments. Lee urged Christians to work for change. One way of doing this, he suggested, would be through the formation of Christian associations in every walk of life 'to draw up a statement of what is wrong in current practice, and of the principles on which Christians ought to act'. Their findings would be collated to formulate 'the general maxims of Christian living' in modern society.[16]

H. Slesser spoke along similar lines. He, too, pictured the middle ages as a time when the mass had been at the centre of everyone's life and all human social and economic activity was affected by this. In the centuries since then, he said, the sovereignty of God had been replaced by the sovereignty of the State, and the profit motive had replaced a sense of corporate responsibility. Once avarice and covetousness had been judged deadly sins; now they were regarded as neither deadly nor venial but as non-existent. If the Catholic revival was to be true to itself, he said, the doctrine of the real presence must be carried from the mass into the world, so that once more the world would be organized on the basis of Christian law, taking its politics, its economics and its sociology from the teaching of our Lord.

Although these speakers were eloquent on the relevance of the Catholic faith to society, they were vague on practicalities. Except for Lee's suggestion about forming Christian professional associations, there was no direct challenge for Catholics to join political parties and trade unions in order to work for change. The only speaker who did this was G. A. Studdert-Kennedy. After the armistice this well-known, former army chaplain – 'Woodbine Willie' – had become missioner of the newly formed Industrial Christian Fellowship. His understanding of both Catholicism and humanity had been tested and broadened by his experiences in the suffering and comradeship of the trenches. Now he was deeply involved as mediator in disputes between unions and management – a ministry, in the opinion of many, of greater significance than that for which he was more famous.

He began by saying that, although the saving work of Christ should bring to individuals a sense of inner peace, the world of work within which Christians lived meant they found themselves torn apart by the struggle they were caught up in. A man found things being done in his name which as a Christian he detested. He was obliged to live in a city which tolerated slums and seemed to do little to improve housing. As a business man he had to accept standards of morality and ideas of what work is for which he would normally regard as beneath contempt. As a worker in a factory he had to submit to conditions and tolerate abuses which his Christian soul abhorred.

One result was that the Christian became a dissociated person, being one kind of a person on a Sunday and another on Monday. Studdert-Kennedy gave examples: 'The churchwarden who owns slum property; the devout layman who will not face the problem of war; the earnest brewer who presents a chalice to the church in the suburbs bought with the profits of the drink shops in the town.' Then came his reproach of those who refused to join a trade union: 'The Christian workman who helps the vicar, and perhaps serves at mass, and leaves his mates to strive for an improvement of conditions which he knows is short of justice and humanity, and takes gladly when he gets it, though he will not work for it – all these are dissociated personalities.'[17]

He was critical, too, of those whose devotions centered on the real presence of Christ in the mass but ignored that presence in daily living:

> There is only one spiritual life, and that is the sacramental life – sacramental in its fullest sense, its widest, and its deepest sense, which means the consecration of the whole of man and all his human relationships to God ... If the Real Presence of Christ in the Sacrament obscures the Omnipresence of God in the world, then the Sacrament is idolatrous, and our worship is actual sin, for all sin at its roots is a denial of the Omnipresence of God ... I have been to Masses in church where I felt it was sinful, sinful because there was no passion for social righteousness in it.[18]

Weston was to say much same thing in his famous challenge at the end of the Congress.

What should be done? Studdert-Kennedy suggested four things: to teach the social implications of the Gospel and the sacraments ('If Christian social teaching were not so rotten we would not have Socialist Sunday schools'); to preach fearlessly on social questions; to pray for the whole world; and to demonstrate that in the Catholic Church there is a power which can knit together in unity men and women of different nations, classes, temperaments and interests. 'If the Christ our Movement worships cannot do this,' he concluded, 'then may the Christ of the ages destroy our Movement and scatter its futilities on the wings of the wind to the seven seas, and give us the glorious Christ who can – and will!'[19]

International affairs were discussed by a bishop who had served overseas and by an Episcopalian priest from the United States. Bishop Ridgeway had died a year after he preached at the opening of the 1920

Congress, and his successor at Salisbury was St Clair George Alfred Donaldson, a former Archbishop of Brisbane. Henson described him as 'the best of men – simple, unselfish, good-tempered and conscientious – but with something of the snugness of a pattern Sunday school scholar, and the reverent pettiness of an Anglo-Catholic zealot!'[20] Like other overseas bishops at the Congress, Donaldson brought with him a world perspective often lacking among English Anglicans. He warned the Congress of great changes which were taking place in countries beyond the Middle East. The war, he said, had revealed that the nations of so-called Christian Europe had been building their lives without God. The same thing was happening among nations such as Japan, China, India and Africa.

'These great races, our equals in capacity, outnumbering our European populations by seven to one, outstripping us in the rate of their progress, have no thought or feel no need of union with God revealed in Christ... They are not prepared any longer to listen to our missionaries merely because they come from the White Race; they are suspicious of our motives, they recoil from anything like white domination, and they are quite prepared to go forward without the knowledge of Christ. This is the one thing that remains for us to give them... Without it they are heading for inevitable confusion; without it there lies before the world a disaster of unparalleled magnitude.'[21]

He challenged the Church of England to become a missionary Church and to concentrate her resources on this world-wide task instead of on herself. If she did, she might begin to learn from other nations and races. 'The Chinese Christians, missionaries tell us, have their own distinctive contribution to make; so have the negroes [sic]; so certainly have the natives of India; so, perhaps more than all, have the Jews.'[22]

After 1918, as we have seen, many church leaders placed their hopes in the establishment of the League of Nations as an international instrument of reconciliation and peace. The Archbishop of Canterbury, prompted by his friends at the Foreign Office, had written to the *Times* that year urging the government to join it. Temple as Bishop of Manchester was also an enthusiastic advocate. He wanted the Irish question to be referred to the League, a suggestion which horrified the Unionists. But the only reference to the League by any of the contributors – and that in an indirect way – was made by Fr J. O. S. Huntington, Superior of the Order of the Holy Cross, New York. He almost certainly had the League in mind in an illustration he gave in his talk on original sin.

He said there had been unparalleled scenes of joy in Wall Street when news of the armistice came through: 'Men and women poured out of the offices and filled Trinity Church... to fall on their knees in thanksgiving to God, and utter strangers threw their arms round each other in mutual embrace.'[23] But the euphoria did not last. Sin quickly returned and persisted as a contagion which had humanity in its grip. He then invited his listeners to imagine how they would feel about a friend who was a citizen of another country which had refused to join an international organization for the promotion of the welfare of the world. Although they wouldn't want to reject their friend, they would inevitably regard him as being in some sense responsible for his country's unco-operative attitude. In other words – though Huntington didn't say as much – the friend was tainted by the 'original sin' of his country simply by being a citizen of it. (Some of his listeners may have wondered if he was referring to his own country. Although President Wilson had been an enthusiastic promoter of the League of Nations, the USA refused to join it, preferring to follow an isolationist policy in foreign affairs up until the middle of the second world war.)

Huntington went on to suggest they would not expect their friend to leave his country but rather hope that he would 'like the prophets of the Old Testament or like St Paul in the New . . . bear the reproach of his people', and look forward to the day when a great leader would arise who could 'call upon his nation to take its rightful place among the other nations of the world.'[24] Huntington's great leader in his illustration was of course, Jesus Christ. The tragic irony is that his illustration was devilishly distorted when ten years later Hitler became what many in Germany regarded as their messianic leader.

Thursday was even hotter than Wednesday, but in spite of the temperature the Albert Hall filled rapidly when the doors were opened. For forty-five minutes the audience sang their favourite hymns, calling out numbers or first lines to the organist, until Weston and the platform party appeared. The *Veni Creator* was sung, and the Lord's Prayer and the Hail Mary said.

Modernists were continuing to attract publicity with their questioning of traditional teaching: Christ had no intention of founding a Church; the churches were human institutions with all the weaknesses of human nature embedded in them; the ordained ministry was not God-given but had developed from the organization of the synagogue; the sacraments are not covenanted means of grace but 'dramatized sermons' which may have a spiritual value for those who participated in them. In these circles the word 'spirit' was used with a variety of meanings from the soul or the immaterial part of a human being to his or her moral and intellectual qualities. Three scholarly Catholics were asked by the subjects committee to refute these speculations – Bishop A. C. Chandler, W. Frere, and J. Howe.

Chandler resigned as Bishop of Bloomfontein because of ill-health and returned to England in 1921. Many felt that he should have been offered a bishopric, but he was content to accept the country parish of Bentley near Farnham from his old friend, Bishop E. S. Talbot of Winchester. He was later to play an important role in the Congress movement. Chandler reminded the audience that when Christians spoke of 'the Spirit' they should remember they were referring to the Third Person of the Holy Trinity. He then went on to describe how the Holy Spirit works through the Church as an institution and in the Christian as a believer:

> The former way is pre-eminently social; it tells the Christian that he is essentially a member of a great society, and offers him God's grace in virtue of that membership. Thus one great Sacrament grafts him into the Body of Christ's Church, and a second strengthens and refreshes him in a life of communion with Christ and his fellow Christians; and in both Sacraments it is the Spirit who is at work, the Spirit who sanctifies the water of baptism, and the Spirit who makes the bread and wine of the Eucharist to be the Body and Blood of Christ. So, too, it is the Spirit who confirms, and the Spirit who absolves; the Spirit who brings the merits and blessings of Christ.[25]

When believers yield to the Spirit, he continued, he works in the hearts of each individual according to his needs and capacities, and strengthens him through difficulties and temptations. It is a spiritual work which is so personal that it cannot be described in general terms.

'It is just the consciousness of a fuller and more abundant life, a life coming to awareness of its own meaning and purpose and destiny, an eternal life, a life hid with Christ in God. Its notes are progress and simplicity: progress in the cleansing of our nature and in our readiness to learn fresh truths, and simplicity in committing ourselves wholeheartedly to the guidance and transmuting influence of the Holy Spirit . . . It is a fatal mistake to oppose or even contrast [the social and the individual], since the Holy Spirit works equally in both.'[26]

Frere followed Chandler by describing the work of the Holy Spirit in the Church in a wide-ranging lecture. People's faith is impoverished, he said, if they rely solely on the corporate worship and the sacraments without personal prayer and mediation. It is equally impoverished if they rely solely on personal prayer and mediation and neglect corporate worship and the sacraments. 'In the unity of the Spirit the two sides, the inner and the outer, the institutional and mystical, combine to produce a religion which can reach out boldly into the sphere of spiritual adventure just because it rests on the Catholic convictions and the garnered experience of the Church.'

The Church, he continued, is presided over by Christ as the Head and guided by the Holy Spirit to shape her character, unity and holiness, to uphold her principles and the moral standards of God's law, and to develop her organization of the ministry and the sacraments. Catholics see these as divine appointments which cannot be modified or dispensed with by human authority. Christ empowered the apostolic ministry and instituted baptism and the Eucharist, but the divine authority of these is witnessed not merely by that original appointment, but also ('and in some ways more convincingly') by the evidence of the operation of the Holy Spirit through them.

He then turned to the tension created between the traditionalist and the Modernist in discerning God's will for his Church in successive ages. He saw the Modernist as the 'critical opposition' to orthodoxy.

'It is one of the glories of her [the Church's] living personality, that she is ever learning the lessons of the Spirit, as he interprets to her more fully, as she is able to bear it, the inexhaustible mysteries of revelation. The critical opposition therefore is of service to her, in that it enables her to advance more securely, scrutinizing the new steps in the road of knowledge as they open out before her, declining those that would side-track her progress, and taking those which the Spirit reassures her to be genuine development.'[27]

He was more concerned by the effects of disunity than the effects of controversy. The great division between the Eastern and Western Churches had been followed by further divisions in the West. At its core were differences between those who saw the Church as monarchical and those who saw her as conciliar, depending on what they believed about the pre-eminence of St Peter within the apostolic college. Much of the trouble arose because Christians allowed themselves to isolate parts of the truth and over-emphasize it.

'Therein lies the cause of past disasters,' he said; but then, perhaps as a result of being at the second round of the Malines conversations in March that year, he added: 'There too lies the hopes of future repair, if only we can learn, that the whole truth to which the Church witnesses is more than all the half-truths to which the Churches, with the Roman Church at their head, so tenaciously cling.'[28]

Howe said it was the primary vocation of every Christian to manifest the Spirit in everyday life through the love of God and the love of one's neighbour: 'The world is quite right when it judges the truth of our religion not by the length of our prayers, nor by any warm feelings of devotion we may, or may not, have, but by the way we treat our cook.'[29]

THE SECOND CONGRESS 1923

He described the Spirit's manifestations in the lives of clergy and religious: the priest in the way he taught and guided the faithful in fulfilling their Christian calling; the religious in the witness of their common life of poverty, chastity and obedience. He thanked God for the fifteen hundred women who were Anglican nuns and appealed for more young men to accept the sacrifice of the monastic life.

What is noteworthy about these three contributions is the stress on the work of the Holy Spirit. Among many Catholics priests there was a fear that over-reliance on the Spirit led to schism and heresy. *The King's Highway*, a manual on Catholic belief and practice, first published in 1924, had very little to say about the Spirit in the life of the individual Christian or the Church. Dominant in much Catholic teaching was the valid use of the sacraments as the essential way to holiness. Chandler, Frere and Howe seemed to be implying that there was a danger the faithful would be so dependent on the sacraments that they would overlook other divine sources of strength and guidance. Later in the century this was described as being 'over-sacramentalized'.

The final session in the Albert Hall had a last-night-of-the-Proms atmosphere. After the opening prayers Weston announced, to prolonged applause, that the target of an appeal for £25,000 for the Congress Committee, made earlier in the week, had been surpassed: £28,000 had been received.

In his closing address Weston, speaking spontaneously, asked his audience to pray that Anglican families would produce as many priests and religious as Roman Catholic families in Ireland and France did. He urged priests to be obedient to their bishops in as far as they (the bishops) obey the Catholic Church (that brought so much applause that he had to call for silence). He challenged them all to live a life of Christian simplicity and to make concern for the poor a priority. Then came the words for which he was famous and which are quoted in practically every twentieth-century church history:

> You have got your Mass, you have got your Altar, you have begun to get your Tabernacle. Now go out into the highways and hedges where not even the Bishops will try to hinder you. Go out and look for Jesus in the ragged, in the naked, in the oppressed and sweated, in those who have lost hope, in those who are struggling to make good. Look for Jesus. And when you see him, gird yourselves with his towel, and try to wash their feet.[30]

The Congress concluded with a service of thanksgiving in St Martin-in-the-Fields on Friday evening. Priests in cassocks and cottas, and bishops in copes and mitres led by Winnington-Ingram, met in Suffolk Street and processed to the church across Trafalgar Square. As happened three years previously in Southwark, the Bishop of Nassau led an overflow congregation round the church steps. Inside the church the Bishop of St Albans called in his sermon for unity. He said that since coming home after seventeen years in Africa he had detected more of what he called 'the Christ-spirit' among clergy and people. 'It is this spirit which I plead with you tonight, at the close of this great Congress, to make the dominant note and characteristic of the Anglo-Catholic Movement in the Church of England. Let it be English – there is nothing to be ashamed about in that. Let it be Catholic, broad-based. But, above all, let it be Christian. If any Movement (or any man) have not the spirit of Christ it is none of his. It may be very successful, but it will be disowned by Christ at the last.'[31]

By the time the procession returned to Suffolk Street thousands had gathered in the Square. Many knelt as the bishops passed. The only protests came from one man holding up a board with the words, 'Priests will be England's downfall' on one side and 'Anglo-Catholics are traitors to Protestantism', on the other, and another man shouting about 'Gospel truth'. Everyone else was singing, 'For all the saints'.

10

Communities, Societies and the *Church Times*

Religious Communities

Before the first Congress Atlay and his committee invited representatives from the Anglican religious orders and the main Anglo-Catholics societies to join in the organization of the event. The success of the Congresses owed much to the support they received from them. Let us take the religious communities first. Those who went to St Paul's cathedral at the opening service of the 1923 Congress were thrilled by the sign of a hundred or more nuns and a smaller group of monks in the transepts. In the Albert Hall the religious orders occupied special tiers of seats, and during the provincial congresses they took part in the outdoor processions as well as the services and meetings. Their appearance was an impressive demonstration that the religious life, itself regarded as a historic sign of authentic Catholicism, was alive and well in the Church of England. Anglo-Catholic propagandists boasted that there were more Anglican religious in the country than there had been at the time of the Reformation, though the statistically minded pointed out that when comparing the numbers proportionately with the totals of the population at the different times, such a claim was questionable. The communities' reputation for good works in the neighbourhoods where they worked earned them pride among Anglo-Catholics and respect among many others. The days of popular suspicion and even hostility towards a religious habit in the streets were long over.

Giving support to the Congresses, however, was not one of their priorities. They had other urgent matters occupying their attention. Mirfield had to re-open the College of the Resurrection (it had been closed during the war) to accommodate the sudden rush of men who had suspended or delayed their ordination training to join the forces. Kelham had to deal with a similar increase. Both communities were receiving more applications then they were able to accept. In Oxford the Society of St John the Evangelist (the Cowley fathers), besides their normal work, were having to deal with the influx of undergraduates who were beginning or resuming their studies. The communities' overseas connections had been disrupted during the war. The Cowley fathers had houses in India and South Africa, and they were helping to establish one in Boston, USA. Mirfield was responsible for St John's College for boys in Johannesburg, for St Peter's College in Rosettenville and for missions in the Transvaal. Kelham fathers were working in Japan, Korea and Northern Rhodesia.

Among the communities there were differences of opinion on the value of the Congresses. At Mirfield Fr H. Jeaves was scornful of the plan for the first Congress, but Fr E. Symonds argued the community should support it.[1] At Kelham Fr H. H. Kelly was anxious that the Society of the Sacred Mission should have nothing to do with an affair which he suspected was tainted with papalism. He disliked the label 'Anglo-Catholic' because he rejected party connections. One of his novices, Fr Gabriel Hebert, who in 1920 had just been sent out to the community's house in South Africa, protested: 'I feel very sore that Kelham has stood out of the Anglo-Catholic show. I fancy it is an idea of old Fr Kelly that the Anglo-Catholic Congress is a party thing.'[2]

One of the most outstanding supporters among the religious was Fr Vernon Johnson of the Community of the Divine Compassion at Plaistow in east London. He preached at the Congress rallies in London and in the provinces and had become something of a celebrity. Fr Paul Bull, the superior of Cowley, joined the organizing committee as an adviser on the nationwide mission which had been discussed. Mirfield had a house in Holland Park, making it easy for members who lived to be involved in the Albert Hall. The little Benedictine community at Pershore was still recovering from the secession of its abbot and many of its members to Rome. The remainder moved to Nashdom in 1927. Gregory Dix visited the community at Pershore while an undergraduate at Oxford and entered the novitiate in 1926. He might have been invited to the later Congresses except that Abbot Denys sent him to join a mission which the community had opened on the Gold Coast (now Ghana) where he remained until illness brought him home. That mission closed in 1931.

The tally of members of the religious communities who spoke at the five Congresses in the Albert Hall is as follows: in 1920: L. S. Thornton CR, W. G. Frere CR, P. Bull SSJE; in 1923: P. N. Waggett SSJE, J. O. S. Huntington OHC, D. Jenks SSM; in 1927: Waggett, Thornton, Hughson OHC; in 1930: Thornton, F. Biggart CR, the Prioress of Whitby; in 1933: R. Tribe SSM, Biggart, Barnard Clements OSB, the Prior of Alton. Their topics were worship, prayer and the Chrfistian life, but not exclusively. Thornton warned of the secular forces which were emerging in society after the war (1920) and later presented a theological defence of the practice of corporate devotions to the Blessed Sacrament (1927). Biggart, in a talk on the international scene, urged Christians to join the anti-war movement as the European situation darkened (1933). These, and other members of their communities, spoke at Congresses in different parts of the country.

In 1920 there were 43 houses for women in England, plus three in Scotland and two in Dublin. Their work included maternity cases and the care of orphans, disabled children, unmarried mothers (in what were still called in some places 'penitentiaries'), the sick and the elderly. They established hospitals and rest homes. In education they ran day schools and boarding schools for boys and girls. Nearly all of them had groups serving in parishes where they were responsible for pastoral work among children, young girls and women. Three were enclosed orders: the Community of the Holy Comforter at Malling Abbey, Kent; the Community of the Servants of Christ, Pleshey near Chelmsford; and the Community of the Love of God at Fairacres, Oxford. Abroad there was the Community of the Resurrection of Our Lord in Grahamstown, South Africa (no connection with Mirfield) and the Community of the Sacred Passion in Zanzibar, founded by Weston in 1911.

The role of the sisters in the Congresses, both in London and in the provinces, was practical and spiritual. They sold tickets and organized parties from their parishes, and manned stalls and assisted at the children's pageants. They kept novenas of prayer and vigils before the Blessed Sacrament during the sessions in the Albert Hall, and offered the hospitality of their chapels to priests who wanted to say mass. Only one sister was invited to speak at the London Congresses; she was the Prioress of Whitby in 1930, and then only at a session for women.

In her talk the Prioress said her community was receiving far more requests for help from parishes than they could respond to. One or two other speakers at other Congresses said they wished more young men and women would hear and obey calls to the religious life. The women's communities were at the beginning of a slow decline in the number of novices which was to continue throughout the century, though with a slight recovery for a few years after the second world war. The reasons for this were varied and complex. One was that until the latter half of the nineteenth century these communities had provided opportunities for single women, living together under a rule, to teach, to nurse and to engage in welfare work, especially in socially deprived areas, in ways they could not so easily do in ordinary life. Now the situation was changing. Improved educational facilities for girls meant they could be more independent. The professions were becoming more open to women. Christian service could be offered by women without the need for a community's support. For example, the British Hospital for Mothers and Babies at Woolwich, with its distinctly Catholic character, was set up before the war by three friends who did not think it necessary to become religious sisters first – one of many such initiatives.

Then the ethos in many religious houses was off-putting. The adventurous spirit which had motivated the lives of earlier communities had been replaced by an anxiety to preserve the past in the midst of change. Loyalty to the vision of the original founder meant mid-Victorian practices were tenaciously upheld. Young women used to twenties' and thirties' fashions were appalled when they entered a novitiate and were expected to wear heavy, uncomfortable garments (including underwear) not unlike those their grandmothers used to have. Convent chapters debated endlessly on modernizations, such as whether or not a telephone should be installed. Worship in their chapels – often devised by a Latin-loving priest who was the founder or first chaplain – seemed out-of-date when contrasted with the liturgical changes which were taking place in parishes. Communities were finding it increasingly difficult to maintain work which had begun when they had more members.

Developments in the Community of All Saints illustrates how an order could gradually overstretch it members. It was formed in the 1850s by W. Upton Richards, vicar of the Margaret Street church, to look after needy cases in the parish. As their membership grew and they took on work outside the parish, they moved to a specially built convent at London Colney in 1907, keeping their original home in Margaret Street as a mission house. By 1920 the community was working in Atlay's parish in Westminster and other parts of London including Finchley, Osnaburgh Street, Berkeley Square, Hammersmith, Lewisham and Hendon. They set up a hospital in Eastbourne and a convalescent home in St Leonards. They had houses in Oxford, Leeds and Liverpool. They assisted in the establishment of communities in India, and in Baltimore and Philadelphia in the USA. Other communities had developed in a similar way – St Mary the Virgin, Wantage, St John Baptist, Clewer, St Margaret, East Grinstead, and St Peter's, Horbury. All this growth meant that they gradually found it difficult to staff their work and had to hand over the administration of their institutions to others.

A beneficial outcome of their involvement in the Congresses was that different communities came to know one another better. Services in cathedrals and meetings in the Albert Hall and in halls across the country resulted in more contacts with each other, and a network of relationships slowly emerged among the communities. It is significant that a few days after the first Congress, the Lambeth Conference had a brief discussion on the religious communities in the Anglican Communion. At the next Lambeth in 1930 a resolution was passed asking provinces to provide ways of enabling communities to be represented in official bodies. Shortly afterwards an Advisory Council for Religious Communities was set up by the Convocations of Canterbury and York which, among other things, gave the communities the right to elect their own representatives to the Church Assembly – something for which Fr E. K. Talbot CR had been campaigning for years.

The Oratory of the Good Shepherd and the Society of the Holy Cross (the Societas Sanctae Crucis)

Besides these established communities there were two other small groups of priests who saw themselves in the tradition of the religious orders rather than as secular clergy – the Oratory of the Good Shepherd (OGS) and the Society of the Holy Cross, the Societas Sanctae Crucis (SSC).

The Oratory of the Good Shepherd was formed in the years before the war when a group of young Cambridge dons began to meet regularly to celebrate the Eucharist and to pray for the university. The first members took vows to form an oratory in 1919. These included John How, Wilfred Knox (brother of Ronald), and Eric Milne-White, Dean of King's College. They were joined by other Cambridge men, including Will Spens, Geoffrey Clayton and E. G. Selwyn.

From the beginning the Oratory was a fellowship of unmarried academics, priests and laymen, united by the observance of a common rule of life. The majority of them were brilliant and immersed in their own interests; and – as was (and still is) common among newly formed communities – each had different expectations of how the Oratory should develop. The celibacy rule was shaken but not relaxed when John How married. Milner-White resigned after a few years because the others would not agree to his vision of the Oratory becoming a religious order. It was a shaky start.

But gradually it organized itself with a general chapter meeting regularly and a superior elected triennially. A house was purchased in Lady Margaret Road in Cambridge in 1921 as the headquarters of the Oratory; it was retained until just before the second world war. There were usually three brothers in residence, but with much comings and goings Wilfred Knox was the only member who remained in the house all the time.

Knox was a model of holy, scholarly eccentricity, and was popularly credited with being the one who until his death in 1946 kept the Oratory in being. Penelope Fitzgerald described the OGS as 'not a community at all, nor . . . a guild, nor an order, nor could it have been in origin anything but English. The vagueness of its definition, and the absolute certainty of its members as to what they are, makes it one of the many and unknown currents that quietly deepen the life surrounding it.'[3] Perhaps her description was coloured by the quizzical outlook of a niece towards the enthusiasms of an uncle.

Will Spens, a layman, Fellow and later Master of Corpus Christi College, Cambridge, took the initiative after the success of the first Congress to suggest to Bishop Burge of Oxford that a theological commission should be appointed by the Archbishops drawn from Anglo-Catholic, Evangelical and Modernist schools to report on doctrine in the Church of England. This was done, and the commission met under the chairmanship of Temple over a period of sixteen years until *The Report on Doctrine in the Church of England* was eventually published in 1938. The twenty-five members included Spens together with two Oratorians, Knox and Selwyn. Besides the last two, other Congress speakers on the commission were Mozley, Rawlinson, Taylor, and Thornton. Their presence ensured that the sections of the report on the ordained ministry and the sacraments expounded Catholic teaching.

Another of Spens' achievements was the publication of *Essays Catholic and Critical*. He persuaded the English Church Union to sponsor 'a volume of Anglo-Catholic essays', but there was resistance from Stone, the chairman, over the appointment of a Cambridge man as editor. Eventually Selwyn was chosen because, as editor of *Theology*, he had close connections with SPCK, the publishers. *Essays Catholic and Critical* appeared in 1926. The book was generally well received as evidence that the post-war generation of Catholic scholars was prepared, as its title indicated, to tackle crucial questions such as those raised by Modernists. That was Sparrow Simpson's judgement, though he added a caution: 'Individual (contributors to the book) must not allow themselves a speculative liberty which is not without its dangers in creating reactions towards the Fundamentalism from which it desires to deliver the believing mind.'[4] Nine of the fifteen contributors to the book were speakers at the 1927 Congress, and four at the 1930 one.

The Society of the Sacred Cross was founded by Charles Lowder in 1855 for priests working in slum parishes, with the intention of helping them through a strictly disciplined life to be more effective in mission. At the end of the war there were between 200 and 300 members. Its Latin title gave the impression that its members were papalist, but in fact the majority were deeply committed to the Church of England. They saw themselves as sort of spiritual militia defending and promoting by example the Church's Catholicity. In certain Catholic circles the initials SSC behind priests' names were regarded as a badge of impeccable orthodoxy. Some parishes insisted on having an SSC priest as their vicar. Officially the SSC boycotted the Congresses. What few references there are to the Congresses in the minutes of the Society are critical of them. They record some members' disgust that the chairman of the 1920 Congress, Atlay, had not only married, but married a widow. But that did not deter individual members, like Weston and Baverstock, from being involved in the movement. Attempts were made during and after the war to limit membership of the Society to celibates, but they failed. The SSC grew in numbers later in the century.

The English Church Union

Besides the religious communities, the Congresses depended on the support they received from various Anglo-Catholic institutions. The Church of England Year Books of the period lists between twenty-five and thirty of them. Officers and members of three took part in planning the Congresses – the English Church Union, the Federation of Catholic Priests, and the Confraternity of the Blessed Sacrament.

The English Church Union (ECU) was formed in 1868 from local unions of clergy and laity to defend priests and parishes threatened by ecclesiastical censure for introducing ritualistic practices. It was governed by a president and a council, but its day-to-day business was in the hands of an executive which met every month.

Charles Lindley Wood, Viscount Halifax, had been ECU President almost from its beginning. A devout High Churchman, he committed his life to Catholic causes. His enthusiasm led him to seek recognition for Anglican orders by Rome which resulted, to his great disappointment, in the papal letter *Apostolicae Curae* (13 Sept. 1896), declaring they were invalid. He also, as we have seen, initiated the Malines Conversations. He retired from the presidency because of ill health in 1919 but continued to play an active role until his death in 1934. After Halifax's retirement the Union had difficulty in finding a replacement. Lord Phillimore, an ecclesiastical lawyer, took the job on as a stop-gap for a few months. Sir Robert Newman MP (later Lord Mamhead) followed him until 1922 when the Earl of Shaftesbury took his place. The Union liked to have a distinguished layman as its president.

For years the general secretary of the Union was Mr H. W. Hill. He and Halifax had more or less run the Union together. Rotund and red-faced, Hill was typical of the militant laymen found in Catholic parishes. As secretary he had fought the good fight for persecuted priests for years. It was his custom to wear a white topper for the Union's annual general meeting in the spring of each year. Someone once remarked that the appearance of that white topper was a sign the London season had begun. He retired in 1920 with a pension from the Union but remained an ex-officio member of the executive until his death in 1926. In his place the executive appointed as general secretary Arnold T. B. Pinchard.

Pinchard was a priest of wide experience and an able administrator. He had served in Argentina (his patch included the Falkland Islands) from 1889 to 1895 before going to St Jude, Birmingham. There he abolished pew rents and built up a mainly working-class congregation. As secretary he recognized the importance of co-operating with the Congress executive in spite of the resentment of some Union members towards the newcomer. A drawing made in the mid-twenties shows him with hair brushed straight back and wearing a monocle.

The Union had offices in Russell Square and was serviced by a small paid staff – the general secretary, an accountant, a legal officer, a librarian and a typist. The district secretaries of the Union, who worked voluntarily, were given £15 a year towards their expenses. Money came from collections at Union events in London and in the provinces, subscriptions and legacies. Halifax was a generous benefactor, as indeed were a number of wealthy laity.

A list of the ECU's committees in 1920 illustrates the extent of its activities and the need for such a staff: Theological and Liturgical, Legal, Finance, Organization and Efficiency, Library and Publications, London Diocesan Conference, Southwark Diocesan Conference, Civil Marriages, Foreign Missions, Religious Education, Women's Work in the Church, Church and State, Life and Liberty Movement, and Prayer Book Revision. Most of these committees were permanent; a few, like the Life and Liberty movement committee, were set up as the need arose to advise the Union on its response to contemporary matters. The Theological and Liturgical committee, chaired by Stone, was particularly busy as it had to deal with the various stages of Prayer Book revision and ecumenical matters. For several years there was a Church Patronage Protection Committee which raised funds to purchase avowsons as they came on the market. This committee also succeeded in getting the Church Assembly and Parliament to pass a series of measures which restricted and then abolished the practice.

In 1923 Charles Harris, a member, proposed that the Union should encourage the production of books by agreeing with publishers (principally SPCK) to cover any losses they might make on the works the Union sponsored. This was agreed, and over the next few years Gore's *New Commentary on Holy Scripture, Liturgy and Worship,* which Harris himself edited, and *Northern Catholicism* edited by N. P. Williams were published by SPCK. The books remained in print for many years, though Williams' contention in third book that there was a *Northern* Catholicism as distinct from a *Roman* Catholicism has been judged as special pleading and historically unsound.

The executive's minutes, quaintly called 'the Acta', for the year 1920 show something of the ECU's day-to-day business. They record the ongoing financial and administrative matters which had to be dealt with, recording subscriptions coming in each month from individuals and parishes, and noting the number of new members. Each committee had to be serviced with minutes and correspondence. A monthly *Gazette* was published giving members news of decisions made by the council and activities of the Union generally. Its library was used by those living in the London area. Requests for support for Catholic causes in parishes came into the office regularly. Some were minor, such as questions on the whereabouts of local Catholic churches from members moving to different parts of the country; others, like disputes with bishops and patrons, needed counselling or, in the more difficult cases, legal expertise.

That year saw the beginning of a wrangle over an appointment to the moderately high church benefice of Sacred Trinity in Salford. It concerned the claim by Bishop Knox of Manchester to make his own appointment 'by lapse' to the parish as the patron had done nothing to fill the living for two years. The Bishop had nominated as priest-in-charge a Revd J. W. Rideout, but the patron, Sir Joselyn Gore-Booth, had been unhappy about the nomination and corresponded with the ECU about it. He had heard that Knox had made Rideout promise to abandon certain rituals at Sacred Trinity as a condition of his appointment. Hill, who was still secretary when the dispute began, had handed the case over to the Union's lawyers. Eventually the ECU Legal Committee decided the patron's complaint was indefensible and Rideout was inducted. The affair attracted a good deal of attention and became known locally as 'the Salford case'.

Another case concerned the vicar of St Nicholas, Guildford. The Revd E. A. Ommaney and his wife had lost a son at the battle of the Somme in 1916 and members of the congregation had raised a fund so that a Calvary could be erected outside the church in his memory. A Protestant group in town was taking legal action to have it removed. Their complaint was that the Calvary faced the road and that people had been seen bowing to it and making the sign of the cross as they passed by on the pavement.

The ECU Legal committee defended Ommaney, and the outcome of the case, which also dragged on some years, was that the Calvary could be retained but moved to a less public position.

The Union was occasionally asked to help parishes financially when diocesan funds were cut off because of episcopal displeasure. On 18 April the committee agreed to donate £25 a year towards the salary of an assistant curate at All Saints, Plymouth, where other help had been refused because of the church's ritualism. A similar sum was agreed for another priest who had been deprived of his living for ritual practices. The ECU's guiding principle was to help clergy financially but not to make grants towards buildings and furnishings.

In ritual matters the Union's policy was to provide legal assistance to parishes taken to court for using the eastward position, altar lights, unleavened bread, vestments, mixed chalice, and incense (its 'six points'). Its lawyers were prepared to argue that such practices were legal or permissible according to the provisions of the Prayer Book and the canons of the Church of England. They would not, however, defend the use of benediction and similar devotions because they recognized these services had little chance of being upheld in the courts and attempts to do so would be a waste of money. This was one of the reasons why the Union was dismissed as 'merely High Church' by papalist clergy.

Other business during 1920 included discussing a letter from the Australian Church Union asking if it could to be affiliated to the ECU: this was agreed. Similar Unions were formed in other parts of the Anglican Communion and in the USA. On 27 October Weston wrote asking for support for his campaign against slave labour in South Africa: it was referred to the Foreign Missions Committee who assisted the Bishop when he was pursuing this matter in England.

At the beginning of Pinchard's secretaryship a leaflet was issued declaring that the Union's purpose was to maintain the doctrine, discipline and position of the Church of England as part of the whole Catholic Church; to encourage research and literature 'in all branches of theology and ethics, and in those departments of philosophy, psychology and natural science which are closely related to religion'; to defend 'all persons, lay or clerical, suffering under unjust aggression or hindrance in spiritual matters'; and to 'promote the interests of religion as to be, by God's help, a lasting witness for the advancement of His glory and the good of His Church'. It was an explicit call to Catholics to take developments in theology seriously. The Congresses did much to promote this.

The year 1920 saw ecumenical matters attracting more of the Union's attention. The first signs were occasions when Nonconformist ministers were invited to preach in Anglican churches. On 28 January it was agreed to send a letter of protest to the Bishop Handley Moule of Durham for allowing Dr J. H. Jowett, a well-known Congregational minister, to preach at a forthcoming service in Durham Cathedral. On 21 July P. H. Leary drew the committee's attention to an interchange of pulpits between the same Dr Jowett and the Revd Holden of St Paul's, Portland Square. Leary also complained that the Prime Minister and Mrs Lloyd-George, who were Presbyterians, had received Communion when the Archbishop of Wales was enthroned at a service inaugurating the disestablished Church in Wales. A group of London clergy had written to Winnington-Ingram, pointing out this had caused 'great distress'. They had received an evasive reply. Hill proposed the correspondence be published in the *Gazette*. Later in the year it was reported that Henson, recently nominated Bishop of Durham following Handley Moule's death, had accepted an invitation to preach in Westminster Chapel where Jowett was minister, and on 15 December the Council agreed to send a letter of protest to him.

On 19 May a letter was received from Mr O'Brien, Chairman of the Bombay branch, asking for help on problems surrounding the proposals for a reunion of Churches in India. This was referred to the Theological and Liturgical Committee. It was the first indication of the South India Scheme which was to trouble the ECU and its successor, the Church Union, for many years to come. A few months later the Theological and Liturgical Committee commented on Lambeth Conference's Appeal and its resolutions, as described in Chapter 5.

One member whose involvement in ecumenical affairs threatened to divide the executive was T. A. Lacey. A mildly eccentric character, he was reputed to be the cleverest clergyman in the Church of England. His colleagues in the Union did not doubt his Catholicity, but they were uneasy about his questioning and exploring mind. He sometimes seemed a shade too Modernist. In January 1920 Lacey went to an ecumenical conference organized by Headlam for Anglican and Nonconformist leaders at Mansfield College, Oxford. The conference issued a manifesto which suggested preparing the way for reunion through an interchange of pulpits, eucharistic hospitality, and a mutual recognition of each others' ordained ministries. Lacey believed he had been instrumental at the conference in leading others towards a more Catholic understanding of faith and order and so felt justified in signing the manifesto, along with Temple, Dearmer and others who were present.

The 'Mansfield Manifesto' was widely reported and Lacey was criticized by many Catholics for putting his name to it. The matter was so serious that it was referred by the ECU executive to the whole council at its meeting on 24 March. After a debate, at which a number showed they agreed with him, Lacey moved:

(1) That corporate groups of Christians, separated by schism, ought to be received into Communion by proper authority, if they show a desire to close the schism and are found to be orthodox.
(2) That they may continue as corporate groups, retaining such features of their former organization as are consistent with Catholic faith and practice.
(3) That their Ministers, if they desire it, and are found to be personally qualified, should forthwith be admitted to Holy Orders, without being required to repudiate their former ministry.

The executive rejected the last paragraph, but that seems to have settled the matter as far as the Union was concerned. It was a significant resolution, however, for Lacey was a representative of an increasing number of Catholics who were seeking acceptable ways of interpreting Church order in the cause of Christian unity.

The overall membership of the Union was about 20,000. Its followers were divided between Members and Associates, the former receiving the Union's monthly paper, the *Gazette*, free, the latter only receiving notices of meetings. Both groups were allowed to vote on Union matters. A new class of Adherents was introduced when, as described in Chapter 6, the constitution was revised in 1923 following the establishment of the Church Assembly. The number of those joining the Union during the Congress years is as follows:

	Members	Associates	Adherents
1921	1,182	1,632	
1922	518	1,127	
1923	512	1,273	186
1924	425	1,076	261
1925	571	1,313	130
1926	456	1,172	132
1927	358	966	115
1928	23	967	95
1929	102	387	108
1930	146	406	158

The sudden drop in the number of new members between 1921 and 1922 – a half – may have been due to the start of the Congress movement, when groups began to form in different parts of the country to promote provincial Congress meetings. The steady decline in new members continued through the twenties. With this came financial difficulties aggravated by the economic slump which began in 1929.

The Confraternity of the Blessed Sacrament

The Confraternity of the Blessed Sacrament (CBS) was founded in 1862 by T. T. Carter in his parish in Wantage to encourage communicants to keep a fast from midnight the day before receiving Communion and to make their confessions to a priest regularly. As its membership increased, the Confraternity became a national body. It then extended its activities to giving grants to poorer parishes for the installation of aumbries or tabernacles in their churches, and for purchasing Communion vessels and vestments. In the early days some clergy who introduced reservation in their churches had little idea of how to do this properly. Stories were told of the Sacrament going mouldy in damp cupboards and or being kept in a cocoa tin.

By 1920 the CBS membership was over 20,000. It was organized into twenty districts, each district coterminous with one or more English dioceses. There was also a district in Wales. Local groups were known as wards, and there were about four hundred of them. Confraternity festivals were popular events. The annual festival for the London wards in the year 1931, which took the form of solemn evensong, sermon and benediction, filled five churches on the same day – St Michael, Woolwich, St Columba, Kingsland Road, St Mary Magdalene, Paddington, St Agnes, Kennington, and St Augustine, Highgate. Similar services were held in different parts of the country.

The Confraternity was governed by a general council meeting under its superior general, who from 1920 was the Revd Lord Victor Seymour, vicar of St Stephen, Gloucester Row. Applications for help were considered by a grants committee. Between 1912 and 1932 grants were made for 216 aumbries and tabernacles, 264 vessels, 121 ciboria, 690 sets of vestments, some of them for overseas wards.

What were regarded as abuses of the Sacrament were also brought to the council's attention. At a meeting on 12 February 1920 the superior general said more teaching was needed on concomitance (administering Communion with the Bread only), especially since some bishops were insisting on reservation in both kinds. He thought that in future years there would be more controversies over practices introduced in the cause of hygiene, such as giving Communion in a number of little cups like some Nonconformists, and wiping the chalice with a purificator after each communicant had received. Then there were the prohibitioners who claimed Communion with fermented wine was a danger to alcoholics. At a later meeting that year he reported it had been necessary to refuse admission to the Confraternity to several priests because they failed to keep the rule of the fast before celebrating mass. In a similar exercise of discipline the Folkestone ward informed the council that a certain lady's name had been removed from the register because she persisted in receiving Communion in a Nonconformist chapel.

In 1924 the council expressed its regret that evening Communions had been started in St Martin-in-the-Fields, especially as that church had been involved in the first and second Congresses. The superior general expressed his satisfaction that more parishes had Sunday masses than when the Confraternity was founded. But there were still many churches which did not have reservation, and some places where reservation was unrecognized. 'Our Blessed Lord would vouchsafe His most holy presence in all our parish churches, but in many of them He is not wanted. In some churches where the Blessed Sacrament is reserved there is no indication, light, or anything to encourage adoration. Thus from morning to evening the Most Holy remains there unhonoured.'[5]

The Confraternity's support for clergy in controversies was largely through letters to bishops and to the church press. Once when it attempted to be more active, it was unsuccessful. It decided to support three Liverpool clergy, who had been placed under an episcopal ban, by asking all its priest members to sign a petition of protest. Some 1,600 copies of the petition were sent with stamped addressed envelopes, but only 725 were returned. Of these, six were marked 'not for publication' and 50 were returned by recipients who refused to sign it. Three priests resigned from the CBS because they disagreed with the petition. Among those who had not replied were nine in the Liverpool diocese itself. Faced with this poor response, the committee decided to take no further action. In 1927 the secretary general told members their most important role in the controversies was to pray: 'The Confraternity is a devotional society, and we have chiefly to do our fighting for the faith on our knees. We have no intention of forcing others except by the force of prayer. If there is contention with others, it is because we contend for the right to go on with those practices which flow from our belief in the Blessed Sacrament.'[6]

Most wards met monthly in church to recite the CBS office when the Blessed Sacrament was taken from the aumbry and placed on the altar, or when the door of the tabernacle was opened. The popularity of these services is an indication that many found them a helpful way of praying together. The Confraternity also provided a rule of life for it members. The extent of the Confraternity's support in the Anglican Communion was illustrated when during the 1930 Congress it organized a dinner at the Belgravia Hotel for oversees bishops who were members: 17 attended and 14 sent apologies. A. E. Cornibeer succeeded Seymour as secretary general in 1932.

The Federation of Catholic Priests

The Federation of Catholic Priests (FCP) was created by bringing together groups of clergy who had been meeting for several years in different parts of the country. The first of these groups was in Lichfield and its members formed the nucleus of a national organization which came into being in 1917. These clergy felt they were not being adequately represented by the ECU which had a mixed clergy and lay membership. It was also a defensive move against the growing suspicion that the proposals for a National Assembly were a threat to the authority of the Convocations and of the parochial clergy.

The first chairman of FCP was Darwell Stone and the first secretary F. Underhill. The Federation's purpose, it declared, was to present 'a united front in the propagation and defence of the faith, worship and discipline of the Catholic Church'. Its members upheld the doctrines of the bodily resurrection of our Lord and the perpetual virginity of the Blessed Virgin Mary. They defended the right of the parish priest to reserve the sacrament and to hear confessions without seeking episcopal permission. FCP members undertook a rule of life which included regular celebrations of the Eucharist and the recitation of the divine office; the practice of mental prayer and the study of the Scriptures and the Fathers; self-examination and confession; and prayer for the Federation.

W. Dudley Dixon, the vicar of Glossop, took over as secretary in 1920, and within a few years its numbers grew to over 1,000. The members met regularly in their own diocesan associations. These provided fellowship for Catholic priests, especially those who felt isolated in town and country parishes where like-minded clergy were few and far between. Meetings began with mass and breakfast, followed by a speaker or a discussion of a paper. Quiet days and retreats were arranged. Although Dixon and his committee were hostile to any hint of compromise, the Federation attracted clergy from different parts of the Catholic spectrum.

Many members were involved in the Congress movement nationally and in the provinces.

Other Societies

Other societies publicized the Congresses and set up stalls in the foyer of the Albert Hall. The Additional Curates' Society, founded in 1837 by Joshua Watson, gave grants to mostly Catholic parishes. In 1930 it reported that it was supporting around six hundred priests with its income that year of £31,000. In making grants it gave priority to churches in working-class areas in England and Wales. Curates often had to wait ten or more years before they became incumbents. There were usually three or four in the big parishes in London and the cities. They either lived in the clergy house with their vicar (as at St Matthew, Westminster) or in a separate house near the church (as at All Saints, Margaret Street). For them it was a kind of extension of their life at college – and often as boisterous. In some cases the curate lived with the vicar who was a celibate. Raymond Raynes, the future superior of Mirfield, served his title in Bury where he had a room in the vicarage, the ground floor of which was given over to parish groups each evening. Curates who married had to provide their own accommodation unless the parish owned a house for them.

The Guild of All Souls promoted prayers for the faithful departed and sold or hired vestments and other furniture for requiem masses. It provided these for the requiem which took place in the Albert Hall at the 1930 Congress. The Guild of St Raphael arranged conferences and courses on the ministry of healing and provided a form of service for the laying on of hands and anointing the sick. Charles Harris was a keen member. He was mainly responsible for persuading the Convocations in the thirties to authorize services based on the Guild's rite of the sick for general use. Curiously for a movement which stressed the importance of the sacraments, very little was said about this particular ministry at the Congresses. The Guild of the Love of God helped Catholic laity to be evangelistic in their prayers and daily life. Guild of the Servants of the Sanctuary aimed to develop the devotional life of its members.

The Anglican and Eastern Churches Association was the agency though which the Congresses formed links with the Orthodox Churches. Leading members of the Association were Athelstan Riley, H. Fynes-Clinton of St Magnus the Martyr, London Bridge, C. B. Moss and J. A. Douglas. Individuals among them had links with the Orthodox Churches in Russia, the Balkans, or the Middle East through visits or serving in chaplaincies.

After the war the Association welcomed exiles from these countries, including the families of deposed monarchies, and helped in practical ways. Fynes-Clinton secured the church of St Philip in Buckingham Palace Road for use by the Russian Orthodox (it was demolished in 1958) and also set up a fund for theological students from Serbia to study at Oxford. C. B. Moss launched another fund for helping Armenian Christians. The Association protested to the British government for leaving the Assyrian Christians to the mercy of the Turks and Kurds at the end of the war, and to the Turkish government for the Armenian massacre. They publicised news of the persecution of bishops and priests following the revolution in Russia. Riley wrote a series of letters to the *Times* expressing concern about the preservation of St Sophia in Constantinople. Such activities explain why Orthodox bishops with their impressive titles and vesture were willing to be present at the Congresses in gratitude for the assistance they had received.

The *Church Times*

The part played by the *Church Times* in informing Anglicans and others about the Congresses was enormous. Without it the executive committee could never have attracted the attention and support they received. George Josiah Palmer, the paper's founder, was the son of a printer. He worshipped in St Mary Magdalene, Munster Square, and it was the clergy of that church who persuaded him in 1863 to launch a cheap weekly newspaper for Catholics in the Church of England. The paper prospered and in 1915 Fred Palmer became the next member of the founder's heirs to assume control. He appointed Ernest Hermitage Day, a scholarly priest who had been a frequent contributor to the paper, as editor. Day lived in Hereford but commuted to London for three days a week, working with Palmer on the production of the paper. Together they were responsible for reporting the first two Congresses, the first Priests' Convention, the provincial Congresses and other related activities

Day retired in 1924 and was replaced by Sidney Dark, a professional journalist with the *Daily Express*. The scholarly conservative parson was replaced by a witty socialist from the popular press. Dark brought a new vigour to the paper and included more reports on the social and industrial affairs of post-war Britain, such as a series on the slums, which did much to inform readers of the extent of the problem. By the 1920s the paper had a circulation of over 60,000. Many outside Catholic circles read it regularly as its coverage of religious affairs was extensive. It was published in two sections, one containing news, comment and letters from readers, the other book reviews and longer articles. Correspondents in different dioceses fed in local items. After Easter there were two or three pages giving a round-up of how Lent and Holy Week had been observed in parishes across the country. There was a weekly 'Anglo-Catholic Pulpit', usually the text of a sermon preached by a well-known priest. Only during the general strike of 1926 was it reduced to a few pages.

The academic standard of some contributors was striking. Their lengthy pieces with quotations (occasionally in Latin and once or twice in Greek) read like discussions in a theological college seminar. Other contributors were anxious or indignant clergy and informed or outspoken laity, many of them able to hold their own and question the assumptions and arguments of the theologians. Some, like Desmond Morse Boycott, H. Wilson and F. Belton, later published their contributions in book form. Occasionally articles were printed from Evangelical leaders, and meetings such as the Islington Conference were sympathetically reported. The paper avoided attacking Evangelicals, except when their bishops made life difficult for priests. In general it took a broadly Catholic Anglican line on most things and was critical of Papalism and Modernism in equal measure. But that did not prevent the editor from accepting letters from such circles. Mayor, the leading Modernist, was a frequent correspondent. The letters columns usually filled two or more pages and, as always, revealed the worst as well as the best in those who wrote.

The paper gave extensive coverage to the preparations for and the events at the Congresses. Speeches were reported in detail over several pages and special supplements issued for the 1927 and 1933 events – the first on the history of the Church of England's liturgy as a background to the revision of the Prayer Book; the second on the story of the Oxford Movement to mark the Centenary celebrations. Annual festivals and meetings of Catholic societies such as the ECU and the CBS were usually give a full-page spread.

Yet the editor was prepared to criticize things about the Congresses which he felt were unsuitable. Every year he or his reporters asked why Congress congregations had to listen to lengthy settings of the mass instead of being able to join in with the music of Merbeck or Shaw. He or his contributors criticized certain speakers for being too intellectually remote for their audiences. He thought Weston's message of greetings to the Pope from the 1923 Congress had been unwise. Hermitage Day was cautious about the growth of Liberal Catholicism, but under Dart's editorship it was accepted as the norm for the movement.

The paper also set out to attract the less academic. It reported the sayings and doings of well-known clergy and laity in the manner of a fan club gossip column, and its reporters included accounts of their own personal observations and experiences when writing about major events, mixing enthusiasm with humour. The paper took care to retain the interest of its readers outside London by printing accounts of parochial news and events elsewhere in the country. At times the paper seemed to read like a nationwide parish magazine. There was an appreciable coverage of the rest of the British Isles and overseas dioceses. More photographs appeared as the paper moved from the twenties into the thirties.

It was assumed its readers had the leisure to appreciate its many pages. In days when clergy were not distracted by the radio, the TV, the telephone, the Internet or the mobile, and middle-class churchgoers had domestics to clean and prepare meals, the *Church Times* was a major source of communication. It created the feeling among Catholics that the fellowship they enjoyed at the Congresses and at the diocesan and national meetings of their societies was maintained through the printed word. They read what others said and did; now and then they read something about themselves – the report of the meeting they had attended, or the text of the sermon they had heard. And when an appeal was issued for a worthy cause, as when the Congress committee needed cash for a new project, they responded generously.

Some of the adverts were similar to those in today's issues of the paper (though none of them as they do today described vacant ecclesiastical situations as 'exciting'). One kind of advert which has now disappeared was put in by clergymen looking for an exchange of livings ('with the Bishop's permission'). When applications for a particular parish were invited, it was usually said to have 'full Catholic privileges' or a similar phrase to indicate it churchmanship.

The paper's approval of the Congresses was evident from the beginning. The leader for 9 July 1920 was headed 'Deo Gratias': 'The Congress was thoroughly representative of English Catholicism: those who gathered in the Albert Hall stood not for themselves alone, but for the hundreds and thousands who could not be present.' The editor then went on, with a belligerence typical of his column, 'This representative assembly many times made it clear that English Catholics will not countenance any experiments with intercommunion which would be inconsistent with the principles of the Church to which they owe their allegiance, experiments which would only delay the real reunion with the Churches of the East and of the West for which they are accustomed to pray.'

In his history of the paper Bernard Palmer, a former editor, pointed out that, although the *Church Times* maintained that line on reunion right up to the 1950s, its leader for the next Congress on 20 July 1923 revealed a less hostile attitude to fellow Anglicans:

> If anything was lacking in what may be termed the Congress message, it was the consideration of our relation, as Anglo-Catholics, to the other parties within the Church of England. For good or ill – possibly for both – our lot is cast in a torn and divided Church, and the question of our relation to our fellow Churchmen who do not see eye to eye with us, and notably to Evangelical and Modernist parties, among whom there is a growing appreciation of our aims which is far more than tolerance, is one of immediate and practical concern. No concentration on the great task of converting England to the Faith can dispense us from readjusting our attitudes towards those within the Church from whom we have hitherto experienced a sharpest antagonism and the most hampering opposition.[7]

The editor was reflecting the growing awareness among Catholics that some of the things Modernists were saying might lead to a better contemporary understanding of the faith. And after the publication of the Lambeth Appeal it became less rigid on certain ecumenical trends. It is ironic that only a few years previously the paper had sacked one of its most valuable columnists – Lacey – for his more open attitude in signing the Mansfield Manifesto.

The July 1933 editions were overflowing with Congress affairs in London and throughout the country. Page after page presented news and comments from far and wide. Advances in technology enabled full-page photographs to be printed as well as two full-page sketches by Donald Maxwell, the paper's artist. These were great days for the paper as well as for the Congresses.

11

The Congress Movement

The 1923 Congress's financial support gave the executive the resources with which to promote their plan for a nationwide evangelistic initiative. In the follow-up to the provincial Congresses nearly two hundred local committees had been formed up and down the country, and the executive realized it was necessary to organize these into a workable communications network. Weston attended the executive's meeting when they discussed this before he returned to Africa, and they accepted his scheme for grouping local committees into eight administrative areas: Metropolitan and Home Counties, North, North West, Midland, Wessex, South West, East Anglia with the East Midlands, and Wales. These local committees were invited to send representatives to area meetings which would elect their own chairman and officers. Inevitably, the response was patchy. The Midland area already had an office in Birmingham which had been established as a result of the Congress there whereas others, like the North, had little organization. To facilitate the scheme the executive proposed that each area secretary should receive an honorarium of £100 a year and up to £50 for travelling expenses. The secretaries were expected to attend the executive's London meetings to report what was going on in their areas.

In London the executive rented an office in Abbey House, and a national committee was set up with representatives chosen by the areas. This committee elected a council which met four times a year and included delegates from the religious communities, the universities, and the various associations of the Congress. The council was made up of lay men and women as well as clergy, though as one observer commented, 'It is necessary for any lady elected to have a sufficiently strong constitution to withstand several hours of fumes from the cheaper brands of empire tobaccos, whilst any layman is expected, for some unknown reason, to be a natural expert on finance.'[1]

Once these arrangements were settled, Wilson went abroad for three months. He said he needed a holiday after four strenuous years at the centre of the movement. He retired as secretary and returned full-time to the staff of St Matthew's. In his place the executive appointed Maurice Child, a librarian of Pusey House. Child had been ordained in 1910, founded the Society of SS Peter and Paul (SSPP) in 1911 with Mr Samuel Gurney, R. Knox and N. P. Williams, served in as a curate in four different parishes, and been a chaplain during the war. His appointment was regarded as risky. His SSPP had a reputation of poking fun at the Anglican hierarchy, importing baroque ecclesiastical bric-a-brac from the Continent and advertising and selling them with cheeky titles ('Ridley Candles' and 'Canterbury Incense'). Consequently he acquired the reputation of being papalist, but in fact at heart he was a committed Anglican and through the SSPP he aimed to encourage clergy to enhance their use of the Prayer Book with rituals from modern Romanism.

He could not have been more different from his predecessor. In personal appearance he was highly unconventional. He never wore a clerical collar, even when in a cassock, and he preferred to be addressed as 'Mister Child' rather than 'Father Child'. To those who did not know him he seemed to be a rather mysterious character. W. L. Lowther Clarke, editorial secretary of SPCK, expressed the feelings of many when he said that while he appreciated the Congresses themselves, he was not so happy about some of the things the Congress secretary said and did in between them. But when Bishop Chandler accepted an invitation to become the movement's president, people like Lowther Clarke felt more reassured. It was only later that Child's detractors realized that he was a skilful organizer, and the success of the next three Congresses was due largely to his energy and abilities.[2]

The former Bishop of Bloemfontein had the reputation of being a devout and scholarly teacher. After his death in 1939, Child paid a grateful tribute to him: 'Bishop Chandler took on the presidency of the ACC when it was rather in the SSPP stage and although popular was not at all proper. He sat through innumerable meetings (which really rather bored him) with benignity and a twinkle which only vanished when anyone became earnest, pompous or flatulent. He just could not bear earnest zealots or folk who "raised the tone". He spoke rarely, but quietly, briefly, and to the point. He approved of ACC and was prepared to back it up in every way and to do all that he was asked. He was keen on the Congresses, always wanted a back seat; worked hard with Lord Halifax and me to bring about the amalgamation of ACC and ECU, and never looked gloomy.'[3]

The work of the movement grew in the run-up to the 1927 Congress, and to handle the extra business the executive appointed C. E. Russell as an organization secretary to visit local committees. The setting up of yet another Catholic organization (it was usually referred to as 'the Anglo-Catholic Congress', 'the renewal movement' or 'the renewal') alongside the ECU, the FCP, and the CBS was criticized by many. Not only did it increase the number of meetings Catholics in parishes were expected to attend; it also unwittingly competed with the other societies for financial support once the collection from the Albert Hall had been spent.

Fortunately, as we have seen, a number of the leaders of these societies were invited to join the Congress executive and that helped to prevent any serious quarrel between the movement and their organizations. Pinchard was astute enough to recognize that the movement had become a popular and effective promoter of the Catholic cause and deserved the ECU's backing. He was at that time involved in reorganizing the Union's national structure, and in talking and writing about this he used every opportunity to explain what he regarded as the difference between the two organizations. The ECU's role, he said, was a defensive one – to protect clergy and parishes from unjust treatment by bishops and others and to advise the priests and laity on the Church Assembly if anything on its agenda compromised Catholic faith and practice. In contrast, he pointed out, the Congress movement's role was a teaching and evangelistic one, and so complemented the work of the ECU rather than competed with it. As general secretary of the Union his views were respected among those who might have been more wary of the Congress movement. Gore and Frere agreed to be on the Congress's council, which was a further reassurance for those suspicious of Child.

During the next ten years the Congress movement represented much that was innovative in the Church of England. This was largely through the associations and other groups which its members initiated and which the executive sponsored financially.

The Fiery Cross Association

To encourage intercession for the evangelization of the country, the Fiery Cross Association was formed. Parish churches and religious communities were invited to take part in continuous prayer according to a timetable drawn up among them. At the beginning of a designated week, the first parish or community in an area undertook to keep a 24-hour vigil of prayer and received a four-foot high wooden cross with the words SIC MUNDUM ENIM DEUS DILEXIT surrounded by red flames painted on it. Special forms of service and intercessions were provided. When one vigil was over, the fiery cross was passed on to the next parish or community for them to keep a similar vigil. In 1924 parishes in the Midlands undertook the vigils in January and February, London and the South in March, and other areas for the rest of the year. The months of August and September were reserved for churches in seaside towns. The *Church Times* regularly printed a list of where the vigils were to be kept in the following weeks.

In his book, *The Romance of the Fiery Cross* (1924) Kenneth Ingram described how the cross was received in various villages, towns and cities, though without identifying any. In a village there was only the vicar and a few people to receive the fiery cross as it arrived in a taxi from a nearby town. In London it was carried through the streets in a procession including the choir, servers, uniformed organizations and clergy to the parish boundary to be handed over to a similar procession from the neighbouring parish. In some places the vigil was kept by large numbers, the men taking over the night hours, with the fiery cross surrounded by candles and flowers, not unlike those provided for the altar of repose on Maundy Thursday. In others it was placed on the altar in a side chapel where a few devout souls came into church for a few minutes during the day. In one town the vicar hired the corn exchange and made the fiery cross the focus of an evangelistic rally. In 1930 eleven London churches held station days to pray for forthcoming Congress. The fiery cross became the logo of the Anglo-Catholic Congress movement and appeared on much of its literature.

In the first year 100,000 copies of a leaflet entitled *What to do during my Watch* were sold, and it had to be reprinted regularly for several years. The fiery cross inspired a wave of prayer across the country throughout the twenties. The project survived until the early thirties and spread to the USA, Australia and New Zealand. It also inspired two other important initiatives. One was the *Fiery Cross* parish magazine inset which provided Catholic teaching for thousands who never saw a church paper or any other kind of Christian literature. The other was the Anglo-Catholic Ordination Fund.

The Anglo-Catholic Ordination Fund

Those who attended fiery cross rallies and vigils were invited to make donations towards the training of priests, and so was launched the Anglo-Catholic Ordination Fund. It joined similar funds established by individual dioceses and other organizations. F. Underhill was one of the committee which launched it. He described how the principals of both

Mirfield and Kelham had told him that they had more applications than they were able to accommodate and that there were many young men who were willing to test their vocations if money was available to pay for their training. Audiences were regularly reminded of the shortage of priests. During a Congress rally in Bournemouth in 1929 one of the speakers introduced to great applause two young clergymen, sons of a mining family in south Wales, whom the fund had helped to prepare for ordination at Chichester theological college. At the centenary Congress in 1933 it was announced that in the nine years since it had been launched the fund had enabled 200 men to be ordained and was paying for a further 192 then in training.

The Women's' Auxiliary

The Anglo-Catholic Congress Women's Auxiliary (ACCWA) – to quote its full name – began when Atlay and Wilson asked members of St Matthew's congregation to help in providing board and lodging for priests coming to London for the first Congress in 1920. The women who did this continued to meet and, when local Congresses were organized, similar meetings for women were formed. In this way the ACCWA became an official arm of the movement as branches sprang up in various parts of the country. The women who attended the meetings often belonged to the Fiery Cross Association and worked for its ordination fund. In some places where the leadership of the Mothers' Union was unsympathetic or narrowly Evangelical, Catholic parish priests found the ACCWA provided a welcome alternative.

By the time of the 1927 Congress the ACCWA had acquired it own secretary and room in the ACC offices. Two of its leading figures were Lady Cynthia Colville, whose activities stretched from being lady-in-waiting to Queen Mary to undertaking work among the slums, and Dame Beryl Oliver, who held important posts in the St John's Ambulance Brigade and the British Red Cross. When Cynthia Colville spoke at a women's meeting in the Brighton Pavilion in 1929, 1,000 turned up and 300 failed to gain admission. She told them the ACCWA was 'a kind of Eve to the Adam of the Anglo-Catholic Congress'.

The ACCWA brought to the clerical planners a dash of feminine commonsense. When Child asked the London committee in 1930 to provide lunch for the 4,000 persons expected to attend the Congress from different parts of the country on the Wednesday 'provincial day', they firmly refused. They told Child that the quotation from J. Lyons was too high and the numbers too great to guarantee satisfactory catering, so they would provide a cup of tea and a cake in the afternoon interval in a marquee in Kensington Gardens instead.

The Auxiliary was active in other practical matters. They made costumes for the children's pageants at the 1930 and 1933 Congresses, and arranged for charabancs and cars to transport the children to the Albert Hall. They organized the women's meetings during the later Congresses. They manned the ticket office, the enquiry desk and the bookstall. Throughout the country they provided speakers for local meetings and gave lessons on how to make vestments and other linen for Catholic churches. When a vicar in Harrogate tried to close down a branch of the ACCWA in his parish, the London office told him sharply that he had no authority to do that because it was a voluntary national organization over which he had no control.

The Green Quarterly

The *Green Quarterly* was launched by Kenneth Ingram as a personal venture in support of the Congress movement. Ingram was a lively freelance journalist with idealistic communist leanings, like many young intellectuals at the time. The title of his quarterly magazine was taken from the cover of the *English Hymnal*. Green was adopted as the standard colour by several Catholic publications, including the Alcuin Club, and for the ECU's suggested revision of the Prayer Book. Ingram invited ordained and lay Catholics to contribute to the magazine on a wide range of subjects – drama, art, music, architecture, social affairs, politics, the economic situation, overseas visits, and so on. There were reports of various Catholic conferences and book reviews. Sheila Kaye Smith, the novelist, wrote a short story for each issue during the first year.

Besides the editorial there were one or two unsigned pieces in each issue which, judging by their content and style, seem to have been written by the editor himself. One was 'Anglo-Catholic Activities' with insider gossip about the movement and personalities connected with it – a sure means of keeping readers' interest and subscriptions. Another was 'Letters from the North Pole' in which an imaginary Catholic who signed himself 'xx' shared his thoughts, usually critical and amusing, with an imaginary friend. In one issue, for example, 'xx' wrote: My dear Charles, I am more and more dissatisfied with our label Anglo-

Catholicism. It is the hyphen and the ism which is doing the harm, for it is giving the general impression that we are a consolidated little sect within the Church of England, with our own doctrines and our own authority, and a definitely crystallized form of religion.' After saying he would like to get away from formal processions with banners and many hymns and elaborate settings, xx went on. 'I want to see a simple sung mass with every encouragement given to silent devotion . . . a simple continentalism, that is to say, a freer and less conventional atmosphere which is homely without being irreverent.'[4] That sounded very much like Ingram himself.

The magazine was welcomed enthusiastically by literary-minded Catholics. In the second number the editor happily reported that the first issue had sold out, and that one young lady had gone to a fancy dress ball in the West End with a costume made up to look like the magazine and a copy of it in her hand. It flourished for ten years or so, but then circulation declined after the Oxford Movement Centenary celebrations and it ceased publication in 1936. Of all the sources available on the movement, the *Green Quarterly* is one of the most entertaining to read today.

The Congress Van

The executive purchased a van with the words 'The Anglo-Catholic Congress' and the logo of the fiery cross painted on its sides. It was equipped with two bunks and the rear doors could be opened to provide a platform with a canopy from which to address open air meetings and lead services. A rota was drawn up for pairs of clergy who volunteered to give up part of their holidays to conduct missions in different places at the invitation of local incumbents. They were warned that conditions were not luxurious. Besides being able to drive, they had to cook for themselves, sleep on narrow hard bunks, and fill the water tank regularly. They also had to beg for permission to use the bathroom in vicarages and endure the rattle of household crockery as they drove down bad roads. One year the van went to Cornwall, another to the mining towns in the Midlands.

It was not an original idea. The use of vans for missionary purposes had been taken up by other Christian organizations. But the editor of the *Green Quarterly* evidently regarded it as a unique facility for the Church's evangelistic ministry. In a 1927 issue he printed a photograph of it and wrote: 'Our illustration shows the caravan complete with folding platform, living accommodation and an ammunitions store of books. Perhaps in years to come, this illustration will be as historic as a print of the first railway engine. For by that time the Congress will be dropping literature on the native villages of Africa and Asia from a fleet of aeroplanes.'[5] The van was used in the late spring, summer and early autumn throughout the twenties, but the executive had to sell it in 1930 when the Congress's finances were low.

The Overseas Association

The presence of overseas bishops at the Congresses thrilled those who went to the Albert Hall. Their presence reassured the faithful that whatever their own diocesans might be like, there were still bishops in the Anglican Communion who kept the faith. With their purple soutanes, purple birettas and pectoral crosses they *looked* like Catholic bishops! Two of them – Zanzibar and Nassau – chaired the five London Congresses.

Clergy from other parts of the Anglican Communion who came to the Congresses wanted to be kept in touch with the movement after they returned, so it was for them that the Anglo-Catholic Congress Overseas Association came into being. Occasional newsletters were dispatched. The Association acted as a post box for individuals and parishes wanting to donate vestments or other liturgical requisites to missions in Africa, the West Indies and elsewhere. It also had the important task of allocating funds raised at Congress meetings to overseas dioceses. The bishops who spoke in the Albert Hall often expressed their gratitude to the Association for what these gifts meant to themselves and their churches. It remained a small body and seemed to exist harmoniously alongside UMCA and other missionary societies.

The Association acted as liaison between the London Congress office and Congresses held elsewhere in the world. A number of successful Congresses were organized by the Episcopal Church of the USA in New York, Chicago, Pittsburg and Washington during the twenties and thirties, and there were Congresses in South Africa, Australia and New Zealand. The Association also provided resources for celebrating the 1933 Oxford Movement Centenary in many parts of the Anglican Communion.

The Anglo-Catholic Pilgrimage Association

The Anglo-Catholic pilgrimages were the initiative of George Napier Whittingham, the vicar of St Silas the Martyr, Kentish Town. He organized the first pilgrimage to the Holy Land in 1924 with the help of

Sir Henry Lunn, the travel agent, and wrote an account of it in his parish magazine in July of that year. His party of nearly two hundred, which included the Bishops of Nassau and Nebraska as well as a number of priests, travelled to Marseilles by train and sailed on a passenger liner to Jaffa. The harbour there was too shallow for the ship to dock so the pilgrims had to disembark in small boats, much to the consternation of some. Whittingham wrote:

> We were greeted on landing first by the local Greek Archimandrite and then by Archdeacon Stacey Waddy as representative of the Anglican Church in Palestine. We said our prayers privately in the Greek Church close to the landing stage, and then we climbed through the steep and narrow little streets in the broiling sun, though it was only 7.30 a.m., past the traditional house of Simon the Tanner to the little CMS [Church Missionary Society] church, bare and severe as a Trappist Monastery, where, led by the lusty and resonant voice of our President, the Bishop of Nassau, we made the roof ring with the joyous notes of *Te Deum*.

That morning they went on to the Bishop's house in Jerusalem where they were greeted by a distinguished company – the heads of various Eastern congregations, the Anglican clergy of St George's, missionaries, and the Governor of Jerusalem. They were gratified to discover the welcoming group included a Roman Catholic priest. Then they began visiting the holy sites:

> The first official visit should have been to the Church of the Holy Sepulchre, but Friday is 'washing day' there, and so we had to alter the order of proceedings. Thus we went to Bethlehem, and in the great square outside the Church of the Holy Nativity we were welcomed by the Archbishop of Bethlehem and Mgr Themelis, Archbishop of Jordan. Then the pilgrims formed into a procession and led by the Bishops of Nassau and Nebraska entered the noble Basilica and were conducted to the shrine of the Grotto.
>
> This sounds simple enough, but in reality it was a most difficult matter. We numbered well over 200, and there is not room in the Grotto of the Nativity for more than 20 people, and as everyone naturally desired to kiss the holy Star this part of the proceedings took at least an hour and a half. We descended the steps cut out of the rock tapers in hand into the Grotto and found ourselves in front of one of the most sacred places in the world, which in spite of many vicissitudes has remained

unaltered. At this altar the Archbishop of Bethlehem chanted the Litany of welcome to Pilgrims, and then in single file each pilgrim venerated the sacred place. When all had made their pilgrimage, we assembled in the Sanctuary of the Basilica and there the Archimandrite Kyriakos read us an address of welcome in excellent English to which our president, the Bishop of Nassau, replied.

The next morning the lay pilgrims foregathered in the Courtyard of the Church of the Holy Sepulchre, and the priests headed by our two Bishops walked in procession through the Greek quarter, Fr Maurice Child and I acting as Masters of Ceremonies. Here we were welcomed by Archbishop Themelis representing the Patriarch, and then were conducted in three parties round the sacred places within. Needless to say the Holy Tomb and Calvary were visited first of all, and at both these the Archimandrite Kyriakos gave a short explanation together with words of welcome. Then followed a delightful reception at the Patriarchate for the pilgrims who were introduced to the Patriarch Damianos by Archbishop Themelis. Everyone received a souvenir from his Beatitude which was greatly appreciated, and afterwards the Committee of the pilgrimage were entertained to lunch at which the Patriarch Damianos presided, and during which an invisible choir sang as only Greek boys can sing . . . It is not possible to recount all the wonders the visitors saw in and around Jerusalem, they would fill a large book, suffice it to say that nothing of importance was omitted.

The next days they visited Nazareth and Galilee and then went back to Jerusalem. Five masses were said each day so that the pilgrims could attend in relays. On one occasion an Orthodox bishop allowed the Bishop of Nassau to borrow his vestments. Eventually the party re-embarked at Joppa and returned home. Aboard ship the five masses continued to be said each day, beginning at 5.30 a.m.

Whittingham noted with satisfaction that the pilgrimage was the first to go to the Holy Land since it had been rescued by the British from 'the blight of Turkish misrule' seven years previously under the terms of the peace treaty. The influx of this large party of pilgrims was evidently of some importance in Jerusalem since the British governor and the Orthodox dignitaries were present for many of the events. The contacts which the Congress had made with the Orthodox in London were evidently appreciated by their fellow believers in the Holy Land, which is why the pilgrims were given such a warm welcome.

However, the pilgrimage created a minor controversy. When Whittingham returned to London he learned that the Roman Catholic Church press had printed stories of Anglican bishops and priests invading the Church of the Holy Nativity in gorgeous vestments. The stories originated from the Franciscans from the nearby convent. They had informed the Latin Patriarch in Jerusalem who had then complained to the governor. The bishops had in fact been in Convocation dress and the priests their academic habits (which they seem to have worn in spite of the heat!). In reply, Whittingham pointed out that on the last day of their stay in Jerusalem, the Bishops of Nassau and Nebraska with six priests called on the Latin Patriarch in Jerusalem, who received them courteously. During the interview, in which controversial subjects were avoided, Whittingham noticed the Patriarch addressed the bishops as 'Monsignor', and the priests 'Father'. He commented: 'Italians rarely forget their manners whatever else they may do.'

During the second pilgrimage led by Whittingham the following year, the party witnessed signs of the Arab–Jewish conflict. In 1917 Mr A. Balfour on behalf of the British government declared that Palestine was to be the homeland of the Jews (the Balfour Declaration). It so happened that the pilgrims arrived in Joppa just after Balfour had made an official visit to Palestine. Arab demonstrations against him were so violent that the minister had to be protected and hustled away by British troops. The pilgrims watched with alarm as demonstrators passed down the street where they were staying shouting, 'To hell with the British and the Jews!' and, 'Down with Zionism!' (the words were translated for them). Whittingham was scornful of the British government's policy. 'Nothing has done more to lower British prestige in the East than the effort to force Zionist rule on a Christian and Moslem population,' he wrote later.

The party left Joppa with relief to continue the pilgrimage by visiting Cyprus, Patmos, Smyrna, Ephesus, Constantinople, Athens and Malta. The president of this pilgrimage was H. R. Wakefield, the retired Bishop of Birmingham. He was a popular figure among the party, and Whittingham commented how much he was missed 'by churchmen in that smoky city' since his successor, Bishop Barnes, was attempting to suppress Catholic practices.

Further pilgrimages to the Middle East were organized in the following years. In addition there were visits to holy sites in the British Isles. Mackay, who was born in Wales, took a group to visit St David's. Other parties went to the northern shrines – Durham, Lindisfarne, Iona. A pilgrimage to the places associated with St Patrick in Ireland took a party from Ulster over the border to the newly established Irish Republic where the pilgrims were relieved to be given a friendly welcome (the British had been very unpopular there since the rebellion).

The annual Glastonbury pilgrimage began when the Bristol Guild of the Servants of the Sanctuary wrote to the vicar of the parish church of St John in 1923 proposing a 'Bristol Anglo Catholic Glastonbury Pilgrimage.' Groups in other southern dioceses joined in, and at the first pilgrimage 1,500 including 30 priests and 400 servers sang vespers in the abbey ruins. The Anglo-Catholic Pilgrimage Association was sponsored by the Congress executive who made small grants to the organizers to enable it to develop into a national event. The Association also arranged for a large party to go to Oberammergau in 1930.

Although some parishes subsidized their poorer members, in general the pilgrimages remained a privilege for middle-class Anglicans. This caused a few SSC clergy to comment that such events should not be called pilgrimages as they were undertaken in luxury without any of the hardship and self-denial which are the marks of a true pilgrim.

The Fiery Cross magazine survived for several years after the second world war. The Ordination Fund was taken over first by the Church Union and then by the *Church Times* as the Lent Train-a-Priest fund. The Pilgrimage Association set the pattern of such visits for similar organizations in later years.

Retreats

The Association for Promoting Retreats, formed in 1912, was supported by the Congress movement. The executive invited it to have a base in the Congress offices and made grants towards its work from time to time. That led to the formation of the Society of Retreat Conductors as the demand for retreats grew.

The Congress years saw an increase in the number of retreat houses opening. Up until then they had been largely run by the religious orders, a link which in the years of the ritual troubles gave rise to a suspicion that retreats were Jesuitical practices. Anglo-Catholics had started taking parties of parishioners to weekend retreats from the end of the previous century, and making an annual retreat was an item in the rule of life for many priests and others. After the war the custom grew of bishops taking the men they were to ordain into a retreat a few days prior to the ordination service. The Chelmsford diocese established its retreat house at Pleshey in 1927 and other dioceses gradually followed. By 1930 there were 20 diocesan retreat houses in addition to the 40 houses run by the religious orders (32 of the latter for women and 8 for men). Obviously making a retreat was only possible for those who could afford the time and the cost, through parishes in poor areas arranged weekend retreats at a subsidized rate for their members.

J. F. Briscoe gave a talk on making a retreat at the 1920 Congress. It was, he said, an adventure – a searching for God. But it required plenty of time in proper surroundings with a strict discipline of keeping the silence to clear the mind of worldly thoughts. Retreatants should review their lives – their work, their possessions, their aims and their relationships – as gifts from God and how faithful they have been in using them. Realizing their failures, they should then make their confession. Afterwards they should spend as much time as is available to recognizing and rejoicing in the presence of Jesus Christ – in the silence of their room and in the garden and countryside, in the chapel before the reserved sacrament, and above all in the daily mass.

He went on, 'It is the most delightful experience of my life to give Communion at the end of retreats. I have seen them, priests who were utterly discouraged, men and women quite away from God, lads and girls whose lives were all in a tangle. But that was three or four days ago. Now in a long row, often with tears in their eyes, they wait, happy and calm, for me to set the Body of Christ upon their lips. I know that the peace which is shining in their faces is no peace of this world, but the peace beyond all understanding which is the gift of God. I know that from the house of retreat they will go, true bearers of Christ, true missionaries of the gospel, true disciples of the Faith, carrying to others the light and the joy they have found for themselves.'[6]

He was insistent that the term 'retreat' should only be used for properly organized exercises such as those he described. A quiet three hours on a Saturday afternoon were not a retreat, he said, however valuable that may be. Retreat conductors should be trained to give meditations each no longer than half-an-hour in the morning and early evening each day, and should be available for hearing confessions and having interviews at set times.

Members of religious orders were usually called on to lead retreats, but a notable exception was Evelyn Underhill. By the time she spoke at the 1927 Congress she was well known through her books and lectures as a student of Christian mysticism. She gave most of her retreats at Pleshey, where there is a memorial plaque to her in the chapel. Although her clientele were mainly women, she was occasionally invited to give retreat addresses to clergy, and she acted as a spiritual director to a small number of priests and others who appreciated the restrained Anglican way in which she expounded her Catholic spirituality.

During the 1930 Congress, talks on this topic were given by G. S. Shaw, secretary of the Association for Promoting Retreats, and P. G. Bacon of the Society of Retreat Conductors. They said much the same thing as Briscoe had done ten years earlier. Bacon in his address included advice for those who led them. He believed that the best kind of retreat was the solitary one, since the purpose of a retreat was to help an individual to review his life and to discern what hindered him from drawing closer to God. Each person was at a different stage in his spiritual pilgrimage and consequently needed individual help from the retreat conductor. But for many it was only possible for them to go on corporate retreats, where conductors were tempted to speak to them as if they were a congregation with common needs and interests. That was a mistake. The conductor, said Bacon, should always remember he is addressing individuals and prepare his talks as if he was in a personal one-to-one situation. That would help the retreatants to feel he was addressing them as individuals and encourage them to make an appointment to see him privately.

12

Prayer Book Revision

The 1927 Congress differed from the previous two in that its main focus was on the liturgy under the general title of 'The Holy Eucharist'. It met during the same week in which the Church Assembly was debating the Revised Prayer Book, and the Congress executive wanted to help those who came to the Albert Hall to understand the reasons for the revision so they could make up their own minds about it.

Many of those who attended the Congress that summer had been children when the process of revision began (and anyone under twenty-one would not have been born!). A Royal Commission on Ecclesiastical Discipline had been set up to advise the Church of England on resolving the problems raised by the ritual disputes following the ill-fated Public Worship Regulation Act of 1874. The Commission published its vast four-volume report in 1906 and made recommendations. The most important of these was that the Convocations of Canterbury and York should prepare a new rubric on the vesture of the ministers and recommend modifications in the existing law relating to ornaments and fittings of churches. The intention was that the Convocations would then submit these proposals for Parliamentary approval. There was no thought at that stage of revising the services themselves. However, it was gradually realized that changes in vestures, ornaments and fittings could not be made without taking into account the rites and ceremonies they were supposed to govern, and so within a few years proposals were being put forward involving the revision of the whole Prayer Book.

The work continued slowly and intermittently. Davidson was unenthusiastic about it: he knew it was a highly contentious project. Difficulties were encountered in providing alternative services for the administration of the sacraments. Evangelicals were upset that the child was still declared to be 'regenerate' in the alternative baptism service as in the old (they argued that regeneration was only possible after personal repentance and faith). Traditionalists protested that in the alternative wedding service the bride did not use the word 'obey' in her promise to the bridegroom. But the greatest stumbling block in getting the Convocations to agree on a revision was the eucharistic prayer.

Frere proposed that with other rearranging of the texts, the prayer of oblation ('O Lord and heavenly Father ... ') could be added to the prayer of consecration by the link word 'Wherefore'. Some Catholics were already using the prayer of oblation in this way. (It became known as 'the interim rite', implying that it was a temporary form of the prayer until something better was authorized.) However, he could not get his fellow bishops to agree. In the meantime, other parts of the Anglican Communion were using revised versions of the Prayer Book – with Frere's advice in South Africa and Northern Rhodesia.

The delay in putting forward a Revised Prayer Book was also caused by the lack of a proper constitutional procedure for accomplishing it. If and when the proposals were passed by the Convocations, they could have been presented to the Church Representative Council, though the CRC had no legislative authority to do more than to signify its approval or disapproval. The next step would have been to submit them to Parliament. Even if Parliament had found the time (especially during the war) to deal with the proposals, many in the Convocations were appalled at the thought of texts and rubrics of the revision being debated by MPs of different denominations or none. The hope was that when the Church Assembly was established, an appropriate constitutional process for dealing with the proposals would be in place.

One of the first things the newly constituted Church Assembly did was to appoint a joint committee made up of members from all three Houses (Bishops, Clergy and Laity) to work through the proposals and make regular reports. Two years later the committee presented a list for the Assembly to discuss and vote on: a new lectionary, a form of burial for an unbaptized child, and an improved order for the visitation of the sick. Later they presented revised baptism, confirmation, marriage and burial services, and wider choices in the offices of morning and evening prayer, together with the optional use of the 'cursing' verses in the Psalms and of the warning at the end of the Athanasian Creed.[1] Last of all came the rite for the revised Holy Communion service.

Hostility to the revision, which had been heard intermittently in previous years, now became passionate as Davidson had feared it would. It came from three quarters – cultural conservatives, Evangelicals and some Catholics. The cultural opponents were older bishops, priests and laity who were deeply attached to the 1662 Prayer Book and said there was no need for a revision. Into this category came a majority of ordinary English people. Although they only heard the Prayer Book used at baptisms, weddings and funerals, they regarded it as a national icon along with the Authorized Version of the Bible. Brides carried a small white-covered edition as an item in their wedding dress accoutrements. The cry of 'Hands off our Book!' was heard in the land.

Evangelicals resisted the revision because they believed that, with the Thirty-Nine Articles, the Prayer Book enshrined biblical and Reformation teaching and protected the nation from the errors of Roman Catholicism. Their foremost champion was Bishop Knox, who devoted the years of his retirement to organizing a vigorous public campaign against the revision. Most of the bishops of the Northern Province were Evangelical, and they hindered the progress of revision by constantly raising objections in their House of Convocation.

Among Catholics reactions were mixed. In the years leading up to 1920, the English Church Union was against any tampering with the Prayer Book. In this, the Union reflected a suspicion among many of its members that the revision was an attempt by the bishops to suppress ritual practices. Its policy, therefore, was to oppose it. In 1922, however, the Church Assembly voted that the Prayer Book should remain untouched and that all alternative services should be optional. When this was understood, opinions in Catholic circles began to change. Many saw that revision might be a promising development. Wiser members of the Union said co-operation was preferable to confrontation. If Catholics wanted to influence change, they had to take their part in making their views known.

So the ECU Council passed a resolution to give consideration to 'the present situation as regards the work of revision of the Prayer Book, especially in respect of a Eucharistic office'. It was 'a magnificent opportunity for removing the blemishes and dislocations from its texts and structure, for enriching it with many of the long-forgotten treasures of Catholic devotion, and for shaping it into something approximating as nearly as may be to the ritual of a perfect instrument for the praise and adoration of Almighty God'.[2] This change of policy was echoed in some of the talks given at the provincial Congresses in the early twenties.

The Union's contribution was to publish its own version of a Revised Prayer Book in 1923. It was known as the Green Book, the colour of its covers matching those of the English Hymnal. It was drafted largely by Darwell Stone and N. P. Williams and included a eucharistic prayer described as 'an attempt to combine the best features of the First Prayer Book of 1549 and the South African revisions'. Provision was made for reservation on an unrestricted basis, a calendar which included such feasts as Corpus Christi and the Assumption of the Blessed Virgin Mary, and the restoration of the chrism in the rites of initiation – practices and celebrations which were observed in many Anglo-Catholic parishes. The Union declared disarmingly that its policy was 'not to resist the process of revision, but to endeavor to guide it on the right lines' and so secure a book that was 'as satisfactory as possible from a Catholic point of view'.

Its eucharistic rite had a clearly Catholic character. It resembled the revised Book presented to the Church Assembly, but with some departures. The prayer of consecration was called 'the Canon'. It included an epiclesis (an invocation of the Holy Spirit), before the institution narrative, and afterwards an anamnesis (act of remembrance) which read:

> Wherefore, O Lord and heavenly Father, according to the institution of thy dearly beloved Son Jesus Christ, we thy humble servants do celebrate and make here, before thy divine Majesty, the holy, pure, and spotless oblation which thy Son hath commanded us to make, and having in remembrance his blessed passion, mighty resurrection, and glorious ascension, we offer unto thee these thy sacred gifts, the holy Bread of eternal life and the Cup of everlasting salvation.[3]

The *Agnus Dei* was followed by the prayer of humble access, the invitation, the confession, the absolution and the comfortable words before people received Communion. Reservation was permitted for the sick, but there was no restriction on eucharistic adoration as there were in the revised Book.

Catholic members wanted the Church Assembly to consider the Green Book as a basis for the revision. One non-ECU priest suggested it should be adopted as it was so as to bring the whole business of the revision to an end. But Evangelical members strongly objected. They opposed the provisions for reservation, among other things, but the focus of their criticism was the eucharistic prayer. They saw it as a means of bringing the Roman rite into the Church of England by the back door. They pointed out that proposals for extending the prayer beyond the words of institution with the phrase 'we offer' could introduce the doctrine of the eucharistic sacrifice into the Anglican worship (reinforced by the words 'a holy, pure and spotless oblation' taken from the Roman canon). The ECU compilers pointed out that the once-for-all nature of Christ's offering was clearly affirmed in the prayer, but their opponents were not persuaded.

Two other groups also produced suggested revisions. The Alcuin Club had published a series of pamphlets on the subject and these, because of the colour of the covers, were called The Orange Books. Members of this group included Congress speakers such as Gore, who was president of the Club, Frere, Lacey and A. S. Duncan-Jones. The Eucharist more or less followed Frere's suggested rite. The Grey Books were a similar collection of pamphlets by a group which included Temple, Sheppard, Dearmer and F. W. Dwelly (the last named, a vicar of Emmanuel, Southport, had a reputation for devising services for special occasions, which was why he was appointed the first dean of the new Liverpool cathedral after it was consecrated in 1924). These pamphlets aimed at greater simplicity in response to the pleas of those who had been chaplains in the war and who found Prayer Book services unsuitable for most situations in which they served. The Grey Books were striking because they attempted to use contemporary language. They received some support, not only from Anglicans who were interested in modernizing their worship but also from a few Evangelicals.

Another division was created among Catholics by the use of an invocation of the Holy Spirit on the bread and wine. Some, led by Frere, pressed for the inclusion of an epiclesis, not only because of its antiquity and of its use in Orthodox rites, but also because they believed that the role of the Holy Spirit in the consecration of the Bread and the Wine should be clearly expressed. Opposing them were others, led by Stone, who said that an epiclesis had never been a feature of the Western eucharistic rite and that it introduced a novel and unnecessary phrase into the prayer. Among this group were those who believed that the 'moment of consecration' was when the priest recited the words of institution over the sacred Elements. Linked with this belief was the ritual elevation when, with the ringing of the sanctuary bell and the swinging of the censer, the Host and the Chalice were lifted by the priest for the congregation to see and adore. In non-communicating masses, this was the climax of the service. It was also for many a highly emotional and awesome experience, kneeling in the sacramental Presence of the Lord and joining in the offering of the holy sacrifice. The introduction of an epiclesis, the group feared, would detract from the moment of consecration and the devotion it invoked.

In the autumn of 1925 the proposed revisions were sent to the House of Bishops for their final approval. This was not as straightforward as had been hoped. Frere complained that few of his episcopal companions had any real knowledge of liturgy. In particular, there were strong disagreements on the rubrics concerning reservation. It was because of this that Bishop Woods arranged the conference at Farnham, described in Chapter 14.

These years witnessed an outburst of books, pamphlets, articles and lectures for and against the revised Book. Many Catholics objected to items which had been made optional – the recitation of the Athanasian Creed, the cursing verses in the Psalms, the words, 'all men are conceived and born in sin', from the Baptism service, and in the Marriage service of the words, 'who didst teach that it should never be lawful to put asunder those whom thou by matrimony hast made one' and the bride's vow 'to obey'. Such options, they said, undermined Catholic doctrine and discipline. The ECU and the FCP, acting together for the Central Council of Catholic Societies, published a memorandum which urged the Convocations to reject the Book because they believed the proposed revision of the Eucharist and was unsatisfactory, especially the proposals about reservation. They said:

> It has by now become clear that a large body of Anglo-Catholic opinion could not accept a liturgy which suddenly reversed the tradition of the English Church since its beginning fourteen hundred years ago. Many could not accept the proposed rubrics as to reservation. Nor could they accept those rubrics, even if they were amended on other points, so long as they absolutely prohibit all corporate worship of our Lord in the Holy Sacrament when Reserved.

To claim that the Prayer Book Communion service was to reverse the tradition of English eucharistic worship for fourteen centuries was an argument which Evangelicals and others could fairly challenge. The Central Council may have sensed this for they went on: 'These objections may be right or wrong. They are, however, held by so substantial a body of opinion and with such conviction as to make it certain that the Bishops' proposals would not produce peace, and could only be enforced, if at all, by a widespread and determined use of ecclesiastical discipline.' The memorandum ended by saying that, if the proposed revision was passed by the Convocations and the Assembly, the disunity it caused in the Church would hardly commend it to the House of Commons.[4]

This memorandum represented the Red and Orange spectrum of Anglo-Catholics. It was also unrealistic. Other Catholics realized this and urged acceptance of the revised Book. Lacey said that although he recognized its defects, he would vote for it because he did not want Evangelicals to overthrow it. Gore, though no longer a member of Convocation, wrote urging Catholics to support it. In the debates in Convocation on 29 and 30 March, Frere, Kidd, Lacey and Harris all spoke in defence of the

Book. Among the bishops all but 4 voted for it, and among the clergy 236 were in favour and 32 against. But the opponents told lay Catholics in the Assembly that they should still feel free to vote against it even though it had been passed by Convocation. The Assembly debated the revised Book on 5 and 6 July and it was passed by 517 votes to 133. The debate and vote took place during the final sessions of the 1927 Congress.

To continue the story of the revision, agitation against the Book became more strident in the days leading up the Parliamentary debate. There were protest meetings in the country and MPs received numerous letters from their constituents – correspondence which was orchestrated by Bishop Knox and Protestant groups. It become a national issue, and many MPs felt they should join in, whatever their religious affiliation or none. Stone advised Catholics not to take part in the public lobbying of MPs as this would give the impression that the authority of the state was greater in these matters than that of the Church. He was not, however, against private lobbying of individual MPs. He chaired an FCP meeting on 11 October in Chelsea Town Hall attended by 500 priests which voted unanimously not to have anything to do with the Book.

The Lords debated the measure for three days, 12–14 December, and passed it by 241 votes to 88. When it was introduced into the Commons on 15 December, it was generally expected it would pass. But its supporters had miscalculated the strength of opposition. Cecil introduced the Deposited Book (as it was now called[5]) with a carefully scripted account of what the revision was intended to do. Observers in the House thought he seemed unusually nervous; he may have been relying on someone else's briefing – perhaps Frere's. But a strong opposition came from the Evangelical Home Secretary, Joyson Hicks, and by MPs from Wales, Scotland and Northern Ireland. The record in Hansard reveals the passion and prejudice of those against the revision. There were many references to the Romanizing character of the Deposited Book, and to the inability of the bishops to discipline their clergy.

Slesser admitted that in the Church Assembly he had voted against sending the measure to Parliament because he didn't think the proposals for revising the Prayer Book went far enough, but in spite of that he urged the House to pass it. He then perhaps unintentionally delivered what must have sounded like a snub to the House by saying he regarded the bishops in Convocation to be 'the only authority which I recognize in the Church'.[6] The most intelligent and eloquent speech in favour of the revision was by John Buchan, who warned the House not to resist change in the Church provided the main tenets of Christianity were upheld. He said, 'An acute English critic wrote in the early seventeenth century of my own Church of Scotland, "Those people think they can find the road to heaven only if they leave Rome behind them." [7] The debate ended the following day with the measure being rejected by 258 votes to 205.

Many Anglicans indignantly pointed out that if English MPs had been allowed to vote separately the measure would have passed. The injustice of seeing the Church of England's constitutional decision blocked by those who did not belong to it – or any Church – highlighted more than before the case for disestablishment. To their honour, Roman Catholic and some Nonconformist MPs who were present in the Commons refrained from voting.

Following the defeat, the bishops convinced themselves that the rejection of the Deposited Book was due to misunderstandings, so they decided to reintroduce the measure to the Church Assembly and to Parliament with modifications which, they hoped, would make it more acceptable. The most significant change was in the provision for reservation. In the 1927 version the arrangements about reserving the sacrament were not prescribed by rubric, but left to regulations framed by the bishops or to legislation by canons. In the 1928 version this flexibility was removed. A rubric was introduced stating that reservation was to be permitted only in exceptional cases with the bishop's permission. The result of these changes was to drive some Catholics who had supported the 1927 book into opposition. These included Kidd and Frere. The ECU urged the Assembly to postpone all further action until after the 1930 Lambeth Conference, but also expressed its hope that all Catholics would follow Frere in his opposition to it. Those who voted for the revision did so more because they felt they ought to support the bishops than because they welcomed it. After debates on 28 and 29 March 1928, the changes were supported by a much smaller majority in Convocation and in the Church Assembly, but the amended book was rejected a second time by Parliament after debates on 13 and 14 June, this time by 266 votes to 220 in the Commons.

This second failure caused consternation among the bishops (except the four who had voted against the revision). They felt the authority of the Church had been weakened. Henson wrote in his diary it was his conviction 'that the Establishment as it has been now revealed had ceased to be defensible'.[8] Lang, who was appointed from York to Canterbury when Davidson retired a few weeks after the vote, was alarmed that disappointed Catholics might convert to Rome. Temple had the same thought. 'We have to face the fact', he wrote to Lang, 'that a considerable Anglo-Catholic section is contemplating secession as a genuinely

1 The Fiery Cross symbol of the Anglo-Catholic movement.

2 Marcus Atlay, Chairman of the ACC 1919–22.

3 Herbert Wilson, Secretary of the ACC 1919–23.

4 Frank Weston, Bishop of Zanzibar.

5 Roscoe Shedden, Bishop of Nassau.

6 Arnold Pinchard, Secretary of the ECU 1920–33.

7 Francis Underhill as Bishop of Bath and Wells.

8 David ('Rosie') Rosenthal, Vicar of St Agatha, Sparkbrook, Birmingham.

9 Darwell Stone.

10 Sheila Kaye-Smith.

11 Evelyn Underhill.

12 Arthur Chandler, formerly Bishop of Bloemfontein, President of the ACC 1924–33.

13 Maurice Child, Secretary of the ACC 1924–33.

14 P. E. T. Widdrington.

15 N. P. Williams.

16 1920 Congress. The cross from St Matthew, Westminster, leading the procession of clergy to St Alban, Holborn, for the opening Mass.

17 The procession.

18 The Anglo-Catholic Congress mission van. Note the fiery cross symbol painted on the side.

19 The poster for the 1926 Manchester Anglo-Catholic Congress. Note the sketch of the cathedral and the cotton mills.

20 The last evening of the 1927 Eucharistic Congress in the Albert Hall.

21 The Bishop of Colombo entering the White City stadium for the High Mass during the 1933 Centenary Congress.

22 Evensong at the White City stadium.

23 The Requiem Mass for the Heroes of the Oxford Movement in the Albert Hall.

24 The Centenary High Mass at Hickleton Hall, the home of Lord Halifax, in 1933.

25 Lord Halifax at the High Mass, escorted by his son, Lord Irwin (left), and Sir Eric Maclagan, Director of the Victoria & Albert Museum.

practical idea . . . I don't know that any of them want it, and most heartily shrink from it, but they are certainly thinking about it.'⁹

The identity of the Church of England had been challenged by the state. The Revised Prayer Book (RPB) may not have been acceptable to many Evangelicals and Anglo-Catholics, but it had attempted to accommodate developments in liturgy and pastoral practice in the previous fifty or more years. There arose a widespread demand that the Church should use the RPB and ignore Parliament's decision. Reluctantly the bishops came to that view, and in 1929 they issued a statement saying that they would allow its services to be used, that each diocesan bishop would exercise his discretion to see that practices inconsistent with the BCP and the RPB would cease, and that the use of the RPB would be conditional upon the goodwill of the PCC or interested parties in the case of the occasional offices. Shortly afterwards the Central Council of Catholic Societies, in a defiant mood, also issued a statement affirming their belief in the real presence and the eucharistic sacrifice and the rightness of adoring Christ in the reserved sacrament. Although signed by over 2,000 priests, Kenneth Ingram was being realistic when he wrote, 'It would have been as impossible in the Church Assembly to plead for services of adoration as to expect Mussolini to allow free speech in Italy.'¹⁰

It was realized that the Assembly needed further powers to be able to decide, without Parliamentary approval, matters which concerned the spiritual life of the Church, particularly its forms of worship. This, it was pointed out (and what Buchan had said in the Commons debate), was what the established Church of Scotland enjoyed. Cecil proposed drawing up a new measure to transfer authority for deciding doctrinal and liturgical matters from Parliament to Convocation and the King in council, but it was not taken up. It was not until 1964–65 that this freedom was secured by the passage through the Assembly and Parliament of the Prayer Book (Alternative and other Services Measure), thus opening the way for the *Series 1, 2 and 3*, the *Alternative Services Book* in 1980, and *Common Worship* in 2000.

The attempt to revise the Prayer Book exposed yet another division among Catholics. A minority were glad the measure had been rejected as it left them where they had been before – free to continue using the 1662 rite with Roman embellishments, and free to reserve the sacrament, with or without corporate devotions before it. Probably a larger number regretted the loss of what they saw as an opportunity to authorize an alternative Communion service which might in time lead to further developments towards a modern Catholic rite. But for a few the whole episode confirmed their suspicion that the Church of England had never been truly Catholic. It had been established and was ultimately controlled by Parliament. That led them to take the final step of submitting to Rome, as we shall see in a later chapter.

Those who organized the third Anglo-Catholic Congress were well aware of these tensions, and they planned its programme to try and help those divided on these issues to learn from one another.

13

The Eucharistic Congress 1927

The third Congress – often referred to as 'the Eucharistic Congress' – began on Sunday, 3 July, with masses and special preachers in over ninety churches in the London area. The sessions opened in the Albert Hall on the following Monday afternoon. The Church Assembly was meeting the same week to vote on whether or not to submit the Revised Prayer Book to Parliament. Presumably the Congress executive knew this when they fixed the dates, unless it happened the Hall was only available that week. Whatever the reason, those attending had a heightened awareness that a decision would be made by the Assembly by the time the Congress was over.

The organizers were particularly concerned lest divisions among Catholics on the revision should spoil the spirit of previous Congresses. They feared the press would headline news of any controversy. It was Stone who proposed that speakers should be asked not to comment on, or express their opinion about, the Revised Prayer Book in the months leading up to and during the Congress. Rather, he suggested, they should give their audiences a theological and pastoral overview of the Eucharist to help them to understand what lay behind the proposals. Since Stone himself was one of the leading opponents of the revision, it was a magnanimous gesture on his part. His suggestion was accepted, much to the disgust of opponents of the revision like Dom Anselm Hughes, who showed no restraint in saying what he thought about the proposals when speaking at a local Congress in Kettering earlier that year (he said they 'smelt of sulphur'). Afterwards he found invitations to speak at other Congress events withdrawn.

The Albert Hall was nearly full that Monday afternoon. On the platform were members of the Congress executive, rows of religious in their habits, and twenty overseas bishops. The only English bishop present was Frere. In his opening remarks Bishop Roscow Shedden of Nassau, the Congress president, said: 'If there are any here who wish to hear the Revised Prayer Book discussed, it is no use whatever coming to the Albert Hall. They must go to Westminster.' The time for talking was over; their task was to pray and 'to storm the heights of Heaven for the guidance of the Holy Spirit'. He went on to say he felt unworthy to follow in Bishop Frank Weston's place as president, and invited the audience to stand for a minute's silence in memory of their hero. Then he asked them to remember that the Church Assembly was meeting, adding a tribute to the Archbishop of Canterbury: 'I have had some experience of the anxieties of piloting a vessel through shoal water in a literal sense. The piloting of such an awkward vessel as the Church of England can have hardly imposed a heavier burden of anxiety and responsibility on any archbishop than at the present time.'[1] Finally he announced that other Congress meetings were being held that week in towns and cities across the country as well as in places as far away as Paris, Colombo, Toyko and Ottawa.

The addresses on the first two days, Monday and Tuesday, discussed the background of the Eucharist. Speakers included N. P. Williams, who spoke about the Christian doctrine of man, and B. E. Butler, a tutor of Keble College, on sacraments in other religions. Butler was regarded as one of the ablest scholars among the recently ordained clergy. We shall meet him again in a later chapter.

Evelyn Underhill was briefed to speak on 'Sacraments and Mysticism' in order to refute a current idea that mysticism was a more spiritual way of entering into the presence of God than sharing in the liturgical worship. Those attracted to this view argued that mysticism was the proper form of Christian devotion in an age of advancing education and science. Church rituals were childish things which could now be put away. Evelyn Underhill was an obvious choice for such a task. She was well known for her book, *Mysticism* (1911), and other publications. Living with her barrister husband in Holland Park, she was a friend of Baron von Hugel and through him had learned to appreciate the importance of the Church and the sacraments in the Christian life. In her younger days she had wondered whether to become a Roman Catholic, but eventually settled in the Catholic tradition of the Church of England. She occupied herself with lecturing, leading retreats, writing, and visiting poor families in Notting Hill. She was made a Fellow of King's College, London, in the same year as the Congress.

In her talk she said the mystics' experiences of God's presence did not replace their need for sacramental grace but rather enhanced it. With illustrations from authors about whom she was a recognized authority, she told how much the Eucharist had been central to their lives – Catherine of Siena rejoicing at her attendance at mass, Catherine of Genoa being given permission to receive Communion every day (a rare privilege at that time), Thomas Aquinas writing some of the Church's greatest eucharistic hymns, and Ruysbroeck expressing a passionate dependence on the sacrament. Since we are physical as well as spiritual beings, she went on, we need outward and visible means of grace as well as an inward awareness of God. Quoting John 6.21 (Thou gavest them bread from heaven to eat), she commented, 'If that gift is to be made to all faithful and loving souls, and not just to persons of spiritual genius, then it must be made in ways which are suitable to a creature who is still immersed in physical life, who is living the life of the senses as well as the life of the Spirit, and is unable to draw too sharp a line between them. It must come, then, by visible signs and deeds, and not by spiritual intimations alone.'[2]

On other days speakers covered topics such as the nature of sacrifice in other religions (E. O. James) and in the Old Testament (H. L. Goudge), on Calvary (K. E. Kirk) and in the Eucharist (E. G. Selwyn). The doctrine of the real presence was expounded by Stone and A. E. Taylor. But the two most important contributions in view of later developments were those by Edwyn Hoskyns and A. E. J. Rawlinson.

Hoskyns and Rawlinson were two of a number of theologians who, while not being paid-up members of any Catholic organization, gave their support to the Congress movement and took part in its meetings. They were Liberal Catholics in the sense that they accepted the findings of contemporary biblical scholarship, but they argued that it must be understood as a development of Catholic tradition, not as a radical departure from it. Both contributed to *Essays Catholic and Critical* and to the booklets issued with the 1923 Congress.

Hoskyns, son of a former Bishop of Southwell (also an Edwyn), was Fellow and Dean of Corpus Christi College, Cambridge. His *Riddle of the New Testament* (1931), which he co-authored with one of his pupils, F. N. Davey, introduced later generations of theological students to the synoptic problem. In his address he demonstrated the continuity of Catholic Christianity with the life and the teaching of Jesus Christ and the apostolic Church, and challenged those who said that what people wanted was a simple Gospel purged of Church dogmas and later accretions of sacramental and ecclesiastical traditions. The New Testament and the Catholic Faith, he said, are not two different systems but are intimately related to each other; and criticisms that Anglo-Catholics are unscriptural are totally unjustified.

Hoskyns then went on to show how the Eucharist developed from the worship of the New Testament Church. We cannot expect to find, he said, a fully developed liturgy in the earliest centuries (some Anglican liturgists had dreamed of finding a rite almost contemporary with the first apostles), but, 'we ought to be able to discover in the earliest Christian writings signs of an adjustment of worship so that the Gospel may be thereby expressed in concrete form'.[3] He traced the development of the Eucharist from the references in Paul, the accounts of the Last Supper, and the 'flesh and blood' discourses in John. There is little evidence of what pre-Pauline apostolic worship in Jerusalem was like, he went on, since Luke did not explain what he meant by 'the breaking of bread'. 'But whatever conclusion we may tentatively accept as to the significance of St Luke's language, it seems abundantly clear that the line St Paul – St John – Catholic worship is one line, and that it finds its adequate explanation and origin only in our Lord's death and in his words and actions at the Last Supper taken together as forming one sacrificial act.'[4]

Catholics can be assured, therefore, that their religion is biblically based and that their opponents have missed the point of Catholicism, not because of any inherent weakness in the Catholic system, but because of their own lack of objective judgement. He concluded, 'Our controversy with the Bishop of Birmingham and with those he represents does not concern primarily the Eucharist, but the Gospel . . . In this particular controversy it must be stated, and stated quite clearly, that we Catholics have the New Testament wholly on our side.'[5]

Rawlinson spoke on 'The Holy Spirit and the Eucharist'. He summarized the New Testament teaching of the relationship between Christ and the Spirit, and the role of the Spirit in the Church and in the believer, and then expounded Paul's teaching on the gifts of the Spirit by drawing on a recently published book by a Presbyterian scholar, C. A. Scott Anderson, *Christianity According to St. Paul*. There is some evidence, he said, that in the post-apostolic Church charismatics such as prophets may have presided at the Eucharist, but the Spirit eventually guided the Church to restrict this office to the ordained ministry. 'The "goodly fellowship of the prophets" has never wholly died out in the Church, and men prophetically inspired to be the bearers of a religious message for their brethren have been in some cases clergy, and in some cases laymen. With an Old Testament writer we may say, "Would God that all the Lord's people were prophets."'[6]

Centuries after Paul, he continued, theologians came to distinguish between the institutional and the charismatic nature of the Church. Many saw these two natures as completely separate, but this was a grave error. He explained why by an illustration from the ordained ministry. 'According to the Catholic or "institutional" conception of the ministry, the purely personal "gifts" of the minister are in strictness irrelevant. The celebrant acts, not in virtue of them, but in virtue of his office. At the same time, it must be claimed that his office itself is essentially "charismatic", that the ministry is the gift of God to his Church, and that it is in the power of the Spirit that the ordained minister is enabled to act.'[7]

The same is true of the individual Christian, he went on. In the New Testament Christ and the Spirit have their distinctive roles in the work of salvation, yet they are essentially united. 'The Spirit . . . must . . . be regarded as actualizing and making real in the hearts of believers and in the fellowship of the Christian Society the presence of Christ, who, except in so far as he is operative in the Church through the Spirit, is to be thought of (to use the language of metaphor and symbol) as being "seated at the right hand of God" . . . We hold communion with Christ; we are inspired by the Spirit. It is through the operation of the Spirit that we are enabled to know Christ or to call Jesus Lord; but the Lord and the Spirit are quite distinct. There is, I think, a real and actual basis in experience (quite apart from the mere language of Scripture) for the kind of distinction which the mind of the Church, under the guidance of the Spirit himself, came eventually to draw more and more clearly between the Spirit and Christ, while at the same time affirming the unity of Both with the Father in the ultimate mystery of the being of God.'[8]

All worship, and especially the Eucharist, he said, is offered by the Church to the Father through Jesus Christ in the power of the Spirit. Studies comparing the role of the Spirit in the New Testament with its role in the ancient liturgies of the Church had been published by Continental scholars 'who are connected with the so-called "liturgical movement".' But he wanted to focus on the consecration of the elements in the Eucharist. He supposed that 'all schools of thought would agree that the Spirit is the Divine Agent of whatever spiritual change is effected in the significance of the Elements as a result of their consecration; if only for the reason that no one (as far as I am aware) would believe that he had genuinely received Holy Communion, if he merely attended the liturgy and proceeded (instead of going up to the altar rails to receive) to consume privately a piece of unconsecrated bread . . . I am persuaded that the best Christian theology refers instinctively to the effects of consecration (whatever precisely they are to be defined or understood) as the work of the Spirit.'[9]

It was for this reason he felt the liturgy of the Eastern Orthodox Churches, with its invocation of the Spirit, expressed this truth better than the Western rite where there had developed a belief that the moment of consecration of the bread and the wine occurred as the celebrant recited the words of institution over them at the altar. He quoted Cyril of Jerusalem's *Mystagogical Lectures* (v.7), 'We call upon God, who loves man, that he may make the bread to be the Body of Christ and the wine the Blood of Christ: for assuredly whatsoever the Holy Spirit has touched is sanctified and changed.'[10] This led him to make a criticism of the 1662 rite: 'I have long been accustomed to think, rightly or wrongly, that the liturgy contained in our present English Prayer Book (more particularly if we take into account the extraordinary jejune provision which it makes for a supplementary consecration to be effected by means of a bare recital of our Lord's words of institution) is perhaps more immediately open to magical misunderstandings than any other liturgy which is known to me ... I believe that the Eastern tradition is theologically right in laying emphasis upon the effectual power of the Holy Spirit, and that the structure of the new proposed consecratory prayer ... in the Deposited Book ... is ... a notable advance upon anything which the Church of England has possessed hitherto.'[11] It would also, he added, bring the rite into line with those of Anglicans in Scotland, the USA and South Africa.

Taken together, Hoskyns' and Rawlinson's sessions reflect developments in the doctrine of the Church and the Eucharist which emerged in the following decades. Hoskyns wanted his listeners not to look for scriptural proof texts to justify Catholic teaching and practice. Rather, they should appreciate how, through the results of biblical criticism, it is possible to detect and interpret the roots of that teaching and practice in the Scriptures themselves. Hoskyns was to return to this theme in his talk on the apostolic ministry at the next Congress. Rawlinson complemented Hoskyns by expounding the biblical revelation of the role of the Spirit in the life of the Church and of the believer, and then applying it to the eucharistic prayer. He showed he supported Frere and those like him who wanted that prayer to include an epiclesis. There were complaints by those who disagreed with Rawlinson's views that he had ignored Roscoe's request to avoid any mention of the Prayer Book revision. But others defended him saying that, given the title of his talk, he could hardly have avoided it. He was the first speaker in the London Congresses to refer to the continental liturgical movement.

These two papers were close to the hearts as well as the minds of many of the hearers because the Eucharist was one of the great cornerstones of the faith. The daily mass was the centre of the spiritual life of many priests in Catholic churches. They saw it as their duty and privilege to offer the Holy Sacrifice for the parish every day of the week. This was particularly true for those working in the slums and the dreary inner-city suburbs of London and elsewhere. They testified that it was this daily offering which sustained them in their demanding ministries. C. Hutchinson represented such priests when he gave a talk on what a daily mass meant to him as vicar of St John's, Lambeth. His description evokes the memories of priests who have had (and some still have) experiences of standing at the altar in a chilly church on a dark winter's morning:

> In the Mass is set forth . . . the consecration of human pain and discipline . . . The priest standing at the altar has behind him the darkness, the gloom, the failure, and the fetters of our poor humanity. Before him stretches the light and splendour of the Kingdom. At that meeting-place of human faith and hope and aspiration, with the downwards sweep of God's wondrous love and power, a marvellous liberation comes to the Christian soul – the light floods over into the darkened, confused ways of men, and we feel within us the fruits of his redemption. 'Who maketh us afraid?' 'I can do all things through Christ which strengtheneth me.'[12]

For clergy such as Hutchinson the doctrine of the real presence was not a theological debating matter; it was the sacramental assurance that the Lord was with them in conditions they would only have accepted in the faith that he had called them there. He was highly regarded for his ministry in the dismal streets round Waterloo Station, and among the boys who lived there. At other times Hutchinson celebrated the mass in pleasanter surroundings:

> [The mass] is highest, noblest, and most satisfying expressions of joy and thankfulness. What other service could I give my boys at camp – the strong sun over us, and the sea sounding in our ears as we come streaming into the little chapel that is as beautiful as we can make it? What else expresses so gloriously the gaiety and the splendour of that experience? Although attendance is quite voluntary, the altars are thronged day by day with sunburnt, bare-legged boys.[13]

In Chesterfield G. Clayton had caused a local rumpus when he substituted a sung mass for morning prayer on the first Sunday after his induction to the parish church. He was one of those robust priests who were prepared to battle for what they believed was right. Speaking at the Congress he said morning prayer was for the conventional church-goer whereas those who came to mass are made aware that it was the real thing. Mass is the corporate offering of the holy sacrifice by the parish, and everything about it – words, music, ceremonial – should express that offering in ways that enable everyone to participate. He noted, 'In some places it is practicable and desirable that all the worshippers should come together in a great service of Corporate Communion, held at an hour when the observance of the rule of fasting Communion is reasonably possible.'[14] He had noticed that that a non-communicating high mass was being replaced by a sung mass with Communion in a small but growing number of churches.

But he warned against forgetting what the mass meant to those who take part in it. 'For the Church to offer the eucharistic sacrifice when the mark of sacrifice is not on her life is formalism indeed. And for us to go to mass and outwardly to take our part in the sacrifice, while at the same time we are living lives of selfishness and self-indulgence, is equally without value. Let us never forget that the mass must be for us the outward expression of an inward reality.'[15] The Reformers, he said, had laid great stress on the close association of the ministry of the word with the ministry of the sacrament. In that they were clearly right. The sermon at the Eucharist is the only Christian teaching many of those present ever hear: 'The men and women, the boys and girls who worship in our churches have to meet all kinds of opposition outside our churches. No opportunity should be missed of teaching them and strengthening them in the faith.'[16]

The *Church Times'* journalist approved of Clayton. It is salutary, he wrote, for London Catholics to hear 'one of those many provincial priests, whose work justifies the reflection, "What do they know of Anglo-Catholicism who only London know?"'[17] Clayton later became Archbishop of Cape Town.

The success of the provincial Congresses led the organizers to plan for parties from different parts of the country to come to London for a day's session. Wednesday of the Congress week was designated 'the provincial day' and an appropriate programme drawn up for it.

Special trains were booked from South Wales, Birmingham, Liverpool and Sheffield. The Liverpool train left at midnight on Tuesday, 5 July, and arrived at Euston early in the morning. The Liverpudlians were taken to a Lyons Corner House for breakfast and then to St Alban, Holborn, for high mass at 8.30 a.m. Afterwards they were driven round London to see places of interest, arriving at the Albert Hall for the 11.00 a.m. meeting. In the afternoon they attended a garden party in Kensington Palace Gardens organized by the Ladies' Auxiliary, and returned to the Hall at 5.00 p.m. for a rally addressed by Fr Vernon. They then went to the evening meeting at 7.30. They had supper at Lyons before joining the train, arriving back in Liverpool at midnight. The total cost for each visitor was 27s. 6d (about £50 today).

Those from Kettering were collected in a 'covered charabanc' from the villages of Kingston and Thrapston and taken to the station. There, with a large contingent from the town churches, they caught a special train at 6.30 a.m. Breakfast was served during the journey to St Pancras. They went to high mass at St Augustine, Queen's Gate, and then joined in the rest of the day's programme. Supper was served on the train during the return journey. The cost for Kettering visitors was £1.00 (£40 today).[18]

The speaker at the Wednesday morning session was Fr Hughson of the Order of the Holy Cross in the USA – a novel opportunity for the visitors to hear an American priest. He spoke on the real presence of Christ in the Eucharist, saying that ordinary folk should not be troubled by theories such as transubstantiation. 'The fact of the Real Presence', he assured them, 'does not depend on any theory. He is there, all that He is and all that He has. Wherever God is, He is to be adored. God dwells in the Blessed Sacrament. Therefore in that Sacrament He is to be worshipped, and this worship is not to be hedged about with cautions and inhibitions.' The *Church Times* journalist, perhaps feeling the strain of taking notes of the academic discourses of the previous day, warmed to this down-to-earth approach: 'Fr Hughson's was the voice of the pastor of souls and not of the professor, and his simple contribution to the Congress seemed to me of great value and charm.'[19]

In the afternoon there was a meeting of the Foreign Missions Association of the Congress. The Bishop of London appeared on the platform and delighted those from dioceses with less sympathetic bishops by addressing them as 'fellow Anglo-Catholics.' He knew how to handle an audience. He caused a murmur of amusement by saying he had slipped away from the Church Assembly hoping the Archbishop of Canterbury would not notice his absence, and then went on to describe a three-month round-the-world tour of Anglo-Catholic dioceses he had recently made.

In Japan he had been met off the boat by Bishop Simpson of Kobe, who was sitting on the platform beside him. His party had travelled by train from Tokyo to the bishop's diocese, and at every station where the train stopped there had been groups of Japanese Christians waiting on the platform to greet them with flags by day and lanterns by night. In Korea (spelt 'Corea' at this time) he found Bishop Trollope, also sitting beside him, working closely with the Roman Catholic bishop and with the Presbyterians. His visit to Ceylon (Sri Lanka) had been a happy occasion because there he had met Bishop Garnier whom he had known as a student. He had preached and celebrated the Eucharist during Holy Week and Easter to crowded congregations and been deeply moved to see British, Tamils and Singhalese all kneeling together at the communion rail. He added that Mackay and the congregation at All Saints, Margaret Street, had presented him with a portable altar before he left and he had used it on many occasions, on board ship as well as on land. When he left, the audience gave him a standing ovation. 'I have never heard the Bishop speak better,' commented the reporter. 'He was obviously moved by the affection with which he was greeted, and no man perhaps ever loved being loved more than he.'[20] The reporter was evidently not restrained from making such a remark about the bishop by the thought that the bishop himself might be reading it in a week's time.

Attendances at the morning and evening sessions were four thousand, but for the 5 o'clock meeting, addressed by Fr Vernon, the Hall was packed to capacity. There is no record of his talk – on such occasions he spoke spontaneously – but the *Church Times* commented:

> It is said that Fr Vernon attracts women more than men, and there were, of course, a large proportion of women in the great audience; but the proportion of men was, I thought, much above the average congregational percentage . . . I find it very hard to explain to myself Fr Vernon's extraordinary power. He is, of course, aboundingly sincere; but sincerity alone will not draw the multitude. He speaks well, but he is certainly not eloquent in the common sense of the term. Sometimes, but rarely, and then as if by accident, he stumbles on an effective phrase or a fine sentence. But simplicity is the note of his teaching, and it is backed by a magnetic personality whose power is sufficiently obvious even if its explanation is hard to discover.

The evening meeting was billed as 'a Social' – another innovation at this Congress. It may have been G. D. Rosenthal's idea. As chairman of the Midland Anglo-Catholic Congress committee he had organized a similar event during the Birmingham Congress of 1922. He argued Catholics should not forget the Eucharist had a horizontal dimension as well as a vertical one: congregations came together to strengthen their unity with one another as well as their devotion to God. First there were two short talks. Rosenthal spoke on unity in a congregation, and Slesser on the duty of Christians to work through the State's constitution as much as possible to fulfil God's purposes in society. Then those present filled the central arena, which had been cleared of chairs, and chatted while a small orchestra played on the stage.

Earlier that day Slesser had chaired a lunchtime Congress meeting in the Cannon Street Hotel for City workers. Elderly gentlemen in frock cloaks, and office clerks in dark suits wearing blue and white Congress badges streamed into the hotel to listen to short addresses by Rosenthal and Slesser. The latter said that when the Revised Prayer Book was sent to the House of Commons for the second time, he would vote against accepting it as he thought it imposed intolerable restrictions on parish priests for reserving the Blessed Sacrament.

For the rest of the week there were shorter talks on a variety of pastoral topics, including the ministry of the priest, preparation for Communion, confession and fasting. Fr Thornton defended the practice of extra-liturgical devotions before the reserved sacrament. But Mgr Germanos, the Metropolitan of Thyatira and the representative in England of the Ecumenical Patriarch, in a short speech of gratitude for the invitation to attend the Congress, pointed out that, although the Orthodox pay due honour to the Bread and the Wine, they have no tradition of services of eucharistic adoration. He recognized that developments in the West which the East had not experienced may have led to growth of the practice, but he gently hinted that the Congress should follow the principle of Vincent of Lerins, '*id teneamus quod semper, quod ubique, quo dab omnibus creditor est*', implying that eucharistic adoration was not in the ancient traditions of the Church.

A joint paper on eucharistic ceremonies comparing Sarum (usually called 'English') and Western Uses, written jointly was presented on the last Friday of the Congress by Maurice Child and Mr Stephen Gaselee, a Foreign Office official who was a member of the Alcuin Club. The Club was formed in 1897 to promote a restoration of the provisions of the Ornaments rubric in the First Prayer Book of Edward VI (1549), together with the vestments and ceremonies of the Sarum liturgy, used throughout much of England in the pre-Reformation era. It sponsored lectures, pamphlets and books on the subject, and guides on how to order the ceremonies.

Alcuin Club supporters argued that Sarum vestments and ceremonial were more pleasing artistically than those of the Western Use as they fitted in with the Gothic architecture of many church buildings. Western supporters, on the other hand, claimed contemporary Roman Catholic practices were more practical and orderly. Debates on the relative merits of the two Uses could become heated, especially among theological students, curates, sacristans and servers. To English users, those who followed Rome were 'Romanizers' or 'spikes'; to Western users, the other side stood for a 'British Museum religion' because much Alcuin Club material was based on research into medieval archives.

Gaselee began by disclaiming any intention of setting one Use up against the other. He and Child were not intending 'to make a gladiatorial show for your amusement'. They both hoped the advent of the Revised Prayer Book would provide opportunities for drawing together what was valuable in both Uses.

He then described the differences between the two Uses in the appearances of the chancel, assuming that many in the audience were unclear about this (which was quite likely, as in some parishes bits of one tradition were mixed with the other, to the disgust of liturgical purists). Western Use churches had an altar standing high up at the east end, with six candles and a crucifix on it and probably a painted or carved reredos behind it. In some a tabernacle for the reserved sacrament replaced the crucifix in the centre of the altar. In English Use churches the altar was long and low, with two candles and a cross or crucifix in the middle. The altar was flanked by curtains coming out at right angles from the east wall, supported by posts usually topped by angels holding candlesticks. If the sacrament was reserved, it would be in an aumbry in the north wall of the sanctuary or in a side chapel. Flowers were sometimes placed on an English altar but never on a Western one.

The vestments of the celebrant, deacon and subdeacon at a Western high mass were different from the English. The Western celebrant's chasuble was short and hung over his chest and back rather like sandwich boards, leaving his arms free: some were cut to the shape of a violin and known as 'fiddle backs'. The deacon wore a tunicle and the subdeacon a dalmatic. The clergy wore birettas and the servers black cassocks and white cottas, sometimes adorned with lace. In contrast the English celebrant's chasuble was much fuller, falling lower and covering the arms: it was generally known as a gothic shape, being developed from medieval patterns. The celebrant was more likely to be assisted by one clergyman wearing a dalmatic or a tunicle rather than two. Other clergy and servers wore albs with coloured apparels. There were no birettas. At certain times the liturgical colour was different – noticeably the Lenten array made of unbleached material.

Those more familiar with the Western Use, said Gaselee, would notice that in the English Use a profound bow replaced a genuflection, that there was an offertory procession when the elements were brought by the deacon or a server from a side chapel to the altar, and that there was no last gospel (John 1.1–14) at the end. Another noticeable omission was no prayers of preparation said by the priest and the server at the altar step before the service.[21] With the new Prayer Book, he suggested, there would be opportunities to create ceremonial which took what was best from both traditions. He thought the offertory procession of the English Use could be introduced into Western Use churches, and the way incense was used at the offertory and the canon in Western churches could be introduced to English ones, where it was only used for the Gospel procession. He wanted to cut out much genuflecting and kissing of books and cruets in the Western Use, but he would like to see the English Use taking the ablutions immediately after the Communion like the Westerners did rather than after the blessing.[22]

'Liturgiology, if it is a live art, as we believe it to be,' he concluded, 'is not fixed for ever in an unalterable mould, but is capable of development. If we can get a large and thinking public, clerical and lay, interested in it, thinking about it, at least it is possible that in time a ceremonial will appear which will be both English and Western.'[23]

The other woman speaker at the Congress was Sheila Kaye-Smith. She delivered a short paper on 'The Eucharist and Art', which was not printed in the official report. Kaye-Smith had been a speaker at two or three provincial Congresses. She represented a growing circle of literary men and women who were drawn to the Catholic movement in the Church of England because of its creation-affirming theology and its appreciation of artistic gifts of all kinds in its worship and teaching. She said she saw the whole of nature as sacramental, and art as one of the ways in which its God-givenness might be revealed. At the last supper Christ used articles which had been created out of natural products by the art of man. The process continued in the mass. The wheat was harvested from the fields and then transformed by man's art and industry into bread. The bread was offered up to God, who receives his own gift back and then bestows it once more to us as his Body. 'Thus we have the chain of evolution – the wheat, the bread, the body or nature, art, and then the supernatural – God himself.' 'It was', said the *Church Times* chivalrously, 'a very suggestive little address charmingly delivered.'

To cope with the numbers wanting to attend, evening meetings were once again held in the Queen's Hall at which some of the papers were repeated. Copies of the texts were sent to be read at meetings in Falmouth, Truro, Edinburgh, Glasgow, Paris, Tokyo, Ottawa, Colombo and elsewhere. Reports from some of the places in Britain said attendance at these had been patchy. But they were attempts to reach out to a wider audience in the years before technology made it possible for national events in London to be transmitted to giant television screens elsewhere. The Congress executive approached the BBC with the idea of broadcasting one or more events from the Albert Hall in 1930, but without success. On Saturday 9 July masses for children were celebrated in several London churches, and the Bishop of Nassau led a pilgrimage to Canterbury. The idea of celebrating the final mass in the Albert Hall had been discussed in the committee but was abandoned when several raised objections. Instead, masses of thanksgiving for the Congress, with special preachers, were celebrated in about ninety parishes around the capital.

The Congress was judged a great success. Over 23,000 registered for it and £21,000 was raised for various Catholic causes at home and overseas. Besides the innovations – the provincial day, the social evening, the masses for children – what was striking about this Congress was the high quality of the academic contributions. Three of the speakers were Bampton lecturers (Williams, Kirk, Rawlinson), and they with other scholars were establishing the reputation of Anglo-Catholic theologians which was to last well into the rest of the century. It was during these years that books were published by them on biblical criticism, doctrinal development, liturgy and pastoral care – and, later, social and political affairs – which became standard reading for the next generation of theological students and clergy.

The academic nature of some of the contributions did not deter ordinary men and women from wanting to listen to them. Figures of attendances on the mornings and afternoons when these papers were delivered did not fall below four thousand, and were often higher – a fact noted with admiration by a visitor from the USA, who said he could not imagine that happening in his own country. By focusing on a single theme – the Eucharist – the Congress provided an overview of Anglo-Catholic liturgical thought and practice towards the end of the twenties. And by avoiding the controversy over Prayer Book revision, contributors were encouraged to look beyond what was proposed and so pointed those who heard them and those who read their papers in the published report to likely developments in the following years.

14

Reservation and the Birmingham Rebels

By the time of the first Congress Anglo-Catholics had established a bridgehead in their 'battle for the aumbries'. The practice of continuous reservation had spread in spite of opposition from bishops and objections by Evangelicals. In early discussions on the revision of the Prayer Book both Upper Houses of Canterbury and York agreed in 1911 that the sacrament could be reserved for the Communion of the sick 'on the same day and with as little delay as possible'. If Communion was not immediate, then the consecrated elements should be kept 'in such a place and after such a manner as the Ordinary shall direct, so that they may not be used for any other purposes whatsoever'. This became known as 'the draft rubric'.[1]

It soon proved difficult to persuade certain clergy to keep within the limits of this regulation. The reserved sacrament had become a focus of private and corporate devotion in their congregations, especially at the monthly office of the Confraternity of the Blessed Sacrament. Increased emphasis on regular Communion meant that for people like nurses and firemen, whose shift-work prevented them from attending mass, arrangements could be made for them to receive the sacrament from the ambry at convenient times. Priests who had encouraged people to make what devotional books called 'little visits to the Blessed Sacrament' for private prayer had no wish to discourage a practice which many valued. They feared that communicants who had grown to love devotions and benediction might be tempted to defect to local Roman Catholic churches if they were denied these services – which happened in some places. They claimed that during the war these practices became even more important for helping the anxious and the bereaved.

A few bishops turned a blind eye to those who disobeyed the draft rubric. Winnington-Ingram's experiences as head of Oxford House in east London and then as Bishop of Stepney made him reluctant to discipline those he knew were conscientious priests when he became Bishop of London. In any case, he hated confrontations of any kind. If some parishes regularly had devotions and benediction, he pretended not to know about it. Gore was incensed when he discovered this. He had played a leading part in persuading the Upper Houses of Convocation to accept the draft rubric, and he felt he had to be obedient to it himself. Consequently he disappointed Catholic clergy in his own dioceses, Birmingham and Oxford, by trying to keep them scrupulously to it. He got very angry with Winnington-Ingram for letting him down and – worse still – flouting Convocation's authority. He was passionate about law and order in the Church. Gore's chaplain said that moral indignation burned in the Bishop like a fire, and he sometimes wondered whether Gore would be consumed by it.

Not that Gore was personally opposed to private prayer before the reserved sacrament, but he doubted the theological justification and canonical legality of it in the Church of England. 'I feel the need of the B.S. openly reserved & wholly delight in it,' he confessed in a letter of 1913. 'I feel no compunction in saying my prayers to our Lord in the Blessed Sacrament. But I cannot but acknowledge the weight of the fact that the whole Church up to 1400, & the Eastern Church till the present, made or makes no such use of the sacred presence, & it tends in fact to obscure the Real Presence of Christ in His living Church. I am therefore in the attitude of one who would gladly welcome it, if authority gave it to me. But I cannot believe that one bishop can sanction so great a change, knowing that almost or quite all the rest would throw him over.'[2]

In 1915 Gore wrote to the Archbishop of Canterbury saying that, as the Bishop of London had 'surrendered' and allowed access to the reserved sacrament for prayer, he was tempted to abandon his own attempts to keep order. In the following year he discovered that some other diocesan bishops were becoming more permissive, so he decided to clarify the situation by reopening the matter in Convocation. He announced that he would be introducing a resolution reaffirming the draft rubric. When this was known, a memorial declaring they could not comply with it was signed by 1,000 clergy and presented to the Upper House before the debate on Gore's resolution took place.

The clergy's memorial was reinforced by a book called *The Reserved Sacrament* by Stone, published the very day the bishops were to debate Gore's resolution (advance copies had been sent to them weeks before).[3] In it he pointed out that in the Western Church from the late middle ages onwards practices such as devotions, exposition and benediction developed out of reverence for the Real Presence, and as the English Church was historically part of the Western Church, Anglicans were at least entitled to consider whether such practices might be spiritually profitable. They had, after all, adopted other practices from the Counter-Reformation era, such as parochial missions, retreats, and the Three Hours' Service on Good Friday. On a personal note he admitted that, while he liked to pray before the reserved sacrament privately, he was not personally attracted to corporate devotions, though he realized that others appreciated them. He suggested what was needed was episcopal permission for these devotions in parishes where they were known to be valued.

A counter-memorandum signed by 2,000 clergy and laity supporting the draft rubric was also presented to the bishops. In the end no changes were made except that the Upper House recognized an individual bishop might sanction permanent reservation in his diocese on the understanding that he acted on his own authority. The bridgehead was made a little wider.

Contention over the subject revived during the early 1920s as the progress of Prayer Book revision slowly continued, and the practice of reservation was defended at the Congresses. In 1920 G. A. Mitchell, principal of St Stephen's House, asked why it was that Protestants, who were always urging Christians should follow the guidance of the Holy Spirit, did not recognize that guidance in the development of the cultus of the Blessed Sacrament. In 1923 Carpenter-Garnier, Librarian of Pusey House, spoke of what reservation meant to communicants: 'Where the Blessed Sacrament is, there is Christ himself. He is present still . . . He is here for the purposes of redemption; to convert, to save, to transform, to feed, to uplift, to sanctify.'[4] In 1927 Mackay described a personal experience early in his ministry when he celebrated a Prayer Book Communion service in a situation where it would have been better if he could have used the reserved sacrament: 'I was called upon to offer the holy sacrifice at two o'clock in the morning in the filthy room of a man in the last stages of septic pneumonia, the floor above being a brothel, and the floor below being a brothel.' Then added, revealing his pastoral sensitivity, 'On the other hand, I should be sorry if celebrations in houses were ruled out altogether. They are greatly valued by devout bedridden people, and have often had a missionary value in a family. Some of our most beautiful memories are connected with sick-room communions.'[5]

But there were still some Catholics who were bothered by the question of the legality of reservation. They were conscious that when they had accepted an office in the Church they had made a declaration promising to use no other form of worship except that provided in the Prayer Book or ordered by lawful authority. They were also uneasy that, as Catholics, they were supposed to respect episcopal authority. How then could they justify reservation when their bishop forbad it? This was the question the Bishop W. Cecil of Exeter put to Seymour as superior general of the Confraternity of the Blessed Sacrament.

In reply, Seymour briefly outlined the development of reservation in England and, following Stone's argument, claimed that medieval canon laws governing the practice had never been rescinded during the years between the authorization of the 1549 and 1662 Prayer Books. There is some historical evidence, he said, that the sacrament was reserved for the sick during those years and afterwards, especially among the Non-Jurors. What Catholics had done was to revive a form of ministry to the sick which had largely been forgotten. Seymour then explained that when priests took the reserved sacrament to a sick person in their home, they used appropriate prayers from the Communion service and so in this way were being faithful to their declaration of assent. Furthermore, the declaration's proviso, 'except in so far as shall be ordered by lawful authority', must refer to changes made after the Prayer Book had been authorized in 1662. It could not refer to the universal practice of reservation since that had been established centuries before.

'In conclusion then, my Lord, I contend that the position of Catholic Priests in the Church of England who reserve the Blessed Sacrament for the sick and dying, not only as of "right" for those on whose behalf the thing is done, but also as a positive duty incumbent on themselves as parish priests, is entirely honourable.' He added that priests were, of course, always ready to celebrate in the sick man's house should he so desire.[6]

Frere disagreed with Stone and Seymour. When he became Bishop of Truro he wrote in the diocesan gazette that parish priests had no right to reserve the sacrament without the bishop's permission (though he was always willing to give it in his diocese). Cases before the ecclesiastical courts in the past had made that plain.[7] He believed Catholics would be wiser to press for the Church of England's law to be revised. To do that, they should emphasize the necessity and convenience of reservation in their ministry to the sick. That, he concluded, would gain a much more sympathetic hearing than appeals to medieval canons.[8]

Apart from the question of legality, some Catholics felt that devotions and benediction were 'un-Anglican'. By focusing attention on the sacramental presence of Christ in the reserved Bread and Wine, they said, didn't that imply a divine absence elsewhere? Shouldn't the faithful be encouraged to recognize the presence of Christ everywhere? And wasn't there a risk that devotion to the sacred Elements might lead an unsophisticated person into something closely akin to idolatry? Other Catholics replied that adoring the reserved sacrament was no more than an extension of the adoration given once the Bread and Wine have been consecrated on the altar at mass. When properly instructed, the faithful would learn to respond to the presence of Christ everywhere in their lives as a result of experiencing his sacramental presence in the mass and in extra-liturgical devotions. At mass they will also hear the words of Scripture and be taught how to be open to the guidance and strength of the Holy Spirit. This should counter errors such as idolatry.

In a pamphlet Stone wrote in preparation for the 1923 Congress he argued that extra-liturgical devotions, besides many other things, can help the faithful to appreciate more deeply what it means to receive Communion: 'The worship of the Lord in the reserved Sacrament aids thanksgiving for Communions already received, enriches preparation for Communions which are yet to come, strengthens the sense of the abiding presence of God throughout his universe and the lasting union of the incarnate Lord with the Christian soul, is a means to deeper penitence and firmer resolve, and a stay for constant prayer. It is one of the resting places of the Eucharistic life of the devout communicant; and it has appealed with a singular force to some who from sin are finding their way back to God.'[9]

During the weekend of 24-27 October 1925 Bishop Woods of Winchester hosted a conference at Farnham Castle on the subject of reservation, with special reference to the practice of extra-liturgical devotions. The controversy over reservation had been heightened by the publicity in the secular as well as the religious press to the events in Birmingham, where Bishop Barnes was trying to suppress it (events described a few pages further on). It may have been suggested to Woods by the Archbishop of Canterbury in the hope the group might find a common mind so as to ease the passage of the Revised Prayer Book when it was debated in the Church Assembly before being presented to Parliament.

The participants represented a wide variety of churchmanship, and included Bishops G. Warman of Chelmsford, W. O. Burrows of Chichester, A. C. Headlam of Gloucester, W. Temple of Manchester, T. B. Strong of Oxford, Frere of Truro, and two retired bishops, E. S. Talbot and Gore. Also present were a number of theologians including H. L. Goudge, O. C. Quick, E. G. Selwyn and Stone. A report of the papers read at the conference with notes on the discussions was published the following year by SPCK. The papers presented by various participants constitute an interesting survey of the historical and theological background of the subject as it was understood at the time, together with references to contemporary scholars, Roman Catholic and Protestant as well as Anglican.

There was much discussion on what was meant by the 'real presence' of Christ in the eucharistic bread and wine. Some found the word 'presence' unsatisfactory as it implied that Christ was absent elsewhere. 'Real' also could be misleading because in ordinary peoples' minds it was associated with a material presence. Goudge suggested that 'real spiritual presence' would be more accurate, provided it was recognized the adjective 'spiritual' was being used in the scriptural sense of the work of the Holy Spirit. Gore disliked using the word 'transubstantiation' as for him, and he suspected for many others, it was associated with the Roman doctrine and the cultus associated with it; he preferred to remain with the patristic understanding of the sacramental presence as a mystery which was beyond the range of human logic.

Quick pointed out that the doctrine of transubstantiation arose in the middle ages as an attempt to refute false ideas of the real presence which had spread in Western Europe. Simple people believed the bread and wine were changed into the actual Body and Blood of Christ through a miracle performed at the altar by the priest, and this had led to all sorts of gross superstitions and primitive practices. When the doctrine is properly understood, he said, it is recognized as an attempt by Thomas Aquinas and his followers to deny the carnal or material presence of Christ (the accidents of bread and wine remained) but to affirm a spiritual presence within them (the substance of Christ's body and blood). At the same time medieval clergy realized that the faith of many in their congregations was deepened by adoring the eucharistic signs in services and processions, and so the associated rituals spread throughout Western Christendom. It was because of this development that the feast of Corpus Christi was instituted in 1215.

Quick had no doubt that, while many Anglicans had receptionist views of the Eucharist, the Prayer Book teaches a real presence of Christ in the sacramental signs, and that the English Reformers would not have condemned the doctrine of transubstantiation in Article XXVIII if they had understood it properly. 'No one who believes in the living presence of Christ in His Church can seriously desire to affirm His absence from the solemn rite of the Church's fellowship with Him.'[10] He went on to say that no true Evangelical would want to deny the presence of Christ in a spiritual sense, just as no true Catholic would want to belittle the necessity of faith for a worthy communion. This, he felt, removed some of the differences between them. It was therefore only in a restricted sense that the doctrine of the real presence was a subject of controversy. For himself, Quick added, he took a neutral view of these devotions. It was not surprising that people yearned for an outward and visible reassurance of the divine presence in an age when scientific discoveries and contemporary philosophies were creating a more secular culture. Rather than attempt to suppress them, he thought there should be more teaching on the divine presence in the Scriptures and in the Christian community.

In the discussions Goudge said greater attention needed to be given to the role of the Holy Spirit in the Eucharist. To worship God in spirit and in truth does not mean to worship with our minds and spirits only; it means to worship by the power of the Holy Spirit in us. So to speak of the 'spiritual presence of Christ' is to acknowledge that Christ is present through the activity of the Holy Spirit, and that attempts to define the precise means by which he is present, using philosophical or metaphysical terms, are hardly relevant.

Stone pointed out that Catholics believed the presence of the Lord in the sacrament was affected through the recital of the appointed words by the appointed person in relation to the appointed elements of bread and wine. 'I do not mean that He is not present before the consecration. He is present throughout the rite; He himself is the true celebrant. But there is a difference. The presence at the consecration is a manifestation of a different kind from that throughout the service – a manifestation which is distinctive. A view that there is not a difference fails to account for our Lord's words, "This is my Body", "This is my Blood", and for the way in which the consecrated elements have been regarded in the Church.'[11] Recognizing that presence, Catholics were moved to reverence the bread and the wine within the Eucharist from the prayer of consecration onwards and in the sacrament when it was reserved.

Selwyn presented an account of the emergence of the cult of the Blessed Sacrament in connection with the Corpus Christi festival in 1215 and how exposition and benediction became regular features in the devotional life of the Western Church. He quoted a pamphlet by Spens: 'The devotional use of the Reserved Sacrament is not something independent of communion or dependent on some separate conception. It has its basis directly in communion. It is because the devout reception unites us to our Lord as our Sacrifice, that the Reserved Sacrament is His Body, that He is present in a special manner, and that He can there be adored as being present.'[12]

Selwyn admitted there was a risk that in the popular mind there might be a tendency to locate Christ solely in the sacrament signs, but he argued the way to correct that was not to underplay the sacramental presence but to teach the truth about the mystical presence of Christ in his Church. In his discussions with clergy in deanery and diocesan meetings, many had told him that devotion to the reserved sacrament was one of the best ways of encouraging people to pray.

It was left to the only layman present to remind the conference of developments outside England. Mr F. C. Eeles, Dearmer's close friend, who was secretary of the newly founded Council for the Care of Churches and an expert on church architecture, spoke as a Scottish Episcopalian. He pointed out that reservation in his Church had been free of any kind of extra-liturgical devotion, and that the practice went back to the penal laws of the eighteenth century in Scotland when the pastoral work of the Church was severely restricted by the Presbyterian establishment. Reservation for the communion of the sick and housebound had been practised in many places, and he had met old communicants who spoke of 'the altar coming to them'.[13]

Summing up the discussions in the introduction he wrote for the published report, Woods said his intention in organizing the conference had been to give those of different theological views an opportunity to listen to one another and to correct misunderstandings. He trusted the publication of the papers would do something to remove the bitterness which the controversy had roused. 'I hope we have heard the last of such phrases as "magic" and "fetish" and "idolatry",' he said. He also hoped readers would admit 'that the great Church of the West has never, in her devotions at least, been lacking in adventurous experiment', and be prepared 'if there be any virtue and if there be any praise' to 'take account of these things'. He concluded by saying that in his opinion 'we shall never reach any definite issue in these high matters until the doctrine of the Holy Spirit has been far more deeply investigated, and especially in our own brand of the Catholic Church. For primarily through the Holy Spirit the Lord's presence is mediated, and only through His influence can we hope to find that wisdom, that freedom from prejudice, that adventurous faith and that mutual forbearance without which our quest must be in vain.'[14] What Woods wrote indicated how much he, as an Evangelical, had come to appreciate Catholic teaching and practice since he became associated with the Congresses.

One reason for organizing the Farnham conference was that for several years there had been a serious dispute between Bishop E. W. Barnes and Catholics in Birmingham which intermittently attracted attention in the national as well as the church press. It was a constant source of frustration for other bishops and those involved in it. Barnes' side of the story is recounted by his son, John Barnes, in *Ahead of His Time* (1979) and the Catholics' side by G. D. Rosenthal and F. G. Belton in *The So-Called Rebels* (1930). Reading these two books is like listening to the prosecuting and defending counsels in a court case. John Barnes was naturally anxious to defend his father's reputation; Rosenthal and Belton had good reasons to feel they were unjustly treated by their bishop. As in many court cases, it is not always easy to unravel what really happened. John Barnes, for example, claims that his father met his opponents to discuss matters with them personally, whereas Rosenthal complained that in spite of several requests the bishop refused to meet him.

The situation arose because during the first brief Labour government of 1924 Ramsey MacDonald, the prime minister, nominated Barnes for the see of Birmingham, evidently regarding him as an ideal cleric for a scientific age. Barnes had been a brilliant mathematician at Cambridge, and he continued to teach there after he went to the Temple as Master in 1915. A former atheist, he had been converted whilst a student and later offered himself for ordination. As a don he was not required to undertake theological training. This may have been a factor in his seemingly total inability to appreciate the other side of the controversy he created. Although a shy man, he could be arrogant and inflexible, and he was fiercely antagonistic to all forms of sacramentalism. He conceived it his personal mission to bring the Church's teaching up to date with his own nineteenth-century scientific outlook. Before his appointment he had made a name for himself as a follower of Darwin, and in the pulpit and in his writings he could rarely resist the temptation to refer to natural selection and the origins of the human race. When he was installed in his cathedral a man standing outside denounced him, shouting, 'This man says we come from apes!' And as Barnes fulfilled his preaching engagements round his diocese, congregations got used to hearing what they called his 'gorilla sermons'.

He was an ardent pacifist; advocated remarriage after divorce and supported the campaign for birth control; flirted with the idea of sterilizing the mentally disabled, and espoused a paternalistic kind of socialism. Brought up in Birmingham, he acted as if the city was his fiefdom (though he was not the only English diocesan who did that!). He had never worked in a parish, and he seemed to regard a bishop's job as being akin to that of a professor. He only kept residence in the diocese during university terms as he had done in his other posts. Yet in personal contacts he was a kindly soul and well liked among the business and working people of Birmingham. They regarded him as their knight in shining Protestant armour, who was nobly defending the diocese from the encroachments of Roman Catholicism within the Church of England.

To some extent, his attitude towards Anglo-Catholics was acerbated by the attacks made on him when his appointment was announced. Sidney

Dark, who had welcomed the arrival of a Labour government in a *Church Times* editorial, felt sufficiently incensed about Barnes' appointment to write a personal letter of protest to the prime minister. Catholics in the Birmingham diocese were even more alarmed. Their previous bishop, H. R. Wakefield, had been relaxed about the spread of Catholic practices. He presided over the Anglo-Catholic Congress in Birmingham in 1922, and when he received complaints about people expressing devotion to the reserved sacrament, he replied that 'not even locked chapels and brick walls would prevent people showing their reverence and saying their prayers'.[15]

One of the most outstanding Catholic priests in Birmingham at the time was G. D. Rosenthal, known to his friends as 'Rosie'. His father, also a priest, belonged to an old Jewish family and was converted to Christianity as a young man. Rosie was trained at Keble College and Ely and ordained by Gore, who thought him 'not inclined to moderation'. He served as a curate in two Catholic strongholds, St Alban's and St Gregory's, during which time he married the daughter of a local doctor. He was appointed vicar of St Agatha, Sparkbrook, in 1918. He soon acquired a reputation as a speaker, writer and organizer, and became a prominent leader in the Congress movement in the Midlands and nationally. He was fortunate to have a curate who did much of the parochial work during his many absences on Congress business.

When news of Barnes' appointment was announced, Rosenthal wrote in his parish magazine: 'We must pray for our bishop, and give him a hearty welcome when he comes, and do everything we can to make his path as smooth as possible.' Barnes evidently felt welcomed by all parties, for in his installation sermon he said, 'It is perhaps natural that Liberal Evangelicals should have sent friendly greetings. But Anglo-Catholics have been generous in offering affectionate loyalty.' Unfortunately he then went on to give a warning that the war had made people spiritually rootless and vulnerable to all kinds of 'less worthy forms of religion'. As an example he spoke of 'a pagan sacramentalism which had entered into the Latin Catholicism, and pretended that they could create the Bread of Salvation by some magic of ritual and formula'.[16]

In spite of this Rosenthal, as chairman of the local branch of the Anglo-Catholic Congress, decided to invite the new bishop to a service of thanksgiving for the Catholic revival in Birmingham which had been organized in previous years. In his letter he pointed out to Barnes that the Bishop's presence would be welcomed as a sign of unity in the diocese. A fortnight passed without any reply, and on the day before the service a copy of a long letter from the Bishop to Rosenthal appeared in the *Birmingham*

Gazette. Rosenthal read it in that paper before the letter itself arrived at the vicarage by post.

The letter began with a note of appreciation for the social concern of the Catholic movement, but then Barnes went on to criticize certain Catholic beliefs by quotations from two contemporary theologians. The first was from a recent visitation charge by Bishop Headlam of Gloucester:

> The doctrine of the Apostolic Succession is taught in a mechanical way. Grace is said to have come down from the Apostles by a golden channel of the laying on of hands. And it is implied that, except in that way, the gift of the Holy Spirit is not given ... We are told that the priest has the power of making the body and blood of Christ. Now all language like this is most harmful. It is bad theology. It suggests a mechanical idea of Sacrament and Divine grace. It puts stumbling-blocks in the way of many people. It is saying what the majority of people can't believe, and won't believe, and ought not to believe.

The second quotation was from V. Storr, an Evangelical scholar: 'As thinking people, we cannot accept the theology which underlies the practice of Reservation. Reservation was not heard of until the Roman doctrine of Transubstantiation was propounded ... The practice ... tends to foster superstition. Why stop at the adoration of the reserved Sacrament? Why not renew the practice of earlier days and carry it with you as a charm against sickness? We are told it is a help to devotion. I do not deny that it may be for some: but the help is gained at the expense of truth ... A prayer in a barn is as valuable and as potent with God as a prayer before a tabernacle.'[17]

Barnes concluded by saying he hoped Catholics would abandon 'illegalities and false doctrine' and unite with all Anglicans 'for that combined witness for Christ, which, as a Church, we ought to be able to give'. He added he was giving a copy of the letter to the press.

Barnes seems not to have realized that this was an unbelievably insensitive way of handling the situation. It could be that the letter to Rosenthal was delayed in the post, but even so the bishop's action in sending a copy to the press suggests he was more concerned to inform the public where he stood than to build up a working relationship with the Catholic clergy under him. Rosenthal wrote a reply, also sending a copy to the same paper, denying that Catholic teaching was erroneous and practices superstitious.

News of the correspondence reached the national newspapers. Reactions were divided. The Protestant papers regarded Rosenthal's invitation as a provocative attack upon his diocesan. The *Church of England Newspaper* called it the result of a worked-up agitation of a group of Catholics and congratulated Barnes on his learned and charitable response. This opinion was picked up by John Barnes who thought Rosenthal's invitation was a declaration of war: 'They cannot have expected him to attend [the service] and must have been looking for a field on which to do battle.'[18] That was unfair. Catholics had been encouraged to invite their bishops to local congresses and other services and many had attended. Since in his installation sermon Barnes had said he wanted to promote unity, Rosenthal was trying to show that the Catholics in the diocese welcomed this.

John Barnes further maintained that his father avoided giving the impression he was opposed to reservation, although he was against the practice, because he knew the proposed Prayer Book intended to allow it under stringent conditions. If that was so, the distinction was lost on Rosenthal and his committee. They naturally assumed the Bishop was trying to banish reservation and, as in their opinion he was acting beyond the bounds of his episcopal authority, they felt they had to defend themselves. Correspondence in the secular and church press became increasingly bitter. But Rosenthal was still anxious to seek reconciliation. In what he hoped was a Christmas spirit, he wrote to Barnes and sent a copy of his letter to the *Times*, which published it on 22 December 1924:

> The difficulties of the situation . . . can be surmounted only by mutual knowledge and goodwill. May I once more urge that if the bishop would meet us, and talk over the whole position in a friendly way, he would find us neither unreasonable nor unsympathetic? Such a meeting must come sooner or later if an end is to be put to a situation which all who care for the welfare of the Church in Birmingham must unfeignedly deplore.

The friendly gesture was not followed up. Instead the Bishop adopted a policy of asking new incumbents to promise they would not continue to reserve the sacrament or initiate extra-liturgical devotions before he instituted them. The first occasion was in 1925 over the appointment of a priest to St Gregory, Small Heath. Barnes met the priest concerned, C. A. Brown, and sought these assurances, but Brown refused to give them. A law suit was threatened to compel the Bishop to institute him so Barnes, unwilling to have the matter brought to court, went through the ceremony in his private chapel. Afterwards he wrote in his diocesan magazine:

> The service of 'devotions' is illegal, and will continue to be illegal when the Prayer Book is revised. It is based on erroneous doctrine. As Bishop,

I have promised to drive away erroneous and strange doctrines; it is my duty to establish law and order in the diocese. I must therefore ask that illegal services such as Benediction, Exposition, Devotions, Processions of the Host, etc., shall cease; and that no consecrated bread and wine shall be kept in receptacles placed in those parts of our churches to which the public are admitted.'[19]

Following this, 166 out of about 260 priests in the diocese signed a declaration of loyalty to the Bishop.

A similar case occurred later in the year when the living of St Mark, Washwood Heath, became vacant and the Bishop demanded that the tabernacle on the high altar of the church be removed and reservation discontinued. Other controversies occurred over appointments to All Saints, Small Heath, and the Church of the Ascension, Stirchley, in 1929. At Stirchley Barnes had ordered the removal of the tabernacle, a statue of Our Lady, and the holy water stoups. That brought a protest from his chancellor, Mr Hansell, who pointed out that matters of faculty should go through him. (Hansell was a member of the English Church Union and a friend of Rosenthal.)

When told that his predecessor had allowed reservation, Barnes said he could find no documentary evidence supporting that claim. This prompted a reply from the retired Bishop Wakefield in the *Church Times* on 19 October 1925 which stated: 'Let me once and for all accept responsibility for allowing Reservation, for forbidding Benediction and Exposition, and for permitting private prayers in that part of the church where the Reserved Sacrament was placed.'

In the meantime Barnes announced that he would not license or give permission for any curate to work in a parish where extra-liturgical devotions took place, and that diocesan grants for their salaries were being stopped. When Rosenthal learned this, he called a meeting of fifteen Catholic incumbents, including the three affected by the bishop's action. They resolved to withhold their parishes' contributions to the diocesan quota and set up their own fund to support one another's curates. Since the parishes affected were comparatively poor, Rosenthal appealed to the ECU for help. The ECU executive had in fact wondered whether they should have protested when Barnes' appointment was announced, but one of their members, Long from Birmingham, had advised saying nothing until the new bishop's attitude towards Catholics became clear. The Union now saw its chance to help – urged on by Pinchard who, as a former Birmingham incumbent, knew the parishes concerned. A special appeal was made to Catholics in the country and raised £3,000 towards the fund. The Union continued to make grants to it until the 1930s when the 'rebellion' faded away. The executive also received letters from Catholics in the Birmingham diocese and from people elsewhere about Barnes' utterances, and reported them in the Union's literature. The Small Heath branch of the ECU urged the executive to begin a campaign for disestablishment to bring the appointment of bishops under the Church's control.

Barnes put what he called 'the fifteen rebel parishes' under a ban, refusing to visit them for confirmations or any other ministration. In spite of this the parishes still contributed to the diocesan ordination and extension funds, and the Bishop on his part did not raise objections when his board of finance made grants to them for building and repair purposes.

The Bishop decided to wait until there were vacancies in any of these parishes and then use his powers of licensing and instituting to enforce his policy. Since the priests concerned had undertaken among themselves to refuse any offers to move elsewhere, vacancies in the banned parishes were rare. However, in 1929 the curate in charge of St Aidan (it was a perpetual curacy) resigned through ill-health and the trustees, who included Frere and Long, offered the living to G. D. Simonds, a curate of Tyneside in the Durham diocese, who accepted it. When Barnes learned this, he wrote to Simonds' diocesan, Henson, asking for information. Henson wrote back warmly commending the candidate, saying Simonds was a moderate Anglo-Catholic. However, when Barnes asked Simonds for an assurance not to reserve the sacrament, Simonds, on the advice of the ECU, refused. So began a legal tangle which lasted for two years.

To his credit, Barnes refused to take the matter to court; he may have had a genuine distaste for such a move, especially as it would be costly. But when the trustees, including Frere, threatened to do so, Barnes said he was willing to go to prison if the court decided against him. When they grasped the implications of this, newspaper reporters were delighted. They gleefully pointed out that if the Bishop of Birmingham went to prison, it would be because the Bishop of Truro had sent him there! The trustees decided to try other legal tactics which eventually involved Lang, who by then had followed Davidson to Canterbury. Eventually Simonds was instituted to the living by the Archbishop himself.

Over fifty pages of the Barnes's biography are occupied by long letters which he wrote (and sent copies to the press) to the Archbishop, and Lang's replies. They reveal Barnes had hardened his attitude towards reservation. Whereas before 1927–28 he had simply discouraged reservation and tried to prevent any priest introducing it, he now forbade it and ordered parishes to discontinue the practice. He believed he had good reasons for doing this. He claimed that since Parliament had rejected the

Revised Prayer Book which incorporated the draft rubric and permitted reservation under certain conditions, those conditions were no longer binding. The 1662 Prayer Book was now the only legal liturgy once more and its provisions (as he interpreted them) forbade reservation. Furthermore, bishops were given permission to exercise their discretion in what parts of the Revised Prayer Book they allowed to be used in their dioceses, and Barnes certainly wasn't going to recognize the rubrics about reservation. Among the massive correspondence in the *Church Times* was a letter in the issue of 5 June 1931 from Alec Vidler, a former curate of St Aidan, asserting that benediction, exposition and processions of the Blessed Sacrament had never been held at that church.

The publicity of these disputes wearied the bishops. Even Henson, who had initially approved of Barnes' attempt to impose discipline, felt he went too far. Lang, having to read and reply to Barnes' letters, at last wrote with exasperation: 'The whole conception of the relation of spirit and matter which seems always to underlie your reiterated utterances on this deep subject seems to me to belong to a past age both of science and philosophy, and in this respect I am bound to say that I wish you were a better Modernist.'[20]

As the long dispute over the Small Heath appointment drew to a close, Barnes wrote an article for the *Record* summing up his views. His main contention was that, if a communicant experiences the divine presence at the Communion Service, such an experience cannot be separated from other experiences of God's presence in life and worship. 'Assertions of spiritual presence in material objects belong to a past phase of religious fancy which humanity is outgrowing. I believe that, as man develops, he will enter into new depths of communion with God. But God is not to be found in articles of food from which He can be assimilated when these are eaten . . . He reveals himself, it may be *through* material channels directly to the soul of man; and, I would add, in such direct revelation there is peace and joy.'[21]

That last expression – 'God reveals himself, it may be *through* material channels directly to the soul of man' – leaves the question whether Barnes was unconsciously approaching a Catholic theology of the sacraments. As Quick remarked at the Farnham conference: 'No one who believes at all in the living presence of Christ with his Church can seriously desire to affirm his absence from the solemn rite of the Church's fellowship in him. On this point, at least, the Bishop of Birmingham agrees with the Council of Trent.'[22]

If Barnes had been less fixated on his campaign, a dialogue between him and the Catholics might have been possible. But the Bishop was not that kind of a person. In his mathematical mind facts were facts but theology could be false. He had a tunnelled determination to preach a Christianity acceptable to what he believed to be the scientific, philosophical and psychological mindset of his age. There is no reason to doubt his son when he tells us that in church Barnes celebrated Holy Communion with great reverence. But the Bishop sincerely thought that any benefit the communicants received through taking the bread and the wine was uncovenanted, perhaps spiritual or psychological, but certainly not sacramental.

For the same reason in the thirties he opposed in Convocation the authorization of a form for anointing the sick as a return to 'religious barbarism'. He told his fellow bishops that they had to choose between the God of reason and the God of magic. Statements like these lost him much of the sympathy he once attracted. The result was that he became more and more an outsider on the episcopal bench. He reached the depths of notoriety with his book, *The Rise of Christianity* (1947), which with its odd treatment of both Scripture and science earned him a formal reproof from the House of Bishops.

Winnington-Ingram's response to those of his clergy in the London diocese who refused to obey his direction that extra-liturgical devotions should cease was totally different. After Parliament's rejection of the Revised Prayer Book he seemed to think that he was partly to blame for the vote because during the debates in the Commons certain Catholic parishes in his London diocese were said to be out of episcopal control. He summoned a synod of clergy and asked them to accept his ruling that the sacrament could be reserved for the sick but not for extra-liturgical devotions. Much to his disappointment only half of the voters agreed to this; the other half rejected his ruling or were non-committal. When he issued the regulations later, many followed Mackay's example and regretfully obeyed, but 21 incumbents wrote to the Bishop saying they would not follow them. They claimed the support of Article XXVIII: it is true, they said, that this article states 'the sacrament of the Lord's Supper was not by Christ's ordinance reserved, carried about, lifted up, or worshipped', but that did not mean that Christ or the authors of the article expressly forbade it. F. Underhill wrote a letter to the *Church Times* criticizing the twenty-one for disobeying their bishop. Dom Anselm Hughes regarded this as an act of betrayal and said Underhill was seeking higher office. Underhill later became Dean of Rochester and then Bishop of Bath and Wells, but his closest friends denied that he was an ambitious man.

After seeking advice from Lang, Winnington-Ingram explained to the 21 that all he was forbidding were services at which the reserved sacrament was censed and lifted up, not private or corporate prayers in the place where it was reserved. He added that of the 170 incumbents who had reservation in the diocese, they were the only ones who objected. In the end, as the objectors guessed, he took no further action except to comment that he would try to enforce his ruling after a vacancy occurred in a parish. There is no record he ever did.[23]

Rosenthal, on his side, was equally determined not to resign from St Agatha's and leave his congregation to the mercy of whoever the Bishop would institute next. So he stayed on, even after it was discovered that he had angina. His doctor and his friends urged him to move to a country living, but he refused. He died on 9 December 1938 after a long illness, leaving a widow and two daughters. He was only 58.

In Rosenthal's many writings, and in a biography written by C. E. Russell and published a year after his death, he comes over as an exceptionally gifted, likeable and able priest. He was a popular speaker in the Congress movement. Many of his suggestions were incorporated into the 1927, 1930 and 1933 Congress programmes. He promoted the Fiery Cross campaign, the Ordination Fund, and the Anglo-Catholic Summer School of Sociology. He was a regular contributor to the *Green Quarterly* on a variety of subjects including art, music and literature, and he wrote stories and poems for the *Fiery Cross* parish magazine inset. If he had moved to a quiet country living, he might have survived longer. But it was against his nature to surrender in a fight. Preaching at his funeral his friend Long said, 'His [Rosie's] devotion to the Blessed Sacrament of the Altar was to him a matter of vital importance, bound up with his faith in the Incarnation. . . . For this he not only deliberately set aside all prospect of ecclesiastical preferment, but also expressed his readiness to die at his post rather then surrender that principle.'[24]

A few years before he died he was appointed to the Archbishops' Evangelistic Committee chaired by C. Bardsley, the Evangelical Bishop of Leicester. When his death was announced, Bardsley wrote: 'I shall always remember him as a man who obviously had great gifts for the ministry, who was a warm-hearted friend, and above all a devoted servant of God.'[25]

Barnes was invited to attend Rosenthal's funeral at St Agatha's on the Monday after Rosie's death, but he declined saying he was unwell. But on the following Wednesday he visited the church to make sure the sacrament was no longer reserved and ordered that the tabernacle must remain empty.

15

Summer Schools, Strikes and Slums

When Charles Gore stood up to speak on the closing night of the 1920 Congress, he had long had the reputation of socialist leanings. From the time when he edited *Lux Mundi* (1889) his name was linked with theologians who taught that faith in the incarnate Lord inevitably led the believer into concern for everything that touches his and her fellow human beings. For Gore that was an essential duty – he described it as a privilege – of what it meant to be a Catholic. It meant applying the principles of the Kingdom of God, not only to one-to-one relationships with others, but also to the structure and culture of society itself, especially to politics which affected how people live. He contended that Jesus' words 'My kingdom is not of this world' are grossly misunderstood if they are interpreted to mean the Church should not concern itself with the whole range of human activity. Rather, the signs of the Kingdom appear in this world when Christ's followers struggle to enable people to live in accordance with the social and moral principles of the Gospel.

He was a great democrat. He saw democracy as being 'in the order of God'. It was an impulse towards justice and liberty in society which came, not just from human ideals but from the Holy Spirit, leading people to live in community as God wanted them to live. But with that liberty came responsibility. In a true democracy men and women are to care for one another in fulfilment of the second great commandment. He summed it up with the words, 'There is no ordered liberty unless the law for each is for the good of all.'[1] This was the social gospel which Gore preached through his lectures, sermons and writings and which influenced many of the rising generation of Church leaders – notably William Temple.

After the war, and freed from the restraints of being a diocesan bishop, Gore became more outspoken, not only on domestic affairs but also on international ones. He was highly critical of the results of the peace conference. The indemnities imposed on Germany by the French were, he warned, exposing that country to an economic collapse and opening the way for Bolshevism to spread into Europe. The effects of the Russian revolution appalled him; he referred to these in his talk at the first Congress. He wanted independence for countries which had been under Turkish rule, particularly those with large Christian populations like Armenia and Cilicia. When a country moved towards a democratic system of government, he wanted it to develop through peaceful evolution, not violent revolution.

Gore was involved in the Christian socialist movements which had proliferated since the days of Stewart Headlam's Guild of St Matthew. One of the strongest was the Christian Social League (CSL), formed in 1906 following an address at Mirfield by Keir Hardie. Its members included Conrad Noel, Percy Widdrington, and Frs Neville Figgis, Walter Frere and Paul Bull of the Community of the Resurrection. Its beginnings coincided with the election of the first Labour MPs to Parliament, of whom Keir Hardy was the leader.

Among Christian socialists there was a mixture of ideas. Many were attracted to 'guild socialism', seeing in the ages before the Reformation a nation in which all aspects of social activity were influenced by the Church. Within this structure, they argued, the guild played a major part in shaping social and commercial life, so that the country became a community of communities in service to its members and to the nation as a whole. It was, however, an idealized notion of the middle ages (reflecting the idealized picture of the medieval liturgy drawn by those who championed the Sarum rite). The guild system could repress workers and deprive them of their rights. Owners of businesses (from the lord of the manor to the farmer and miller) could behave like tyrants and treat their workers abominably. Strikes were common. The evils of capitalism did not emerge, as some claimed, as a result of the Reformation; they only became more widespread as a result of the dissolution of the monasteries and the increase in trading opportunities.

Others championed distributism. It is not easy to fathom what distributism meant, though it was fashionable among the literary intelligentsia such as G. K. Chesterton and Hilaire Belloc. Distributists were socialist in that they opposed capitalism on one hand and state-controlled collectivism on the other, but were vague about political and economic practicalities. Yet others supported the Labour Party's agenda – the nationalization of the major industries and the legal entitlement to a fair wage. Besides these, there was a small minority of those like Kenneth Ingram who read Karl Marx and argued that communist principles could be the basis for a truly Christian society.

With such a variety of ideas around it was inevitable that divisions arose in Christian socialist circles. Conrad Noel, perhaps best described as a romantic communist, wanted the CSL to become affiliated with the Labour Party, but Widdrington was unwilling to do this. Although Widdrington was a Labour supporter and had worked for the party in his younger days, he was a disciple of Gore in believing it was unwise to link the Christian socialist movement too closely to any one political party. Consequently Noel broke away from the League and in 1918 formed the Catholic Crusade of the Servants of the Precious Blood. With a small band of supporters, the Crusade was at first marginally involved with the British Communist party but split over attitudes to Russia. Noel in time gave it less attention as he became engrossed in his ministry as vicar of Thaxted. There he combined Catholic faith and practice with controversial revolutionary ideas which attracted hostile publicity but drew to the picturesque country town a small group of left-wing sympathizers. These included the poet Charles Dalmon, the actor Franklyn Dyall, and the composer Gustav Holst. The latter was Noel's choir master for several years and wrote much of *The Planets* suite while living there.

Percy Widdrington pursued a different line. During the war, as vicar of St Peter, Coventry, he had been asked by his bishop to become the diocesan promoter of the National Mission of Repentance and Hope in 1917, and he threw himself into this with great enthusiasm, visiting parishes and deaneries and speaking on the Gospel in its relation to social and economic issues. After the war Lady Warwick nominated him to the living of Great Easton on the Essex–Suffolk border, one of the parishes of which she was patron. She was a critic of class divisions and, living in Easton Lodge, liked to have Catholic socialist priests around her. Years before, she had nominated Noel for Thaxted. Widdrington accepted Great Easton because he was exhausted after his diocesan work. He believed he would only be there a few years before returning to an urban parish, but in the event he stayed until he retired in 1955. He found the quiet country parish freed him to pursue his various interests, and his wife took a lead in village and county affairs. The parish is not far from Thaxted, and Widdrington and Noel remained friends in spite of their disagreements. Biographers have remarked on the irony of the fact that these two socialist priests owed their livelihood to a system of ecclesiastical patronage which they wanted to abolish.

When he was settled in Great Easton, Widdrington organized meetings in nearby Coggeshall for those of his friends who remained in the CSL after the defection of Noel and his followers. At these meetings the affairs of the CSL were wound up, and the League of the Kingdom of God (LKG) was formed in 1923. Its president was Henry Slesser. Fr Tribe

SSM joined as director of studies; others on the committee included R. H. Tawney the economist, Ruth Kenyon the sociologist, Maurice Reckitt (a member of the family which established a famous soap factory), F. Underhill and G. D. Rosenthal. The LKG came to be known as the 'Christendom Group' after the book *The Return of Christendom* was published in 1922. It was edited by Reckitt with contributions by Widdrington and other members of the League.

Reckitt had worked for the Labour Party in London and during the war joined the Church Socialist League. When the CSL split, he was one of those who went to Widdrington's meetings and, living in London, was a frequent visitor to Great Easton. Reckitt was a committed Anglo-Catholic layman, an author of many books on Christian sociology, and an able speaker. He summed up his views on the role of the Church in politics in these words: 'If you had told any typical Christian thinker in any century from the twelfth to the sixteenth century that religion had nothing to do with economics, and that bishops must not intrude in these matters upon the deliberations of laymen – propositions which to many of the correspondents to our newspapers appear to be axiomatic – he would either have trembled for your faith or feared for your reason. He would have regarded you, in short, as either a heretic or a lunatic.'[2] He used his wealth to finance the group when the Congress committee could no longer afford to do so, and before his death established the Christendom Trust to promote Christian social thinking.

By the mid twenties the LKG's membership had grown to 1,200. Widdrington expressed the task of the Group as seeking a theology of the Kingdom of God as the authoritative guide for a Christian sociology. 'The Church', he wrote, 'once delivered from ecclesiastical-mindedness and aflame with the faith of the Kingdom, will be compelled to adopt towards our industrial system the same attitude which our missionaries took towards the social order of heathendom.'[3] The group hoped that by calling themselves a 'league' they would attract Catholics who were suspicious of the word 'socialist'. Yet they did not want to compromise their objective by allowing into its membership those with little or no concept of the Catholic doctrine of the Church.

While Widdrington and his friends were reorganizing themselves after the break-up of the CSL, Temple was following up what he had learned during the war as a member of the committee which drew up the Industrial Report of the National Mission of Repentance and Hope. On that committee he was impressed by Gore's advocacy of the Church's social mission and was moved to join the Labour Party in 1918. The following year he became chairman of an ecumenical group which commenced preparations for an international conference on post-war problems. This was held in Birmingham in April 1924 as a Conference on Christian Politics, Economics and Citizenship (COPEC).

Temple, who by then was Bishop of Manchester, chaired the 1,500 delegates, 80 of them from overseas. The conference passed reports which urged, among other things, that the Churches needed educating in their social responsibilities and that they should prepare 'textbooks for social study of the same type as those already issued for examining the problems of the mission field'. Perhaps it was unrealistic to expect such a gathering to produce anything more challenging. Its resolutions would only come to life if those who voted for the reports were willing to act on them. Gore saw this and warned the conference: 'We need tremendous courage to ask ourselves frankly whether we are really prepared to accept these fundamental principles and to apply them whatever their effect upon party politics.'[4]

However, COPEC was a step towards wooing the Church of England away from a Tory-establishment attitude to contemporary problems and urging it to fulfil its social responsibilities more forcefully. But not everyone was persuaded. Henson called the conference 'sentimental socialism' with Temple as its 'pope'. Yet even he was faced with the realities of the economic situation when, during a Durham miners' strike a few years later, he found five of them trespassing on the episcopal estate in Bishop Auckland to help themselves to an outcrop of coal on its land. He sat on the grass listening sympathetically to them and before he left told them to fill their bags. For the majority of those taking part, COPEC was a learning experience which was to affect their outlook and their activities in the future. Perhaps most important of all as far as Britain was concerned, it led Temple to be regarded as the leading figure in expounding the Church's social responsibilities. By a quirk of history, COPEC met in the same year as the first short-lived Labour Government.

COPEC also passed another resolution condemning war as 'contrary to the spirit and teaching of Jesus Christ' and urged the churches to refuse to support a war waged before, or in defiance of, arbitration. This led to similar resolutions passed by international ecumenical conferences in 1928 and 1929 and the Lambeth Conference of 1930. All of them called for support for the League of Nations, and indirectly they backed the peace movements as well as the growing number of pacifists. These resolutions, however, turned out to be more ambiguous when the dictators began their invasions in the thirties.

Anglo-Catholic Summer Schools of Sociology

In the spirit of COPEC, Widdrington and the Christendom Group organized the first of their annual conferences the following year. The Congress executive provided financial support and the conferences were given the name the Anglo-Catholic Summer Schools of Sociology. These met in July of each year for three days in Keble College, Oxford. Papers were introduced and discussed in groups, which reported back. Attendance was around one and two hundred. The final School was in 1952 by which time its speakers had included well-known names – Lewis Donaldson, Harold Buxton, V. A. Demant, T. S. Eliot, Gresham Kirkby, Lionel Thornton, Eric Mascall, Dorothy L. Sayers, Ruth Kenyon, Temple and Michael Ramsey.

Each year the School chose a particular theme: a survey of contemporary society from a Catholic viewpoint; the implications of the sacraments to social life; the Church's teaching on economic matters in the past and their relevance for today; and Catholicism and the world order (the state, the economic order, and the home). The addresses were printed by the CLA. In later years the group published its own journal, *Christendom*.

We can take the summer school of 1927 as typical. The topic chosen for it was 'Property'. Temple gave the opening address on the Christian conception of the relationship between the individual and property. He pointed out that an individual only finds fulfilment in relationships with others, and that if such relationships are be harmonious there must be a willingness to share in material things as well as in spiritual blessings – the ethic of the Gospel. This could not be justly achieved through capitalism or communism: 'If the right to property is made absolute, sacrosanct rather than sacred, the effect in the long run is to deprive most citizens of any real property. Sheer collectivism, on the other hand, the complete polarization of property, enormously diminishes the freedom of self-expression.'[5] He admitted that contemporary economic problems were so complex that the practicalities of applying Christian principles were equally difficult. He echoed the view of his friend R. H. Tawney (they had been schoolboys at Rugby together) that education over two or three generations was the best hope. He said that where they could not see their way forward, it would be right to put the spiritual first and expect that it will be more important in the issue than the merely material. He was a great believer in the power of education – and particularly Christian education – to change society.

G. Gillett, the editorial secretary of the Society for the Propagation of the Gospel, put the case for distributivism. Its proponents claimed that the solution to problems of property was to distribute it so that each person and family had enough to live comfortably and to fulfil the work that God called them to. He warned that if capitalism was replaced by socialism in three or four generations people would be brought up to expect security, high wages, leisure time and state provision for old age and sickness. Ownership through the equal distribution of property would make possible 'the return to civilization'. But many in the audience regarded this as unrealistic. In the discussion which followed a Mr Currie, described as 'a practical business man', warned that distributivism would be difficult to apply in modern economic circumstances.

W. G. Peck gave a long and complicated paper on dividends and investments, in which he began by explaining that the scholastic condemnation of usury assumed a Christian society in which everyone was a neighbour in the literal sense: therefore to charge interest was to take advantage of the man-next-door's need. In the modern financial system all sense of neighbourliness had vanished. The key industry was money-making, and the majority of human beings were simply instruments for the production of money. The right objective of work, to supply human needs, has been lost sight of altogether. No Catholic can accept that situation. We believe, said Peck, that human life is supernatural, a gift of God, and that it is corporate. Therefore it follows that all human resources must be corporate and money recognized as an ethical and social instrument for serving everyone, not just a few. He noted that according to a Labour Research Department report only 15 per cent of the population in England had any personal savings at all. Like other speakers he had no practical suggestions on how this change was to be effected. There was much discussion but no conclusion on what constituted a 'Just Price.'

Critics – and there were plenty of them – said the Schools were out of touch with the realities of industrial and commercial life. Theories were expounded at them which sounded like inspired solutions to the ills of society on a sunny morning in an Oxford college, but which were hardly practical when applied to the real world beyond. Those who went to them, it was said, had little experience of work in the mines and industries. One wrote that those who went were the kind of people who looked out compassionately on the slums from the windows of a first-class railway carriage.

In reply Christendom supporters said the critics misunderstood the purpose of the Schools. They were not intended to be anything other than providing opportunities for sharing ideas. Fr Tribe defined their role as 'an intellectual one; to make clear the theological basis of our social action, as well as to show the social implications of our Catholic convictions'.[6]

If some of the speakers' theories seemed impractical, at least they were stirring minds for alternatives to rampant capitalism and state-centred socialism. They set out to demonstrate what was distinctive about a Catholic approach to the problems of society. Evangelicals, with a few exceptions, were suspicious of anything that sounded like a 'social gospel'. In their view Christians should witness to their faith by the way they lived in the midst of a sinful world and seek to rescue individuals by leading them to become disciples of Jesus Christ. Other Anglicans would have said that their faith had implications in working for reconciliation and justice in all sections of society, but that did not necessarily mean becoming actively political. What the Christendom group did was to insist that the social order needed to be rescued, too.

The Schools were in fact theological and economic think-tanks in which the Church's social responsibility was explored as an integral part of her mission. This meant in practice that Christians should not only be at the forefront in charitable works; they needed to be more than Good Samaritans. They must also work strategically to influence the forces which shaped that society – political, economic, ethical, and spiritual – and enable its citizens to find fulfilment according to God's purposes for them. To do this, Catholics said, they must understand these forces in order to engage with them, and the Schools helped them to do this.

For this wider mission, they went on, Christians needed to be able to discern those trends in modern society which were for or against the Kingdom of God, and support or oppose them accordingly. They saw the servants of the Kingdom acting – as Jesus himself had said – like the seed growing secretly, or leaven in the lump, penetrating every area of human life, including politics, until it reflected the values of heaven here on earth. A social order which was based on any other principle than the will of God was bound to fail, because it did not accept the truth that human nature was fallen. As Christ had taken human nature to himself and redeemed it as a sign of his Kingdom breaking into the world, so the Church had to embrace human society in all its many aspects and work for its redemption in the power of the Kingdom. The Church's mission flowed from the sending of the Son by the Father to redeem the world by the power of the Holy Spirit working through his people. Hence the purpose of the papers and discussions in the Schools was to awaken the Church to its mission to transform society.

Ruth Kenyon put it this way: 'The Anglo-Catholic School of Sociology is our attempt to enable the Anglo-Catholic Movement to bear its part in the restatement of Christian ethics in terms of the present day; and its motive for doing so is the faith that Christ is King, and the hope that understanding the recognition of his Kingship may effect by grace the return of Christendom.'[7] She noted that in 1925 Pope Leo XI had instituted the feast of Christ the King as a defence against the 'plague of secularism' and a declaration that the rule of Christ was not merely over the individual soul, but over societies as societies and not as collections of individuals. The Pope went on to declare that the state must reverence and obey the law of God proclaimed by the Church. Kenyon hailed this as a vindication of the Christendom group's own objective. She might have been less enthusiastic if she had realized that Leo XI was a bad-tempered autocrat, who smashed the French Church's links with political liberalism and whose concordat with Mussolini (whom the Pope welcomed as 'a man sent by Providence') undermined Italian democracy. The School's main achievement, then, was to make more and more members of the Church of England open to what socialists were saying, and to help them realize that the study of sociology was necessary for a better understanding of the world in which the Church's mission and service were to be fulfilled.

It is significant that when Temple set up a committee to organize the Malvern conference of 1941 to review progress since COPEC, he invited a number of the Christendom group to join it. His book, *Christianity and the Social Order*, published the following year, was one of the fruits of his experiences in the years between COPEC and Malvern. It sold over a hundred thousand copies and helped Anglicans and others to welcome the Beveridge Plan (William Beveridge was another of Temple's friends) and the launching of the welfare state by the Labour government after the second world war. The Summer Schools played a minor role in bringing about this change.

Unemployment

The Church of England's response to unemployment problems was uncertain and limited. There was little it could do as an institution nationally except make appeals and pray. Power to reduce the statistics of those on the dole seemed to be in the hands of the employers and the trade unions. The Church Assembly in 1923 set up a Social and Industrial Commission to gather information about the social work done in dioceses and parishes. Its purpose was to provide data for bishops and Assembly members to use to propagate the Church's aims. (The editor of *Crockford* remarked that, after a discussion on a report of this Commission in the Church Assembly one year, its members would have done more good if, instead of talking about it, they had all gone home and paid their bills promptly!)[8] The Industrial Christian Fellowship was formed after the war from a merger of the older Navvy Mission and the Christian Social Union. It engaged lay people in factory visiting. Studdert Kennedy, its missioner, toured the country addressing meetings and involving himself in industrial disputes. He overworked, was frequently in hospital, and at the age of 45 died in Liverpool in 1929 where he had gone to give the Lenten addresses.

Locally, however, congregations in various places used their premises to provide the unemployed and their families with cheap meals, second-hand clothing and workshops for repairing furniture. During strikers' marches they opened church halls for meals and overnight accommodation. Often these activities were organized ecumenically by a group of churches, continuing the co-operation which had been initiated during war.

The nine days' general strike, which began on 3 May 1926, was the most important industrial conflict in the Congress era. Its impact affected the whole of British society. One and three-quarter million trade unionists came out in support of 800,000 coal miners who had been locked out for refusing to accept wage cuts of 10 and 20 per cent. More than any other event during the inter-war years it divided the nation between those who sided with the miners, and those who feared there would be a revolution like those which had taken place in Russia and elsewhere in Europe.

Davidson used his position as Archbishop and his membership of the House of Lords to discuss the situation with Stanley Baldwin and other ministers. He got a group of national church leaders, including the President of the Free Church Council and Cardinal Bourne, the Archbishop of Westminster, to issue an appeal that the strike should be cancelled and the mine owners' new wage scales should be withdrawn to make time for further negotiations. Afterwards delegates from the TUC thanked Davidson for what he had done.

Two local reactions from clergy illustrate the differences in the way the strike affected clergy in different parts of the country. Mackay at All Saints, Margaret Street, wrote in his magazine that it had made little difference to the size of the congregations in his church on the Sunday of the strike. But in the Midlands A. Blunt, who was vicar of St Werburgh, Derby, at the time of the strike, was so shocked by what he saw in and around the city that he joined the Labour Party. He had seen the effect of strikes before. While out visiting when he was a curate at St John the Baptist, Newcastle upon Tyne, he had to avoid stone-throwing rioters and police baton charges.

Probably as a result of these experiences, Blunt was the most outspoken of the bishops on the problem after he was appointed to Bradford in 1931. Unemployment peaked again in the 1930s and he took every opportunity to criticize the capitalist system in industry. He called a conference of his clergy and 120 of them unanimously signed a petition urging Parliament 'to address itself at once to a survey of the issue, without any respect to political partisanship, or to industrial or monetary conventions'.[9] They also urged parishes to stimulate discussions, to spread information and to call public attention to the plight of the unemployed. Blunt visited factories and occupational centres for those on the dole in the diocese. He was disgusted at the views of some members of the Church Assembly as they debated a report on unemployment presented by the Social and Industrial Committee, and told them so. In the nervous atmosphere in the country at the time, he and his clergy were regarded as inciting revolution. When told that the Church had no business in politics, he retorted in his diocesan paper:

> The mechanization of industrial processes continues to displace labour; and most of that displaced labour will never find continuous employment again. The problem therefore becomes not only of increasing opportunities for work, but of providing for those who are in a condition of enforced leisure. And this is a human problem, before it becomes one of economics. Our interest as a Church in it is in the demoralizing effects of pauper leisure upon our fellowmen, and especially upon adolescents who leave school every year to find either no place for themselves in the labour market or only blind alley employment. These are boys and girls who we often have to teach and shepherd. It is a condition of affairs in which they are liable to be thus exposed to the frightful temptations of compulsory idleness, of disheartened resentment at their lot, or of demoralized acquiescence in it. It is not one which we as a Church have any right to leave uncriticized or unattacked.[10]

Blunt's sympathies with the working classes and with the Congress movement made him a champion among Catholics. When the TUC instituted a church service before its annual conference in 1933, its committee invited Blunt to be the preacher at it. In the same year, when he walked in the procession of bishops at the Centenary Congress, he was loudly cheered by those standing by. However, his reputation for outspokenness caused a national sensation a few years later. In an address to his diocesan conference in December 1936 in which he mentioned the forthcoming coronation of Edward VII, he pointed out that the crowning took place in the context of a Holy Communion service and, almost as an after-thought, added that some wished the future king showed more positive signs that he needed God's grace. Those words were seized on by the press as a sign that the Bishop was aware of the king's intention to marry a divorced woman, Mrs Wallis Simpson. (There had been speculation in continental papers about this for months.) Blunt was astonished his chance remark should cause such controversy. He had not mentioned Mrs Simpson's name.

Housing

If the Church of England could do little about the unemployment situation, its members felt they could campaign for better housing. Its clergy lived and worked in the midst of the slums, and bishops and others who visited them were well aware of the situation. The problem was raised regularly in the Houses of Convocation and in the Church Assembly, and Davidson and other bishops expressed their concern both in the House of Lords and privately with government ministers when they had an opportunity. Bishop C. F. Garbett of Southwark set up a working party to gather information about the extent of slum housing in his diocese so that he could speak authoritatively about it in the House of Lords and the Church Assembly.

Under its socially conscious editor, Sydney Dark, the *Church Times* for three weeks in February and March 1924 published a series of articles on the slums in London and in other parts of Britain. They were unsigned but the writer had clearly done his (or, less probably, her) homework, quoting statistics from local government reports.

He pointed out that within a few minutes' walk of the Houses of Parliament there were some of the poorest homes in London, and went on to describe one of them which, he claimed, was 'neither very bad nor very good.' The terrace house in a side street had a basement, a ground floor and two upper floors. All the floors were let to different families. On the top floor nine people lived in two rooms – father, mother, and seven children aged 3 months to 12 years. On the day of the visit the mother was sitting by an open fire with a young child on her knee who was gasping for breath, a baby lay on a pillow on the floor, and another small child obviously ill was in a battered pram by the door. The only toilets were in the yard outside, and all the water had to be carried up from a tap beside them. Cooking was done on a gas ring on the landing. The rooms had not been decorated for years, the furniture was battered and broken, and there were two double beds crammed into the second room for the whole family. The husband worked on the docks. When work was available – there were times when it wasn't – he earned just over nine shillings a week. When the rent and the National Insurance stamp were paid for, there was five shillings a week for food and fuel.

In other districts, he wrote, conditions were far worse. Dilapidated buildings, leaky roofs, broken drains, rubbish-strewn streets and alleyways were common. Landlords did nothing to care for their tenants. It was the same elsewhere in Britain, especially in Birmingham, Liverpool, Manchester, Sheffield, Leeds, Newcastle, Edinburgh, Glasgow, Cardiff and the Welsh valleys. In Leicester the medical officer of health reported there were over 500 homes unfit for human habitation; in Kingston-up-Hull there were 7,000. Labourers' cottages in country towns and villages were little better.

The contrast between the health of children and adults in the slums with that of those living in better areas was shameful. The death rate among children from measles in Manchester was the highest in the country, yet those who died all lived in slums such as those in Hulme and it hardly touched the children of better-off families in the suburbs. Among slum dwellers everywhere deaths from tuberculosis, diphtheria, pneumonia and other illnesses were between ten and twenty times higher than the rest of the population. At the beginning of the twenties, the journalist continued, local authorities had begun demolishing the slums and building new estates, but demand was far outstripping supply. 'Great riches were made in Manchester, and conditions have improved in the last thirty or forty years, but still the stamp of a despair of ugliness is set upon the lives of many of its citizens, and the terrible exploitation of its work people in the early days of the cotton mills is still working out its dreary results in moral and physical enfeeblement.'[11]

At the end of each article he asked his readers questions. How could the Church expect young couples to bring up children in such conditions? How could families maintain moral standards when men escaped the misery in pubs and clubs, and when bedrooms were shared by different generations? Very occasionally, he admitted, a mother 'with Madonna-like gentleness' can make a Christian home in such conditions, but not often.

It was calculated, he wrote, that with a population of 38 million, 1,400,000 new homes were required in England, Scotland and Wales to meet the needs. This obviously could not be left to private landlords. Nor could it be left to housing schemes set up by churches and other charities. It required a great increase in the amount of publicly owned property and this should be a priority for national and local governments. Could they as an interim measure provide accommodation in quick-to-build houses on waste land until the new estates were ready? (This was done after the second world war, when tens of thousands of 'prefabs' were erected on open spaces. They were remarkably comfortable, and a few are still inhabited and prized as a national heritage.)

One Catholic priest who inspired Church action on the slums was Basil Jellicoe. When in 1922 he went to the Magdalene College Oxford mission attached to St Mary, Somers Town, next to Euston Station, he found some of worst living conditions in London. He gathered a group of friends to form the St Pancras Housing Improvement Society and they raised money to buy eight houses and renovate them into self-contained flats with bathrooms – a luxury for the previous inhabitants. From then on the work escalated. A piece of vacant land was purchased for the erection of new flats.

The initiative was described by Morse-Boycott who was an assistant priest at St Mary at that time: 'It is perhaps unnecessary to say that, although the Housing Scheme began as a religious endeavour, and is so maintained, there has never been, and never will be, any creedal test for the occupants. If they are dispossessed for a time, during renovation, they are helped to find alternative accommodation; and, be they Jew, Turk, Infidel or Heretic (to borrow the quaint Prayer Book language) they are welcomed back as soon as their old homes are ready. Soon the restless pioneers were looking for other property, and negotiations began with the United Dairies for about thirty-six houses, which were at a cost from £10,000 to £12,000. Owing to competition it was found these houses could only be secured by purchasing a great many more as well (seventy in all).'[12]

For Jellicoe the slums were the devil's own hunting ground, and he set about publicizing the problems they caused with a passionate faith that he was fighting evil in the name of Jesus Christ. He had one great advantage – his surname. His father, a Sussex vicar, was a cousin of the first Earl Jellicoe, the admiral who had commanded the British fleet at Jutland and was a national hero. There is no evidence Basil ever deliberately used his family connection in his campaigns, but it certainly helped. Cecil heard of his work and appealed for funds through letters to *The Times* with the backing of Neville Chamberlain, the housing minister. The project attracted visitors, including Queen Mary (encouraged by her lady-in-waiting, Cynthia Colville) and the Prince of Wales. More houses were reconditioned and more flats were built.

By 1927 Jellicoe was being invited to different parts of the country as groups – some ecumenical as well as Anglican – sought his advice for starting similar schemes. Local churches formed housing associations at Penzance and Stoke-on-Trent as well as other places. The Church Army formed an association beginning with a scheme in Bermondsey. The ECU launched a fund to aid affiliated parishes. Many other bodies did the same, locally as well as nationally. Jellicoe was constantly on the move, and it was decided he should sever his links with St Mary's while retaining the chairmanship of the association. He eventually attached himself to St Martin-in-the-Fields. When his Catholic friends expressed their surprise that he went to a church which did not have reservation, he replied that if St Martin's did not have Christ in a tabernacle, the church had Christ in the crypt (where the homeless were fed). He spoke at fringe meetings at the last two Congresses. After a long illness he died in 1935 in a Sussex nursing home at the age of 36.

Jellicoe's outstanding commitment to the cause meant that his name has been associated with those early Anglo-Catholic priests who gave their lives to serving the Lord in slum-dwelling. His achievement was summed up by Daphne Young, who as a small girl was prepared for confirmation by him. She wrote, 'He was determined to change things. It was no good, he said, giving the poor a day out at the seaside, only to return to their squalor. He began, in faith and with no money, the St Pancras Housing Association and began changing things himself.'[13]

Another Catholic priest who worked for the abolition of the slums was Charles Jenkinson. Son of a poor family, he was taught the faith by the clergy of St Saviour, Poplar. In 1912 he become Conrad Noel's secretary (Lady Warwick paid his wages) and was strongly attracted to Noel's Catholic teaching and radical socialism. He joined the Labour Party, sided with a strike by local farm workers, and married a Thaxted girl. As a pacifist he served in the medical corps during the war. He was ordained in 1923 and became a curate in Barking. He gave support to the strikers in 1926 and was invited by his local unions to attend the service of thanksgiving in St Paul's cathedral at the end of the strike.

In 1927 he was appointed vicar of St John and St Barnabas, Holbeck, Leeds. Almost immediately he undertook a survey of the slums in his parish and arranged meetings to publicize the problem. While still a vicar he was elected to the Leeds City Council and became chairman of the housing committee. Under his energetic leadership – and amidst much controversy – 14,000 slum dwellings were demolished and over 15,000 council houses were built. The climax of Jenkinson's work was a huge block of flats based on the design of the Karl Marx-Hof in Vienna, to provide homes for those who worked in the city centre. The Quarry Hill flats had communal facilities for the tenants, formal gardens and courtyards, playgrounds, kindergartens and laundries and shops. Building began in stages in 1934 and continued until 1941, but the estate was never finished. Within forty years disintegration and corrosion in the concrete and steel structure had created problems and it was demolished.

Jellicoe and Jenkinson approached the task of slum clearance in contrasting ways. Jellicoe took the initiative by tackling the problem through forming a trust and renovating or replacing poor housing. He showed what could be done by a local church with the aid of volunteers and supporters. Jenkinson, on the other hand, got himself elected to the city council where he was able to press forward plans for rehousing thousands of Leeds inhabitants. Jellicoe is regarded by many Catholics as a martyr for a sacrificial ministry which resulted in his early death, whereas Jenkinson is hardly known now. After leaving Leeds he became vicar of St Silas, Hunslet, and still involved himself in housing. He gave to the Church a large part of the £1,500 a year he earned as chairman of the Stevenage Development Corporation.

16

Conversions to Rome

In the twenties becoming a Roman Catholic had lost much of the social stigma once attached to it. Previously it had been a drastic step to take. Converts were generally regarded as having disgraced their families and dropped out of society. The inflexible rule that marriages had to be solemnized in a Roman Catholic church, coupled with pressure on the non-Roman partner to convert, was resented by relatives and friends of the individuals concerned. Now attitudes were changing. During the war Roman Catholic men and women showed they could be as patriotic as the rest of the nation – suffering the same hardships, grieving the same losses – and this did much to soften inherited prejudices. The professionalism of Roman Catholic chaplains in exercising their sacramental ministry at the front was much respected by troops, and contrasted with the amateurism of some Anglican padres. The better educated among the second and third generations of Irish immigrants were being accepted as members of the middle classes.

But there were reactions against this tolerance among some. Strict Protestants feared for the eternal salvation of the converts. Citizens of places like Liverpool, Manchester, Preston and Glasgow, where Irish Roman Catholicism was strong, felt they were being outnumbered (which in some districts they actually were). They suspected that among the Roman Catholic priests and congregations there were supporters of the recently self-proclaimed Irish Republic. Anglo-Catholics felt their faith in the Church of England threatened when their best friends 'poped'. It was a situation on which Evelyn Waugh based a comedy script he wrote for a short amateur film called *The Scarlet Woman*, which depicted the Pope planning the evangelization of Britain.

To reassure Anglo-Catholics, speakers at the Congresses unswervingly claimed that Anglicanism was a more biblical, traditional and rational expression of the Catholic faith than Rome. That claim was visually reinforced by the presence of bishops from other parts of the world at the Congresses. They were living witnesses to the fact that the Anglican episcopate was truly Catholic, and that the Anglican Communion was, like Rome, an international Church. But doubts persisted. Individuals, and occasionally groups from congregations and religious communities, joined the queue over the Tiber. Critical occasions for this were when events seemed to weaken claims for the Church of England's Catholicity, as when Parliament rejected the Revised Prayer Book, and when bishops tolerated extreme Modernism in the cause of Anglican comprehensiveness. Those who 'converted' (the usual description: the less charitable said 'perverted') were welcomed as reinforcements by English Roman Catholic families whose forebears, in spite of persecutions and restrictions, had remained faithful during the centuries since the Reformation. With the influx of the Irish from the 1840s onwards they had become a separate minority, clinging to the simpler English traditions of their religion.

During these years five well-known speakers at the Congresses were among the Anglicans who converted: G. K. Chesterton, Sheila Kaye-Smith, Fr Vernon Johnson SDC, Basil Butler and Henry Slesser. They were all, directly or indirectly, helped by Ronald Knox, who preceded them to Rome by a few years. Knox, Chesterton, Kaye-Smith, Johnson and Slesser published books on why they had become Roman Catholics, and these provide us with some insights into their doctrinal and spiritual reasons for doing so. But as we read these books we have to remember their authors wrote under some constraints. On the one hand, they were eager to justify what they had done to their Anglican friends; on the other hand, they were anxious to show their co-religionists they had left the Church of England because they had become convinced that only Rome was the true Church. However, what they said about themselves gives us hints of other – if very secondary – reasons for their conversions. We can note these without questioning their personal integrity, or the pain of the personal struggles they went through in reaching their decision.

Ronald Knox

Ronald Knox submitted to Rome in 1917. His conversion was widely publicized because he was a son of the Bishop of Manchester. He had the reputation of being one of the outstanding classics undergraduates of his generation. In *A Spiritual Aeneid*, written during his first months as a Roman Catholic, he told how he had been intrigued by stories of Anglican converts to Rome while still a boy and how, when he went to Balliol College, Oxford, through the influence of Pusey House and the Cowley fathers he entered the university's Anglo-Catholic sub-culture. He kept the disciplines of fasting, went to mass, and made his confession. He was elected to a fellowship at Trinity College and ordained in 1911. His wide circle of friends included N. P. Willliams, A. E. J. Rawlinson and Maurice Child. During vacations he did what many such young enthusiasts did – visited famous Anglo-Catholic parishes and religious houses (the Anglican Benedictine community on Caldey was a favourite), and toured Belgium where he was impressed by the size and devotion of Roman Catholic congregations there. It was while he was abroad that he met Maurice Child and Samuel Gurney, a proprietor of the Medici Gallery in London, and planned with them the launch of the Society of SS Peter and Paul.

He said his first mass at St Mary, Graham Street, using parts of the Latin rite silently – a custom he maintained during his Anglican days. He also began saying the breviary and took a vow of celibacy. He was typical of a younger set of Anglo-Catholic clergy who seemed to delight in defying the establishment by adopting certain forms of Roman Catholic teaching and practice. Knox admitted – with a streak of impish humour – that when invited to preach in an ordinary parish church, he deliberately chose controversial subjects such as the assumption of the Virgin Mary and the doctrine of transubstantiation.

In the preface to *A Spiritual Aeneid* he said he had tried to be objective in his account of why he left the Church of England, and invited any psychologist to probe his motives. 'God knows,' he protested, 'I do not think my own conversion was temperamental.' Then he added, 'But if you put the temperamental altogether outside your reckonings, the whole human value of your document is lost.'[1] That was a hesitant invitation to his readers to see if they could detect other reasons for his conversion behind the assurance of being in the fold of the true Church.

Knox followed the fashion of his contemporaries in wearing outdoors as well as indoors the garb of Continental priests: a soutane, a biretta and buckle shoes (Roman Catholic priests in Britain wore black suits out-of-doors). It was their way of letting others know they believed they were validly ordained priests of the Western Church. But we may suspect that in Knox's case the dress was also a demonstration of his rejection of the Evangelicalism of the family in which he grew up, and particularly that of his father. In his book Knox wrote as loyal and loving son, and expressed gratitude for all that his father meant to him. But his niece, Penelope Fitzgerald, said relations between the two of them were anything but easy. Although the Bishop supported Ronald's decision to be ordained, he was alarmed at the way his son was adopting Anglo-Catholic practices.

At one time tensions between them were such that they only communicated with one another through notes left on the hall table.

Knox's doubts about the Catholicism of the Church of England were revealed in the pamphlets he wrote for the SSPP before and after his ordination. They were brilliant depictions of the weaknesses of the Church of England, but they may have also unwittingly hinted at a deep uncertainty. Knox insisted that he had no thought of becoming a Roman Catholic in the early years of his ministry. But the war altered that. As a clergyman he was barred from conscription, so he went to Shrewsbury School as a temporary classics teacher to release a member of staff who wanted to volunteer for the army. There he missed his Oxford and London companions. He spent much of his spare time keeping in touch with them when they joined the forces, writing letters and travelling up to London to meet them before they embarked for the front. What disturbed him was that some of them afterwards wrote to tell him they had became Roman Catholics because, knowing they might be killed, they wanted to be sure that the last rites they received were valid sacraments. Knox found this almost unbearable when he heard that individuals among them had died in action.

Guy Lawrence was one of Knox's closest friends at Oxford. He went to Trinity a year or two after Knox. He was also a classical scholar, and common interests – religious and academic – drew them together. Lawrence had intended to be ordained, but with the outbreak of war he joined the army. From France he wrote to Knox to say he had become a Roman Catholic, and urged Knox to do the same.

In his book Ronald said it was while he was attending his brother's first mass in St Mary, Graham Street, that he finally made up his mind. Watching Wilfred presiding at the altar, he suddenly discovered he could no longer believe he was attending the offering of a valid Eucharist. We might ask, what was the significance of reaching that decision at that particular moment? Ronald was the youngest of four brothers, and Wilfred was next to him in age. Did a younger brother's wish to do better than a senior sibling give the final nudge for Ronald to fulfil a subconscious dream? When he heard the news Knox's father was horrified. Ronald tried to explain that he needed an absolute spiritual authority. He compared the Church of Rome to a shop window in which there was no need to examine the goods because over the door was a sign, 'This is the true depot ordained by Christ himself.' In his memoirs the Bishop said it was 'the saddest of the experiences and remembrances of my life'.[2] He thought Ronald was 'lost' and determined not to communicate with him for a year. Lawrence was delighted. 'Ron, dear', he wrote from the front,

'I am so glad you're back with me again. It makes a lot of difference to me . . . Be quick and become a priest.'[3] In the summer of 1918, less than three months before the armistice, Knox learned that his friend had been killed.

Knox went to St Edmund's College, Ware, for re-ordination. Because of his academic reputation, Archbishop Bourne of Westminster told him to remain there on the staff. They were unhappy years. He found teaching boys Latin and other subjects unrewarding, and the living conditions were spartan. His friends commiserated with him; they said his gifts were being wasted. It was a relief to be appointed to the Roman Catholic chaplaincy at Oxford in 1926 and later, to his delight, invited to resume the fellowship in his old college, Trinity.

In his pastoral work he said he did not deliberately set out to proselytize; he tried conscientiously and fairly to advise those who took the initiative to come and see him to talk about spiritual matters. Brought up in childhood to read the Bible regularly, he was disappointed to see that few Roman Catholics read their Douai version of the Scriptures. He decided that he should provide his co-religionists with a more modern version of the Vulgate. His Anglican friends questioned his decision. Why the Vulgate? Why not follow the Revised Version and go back to the original and more reliable Hebrew and Greek for a translation? But Knox was anxious to demonstrate his submission to Roman traditions, and that meant using the Vulgate. He resigned the chaplaincy in 1939 to begin work on this, living in friends' country houses as a domestic chaplain for the rest of his life.

Knox had much trouble with the English hierarchy in getting his translation accepted by them. But in the end it was authorized for public use in 1955, two years before his death. During these years he also wrote books of popular apologetics and novels. He did this to earn a living; he never received any regular payment from the Roman Church.[4] Had Bishop Knox known that his son would one day make the Scriptures more accessible to English-speaking Roman Catholics, the old man might have seen the Lord's hand in Ronnie's conversion after all.

G. K. Chesterton

Chesterton became interested in Roman Catholicism early in his life when, as a young journalist, he investigated scandalous stories which were circulating about that Church and discovered they were either unjust or untrue. He had been baptized as an infant in an Anglican church, but was involved briefly with Nonconformity before being attracted to Catholicism, which he regarded as the historical and most rational form of Christianity to answer the critics of religion around him. He enjoyed arguments about the faith with his atheist friends, including George Bernard Shaw. He joined his wife, Frances, in attending Anglo-Catholic worship because he approved of a movement which aimed to restore the Church of England to its Catholic heritage.

But by the end of the war disillusionment was beginning to seep in. He told a correspondent he found Anglo-Catholicism only a pale imitation of the real thing. At the same time, he was alarmed by the changes taking place in society – the effect of a capitalism system on the working classes, the increase in the number of divorces, the practice of birth control, and the talk about eugenics. It seemed to him that, much as he admired individual Anglo-Catholics, the Church of England itself was powerless to stand against these errors and threats because she was infected with Modernism and crippled by her establishment status. 'We do not want, as the newspapers say, a Church that will move with the world', he wrote. 'We want a Church that will move the world . . . It is by that test that history will really judge, of any Church, whether it is the real Church or no.'[5]

GK liked the world-affirming character of Catholicism. He saw it as the unacknowledged inspiration for all that was true in philosophies and social theories. Humanism taught the value of each individual but without relating it to the Catholic faith in God as man's Creator. Socialist campaigns for justice and equality were rooted in the Catholic doctrine of man but without relating their aims to the Gospel. After the war he was worried by the spread of Bolshevism. He disliked state-controlled socialism and communism imposed by commissars. He slowly came to the conclusion that submission to Rome was the only solution, not only for the problems of individuals and society but for those of the world as well. To be a Roman Catholic, he said, was to become a real internationalist, not – as the communists trumpeted – by joining their party. A literary man, aware of the way words subtly change their meaning, he was revelled in what he called 'the iron immortality of the Latin Mass'. Discussions with Hilaire Belloc, Ronald Knox and others helped him make up his mind. Perhaps it was made easier by the fact that he had chosen a Roman Catholic priest, Father Brown, as the hero of his most popular novels.

He acknowledged there could be many reasons why a person submitted to Rome. GK shied away from writing about himself. But this description of his own conversion process is revealing. With typical Chestertonian paradoxes, it described the fears and questions which he (and, no doubt, other Anglicans) went through in reaching his decision. It may also echo the memory of what it felt like when he asked Frances to marry him.

'He (the enquirer) has come too near to the truth, and has forgotten that truth is a magnet, with the powers of attraction and repulsion. He is filled with a sort of fear, which makes him feel like a fool who has been patronizing "Popery" when he ought to have been awakening to the reality of Rome. He discovers a strange and alarming fact that . . . the moment men cease to pull against it they feel a tug towards it. The moment they cease to shout it down they begin to listen to it with pleasure. The moment they try to be fair to it they begin to be fond of it. But when that affection has passed a certain point, it begins to take on the tragic and menacing grandeur of a great love affair. The man has exactly the same sense of having committed or compromised himself; of having been in a sense entrapped, even if he is glad to be entrapped. But for a considerable time he is not so much glad as simply terrified. It may be that this real psychological experience has been misunderstood by stupider people and is responsible for all that remains of the legend that Rome is a mere trap. But that legend misses the whole point of the psychology. It is not the Pope who has set the trap or the priests who have baited it. The whole point of the position is that the trap is simply the truth. The whole point is that the man himself has made his way towards the trap of truth, and not the trap that has run after the man. All steps except the last step he has taken eagerly on his own account, out of interest in the truth; and even the last step, or the last stage, only alarms him because it is so very true.'[6]

GK was anxious to show that becoming a Roman Catholic was a rational and sensible thing for any person to do who was seeking the meaning of life. In the background of the passage we sense GK was trying to excuse himself for delaying so long. He said he postponed submitting to Rome for years because he hoped his wife would submit with him. Yet it is also likely he hesitated because he was conscious that, as a well-known essayist, dramatist, and poet, such a step would attract great publicity and shock many of his friends and admirers.

He was still in this crisis of indecision when he addressed the first Congress. It was almost certainly that occasion which he recalled later when he wrote (mistaking the Albert Hall meeting for the 1920 Lambeth Conference – he was embarrassingly forgetful): 'The insecurity I felt in Anglicanism was typified in the Lambeth Conference . . . The crowd there cheered all references to the Pope, and laughed at every mention of the Archbishop of Canterbury. It's a queer state of things.' He was received in July 1922. A few days afterwards he wrote to his mother: 'The fight for the family and for the citizen and everything decent must be waged by the one fighting for Christianity . . . I have thought this out for myself and not in a hurry . . . I believe it is the truth.'[7]

His conversion was splashed in headlines across the national press and, as he feared, caused a sensation. In an age when it was fashionable for intellectuals to be atheists or dilettantes in other cults, here was one of the most well known among them taking the Christian religion so seriously that he had become a Roman Catholic! For Roman Catholic propagandists it was a moment of divine intervention. If such a thoroughly English and distinguished person as GK could become one of us, they cried, why not you? Letters of welcome were sent to him from Roman bishops, priests and lay persons from all over Britain. G. B. Shaw sent a brief note: 'My dear GK. This is going too far.'

Chesterton's conversion did not in fact involve much change in his way of life. He still made his confession and went to mass as he had done in his Anglo-Catholic days. Nor did it appear to affect his literary output and style. The main difference was that he felt vastly relieved that at long last he had taken such a step, especially when Frances joined him in 1926. Years afterwards he quoted with approval another convert who said he could not explain to others why he had become a Roman Catholic because, having become one, he could not imagine himself as anything else. When GK died Fr O'Connor, his friend and father confessor for many years, and his model for the Father Brown stories, gave him the last rites. It is said that afterwards the priest picked up the author's pen from the bedside and kissed it as a gesture of thanksgiving to God for all GK had written.

Sheila Kaye-Smith

Sheila Kaye-Smith was already a recognized novelist when she appeared on the Congress scene in the 1920s. She wrote thirty or so novels, mostly with a rural background, some of them with a religious theme. One of her most successful was *The History of Susan Spray the Female Preacher* (1931)[8] which was inspired by a visit to England of Aimee Semple MacPherson, an American evangelist. It tells the story of the personality changes which occurred in a girl who, brought up in poverty, rose to become an apparently inspired preacher of a little-known sect in the south of England. In the tale Susan became ambitious, selfish and greedy for money as success overtook her, and she had unhappy relationships with men.

Kaye-Smith's family lived in St Leonard-on-Sea and as a teenager she became attracted to the Anglo-Catholic Christ Church, though forbidden to go there by her parents. While working in London during the first world war she went to St Alban, Holborn, where she felt at home worshipping in 'a luxurious High Mass'. She described how she was stirred by 'the warm incense, smelling shadows, the inking red lights . . . It gave me back my perception of what has been called the numinous side of religion – the shining cloud, the Shekinah, without which the Temple is merely a heap of stone – the gleam.'[9] Like Chesterton, she supported Anglo-Catholicism because she saw it as a divinely appointed means of restoring the Catholic faith to England. It was the theme of her one and only Anglo-Catholic novel, *The End of the House of Alard* (1923), which told in part the story of a young priest's struggles to fulfil that vision. Inevitably this led her to take a growing interest in Roman Catholicism. When her literary agent told her she might offend that Church in one of her books, she pointed out that, on the contrary, her approach had been a sympathetic one, for in it she had shown that Romanism at its worst had the advantage over Anglicanism at its best.

In 1924 she married the Revd Theodore Penrose Fry, curate of Christ Church. He had to resign as it required its clergy to be celibate. He accepted a curacy in St James, Norlands, then in run-down North Kensington, and then in 1926 moved to the more extreme St Phillip, Gloucester Road. By then Kaye-Smith was accepting engagements to speak at Congress meetings in different parts of the country. She wrote a short book on Anglo-Catholicism in 1925. It followed the pattern of similar books on that subject appearing in those years, but she went further than others by expressing her admiration for Rome: 'We want a Catholicism which is alive, progressive and modern, and this the Church of Rome provides. It requires only a slight contact with her to learn that . . . her living voice proclaims the needs of each successive generation. She is more modern than any modernism, for her care is for the whole man, not only that part of him which reads the *Spectator*.'[10]

Also like Chesterton, she became uneasy by the way certain Anglo-Catholic clergy ignored the authority of their bishops. She described one occasion when her parish priest (she did not identify him) told her that it was her duty to attend services of benediction even though the Bishop of London had forbidden them. One effect was that she felt she could no longer be completely sincere when she addressed Congress audiences. A conscientious as well as a strong-minded woman, from about 1927 she decided to decline further invitations. Other disappointments followed. Kaye-Smith and her husband were saddened when they heard that the

Malines conversations had ceased. The hopes of many Anglo-Catholics had been raised by the news of them. They were unaware of the realities of the relationship between Rome and Canterbury. The Revised Prayer Book fiasco was another blow.

The couple shrank at the thought of leaving the Church of England. They feared it would appear a cowardly act, letting their friends down by giving up a fight. To try and resolve this tension, they went on a cruise to Italy in September 1928, hoping their experience of Roman Catholicism in an Italian culture would cure them of their leanings. But instead they were enchanted. They were astonished and delighted ('in spite of the fleas and smell of garlic') to worship in Palermo cathedral which was crowded with the poor as well as the well-to-do. Congregations at mass or benediction included flocks of children, who genuflected, knelt and made the sign of the cross as naturally as everyone else. Clergy in soutanes and religious in their habits were everywhere. It was so different from what Kaye-Smith and her husband experienced in England. The international character of the Roman Church, signified in the use of the same Latin rite, impressed itself on them.

They returned home with their minds made up. After Fry had resigned from the parish, they were received into the Roman Church together in 1929 by Fr Martindale SJ (she called it 'dropping the hyphen'). The sales of Kaye-Smith's books – successful because many Anglo-Catholics who heard her at the Congresses bought and read them – had made her a comparatively wealthy woman. With her royalties she and her husband purchased a small farm in Sussex, and settled down to country life.

At the farm they found themselves nine miles from the nearest Roman Catholic church, so they donated a patch of land for the building of a small church. It was dedicated to St Teresa of Lisieux and the first mass was held there in 1935. Kaye-Smith found herself unexpectedly but happily becoming an unofficial lay pastor in a growing congregation. She wrote later, 'To visit the sick, round up the back-sliders, teach the children, care for the sanctuary, take the collection, "answer the mass" are all things that I would never have dreamed of doing in either of my husband's parishes. Indeed, I have never felt more of a clergyman's wife than since I ceased to be one!'[11]

However, she was critical of certain Roman Catholic practices. She thought the granting of indulgences was a medieval relic that should be forgotten, and said the Archbishop of Westminster's instructions on the keeping of Lent one year showed he was out of touch with people's daily lives. She was glad that, when her church was officially linked to the then new church at Tenderden in Kent, the parish priest there was English and not Irish. Her conversion did not attract so much attention as that of GK, but it caused disappointment and unease among her admirers and readers, especially Anglican women. Later she promoted the novels of Jane Austen, who was not much read by the public then, and wrote books about her. She died in 1956.

Father Vernon Johnson

Vernon Johnson was a contemporary of Knox at Trinity College, Oxford. He was ordained to the priesthood in 1913 and served as a curate at St Martin Church, Brighton, before joining the Society of the Divine Compassion in 1918. The community had been founded in 1894 with a rule similar to that of the Franciscans. It was based in a house in Balaam Street, Plaistow, where it was pastorally responsible for St Philip Church. Later the community acquired a farm at Stanford-le-Hope in Essex for the training of novices. It acted as spiritual directors to a group of Sisters of the Divine Compassion which had opened a leper hospital at East Hanningfield some miles away.

Johnson was soon recognized as a gifted evangelist and invited to lead parochial missions all over Britain. Obviously sincere and youthfully attractive in his brown habit, he was a popular speaker at the Congresses. He was usually assigned the last slot in the day's programme so that he could send congregations and audiences home inspired by what he said. He was committed to a vision of the Church of England as the best means under God for the conversion of the nation, provided it remained faithful to its Catholic heritage. He was aware that not all Anglicans shared the same vision, but he was hopeful for the future. He wrote: 'So far as I had thought of [the Roman Church] I had regarded her as the greatest indeed of all the Christian bodies but one which had made many and great mistakes—notably her insistence on the papal claims. These mistakes completely separated her from the Church of England, and vaguely, I suppose, I hoped that she would one day find her proper place in the final reunion of Christendom which, however, was too far off to worry about very seriously.'[12] He was saddened when he heard from time to time that friends had converted to Rome.

In 1924 he was leading a retreat in a convent when the mother superior suggested he should read a recently published book about St Teresa of Lisieux. Johnson did so and found himself emotionally stirred by the story of a young girl who had been admitted to the local Carmelite convent at the age of 15 and who, after a long and painful illness, had died in 1897 at the age of 24. On the orders of her superior, Teresa had written a spiritual journal of her sufferings and, after her death, the reverend mother arranged for this journal to be edited and published – to edify readers but no doubt also to publicize the convent. *L'Histoire d'une ame* (*The Story of a Soul*) became a best seller. Stories began to circulate of how individuals had been healed after invoking Teresa in their prayers, and this led to her being beatified in 1923. Johnson was fascinated by her. He wrote later:

> Here was someone who had loved Our Lord to a degree beyond anything I had met before: a love as strong as that of the martyrs of old, yet with the delicacy and tenderness of a little child, so delicate and so tender that one almost fails to realize the furnace in which that love was so wonderfully refined. Above all else it was the saint's gospel of suffering as being the most blessed gift by which alone we could really be united to our Blessed Lord in unfettered love, and her interpretation of pain and suffering as something which can be offered in union with our Blessed Lord's cross for the sake of the Church and for the salvation of souls – it was all this which, coming into my life when things were getting exceedingly difficult, lit up and made real to me certain spiritual truths towards which I was dimly groping; truths from which I had been discouraged from holding as being morbid and so forth, and which I now found were the very foundations of the saintly life. For the first time I understood St Paul's words, 'I fill up that which is behind of the afflictions of Christ in my flesh for his Body's sake, which is the Church' (Col. 1.24).[13]

When he heard the ceremonies for the canonization of the nun were to take place in Lisieux, he went to France to be present. While he was there he visited Teresa's home and inspected an exhibition of her personal possessions – her habit and sandals, her school books and pictures she painted, the bed on which she had been nursed in her illness, and the signs of mortification (including, apparently, a knotted cord for discipline). He experienced a profound spiritual awakening which he could not describe. Finding that Teresa had been a girl brought up in a working-class home only forty or so years previously, he believed God had wonderfully revealed to him that sainthood was possible for ordinary people living ordinary lives. Afterwards he encountered a Belgian priest in the garden of the convent and the two of them were so absorbed in a discussion about Roman Catholicism that they were accidentally locked in and had to climb over a wall to get out.

Johnson made a second visit the following year and met people who had known Teresa personally. He marvelled again that such a young girl could become so saintly through suffering. But then he faced a worrying question. Teresa had become a saint as a Roman Catholic: could she have led such a holy life if she had been a member of the Church of England? When he returned to Plaistow, Johnson began reading and praying about his experiences and slowly became convinced the Roman claims were justified. Rome was 'the one true Church founded by Jesus Christ to guard and teach the truth to all men until the end of time', he concluded.

All this Johnson described in *One Lord, One Faith*. In the introduction to the book he said he had written it because he was aware his submission to Rome would distress the many people who knew him. Yet if English people knew what the Roman Catholic Church was really like, he went on, instead of being prejudiced by misunderstandings and lies about her, they would appreciate why he had made that choice. He knew he would feel like an exile in his own land. But recent events in the Church of England had made him realize that he could no longer expect it to be an authoritative teacher and defender of the Catholic faith. 'The Anglican Church is more like a debating society than a teacher of eternal truth revealed for the spiritual and moral guidance of the spiritual life of the world.'[14] He was received in 1929, re-ordained and attached to one of the religious orders. At the end of his book he wrote: 'The human ache and sense of loss was just as acute, but there was a foundation now which made it less difficult to bear.'[15]

In *One Lord, One Faith* he expounded the scriptural basis for the papal claims (much to the appreciation of Roman Catholic reviewers) and listed what he saw as the defects of the Church of England and the weakness of the Anglo-Catholic position as reasons for his conversion. It was the same argument that the other converts presented. Yet, reading Johnson's book, it is difficult to resist the impression that, entangled with the search for spiritual authority, there was also a romantic attraction of a Christian man to the picture of a devout young woman whose holiness through suffering was widely acknowledged and publicized. That is not to say, of course, that his conversion was insincere. He would not have remained a Roman Catholic priest if it had been. But Johnson confessed that he had been given Teresa's book to read while he was going through a difficult time in his life (the demands made on him as a popular preacher, problems of relationships in the community from which he was often absent?) and this may have been another unconscious reason for his decision. There was also the strain of being a star evangelist in the Anglo-Catholic sky and of all that involved. Mackay, when he heard the news, commented that the friar had become lonely and was feeling the need for more personal support. If that is true, then Johnson's fascination for St Teresa becomes more understandable.

His conversion caused such concern in the Anglo-Catholic constituency that within a few months Wilfred Knox and Eric Milner White hurried into print with *One God and Father of All: A Reply to Father Vernon* (1929). They spoke of him as 'an old and intimate friend' and said they had no intention of belittling Roman holiness. 'But,' they went on, 'for the sake of those who may be troubled at his going, we feel bound to set down, with equal sincerity to his, the reasons why we consider his point of view mistaken and his reasoning weak.'[16] The book was an able defence of Anglicanism.

Some years later Johnson was appointed to the Oxford chaplaincy as successor-but-one to Knox. The post was often held by ex-Anglicans, presumably because the Roman hierarchy thought that, as they were graduates of the university, they were strategically placed to win others to the faith. In 1946, the year before he left Oxford, he reported to the governing board that 27 nationalities were represented in the chaplaincy which now numbered 250 undergraduates. His transfer of allegiance to Rome had evidently not deprived him of his evangelistic charisma. While he was at Oxford he founded the Association of Priests and Laity of St Therese of the Child Jesus and wrote *The Spirituality of St. Thérèse of Lisieux* to promote interest in and devotion to the saint. It is interesting to reflect that such popularly as there is among English Roman Catholics today for 'the Little Flower' owes much to this former member of the SDC. For his work Johnson was made a monsigneur.

Basil E. (Christopher) Butler

When the young Basil Butler gave a paper on 'the Sacraments in Other Religions' at the 1927 Congress, those who listened said he would one day become a leading theologian. His paper revealed he had researched his subject thoroughly. He drew on ancient texts, primitive Christian wall paintings and references in the early fathers, to demonstrate that 'Christian Eucharistic ideas and practice, at the stage of their development represented by St Paul and St Mark, are in all essentials free from the influence of the mystery religions.'[17] As a scholarly treatment of the subject it could hardly be improved today.

He was born in 1902, one of the six children of an Anglo-Catholic family in Reading. His intellectual abilities took him on a scholarship to St John's College, Oxford, where he collected prizes and gained three firsts. In 1925 he was appointed a tutor at Keble College. He had only been ordained a priest for a year when he spoke at the Albert Hall. It was while he was at Oxford that he began to doubt Anglo-Catholic claims. He spent a vacation in Germany and was impressed by the way in which so many of the inhabitants of a Black Forest village attended Sunday mass. The contrast with what he had experienced in English services could not have been greater. It was from then that he saw the Church not only as a hierarchical institution but as a gathering of the local community for worship. It also struck him that the Roman Communion as the international body was able to create such local communities in any part of the world and yet remain united. Its Catholicity was demonstrated in its local manifestations as well as in its universality. Back in Oxford, he was going through the streets one day in cassock and biretta to take a service in a church when a working man stopped him and asked, 'Where can I get mass, Father?' Butler wanted to say, 'Come with me', but he knew he couldn't. After a moment's painful indecision, he directed the man to St Aloysius Roman Catholic church. The incident increased his doubts.

A close friend at St John's, Martin Hancock, the son of an Anglican priest, was also attracted to Roman Catholicism, and Butler once described how they went for a walk together on Cumnor Hill to discuss what they should do. They knew that if they submitted to Rome their families and friends would be deeply hurt. Absorbed in their conversation, they sat down on a barrel beside the road. When they came to go, they found they were stuck; the barrel contained tar.

After the Congress Butler discussed his doubts with Dr Kidd, the Warden of Keble, who suggested he went to Downside to talk the matter over with Abbot Ramsay, whom Kidd knew. Butler also had many talks with Ronald Knox. Eventually he resigned his post at Oxford and was received into the Roman Church. In 1928, he returned to Downside to teach at the school. He entered the Benedictine community there in 1929, assuming the religious name Christopher, and was re-ordained priest in 1933.

For Butler it was anything but an easy decision. For several years afterwards he wondered if he had done the right thing. Those who knew him said that his conversion was not because he had any enthusiasm for Rome, nor because he had become disillusioned with the established Church. He did it simply out of a sense of duty that he should follow where his convictions led him. But he retained a deep attachment to the Church of England for the rest of his life. He had many Anglican friends and admired their attempts to grapple with the philosophical problems which confronted the Christian faith as the twentieth century unfolded.

He continued to teach at Downside for many years and edited the *Downside Review*. He was Abbot from 1950 to 1966 and elected president of the English Benedictines in 1961. It was as president that he attended the Second Vatican Council from 1962 to 1965. His fluency in Latin (the language in which the Council conducted its business and wrote its constitutions) was an advantage in that gathering and, representing the religious orders, he was free from any sense of obligation to the English bishops. He was a member of the commission for doctrine and contributed to *Lumen Gentium,* the important constitution on the Church. On this commission he was supported by other theologians like Cardinal J. Suenens and Hans Kung. The constitution was framed in such a way that it presented the Church as the gathering of the priestly people of God, with the Pope presiding over an episcopal college instituted by Christ. Butler became an acknowledged expert on the Council and was a regular speaker at meetings and services for Christian unity in all parts of Britain.

We must not exaggerate Butler's influence in Rome; his was, after all, only one voice among two thousand. But nevertheless it was a Roman Catholic commentator who said, 'If Cardinal Newman was "the invisible father" of the second Vatican Council, then no one was better suited to be his spokesman than Christopher Butler.'

Sir Henry Slesser

Sir Henry Slesser did not become a Roman Catholic until 1946, six years after his retirement. Although he was the Labour Party's leading solicitor, he was always something of an outsider. His parents were German and their son (whose second Christiàn name was Herman) changed his surname from Schoesser, following the custom of many such families – including the royal family – in 1914. His Anglo-Catholic views on subjects such as birth control and divorce made him unpopular among his Parliamentary colleagues, and the promotions he received through the Labour Party were criticized by his contemporaries in the legal profession.

He retired in 1940 and went to live in Devon, serving for more than twenty years as a county councillor and as chairman of the Dartmoor National Park Committee. He was received into the Roman Catholic Church in 1946. In that year he published *The Anglican Dilemma* in which he traced the legal history of the Church of England from the time of the Reformation up to 1928, including Tudor legislation and the Public Worship Act of 1874. In this way he sought to demonstrate how the

Church had always been subject to the State and therefore was never free to be truly Catholic. Passages in it read like a barrister presenting a case for the prosecution.

The Anglican Converts

Knox and the five Congress personalities listed in this chapter were members of a steady stream of Anglicans who converted to Rome during these years. Statistics are not easy to obtain. W. S. F. Pickering suggested that from the years of the ritualist controversies until 1939 there were between ten and twenty clergy converting each year. That being so, then probably two hundred or more clergy submitted in the years between the wars. Their reasons for doing so were probably similar to those just described. Obviously an important one was disenchantment with the Church of England. Their experience of its life and worship, and that of the laity, convinced them that it was not truly Catholic, and for those wanting the security of such teaching and practice, Rome was the Church to join.

That, of course, is one of the things the Congresses hoped to prevent. Their message was that the Church of England (with the Anglican Communion) is a branch of the one, holy, catholic and apostolic Church. The Anglo-Catholic's prayer and hope was that one day Anglicans, Roman Catholics and Eastern Orthodox would be joined in one Communion and fellowship (with the Nonconformists, too, if they accepted the Catholic faith and order). But it leaves us with the uncomfortable thought that the Congresses may have been one of the unintentional causes of leading others to do what Chesterton and the rest did. What was said at those exciting and crowded sessions may have raised expectations which were not achieved as the years went by. The kind of Anglican Church they depicted seemed unrealistic when compared with what some Congress members experienced in the Church of England. They were made only too aware of what Pickering called 'the ambiguity of Anglo-Catholicism'.[18] Was the Church of England truly Catholic? Or was she merely Protestant in Catholic vestments?

Knox had grown up in a household of Evangelicals who were opposed to Catholicism, and he knew there were many others in the Church of England like them. He could not foresee a time when they might change. Fr Vernon doubted whether the Church of England could ever be a school of Catholic holiness like the Roman obedience. Butler found the theological and historical claims of Rome so convincing that, with much regret, he transferred his allegiance to it. Chesterton and Kaye-Smith were both disturbed by the attitude of Anglo-Catholic clergy who emphasized the apostolic succession and all it signified, yet were prepared to disobey their bishops when it suited them. Slesser, too, may well have shared in this feeling, since he met many similar priests through his involvement in the Congress movement.

But, as we have speculated, there may well have been other factors which led them to make the decision to convert. An adolescent reaction against anti-Rome sentiments in the family seems to have been a fairly common one. Chesterton recognized this when he wrote of his own conversion: 'The father of some . . . Anglican or American Puritan family will find, very often, that all his children are breaking away from his own more or less Christian compromise (regarded as normal in the nineteenth century) and going off in various directions after various faiths or fashions which he would call fads. One of his sons will become a Socialist and hang up a portrait of Lenin; one of his daughters will become a Spiritualist and play with a planchette; another daughter will go over to Christian Science and it is quite likely that another son will go over to Rome.'[19]

Close relationships with others also played a part. Knox and Chesterton had Roman Catholic friends. Kaye-Smith's doubts about Anglo-Catholicism were confirmed when she discovered her husband was of the same mind. With Butler it was the intellectual difficulties. Any emotional involvement was regret at leaving a Church he genuinely respected. Slesser, with his legal mind, may have felt much the same after he retired and was able to look back on his association with the Congress movement with greater detachment.

The period witnessed a remarkable growth in the numbers of Roman Catholics in the country. Converts had the impression they were joining a Church which was becoming successful in its mission. Hilaire Belloc was a propagandist for this view, and many listened to him. During those years Rome attracted some remarkable people – Maurice Baring, W. E. Orchard, Alfred Noyes, Rosalind Murray, Arnold Lunn, Eric Gill, David Jones, Evelyn Waugh, Graham Greene and Frank Pakenham. They accepted the current Roman Catholic doctrine and practice without questioning. Papal authority was a shelter from the intellectual and ideological turmoil of contemporary society. Among them were those like Chesterton who believed that the Roman Church was the one force that could save England from social disintegration, and from the political movements unleashed in Europe in the aftermath of the war. GK hoped that Rome would one day become the focus of a new Christendom which would bring in a Europe united in peace and justice. Among them, too, were those – but certainly not GK himself – who initially admired Mussolini as the one who saved Italy from communism, and who fought on Franco's side in the Spanish Civil War.

Commentators have said that in time these converts gave an Anglican flavour to Roman Catholicism in England. They did not leave behind them all they had learned and experienced as members of the Church of England. Many had been trained at public schools and were graduates of Oxford or Cambridge, and they formed a distinct social elite among their co-religionists which gradually became more influential. At a local level they contributed to the fulfilment of that vision of the Church as the people of God as Butler did at the Second Vatican Council.

But not all converts were so happy with their change of allegiance. Some of the less socially privileged priests, placed in northern parishes after re-ordination, found their ministry among predominantly Irish families very different from what they had imagined. Rome's way of exercising episcopal authority irked those who had been used to the benign oversight of Anglican bishops. Those who were married had to revert to lay status and, as the years went by, missed the opportunities of fulfilling the pastoral ministry to which they believed they had been called by God. They lost a sense of personal and spiritual fulfilment. They also found it difficult to maintain old friendships and missed the clerical camaraderie of their Anglican days. One vicar wrote to the *Church Times* saying he knew of four priests who had submitted to Rome but within the space of one year had returned to the Church of England. The passage over the Tiber was not all one way.

17

The Fourth Congress 1930

When plans for the 1930 Congress were publicized, the protests made on previous occasions revived. There were complaints that it was a waste of money, it diverted priests from their work in their parishes, it was a show of strength by the London clergy that would exacerbate divisions in the Church, and it was an attempt by the Congress committee to raise more funds for itself. A prominent critic was M. Bartlett, vicar of St Wilfrid, Harrowgate. In letters to the *Church Times* he acknowledged the value of the first Congress but said the later ones had become too partisan. He had no intention of going to London for the Congress and he would not encourage any of his congregation to go, either. Others agreed with him. R. C. Wainwright, vicar of St Mark, Washwood Heath, Birmingham, complained a leader of the movement told a meeting he had been at that the Congress was a rallying point for Catholics and they should support it whether they agreed with it or not. Yet as far as he was concerned, what happened in London had no relevance to what he was trying to do in his parish.

The organizers justified the decision to hold the fourth Congress by pointing out that the rejection of the Revised Prayer Book by Parliament had created a crisis in the relationship between the Church and the State. Furthermore, 1930 was the year of the next Lambeth Conference and the scheme for a united Church in South India was to be put before the bishops. These were grave matters, and the Congress would provide an opportunity for Catholics to make their views on them known. With these concerns in mind the Congress executive chose to make the doctrine of the Church the theme for the main speakers. They reasoned that talks on the scriptural and doctrinal foundations of Catholic ecclesiology would set out the case for the Church to be free of State interference, and truths about the nature of the Church which the Lambeth bishops ought to consider when they discussed the South India scheme.

When it was known that the opening high mass of the Congress was to be at Stamford Bridge, there were further criticisms. Protesters said that a football field was not a worthy place for such a service, and that it would dishonour the sacramental Presence by making it a public spectacle. Wilson, now chair of the executive, published a letter explaining that, when he was invited to draw up an outline programme for the Congress, he realized that there was no church in London big enough to hold the numbers expected at the opening mass. He had put the Stamford Bridge proposal before the general council of the Congress, consisting of seventy priests and laymen from all over England and Wales, and they had accepted it unanimously. He had also sought the permission of the Bishop of London, who had warmly approved of the idea and agreed that the President of the Congress, Bishop Roscoe of Nassau, should be the celebrant.

At an early stage in the planning the executive arranged for the band of the Life Guards to play at Stamford Bridge. When he heard of this, J. A. Kensit, the secretary of the Protestant Truth Society, wrote to King George V, asking him to tell the Bishop of London to forbid the service as it was 'an affront to your Coronation oath' to let the band play at 'an illegal service'.[1] The letter was passed on to Stanley Baldwin, the prime minister, who asked the executive to withdraw their invitation to the Life Guards. The executive reluctantly agreed and began making other arrangements. When he heard this, the prime minister wrote to thank them. Kensit got up a petition against the service signed by nearly 25,000 people; but when he took it to Winnington-Ingram, the bishop told him there was nothing illegal about a Prayer Book service being arranged out-of-doors with his permission.

These various controversies were so widely publicized that Bishop Roscoe referred to them in his opening remarks in the Albert Hall. The whole Congress, he said, had been carried out under a fusillade of opposition and criticism which was worse than anything encountered before. They came not only from the Protestant front but from 'our very own rear and flanks'.[2] He added the executive had decided that after the commemoration of the centenary of the Oxford Movement in 1933, the next Congress would not be until 1940, to coincide that year with the next Lambeth Conference.

Archbishop Lang sent a letter welcoming the Congress for 'your devotion to the Lord Christ and to the Church which is his Body, your thankful use of the Sacraments of his grace, your efforts to extend his kingdom at home and throughout the world' (though he added ironically, 'I dare say some controversial things . . . may be said or done . . . of which I might not personally approve').[3] Temple at York also signified his support. The executive could now feel they had friends in high places.

THE FOURTH CONGRESS 1930

The high mass at Stamford Bridge on Sunday, 29 June, look place as arranged. The weather was fine, and by the time the service was due to start the altar was surrounded by 2,000 priests, servers, and religious, and there were about 15,000 in the stands. A Captain Francis Burgess conducted a brass band and a large choir. A long procession of bishops from overseas, distinguished guests, Meletios, the Pope and Patriarch of Alexander, and the bishops of the Greek and Syrian Orthodox Churches, came in, followed by Bishop Roscoe and the sanctuary party. The mass was that for SS Peter and Paul. The only mishap was during the consecration when a gust of wind blew over the tall candlesticks on the altar. Five young men received Communion. At the end of the service fiery crosses were blessed and sent to eleven London churches where 24 hours of continuous intercessions were to be offered until the Congress opened on the Monday afternoon. A nurse in the congregation wrote afterwards, 'Our Lord, born for us in a stable, does not disdain to become incarnate in our offerings of bread and wine – on a football field.'[4] Protestant demonstrations were limited to a few people delivering leaflets outside the grounds, and a man in a car with a loudhailer shouting texts from the Bible.

During the week there were four main sessions with talks on the marks of the Church: one, holy, catholic and apostolic. At other times there were short instructions on going to confession, preparing for Communion, prayer and retreats. Separate meetings were held for priests, men and women. Those who addressed the priests' meeting were embarrassed because the women ushers, contrary to instructions, remained in the hall on chairs by the exit doors. Their presence meant the speakers felt inhibited in what they could say about moral issues in the personal life of the clergy. Evensong was sung each afternoon led by choirs from different London churches, and a Children's Day was arranged for the final Saturday.

In the ten years since the first Congress the ecumenical movement had moved a few steps forward. The conversations between the Church of England and the Nonconformists following the Lambeth Appeal had been friendly, but nothing much practical had emerged from them. More was happening locally. The war helped to break down the social divide between 'church' and 'chapel' which had persisted in many places. In Manchester during the war Anglicans and Nonconformists formed a consultative committee with a part-time secretary and arranged ecumenical meetings in the Free Trade Hall. Bristol continued to have united services of Anglicans and Nonconformists in spite of Anglo-Catholic hostility. Congregations in some towns formed joint committees to create housing associations and other social projects, such as helping families during strikes and periods of unemployment. The Swanwick conferences organized by the Student Christian Movement brought together young people of different traditions, some of whom would later become leaders in their respective denominations.

Significant developments were taking place internationally. In 1925 a conference was held in Stockholm to consider the Christian response to the social and economic problems of the post-war age, which resulted in the formation of the Life and Work committee. Two years later another conference in Lausanne tackled the theological problems of unity and set up the Faith and Order committee, with Gore, Temple and Headlam as the Anglican leaders. In 1948 these two committees merged with the newly inaugurated World Council of Churches.

The Malines conversations had been the only sign of a slight temporary rapprochement between Anglicans and Roman Catholics. Their significance was not recognized until the setting up of the Anglican–Roman Catholic International Commission after Second Vatican Council. Here and there were personal friendships between individual Anglicans and Romans. A box in the Albert Hall was reserved at the later Congresses for the Jesuits from Farm Street. Relations with the Eastern Orthodox were hopeful. Some Anglicans, like Frere, had a special interest in the Churches of the East, and an Anglican and Eastern Churches Union had been formed in 1908. There was talk of a possible recognition of Anglican orders by some of the Orthodox and the Old Catholics.

This, then, was the situation reflected in the talks given by W. Knox, W. G. Peck, rector of St John the Baptist, Hulme, Manchester, and G. D. Rosenthal.

Knox had moved away from his earlier papalist leanings (perhaps in reaction to his brother's submission to Rome?) In his talk he explained how the unity among the scattered Christian communities of the New Testament era sprang from their common belief in Jesus as their Saviour and Lord, and from their baptism which made them members of Christ and of one another. That unity still existed in the sight of God, and Christians must always be seeking to fulfil it. At the present day, he said, two ideals for achieving unity were being put forward. One was to draw all Christians into accepting a uniformity of faith, discipline and practice, and to be ready to expel any who would not conform. That was the Church of Rome's ideal. It was an impressive exhibition of unity, but it excluded Anglicans, Protestants and the Orthodox. The other ideal was simply to regard all who declared their allegiance to Christ as members of the Church. That was attractive since it was motivated by a spirit of

Christian charity and by a longing to bring disunity to an end, but it represented a false idea of what the Church is. It ignored the need to hold together in one organized body those whose devotional life is centred on the sacraments.

These two ideals, Knox went on, existed in varying degrees within the Church of England. They created tensions, but he would not want to excommunicate those on either side who sincerely held them. Faith is not stimulated or built up by compulsion: that had been demonstrated too often in the Church's history. Rather, he said, 'the weapons by which we must abolish error are Christian weapons – the weapon of love, which loves the heretic while it hates his heresy; the weapon of Christian life, which shows him our faith is a deeper and stronger thing than his; the weapon of Christian learning, which is free to establish the truth and overthrow falsehood ... This is the warfare that the Church of England has waged for the defence of Christendom ... Her comprehensiveness may seem weak to those who only shut their ears against the danger of hearing any false doctrine; but it is the glorious privilege of Anglicans, and of Anglo-Catholics in particular, to wage the only effective warfare for the overthrow of error and the vindication of the truth.'[5]

He respected the reasons why many in India wanted to bring different denominations together into one institution, but the Church was a divine creation not a human institution. Those involved in such schemes must be prepared to accept the historic creeds and the Catholic ministry. Those who reject these should not be admitted to Communion but, he added, 'It is not for us to be too dogmatic in unchurching them.'[6]

In this last remark Knox showed that he was one of an increasing number of Catholics who, through personal contacts and experiences of co-operation in practical matters, found it difficult to un-church Nonconformists. Not all Catholics shunned local ecumenical meetings. Some, like Mackay, had regular meetings with ministers of other denominations – the beginnings of the later clergy fraternals. The Mirfield fathers joined Nonconformists in support of the Labour Party. Speakers at the Congresses quoted with appreciation Nonconformist scholars like P. T. Forsyth and C. A. Anderson Scott. In a Congress leaflet Thornton said he had been made to feel very humble when he encountered the faith and lives of Salvationists and Quakers who had not even been baptized.

Peck, the next speaker, began by saying he knew more about Nonconformists than most Catholics since he had been brought up as a Methodist. (He had once been a Methodist minister.) He warned his audience that Anglicans and Nonconformists whose only mutual contacts were ecumenical meetings at Swanwick or Lausanne could go home with misleading impressions. Such gatherings tended to attract participants who were unrepresentative of those they were supposed to represent.

However, he admitted, things were changing. When he was young the attitude of Nonconformists to Roman Catholics seemed to have been derived chiefly from Foxe's *Book of Martyrs*. But more recently a new note was being sounded. People were becoming more objective. It was suggested that Catholicism and Protestantism are forms of Christianity adapted to various psychological and racial types, and that an acceptance of this by all concerned was a sufficient basis for unity. Such a suggestion was absurd, he said, but at least it indicated some prejudices were being erased.

The Catholic vision of unity was quite different. 'We mean the reunion of the separated with the one visible organism continuous throughout history and guaranteed by the succession of its Bishops. They [Nonconformists] may come, bringing their sheaves with them, but to that Church they should come.' He realized he was being more hard line than Knox, for he added: 'It may be that in seeking visible unity we are but seeking the outwards expression of a spiritual union which in God's eyes exists – unity in which Nonconformists are included. I think Father Knox would go as far as that. I do not want to quarrel with that position; but I am sure that the profound mystical fact of unity cannot be visibly set forth by the repression of sincere conviction on either side . . . Therefore intercommunion as a step towards organic unity, and all the fantastic flirtation which is going on in some places, seems to me to be mere sentimentalism devoid of philosophy.'[7]

Rosenthal distinguished between unity and union by an illustration from the human family. The members of a family had a unity, he said, because they were all related to one another and they had family likenesses; but if there was disagreement among them they were not in union with one another. The Church was in a similar position. Its unity had been given to it by God through Christ and it had certain family likenesses in its sacraments, worship and organization; but its union would only be realized when all it members came together in the sacraments of the Church with Jesus Christ as its head. The Roman Church and the Orthodox had these 'family likenesses'; so did the Church of England. But Nonconformists did not. Anglicans, therefore, should not compromise their Catholicity by joining schemes of reunion with them. 'No desire to conciliate, no local advantage, no apparent expediency either in South India or anywhere else, could possibly justify a violation of the essential principle of family unity, on which our very status as a true part of the universal Church of Jesus Christ is based.'[8]

He was more hopeful of improved relationships with the Orthodox, demonstrated in the presence of the Patriarch of Alexandria and the other bishops at Stamford Bridge. 'The Orthodox Church meets us on the true ground of family unity. It does not ask, as Rome does, for unqualified submission. It simply asks: 'Do you hold the Catholic Faith? Do you use the Catholic Sacraments? Do you exhibit the Catholic likeness?' But the breach with Rome was wider and more difficult to heal. Anglicans could concede that the Pope should have a position of honour and primacy among the bishops, but not of jurisdiction. However, he went on, 'To say that Rome will never . . . change is to ignore the lessons of history and to deny that the Spirit of God is guiding the destinies of His Church. Can we claim that there is a special divine guidance to the Church of England, so that we can hope for such a revolutionary change in its outlook as it is the aim of the Congress movement to create, while at the same time we refuse to credit the possibility of such a change of outlook among Roman Catholics?'[9]

The *Church Times* commented: 'As so often happens, it fell to the Revd G. D. Rosenthal to make the last speech of the evening. Perhaps the arrangement was made on the principle that it is well to keep the best wine till the last; and certainly Fr Rosenthal's is a choice and sparkling vintage such as puts gladness and courage into the hearts of those who enjoy it.'[10]

These three talks reflect Catholics' varying attitudes towards the developing ecumenical movement. All, however, were opposed to the South India scheme. They rejected the arguments of theologians like Headlam who said Nonconformists should be accepted as members of the Church because they were already united with all who had been baptized. Rosenthal's hope that Rome herself would one day change was notable when most of his contemporaries regarded that Church as immovable. Like some other things said at this Congress, it had a prophetic quality about it when seen from the years after Second Vatican.

In the session on holiness E. G. Selwyn spoke on the scriptural roots of holiness. Christian belief in holiness, he said, was drawn from Israel's teaching on the Mosaic law and the transfiguration of that teaching in the example and words of Jesus the Messiah. Christ's followers, the people of the new covenant, were to reflect that holiness in their lives: 'Ye shall be perfect as your heavenly Father is perfect.' This, of course, was Catholic teaching in the widest sense, Selwyn went on. All Anglicans would have said Amen to it. But beyond that there were differences between Evangelicals and Catholics. Evangelicals regarded the Church as a congregation of men and women who gave each other mutual support in their search for holiness. Catholics believed the Church was a community sanctified by the Holy Spirit to be the Body of Christ, providing through the sacraments forgiveness and strength for the building up of holy lives among its members.

While Catholics did not deny the signs of holiness among Evangelicals and other Christians of other traditions, they held that the spiritual pilgrimage to the holy mountain was more difficult unless those who undertook it relied on their baptismal life and all that life provided. So he commented: 'Our devotion to [Christ] has not grown to maturity until it has come to include devotion to his Body, the Church, and through that to all our neighbours. Loyalty to the Church means loyalty to the world in the sense of accepting the obligation of an infinite loving-kindness and charity to all men.'[11] He outlined Catholic teaching on the three degrees of sinfulness (original, venial and mortal), on forgiveness, on the need for discipline, and on the danger of the Church's holiness being jeopardized by worldliness, especially through involvement with the secular powers.

N. B. Hudson, vicar of St John the Baptist, Newcastle, followed this by taking as an example of the Church's worldliness the attempt to persuade Parliament to authorize the Revised Prayer Book by modifying its contents and presenting the measure a second time in 1928. The Church had been tempted to betray its true calling in seeking to maintain its privileged position by compromising what the Convocations and the Church Assembly had agreed. Parliament's second rejection was a bitter lesson. As individual members of the Church, he said, we could fall into the same temptation by toning down our Catholic beliefs and disciplines to make the faith more acceptable to our worldly friends.

'Am I wrong when I say that the power of the Church of God in this land is the feeble thing it is precisely because thousands upon thousands of her children have found her ideals too high? Surely there never was a greater need than that we should seek to regain that spirit of heroic adventure which, really believing that all things are possible with God, endures to the end with an unresting perseverance in the quest for that true supernatural holiness to which every member of the Holy Church is called.'[12]

It was left to Bishop W. V. Lucas of Masai to remind the audience that holiness also depended on how Christians faced suffering – not only ill-health and physical suffering but also the sufferings of the mind, anxieties, perversities, doubts, wonderings and bewilderments. 'We shall try to use those sufferings, to accept them willingly and even gladly, because by them we may be made more like our Lord and Master himself, for suffering marked that royal road of the Holy Cross by which he himself went before.'[13]

He was speaking out of his own experience of the sufferings he had seen among the African towns and villages he visited. He was also thinking of his personal disappointments and frustrations. Coming back to England he was reminded of the great gap between the comparative wealth of the Church of England and the poverty and lack of resources which affected the Church in his diocese. But he ended on an encouraging note: 'We are not called to make ourselves good. God the Holy Ghost in his life has undertaken our sanctification. He has begun a good work in us, and if we will only respond and co-operate and never say him nay, then because he is almighty and all-loving, and longs for our perfection more than we even in our best moments could long for it, the victory is his beyond all doubt, for he is God.'[14]

In their contributions Frederick Hood and Humphrey Beevor, Librarians of Pusey House, affirmed the Catholicity of the Church of England against those who might be seduced by trends in contemporary society. Hood wanted Catholics to be sure they were not only well instructed in their religion but also living it. Beevor wanted them to avoid controversy and to serve the truth by persuasion and conversion. The third speaker in this group, Fr Thornton, tackled one of the most difficult problems facing the Church: reconciling continuity with change. How do Catholics respond to developments in the world around them without forfeiting their Catholicity? He was ill, so his paper was read for him.

Thornton began by pointing out that Catholicism is not a system but a way of life. As a way of life it is expressed in terms of human fellowship, but at the heart of that fellowship is an attitude of devotion to the incarnate Christ based upon union with him in the Church. The incarnate Christ is both God and Man. As God he is universal, 'for all times and for all places, for all sorts and conditions of men'. But as Man he lived, died and rose again during a certain period of time and in a particular place in human history. The Catholic Church, therefore, is also characterized by these two qualities – universality and historicity. And it is this which gives rise to the problem of how far the Church can change in order to relate meaningfully to people at different times and places without being unfaithful to the universal and unchanging Gospel.

Thornton admitted there was no easy answer to this, but he believed the key belonged 'to those who are in daily communion with our Lord through the fellowship of his mystical Body. Without that key of the living religious experience, Catholicism will seem to be no more than a vast historical relic, a system which has had its day and whose claims must now be brushed aside.'[15]

By appealing to experience, Thornton may have caused unease among his hearers. Some Catholics associated religious experience with the wilder forms of Protestantism. But those who read his script afterwards would notice that he had used the word in a qualified way. He was referring to the experience of those who prayed 'through the fellowship of his [Christ's] mystical Body.' Such individuals were not free-roving self-appointed prophets; they were believers who were devoted to Christ within the discipline of the Church. He used the word 'fellowship' in the Pauline sense of the common life in the Body of Christ (the title of a book he published a few years later), and the phrase 'mystical Body' to indicate he was distinguishing it from the institutional Church which is not always faithful to the guidance of the Spirit. In seeking God's guidance for the future, he went on, it is necessary to hold the universality of the Catholic faith in balance with its historicity. To emphasize one at the expense of the other is a grave error. He illustrated this with reference to contemporary developments in scientific medicine:

'As we cannot play fast and loose with the structure of human life without disaster, so we cannot treat the historical life-structures of the Catholic Church as mere human conveniences, by-products of history, upon which men may lay violent hands and bend and twist them to win some temporary advantage. The comprehensive principle of Catholicism has a definite embodiment. There is nothing formless or vague about that inner reality which finds its outward manifestation in sacraments and hierarchy, its liturgies and creeds, and in the many garments wherewith the spirit of Catholicism has clothed itself ... If human nature is divinely given, it is also a growing thing which has not yet reached its final goal. So, too, Catholicism is not only divinely given; it has also had a long development in the past, and in its human aspect it is still unfinished. It must continue to grow towards a destiny which lies in the future. We have therefore not only to hold fast the Catholicism to which we are heirs. We have also to strive towards the fuller Catholicism of the future, which St Paul describes as "the measure of the statue of the fulness of Christ".'[16]

He acknowledged that Anglo-Catholics owed much to the Roman Church in reviving the Catholic claim and mission of their Communion, but they should not allow their gratitude to obscure Rome's limitations. 'The issue may be summarized in a sentence,' he said: 'Catholicism is much larger than Roman Catholicism [sic].'

Working that out in practical terms was an uncomfortable process, he said, especially if unity is perceived in terms of uniformity. Catholics cannot with justice demand wider liturgical liberties while at the same time demanding restrictions on intellectual freedom. He was glad that during the past century the Church of England had, with some deplorable exceptions, allowed room for different movements within it to develop and prove their worth. He felt the parties in the Church were now treating each other more courteously and showing signs of being willing to learn from one another. 'When men speak of disorders in the Church of England, we can point them to this more excellent way of ordered charity, which relies on the power of truth to win its own battles. The so-called 'disorders' may be a sign of life more precious than any enforced uniformity.'[17] He ended with a warning that the Church needed to discern the difference between true and false developments, as the time may come when secular civilization becomes increasingly hostile to Christian standards culminating in a world-wide apostasy.

Two years before the Congress *A New Commentary on Holy Scripture* (1928) edited by Bishop Gore was published. Written by fifty contributors who were generally sympathetic of the Catholic tradition, it was intended to show that a critical and historical interpretation of the Bible was possible alongside a devout interpretation of what was revealed through its texts. Some conservative Catholics were disturbed by it. The synod of the SSC condemned it as heretical. But the *Commentary* reflected the new approach to biblical studies which was evident in the addresses given at previous Congresses. At the 1927 Congress E. C. Hoskyns had demonstrated how the Catholic doctrine of the Eucharist could be traced back to the New Testament itself. At this Congress he set out to do the same with the Catholic doctrine of the Church.[18]

Hoskyns began by pointing out that apostolicity was part of the essential nature of the Church because it was sent by our Lord himself to proclaim the Gospel. Furthermore, it was sent until the end of time and therefore its work was permanently eschatological, not in the sense that the End was near but in the sense that the Gospel demanded a response here and now. What the Lord initiated as the Messiah of God was for all times as well as all peoples everywhere.

The first apostles, he went on, had the task not only of proclaiming the Gospel but also defending it against misunderstandings and heresies. They were teachers of the Word before and during the years in which the books of the New Testament were being written, and this task they handed on to their successors who were called, trained and authorized through prayer with the laying on of hands. The emergence of the episcopate was parallel with the process in which the Scriptures were canonized. Therefore that office is part of the God-given nature of the Church to which the Scriptures bear witness.

'In our modern controversies we Catholics are not concerned primarily with organization. We are concerned with the nature of the Gospel, at a time when there is much vague talk about the independent motions of the Holy Spirit. Taught by the New Testament, we are bound to think of the Episcopate as preserving the witness of the Apostles, and to demand this of the Bishops. The Bishops are not mystical figures to whom we owe some strange kind of undefined mysterious obedience. The Bishops are responsible for bearing witness to Jesus Christ, the Son of God, and to hold the Church to that witness.' Then came a comment on bishops who used their position to enforce their own opinions, no doubt with Barnes of Birmingham among others in mind: 'The Episcopate [does not] offer an opportunity to gifted individuals to occupy an exalted position and to tyrannize over those who are endowed to a lesser degree with intellectual or other gifts. The authority of the Bishops depends solely on their link with the Apostles, though we may hope that this link may be productive of virtue and courage and of intellect and spiritual insight. Such resultant powers are, however, wholly secondary.'[19]

Hoskyns challenged those of his contemporaries who followed Headlam in regarding the episcopate as being of the *bene esse* of the Church. For him it was of the *esse* of the Church. He did not specifically identify the apostolic succession of the laying on of hands as the essential sacramental sign for admission to the episcopal college, but he implied this in what he said about the authority of the Bishops depending 'solely on their link with the Apostles'.[20]

The movement owed a great deal to Hoskyns. He demonstrated more than any other theologian at the time that the Catholic faith is founded on the Gospel, and this teaching helped perceptive Evangelicals and other Anglicans outside the movement to take its claims more seriously. That theme was taken up in the first book of one of Hoskyns' students at Cambridge, Michael Ramsey. *The Gospel and the Catholic Church* was published in 1936 – the year of Hoskyns' death at the age of 52. In his book Ramsey, brought up in a Congregational church before he became an Anglican, expounded the doctrine of the Church in the New Testament and the early fathers with a gratitude and respect for his early nurture in the Christian faith. He proclaimed the centrality of the cross of Christ in a manner more usual among Evangelicals, but he also criticized those who undermined the authority of the Bible, the creeds, the sacraments and the ordained ministry in a way worthy of the Congress speakers on those topics. It is a tribute to Hoskyns that *The Riddle of the New Testament* and *The Gospel and the Catholic Church*, both inspired by his teaching, have survived as two of the most widely read books of the Congress years.[21]

C. S. Gillett, Dean of Peterhouse, Cambridge, warned against those who claimed to be following the Holy Spirit in ways incompatible with Catholic Christianity. Of their sincerity there was no doubt, but they were surrendering to an emotional desire for Christian unity without counting the cost to the Christian faith. Such people spoke of 'the Catholic tradition' and 'the historic episcopate' without believing the doctrine which these phrases enshrined. Those who supported the South India scheme were in danger of making this error. The mission of the Holy Spirit, he went on, is to be discerned in the emergence of the episcopate from Jesus' commissioning of his apostles who, in their turn, commissioned others to succeed them through prayer and the laying on of hands. From this there came the three-fold ministry of the Catholic Church under the guidance and authority of the same Spirit. The episcopal ministry, therefore, formed a permanent and essential link in the Church back through Pentecost and the apostolic Church to Jesus Christ himself.

'If we Catholics are resolute to retain the episcopal office in the Church, it is not because we have a superstitious reverence for the title of Bishop itself (there are many other titles which could serve us just as well); it is simply because we believe that the Bishop is in fact an Apostle, and embodies a doctrine of ministerial succession that is absolutely vital to the Church – the doctrine that alone can ensure not only the continuity of the Apostolic witness, but the secure and certain celebration of those Holy Mysteries by which we are assured that the significance of the work wrought in the very flesh and blood of Christ's humanity is ultimate and universal.'[22]

So Gillett skilfully summed up the classic Anglo-Catholic doctrine of the historic episcopate as being essential for the Church and the sacraments. It was a doctrine which Catholics steadfastly upheld – some in the *esse* school, others in the *bene esse* – for the rest of the century and beyond in discussions about Christian unity.

On the Thursday evening five thousand men attended benediction at St Stephen, Gloucester Row, and then processed to the Albert Hall to hear a series of short talks on the precepts of the Church. Fr Biggart CR spoke on marriage, divorce, the South India scheme, and going to confession. Rosenthal pointed out that twice as many women went to church as men, and that, except in the matter of ordination, both sexes were equal in the sight of God. He referred to the practice (in churches where men and women sat on opposite sides of the central aisle) of men going to the communion rail first, and he quoted what a woman had said about it:

'No doubt it is on the same principle as that on which men give precedence to women in the world; in church, poor dears, men are the weaker sex.' There was much truth, he said, in the satirical verse:

> In the conflict for Religion,
> In the turmoil and the strike,
> You will find the Christian soldier
> Represented by his wife.[23]

As if to confirm Rosenthal's figures, nearly twice the number of women attended their special session the following day. As they were queuing to enter the Albert Hall, a small group led by a Wycliffe preacher addressed them and distributed leaflets until a priest came out and led the women in singing the hymn, 'Jesus shall reign'. As they entered the building they heard the protesters outside joining in. The same group appeared outside the Hall on Saturday afternoon as children and parents were queuing to go in. They shouted 'Down with priests!' until stewards came, and there was a scuffle when the police arrived. The Wycliffe preacher was arrested and appeared a few days' later in the Westminster police court; he was fined five pounds and bound over to keep the peace for six months.

The Prioress of Whitby described the role of religious orders in the Church and the need for more vocations. Ethel Allanson, an educationalist, spoke on the mothers' responsibility for teaching the faith to their children. Ruth Kenyon gave a talk on social conditions in the country. As secretary of the Anglo-Catholic Summer School of Sociology, she was well informed on the situation. In her address she urged her listeners to become more involved in local and national politics. She was obviously aware that the effects of the American slump were affecting those in the northern industrial cities most for she was critical of 'the comfortable classes in the south of England' who dismissed the unemployed as idle 'dole-snatchers'. She quoted the Congress hymn to the Virgin Mary:

> May the Mother's intercessions on our homes a blessing win:
> That the children all be prospered, strong and fair and pure within

Then she challenged her audience: 'Do we mean it? *Strong*? In these homes of unemployment? *Fair and pure within*? The Mother will not do it without us. What are we doing and what are we feeling towards bringing it about? That is what we want to ask you today. . . That is our vocation as Catholic women in the world.'[24] People commented afterwards

THE FOURTH CONGRESS 1930

that it was the kind of speech Kenyon might have made at an election rally. It seems to have been the only reference to the effects of the 1930s depression at the Congress.

In view of Henson's criticisms of Catholics, many were surprised to see that the Bishop of Durham was to be the guest speaker at the English Church Union's annual anniversary meeting on the Thursday afternoon of the Congress. The reason for this was a change in his views on the establishment of the Church of England after the Commons' rejection of the Revised Prayer Book. Although not in favour of the revision, he had been shocked that what had been passed by the Convocations and the Church Assembly should have been turned down by MPs who represented neither English constituencies nor the Church of England. To the astonishment of his friends, he began to write letters to the press, articles and a book advocating disestablishment, and to accept invitations to express his views – including one to speak in the Albert Hall.

The Hall was crowded. Halifax was in the chair and, after welcoming the speaker, Henson stood to give what was afterwards regarded as a brilliant case for disestablishment. He began by saying that others, such as the Bishop of London, had like him changed their views since the rejection of the RPB, and he was glad that the two Archbishops had appointed a commission to examine the relationship between the Church and the State (its report was published in 1936). Furthermore, the fact that the Lambeth Conference was assembling in a few days' time showed that the Church of England had outgrown its national boundaries and that its links with the State had to be 'mended or ended'. As one who had originally opposed the setting up of the Church Assembly, Henson perhaps had some satisfaction in pointing out that the Enabling Act, far from giving the Church the desired 'life and liberty', had in reality made it more subservient to the State.

'That Act... was widely hailed as a victory of spiritual enfranchisement, the Magna Carta of the Church of England. In point of fact, the change which the Enabling Act effected, so far from increasing liberty, subjected the Church more completely to the control of Parliament. Before 1919 the spiritual supremacy of Parliament could only be expressed through the solemn and gradual method of legislation. A Bill had to be introduced by the responsible Government, read three times, debated in Committee with meticulous detail, agreed upon by both Houses, and finally approved by the King. Through the Lords spiritual in the Upper House the voice of the Church could at least be uttered. But under the new procedure of the Enabling Act, the hasty vote of a single House and that perhaps a House in which the spiritual estate is whole unrepresented, avails to impose the supremacy of Parliament over the Church of England.'[25]

The RPB never had a chance of being discussed in the Commons on its merits, he said. Instead MPs became agitated over the issue of reservation as a papal intrusion. This resulted in 'scenes of excitement and religious passion rarely seen in a secular body'. Although there may be differences on when and how reservation should be permitted, it was entirely within the Church's authority, not Parliament's, to ensure adequate provision was made in parishes for the Communion of the sick. Since he reckoned that not more than one in fifteen among those who had the right to vote in Parliamentary elections was a communicant (about 2,750,000), it could not be argued that MPs spoke for them. (This last point indicated another shift in Henson's views. In debates about the constitution of the Church Assembly, he had opposed Gore and those who wanted to restrict the franchise to communicants, saying that all who were on baptismal registers and were of age had the right to be on parochial electoral rolls.)

The whole controversy had revealed that masses of people outside the Church still had strong 'No Popery' feelings. This, Henson thought, was a situation that should engage 'the penitent consideration of our Roman brethren'. It certainly made it very difficult for the Church of England if she had to consider the reactions of non-Churchmen and non-Christians to any measures it may want to put forward. It also upset the working of the Church Assembly. Reminding his hearers of the way Evangelicals had urged their non-Anglican friends to lobby MPs, he went on, 'It is not wholesome that one party within the Church Assembly should be tempted to depend, not on its powers of argument and persuasion, but on its allies outside the Church. The growth of solidarity among English Churchmen is hindered by this cause.'

He closed by making four final points: (1) 'The spiritual supremacy of Parliament... is indefensible in principle and clearly mischievous in practice.' (2) 'The... nomination of the Bishops by the Prime Minister, who may or may not be a Churchman or a Christian – is difficult to justify, is clearly resented by many, and tends to destroy the moral authority of the Bishops.' (Henson, a Conservative to the core, was appalled at the thought that a Labour prime minister should make such appointments.) (3) 'The appellant jurisdiction of the Privy Council stamps an Erastian colour on the ecclesiastical courts and in the eyes of a large section of the clergy and laity robs legal decisions of moral authority.' (4) 'The parochial system clothes with ecclesiastical rights men and women who break ecclesiastical rules, and even deny the Church's authority altogether. This lowers the level of ecclesiastical life in the parishes, brings

THE FOURTH CONGRESS 1930

discipline into open contempt, and tends to destroy the very notion of Christian obligation.'[26]

A few days later at the Lambeth Conference, he noted in his diary, several bishops who had been present in the Albert Hall thanked him for his address. 'The most part of the English bishops are, I suspect, in the same mood of reluctant acquiescence. They cannot see their way to resist what nevertheless they cordially abhor. That, indeed, is mainly my own point of view. The subject is repulsive, why not let it fall into the background, and be suffered to pass from mind? I do not doubt that this expresses the real mind of the Anglican rank and file. They cling to the hope that the Archbishops' Commission may find a Scotch road out of the mess!'[27]

For the first time at a Congress one day was organized for children – the Saturday. Children's masses were held in different London churches in the morning, and then in the afternoon hundreds of children of all ages processed into the Albert Hall to present a pageant depicting the sacraments and the saints before an audience which filled the building to overflowing. The event was produced by E. S. Cheetham, the vicar of St Stephen, Gloucester Road, who acted as pageant master with the help of a group from the Women's Association. Off-stage he explained to the children that the subject of the performance was the motto of the Congress – The Church is One, Holy, Catholic, Apostolic – and he directed the proceedings from start to finish: there had been no rehearsal.

The first procession led a girl representing Mother Church down the steps into the arena, with a boy carrying the Cross of the Saviour surrounded by children holding pennants of scarlet and white. Mother Church ascended the steps onto the stage and took her place in the centre. After her came seven processions of the Sacraments of the Church. Baptism was headed by black-cowled boys with red and black pennants, and children in white veils with candles in their hands. Penance was represented with children carrying the symbols of the Passion – the crown, the robe, the lash, the ladder, the nails, the spear – and after them a penitent in sackcloth. Confirmation had boy and girl candidates, suitably dressed. Children, carrying a monstrance (empty) under a canopy adorned with a stream of yellow pennants, depicted the Blessed Sacrament, followed by acolytes and a sub-deacon, deacon, and priest. For Holy Matrimony a boy and a girl in medieval costumes came in next, preceded by children carrying a ring and a book. Holy Orders were represented by the banners of the English theological colleges and a vested ordination candidate holding a chalice and paten. Holy Unction was represented by a young sufferer borne in on an improvised stretcher and children holding a vessel of oils and a prayer book.

Next came a long procession of the Blessed Saints, all participants appropriately dressed. This was followed by the procession of Mary, the Queen of Heaven, with a girl wearing a golden crown and white veil over her blue cloak, carrying a sheaf of lilies. Acolytes in blue preceded her; behind her were angels with lighted candles. She ascended the steps to the stage, up to the highest platform under the great crucifix, to take her place on her throne.

Finally St George entered with a procession carrying his banner inscribed, 'The Faith of England', and an enlarged model of the Fiery Cross. By now the platform and the orchestra rises were crowded with performers and banners. At a given signal, Mary, high in the centre, stood and stretched out her arms in a gesture of welcome, and the audience rose to sing:

> I shall not cease from mental fight,
> Nor shall my sword sleep in my hand,
> Till we have built Jerusalem
> In England's green and pleasant land.

'The Youth Pageant', concluded the reporter, obviously moved, 'was a magnificent and an inspiring finish to the Fourth Anglo-Catholic Congress.'

The Congress was rounded off the following Sunday with special preachers at masses in London churches and in various towns and cities throughout the country. At the end of the Congress it was announced that 28,873 tickets had been sold. Although the executive had decided not to make any public appeal for funds, the collections at the various services and sessions raised £12,000. 'The crowded audiences and the enthusiasm at all the gatherings were beyond doubt an answer to those critics who questioned the advisability of such an undertaking in 1930,' noted the editors of the report triumphantly.[28]

18

The Parishes

Anglo-Catholicism and military terminology seemed to go appropriately together. In the early days of the ritual movement Catholic churches were 'besieged' by rioters. Priests had to 'fight' against bishops and others who tried to suppress their ministries. Protestant groups were 'enemies' who 'attacked' those who introduced candles, vestments, incense, and so on. The right to reserve the sacrament was won after a 'battle for the tabernacles'. To succeed in these things was to 'advance', and parishes which had imported the full Western rite and ceremonies were known as 'very advanced'. For them the fight was almost over, the battle won (as far as worship in their churches was concerned). The priest who willingly or unwillingly abandoned some practices was said to have 'retreated'.

After the war the Catholic Literature Crusade began publishing an annual *Church Guide for Tourists*, listing parish churches which promoted Catholic faith and practice. The extent to which that faith and practice had advanced was indicated by signs against each entry: one asterisk (*) indicated that there was a daily eucharist; two (**) a choral eucharist on all Sundays; (***) confessions heard at fixed times; and four (****) continuous reservation. If while you were on holiday you wanted to find a church with the full works, you made for one marked with four asterisks.

Various factors helped or hindered advances. The appointment of the priest was obviously a major one. Where the bishop had the right of appointment he could nominate the successor when a vicar or rector moved on, retired or died. Parishioners could make their views known, and so could influential lay persons – a local land owner, a magistrate, or a politician in a conversation with a bishop at dinner in the Athenaeum. Some bishops resisted such pressures. Winnington-Ingram in London used his personal charm to soothe Evangelical fears. Temple told objectors there was a place for Anglo-Catholics in the Church as well as for others. Burge of Oxford did everything he could to avoid trouble and told his archdeacons to deal with any problem. For all his reservations about Catholic practices, Henson in Durham tried to appoint priests who would build on the good work a predecessor had initiated, whether Catholic,

Evangelical or whatever. Like his episcopal contemporaries, he was glad to see an ineffective or troublesome priest accept a post in another diocese, but he was anxious to use vacancies to keep able young priests in Durham. However, diocesan bishops had only between a quarter and a third of livings in their gift, so Catholics had to rely on private patronage for preferment.

Private patronage varied enormously from the monarchy, cathedrals, incumbents of certain parishes, institutions such as colleges and professional bodies as well as individuals who inherited avowsons through their families. As we have seen, Lady Warwick used her patronage of parishes along the Essex–Suffolk border to appoint Catholic priests who established traditions which survived years afterwards. The avowsons of some parishes were acquired by a number of Catholics trusts which secured a succession of 'sound' priests. This meant that, although a diocese like Manchester had a succession of Evangelical bishops until Temple's appointment in 1922, it had enough Catholic parishes to become the centre for two successful provincial Congresses in the 1920s. Of course, bishops always had the option of refusing to license any priest nominated by a patron. But since that might mean referring the case to the ecclesiastical courts – and was therefore an extremely lengthy and expensive procedure – most bishops or the priests concerned were reluctant to resort to it.

The geography and sociological character of the parish, along with the size of the congregation the new incumbent inherited, was another factor in helping or hindering change. It was generally easier to introduce the Catholic faith and practices in a working-class inner city parish where churchgoers were used to following ordained leadership, than in a middle-class suburban one where there were strong-minded professionals in the congregation. It was also easier in a new mission church established in a growing suburb of a provincial town than in the central church near the market place. In cities and towns people who disliked the changes could opt to attend services elsewhere. But in the countryside, where the parish church was the only place of worship for miles around, that was not so easy. There changes had be introduced very slowly – we might say almost unobtrusively – and then with the simplest ritual. Priests like Baverstock in Hinton Martell and Briscoe in West Bagborough had long incumbencies during which they came to be trusted by their parishioners and so could introduce changes – Briscoe a plain Sarum ritual, Baverstock an elaborate Western one. In other country places change might be effected more swiftly in the country where the new incumbent had exceptional gifts, as at Walsingham in Norfolk and St Hilary in Cornwall.

A third factor was the strategy adopted by the new incumbent. A few Catholic priests believed in changing the worship of a church as soon as possible. 'Start as you mean to go on,' was their advice. An example was one who announced at his induction that the following Sunday the usual monthly 8 o'clock Communion service would now be celebrated weekly and that morning prayer would be replaced by a sung mass. The bishop and the archdeacon present must have shuddered when they heard that. The result was almost always arguments and divisions among the congregation, with some deciding to cease attending worship or going elsewhere, and a remnant vowing to hang grimly on – with, perhaps, a few Catholics secretly rejoicing that their church was at last 'moving forward'.

The advent of parochial church councils (PCCs) from 1920 onwards had to be taken into account by bishops and patrons. Although their powers over the appointment of a new incumbent were marginal – at the most they could only let their views be known – their support was needed if changes were to be introduced into worship, especially if any expense was involved. For clergy who were used to making such decisions without reference to anyone else, this restriction was irksome. Some incumbents could dominate or manipulate their PCCs into agreeing with almost anything. Others had to learn the art of leading the council to accept decisions democratically. It was not unknown for a dissident group to attempt to pack an annual general meeting of the parish with their supporters to ensure they were elected to a new PCC to continue their opposition to the vicar's schemes. One favoured method of introducing, say, vestments or a statue into a church was to find someone who was willing to pay for it as a memorial. PCCs were more amenable to this kind of change if they knew it would not cost them anything.

A majority of clergy were wiser and introduced change only after careful teaching. The more astute among them provided opportunities for their congregation to experience Catholic worship elsewhere – at open days in a local religious community, or at the annual festivals of the diocesan branch of the English Church Union or one of the other Catholic societies. The Congress movement gave encouragement to many clergy who wanted to develop Catholic teaching and practices in their parishes. The executive's initiative in promoting local Congresses was important for this policy. These gatherings, enthusiastically supported by large crowds in churches, cathedrals and public halls, enabled priests to take groups from their parishes to hear Catholic speakers and to catch something of the spirit of the movement. They also helped some who were less sympathetic to learn what the movement really stood for. As we have seen, the Congress executive in London stressed the importance of inviting 'those of other schools of thought' to the meetings and services.

How many parishes 'advanced' during the Congress years? Nigel Yates researched the effect of the Oxford Movement on parish life in various parts of England; Peter Cobb did something similar for Bristol; and John Hawes for Brighton. But with some exceptions most of their work deals with the late nineteenth century. More needs to be done to clarify the picture (this is one of the aims of the Anglo-Catholic Historical Society). By 1939 the dioceses of London, Southwark, Chichester, Exeter, Bristol, Bradford, Ripon and Newcastle had a fair proportion of Catholic parishes. But here I can only mention as samples a few parishes where I had access to books by local historians, old parish magazines and other records, plus a few personal memories.

St Augustine, Kilburn

One of the strongest supporters of the Congresses was P. H. Leary, vicar of St Augustine, Kilburn, until he retired in 1930. Leary was a close friend of Mackay and a member of the 'Wise Men of the West' which met in All Saints' vicarage during the war years. He was part of the original group which planned the first Congress. St Augustine's was one of J. L. Pearson's grand gothic designs; its tall tower and spire dominated not only the parish but also the north London skyline. With four curates and two communities of sisters in the parish (the Sisters of the Church and the Community of St Peter, which ran an orphanage and young women's home), its life is vividly depicted in its parish timetable:

> Services
> *Sundays*: Mass 7, 8, 9.30 (for children, sung); Matins and Litany 9; High Mass and sermon 11; Catechism 3 p.m.; Evensong, sermon and Adoration 6.30 p.m.
> *Weekdays*: Mass 7 and 8; also Tues 6.30 and Wed 9; Matins 7.40; Litany Wed and Fri after Matins; Evensong 6 p.m., except Sat 6.30 p.m.
> *Holy Days*: Solemn Evensong on Eve; Mass 6.15, 6.45 and 8.0 (sung).
> *Baptisms*: Sun 2.30 p.m.; Wed 5.0 p.m.
> *Churchings*: 5 minutes before any weekday service.
> *Confessions*: Vicar Fridays 2.30, 6.15, and 8.0; Sat 8.0. The curates also had set times.

The church had numerous organizations for children, young people, men and women, as well as branches of the English Church Union, the Confraternity of the Blessed Sacrament, and the Guild of All Souls. The annual round of festivals was popular, and events were organized to involve as many in the congregation as possible. An example of this was in the week of 19 June 1922, when it was decided to commemorate the jubilee of the day when the first mass was celebrated in the church.

> *Mon*, High Mass 11, preacher Bishop of London.
> *Tues*, High Mass 11; lunch at a hall in the orphanage.
> *Wed*, Solemn Requiem 8.0. Children's day with outdoor procession to a Mass 10, followed by pageants depicting St Augustine of Canterbury, the history of the parish, and scenes from African church life. The day ended with an afternoon of games and sports.
> *Thurs*, Social and Dance in the church school, 6.30–11.00 p.m.
> *Sun afternoon*, a procession (including the Bishop of Willesden) through the streets ending with an outdoor service in the churchyard.

During the procession the wind was so strong that, Leary wrote later, 'It looked as if it [the procession] was going to be levitated every moment... But it stuck to its feet with Catholic pertinacity, and the mighty wind, and the flying veils of the girls and the sturdy struggles of the lads with the banners made a picture full of delightful colour, and, if one thinks of it a little – a beautiful symbol of the Church Militant, as it battles through the world in a long white line of the Pilgrim's Progress.'[1]

It was communicants from the London parishes such as this who made up the great congregations at the masses on the football fields, who filled the Albert Hall and whose children took part in the Saturday pageants at the 1930 and 1933 Congresses. The movement of people out of London to the outer suburbs was only just beginning to affect the numbers who went regularly to these churches. The lunch on the Tuesday of the festival at St Augustine's was arranged to enable former parishioners living outside London to meet their friends after they had attended the mass.

St John Baptist, Tuebrook, Liverpool

The same kind of support came from the main Catholic parishes in the places were the provincial Congresses were held – Bristol, Birmingham, Liverpool, Manchester, Leeds and so on. If they were not as fruitful evangelistically as the organizers had hoped, they were encouragements to priests and congregations struggling to promote Catholic faith and practice in difficult circumstances.

This was the case at St John Baptist, Tuebrook, one of the Catholic parishes in Liverpool diocese. R. T. Brockman was vicar from 1896 until 1925. For most of his incumbency his bishop was F. J. Chavasse, diminutive of stature but fiercely Evangelical. Chavasse was vigorously anti-ritualist because he was conscious of being in a city in which practising Roman Catholics outnumbered practising Anglicans. Consequently he put the Tuebrook parish under a ban because the sacrament was reserved in the church. In spite of this Brockman gradually introduced more Catholic practices: the Christmas midnight mass in 1917; Vespers of the Blessed Sacrament and Devotions in 1919; and a statue of Our Lady and Child as a war memorial in 1920.

Brockman attended the 1920 Congress and came home saying it was a 'stupendous success, which surprised friends of the Catholic cause and astounded its opponents'. He was, as we have seen, the prime mover in forming a committee to launch the Liverpool Congress of 1922. The event was regarded by Catholic clergy in the diocese as a triumphant if long delayed vindication of their ministry. It also confirmed Brockman as the leader of the Catholics in the city. In a report of the local Congress one correspondent said, 'At every step we looked to him for leadership, and always his guidance was given with the single purpose in view of the advance of the Catholic cause in Liverpool.'

In 1923 Chavasse retired and was succeeded by A. A. David, translated from the see of St Edmundsbury and Ipswich. Son of a High Church canon of Exeter and a German mother, he inherited his father's High Church principles and his mother's 'Prussianism' (as his clergy called his authoritarian attitude). During his Liverpool episcopate David did much to improve the administration of the diocese, issued regular pastoral letters and material for days of prayer, and summoned clergy synods – though the complaint was made about the latter that they were called to enlist the clergy's support for actions the bishop had already taken. One of David's first acts after his translation was to lift the ban on St John's. He visited the church in 1925. It was, reported the parish magazine, 'historic in that it was the first time that the Bishop of Liverpool had been present at a service during the incumbency of the present vicar'. Boardman died shortly after the visit and his successor, T. Brancker (1925-37) pressed ahead with his predecessor's policies. Holy water stoops were fitted in the church in 1926. In the same year a Children's Eucharist at 9.45 a.m. displaced matins at 10 a.m. Brancker joined other Catholics in opposing the revision of the Prayer Book. He took a party from the parish to the

1927 Congress, travelling with the Liverpool contingent in the special train hired for the purpose.

But following the bishops' decision to let the Revised Prayer Book be used in church, David felt he must be stricter. At a special synod of clergy in the cathedral on 21 October 1929, he declared that three parish priests were excluding themselves from the fellowship by disobeying his request that there should be no extra-liturgical devotions before the reserved sacrament. Brancker criticized him for this. The offending priests, he said, could 'at the worst only be accused of excess of devotion'. Pinchard came to Liverpool shortly afterwards to assure the priests of the support of the English Church Union.

Undeterred, Brancker introduced the Mass of the PreSanctified on Good Friday in 1930. He took a party by train to the 1930 Congress. In 1932 *Ancient and Modern* was replaced by the *English Hymnal*. The following year three coach loads of parishioners from St John's attended the mass in the White City Stadium, and masses were celebrated in many Liverpool churches in thanksgiving for the Oxford Movement Centenary.

Brackner retired in 1937. His successor, W. H. S. Tayler (1937–46), introduced further changes – the *Gloria* at the beginning of the mass, the blessing and distribution of candles at Candlemas, ashes on Ash Wednesday, tenebrae in Holy Week, asperges at the Sunday mass, a Corpus Christi mass with a procession, and Stations of the Cross on Saturday evenings in Lent. Eventually a tabernacle was installed on the high altar – the summit of achievement in bringing the Roman Use into a church. As for Bishop David, he gradually became more tolerant of his Catholic parishes and attended a small local Anglo-Catholic Congress in Liverpool in 1942.

St Augustine, Kilburn, and St John the Baptist, Tuebrook, represent those churches which were either advanced in their ritual before the Congresses, or who were emboldened by the success of the Congresses to introduce the Roman Use step by step during those years.

St Matthew, Northampton

John Rowden Hussey (1893–1937) was sent to establish the parish of St Matthew in the Kingsley Park area of Northampton. Regular worship began in a schoolroom, then in an 'iron church', until the present church was built. It was designed by Matthew Holding, a Northampton architect, and was consecrated in 1893. From then on Hussey had a sung mass and sung evensong on Sundays and daily mass and offices. He said the Prayer Book was his authority for doing this. '[The Eucharist]', he told the congregation 'is the weekly Festival of Our Lord's Resurrection, a weekly rejoicing for His victory over sin and death. We must go back to the Prayer Book and see its true meaning.'[2]

The church supported a local Congress in 1925, when W. J. B. Couch of the ECU preached at the Sunday mass and Fr Wallis of Cowley at evensong. Speakers at the Congress included a striking episcopal line-up: the Bishops of Buckingham, Truro, Monmouth and Woolwich.

The following year Hussey proposed to the parochial church council that incense should be used at the sung mass on Sundays, and it was agreed that a poll be taken. One hundred and three took part. The results were thirty-three against, twenty-six 'not opposed', and forty-six in favour. At the next PCC meeting twenty-two were in favour and six against. On the basis of those votes, incense came into regular use from the Sunday after Epiphany 1927. To reassure the opponents and the undecided, Hussey wrote in his magazine that the reasons for introducing incense were (1) that it is used in Catholic churches world-wide, (2) that it is referred to in the Prayer Book and bears the mark of Divine approval, (3) that it gives honour to God and helps the worshippers to lift their hearts and minds to Him, and (4) that it is a mark of unity throughout the world. Hussey persuaded a wealthy parishioner to purchase a silver censer and matching incense boat, together with a pair of processional candle holders and extra cassocks and surplices for the servers. In 1930 he got permission to reserve the sacrament permanently. For the Centenary celebrations in 1933 he gave an introductory lecture with lantern slides in the church, and on Sunday 7 July there was a solemn mass and procession with Bishop Fyffe, formerly Bishop of Rangoon, as president and H. L. Goudge as the preacher.

When Walter Hussey succeeded his father as vicar in 1937, he followed the Catholic tradition of sponsoring the arts and commissioned a Madonna and Child by Henry Moore (1944), Graham Sutherland's Crucifixion (1946), and music by Benjamin Britten and Michael Tippett. He continued that tradition when he became Dean of Chichester cathedral (1955–77).

During Hussey's incumbency the diocesan bishops of Peterborough were F. T. Woods (until 1923) and C. C. B. Bardsley, Evangelicals who understood and supported Catholics provided they were not aggressively awkward. In any case, Hussey introduced change only after consulting the congregation and getting the approval of the PCC. Hardly any bishop would want to object to that.

Country Parishes

The Catholic movement was much slower to make progress in country parishes, except where the patron and the local squirearchy were of one mind about the faith, as at Hinckleton in Yorkshire where Halifax lived. Country clergy tended to be overawed by the life and worship they encountered in the large city parishes. They compared the hundreds who attended the high masses, and the queues for the confessionals, with their own small congregations. They counted themselves blessed if they had a few assistants in the sanctuary and choir stalls, and an occasional – if any – penitent. For many of them a daily mass was only a dream, unless there happened to be living nearby a devout elderly person who was prepared to come to church before breakfast each morning.

Their champion in the Congress movement was J. Briscoe, rector of West Bagborough, a village in the Quantock Hills. He was one of the most respected clergy in the West Country and remembered with affection for years after his death. He had been in this small parish for eighteen years when he spoke at the first Priests' Convention in Oxford in 1921. In his address he said that, unlike the town parish with its population of many thousands, in a village the population may only be a few hundreds and the priest has to minister to all of them, whatever their social status. Conscious that some of his hearers had sided with the miners and mill workers in their strikes for better pay and conditions, Briscoe pointed out that this kind of social action was not so easy for the country priest.

'It is true that the Church . . . should have done very much more in the past to help the labourers in their struggle for happier conditions of life: we must do all we can to help them now. Nevertheless, our mission today is to the squire and his family no less than to the farmers and labourers. We must never be content until we see the squire and the farmers and the labourers kneeling side by side at Mass on Sunday, and coming together to the sacraments.'[3]

Country people are intensely conservative, he went on. That is why proposals for revising the Prayer Book, uniting benefices, and allowing women and Nonconformists to preach in church were unpopular. In his parish he only used the Prayer Book with the exception of the collects for Corpus Christi and for the dead. Ceremonial at mass and at other services was simple and well rehearsed. 'We should not expect country people to be interested in the second year of Edward VI or the fashion plates of Doctor Dearmer.'[4] It may take years for the priest to be respected and win the affection of his flock; but once he has done that, he can quietly introduce vestments and incense for the great feasts without the involved explanation which invites controversy. 'Provide the Mass for the chief service on Sunday: there will be no need to talk much about it: the change will justify itself.'

Regular visiting to every house in the parish – possible in the country in a way that is not possible in large city parishes – and the right kind of teaching by the rector in the church school will slowly build up a Catholic congregation of a truly English kind. What impressed people was not a priest's preaching but his life evolving round a daily mass each morning and evensong each evening before the sanctuary lamp showing where the sacrament is reserved. Looking back over the years, there had hardly ever been an occasion when he was prevented from saying mass because no one had turned up for it.

Briscoe spoke on the same subject at the second Priests' Convention in 1932. This time he gave advice about what was appropriate in the celebration of mass in a country church. Keep everything very simple, he said, and avoid fussiness about ritual details. Two candles were sufficient. Only use incense at greater festivals, and then only cense the altar. Don't have processions round the church: they don't mean anything to country people. Just have one on Palm Sunday when it dramatizes the gospel of the day. Never chide people because they don't genuflect or make the sign of the cross: wait until they ask why you do it and let them decide for themselves. Evidently sensing that the non-communicating sung mass was losing favour in some quarters, he declared defensively that it was the best service for a parish on a Sunday morning, with opportunities to receive Communion at an earlier celebration. Again he stressed that changes can only be made in a country church when a vicar has been there a long time.

When people begin to appreciate Catholic worship, he said, they see the need to beautify the interior of the church. He had asked Ninian Comper to design a rood beam as a war memorial, a font cover painted with scenes from the Passion, and some stained-glass windows. He also had a gallery built and the organ moved from the chancel to the rear of the church. A year later, after attending the Centenary Congress, he described how he had slipped away from the Albert Hall one morning to visit Covent Garden market to buy some raspberries. Seeing a notice over a banana stall which read 'Green but Turning', he said it spoke to him of the Catholic movement in the countryside.

A different policy was adopted by A. Baverstock SSC, rector of St John the Evangelist at Hinton Martel in Dorset. Within a few years he had introduced the Western rite (in English) with a daily mass, and outdoor processions on the festivals of Corpus Christi with the Blessed Sacrament, of the Assumption with a statue of Our Lady, and of St Joseph (he had established a home for mentally handicapped children under that saint's patronage). He was warden of a society which cared for handicapped children in London, and helped to establish a small sisterhood for the same purpose in Dorset. He was one of the founders of the Catholic Literature Association and wrote many pamphlets and articles.[5] He was also one of the Guardians of the Shrine of Our Lady at Walsingham and Chaplain General of the Society of Mary. Visitors to Hinton Martel remarked that in religion it seemed little different from a similar village in Belgium.

Country parishes provided a base for a number of Catholic clergy who embarked on personal enterprises. A. Hope Patten, appointed vicar of Walsingham in 1921, got to know his parishioners in his early years though regular visiting and was able to involve them in his ambition to make the Shrine of Our Lady a centre for pilgrimage. In the late thirties, just before travel to the Norfolk coast was restricted by the outbreak of war, an increasing number of pilgrims came to the annual summer festival at Walsingham. Villagers got used to seeing — and some of them taking part in — Marian processions from the parish church through the streets to the Shrine. Hope Patten's relationship with Bishop B. Pollock of Norwich, an old-fashioned Evangelical, was never easy, but it did not prevent him from pursuing his vision. His support came from London parishes such as St Magnus the Martyr, where H. J. Fynes-Clinton was a friend, and from wealthy individuals such as William Milner, who provided the land for the Shrine and whose firm of architects designed most of the buildings. Halifax was also interested in the project though never visited it. One result was that several Marian societies merged together in the Society of Mary in 1931.

Conrad Noel's parish in Thaxted was the basis of his campaign for his own form of radical Christian socialism. He experienced hostility from landowners — especially when he backed the strikes by farm labourers — but in his later years the inhabitants came to accept him as a national if somewhat notorious figure. With his wife's folk dancing and religious processions he brought colour and fun into the town. Political opposition weakened into tolerant amusement. Through him the name Thaxted became well known in the country and, like Hope Patten's Walsingham, attracted visitors. The villages of St Hilary in Cornwall and Great Bardfield in Essex also became well known through the ministries of their respective vicars, Bernard Walke and Percy Widdrington.

The spread of Catholicism into rural parts was patchy. It was strongest in parts of the West Country, the Essex Suffolk border, villages round

Northampton, and the mining villages of the North; less so in Kent, the Midlands, and the North-West. Generally speaking, its success depended on a priest remaining in a parish for many years to win the trust of his parishioners (or most of them) and being sensitive enough not to push them further than they wanted to go.

19

The Faithful

Teaching the faith was regarded as the most important task of the parish priest after saying mass and administering the sacraments. Those who spoke on this subject at the Congresses emphasized that teaching was necessary from babyhood to old age. What people were taught depended on the priest or the teams of curates working under their vicar. Going back to our earlier classifications, clergy in the Red to Orange zones of the spectrum meant that in one parish there was greater stress, say, on going to confession, compared with those in the Blue to Violet zones. Social circumstances influenced individuals' and families' Christian observances, too. The couple with two children living in Kensington and with a cook, a maid and a nanny were obviously in a better position to keep certain precepts of the Church than the woman with six children in a working-class area of Kilburn whose husband was an unbeliever and unemployed (though a few did with the extraordinary grace of God). There were also differences for Catholics living in cities, towns and country.

Whatever their circumstances, they were 'the faithful'. Clergy spoke of them with a hint of self-satisfaction: 'The faithful in my church would never accept any priest who wasn't a Catholic.' Modernists derided the name: 'the faithful', they said, implied people who were passive and obsequious to their priests rather than to God. Evangelicals said what mattered was that worshippers should be born-again Christians, not just faithful church-goers. In response Catholic clergy quoted the opening phrase of the Athanasian Creed: 'Whosoever will be saved before all things it is necessary that he hold the Catholic Faith.' If saving faith really is the assurance of things hoped for and the conviction of things not seen, they said, then Catholicism properly taught and obeyed offered believers the way to that assurance of salvation.

To instruct and encourage the laity in their worship and private devotions numerous small manuals were published containing liturgical texts, forms of self-examination and confession, and prayers for private use. Among them were *Catholic Prayers for Church of England People, Before the Altar, The Anglo-Catholic Prayer Book*, and *St Swithin's Prayer*

Book. The last named was especially popular. In its attractive blue hardback covers it slipped easily into a pocket or handbag. When people arrived in church it was common to see them kneel down in the pew and open their *St Swithin's* to say the prescribed prayers before mass began.

Books such as *The Ceremonial of the English Church* and *The Ritual Reason Why,* instructed the faithful in what happened at services. First published at the turn of the century, they were re-edited in the twenties to go through three or four reprints. Their authors drew on contemporary Roman Catholic publications and justified the kind of liturgical practices the faithful would encounter in church by referring to sources of the past – canons (both pre- and post-Reformation), the 1549 Prayer Book, the Homilies and the works of early Anglican worthies. When the friends and neighbours asked Catholics why they went to a church where there was so much 'bowing and scraping', these books provided ready-made answers.

A manual often found on church bookstalls was a paperback called, *Good Manners in Church and out: a Guide to Church Customs for the Laity,* published by the Catholic Literature Association in 1932. Its author was Leslie V. G. F. Lean, who was a curate of St Mary, Paddington.[1] It offered a detailed picture of what was expected of the faithful in the Congress era (and an intriguing comparison with behaviour in church today). *Good Manners* reflected the ideals of the clergy in the Yellow and Green zones of the spectrum, with borrowings from those in the Red and Orange zones. It insisted on loyalty to the Prayer Book, though with additions from the Western rite to enrich a parish's worship. Bishops at the time would have approved Lean's vigorous assertion that 'he has no sympathy whatever with those who sneer at the Book of Common Prayer and despise its rubrics', but they would have frowned when they read that he included benediction among his list of 'other services'.[2]

The manual assumed that readers knew that the Church of England and the Anglican Communion are part of the one, holy, catholic and apostolic Church, and that it is their duty to attend their local parish church. It also assumed that their parish would have what were known in advertisements as 'full Catholic privileges'. But if they happened to be in, or move to, a low church parish, Lean said, they should still attend and, when necessary, go elsewhere to make their confessions. By identifying themselves with a congregation of a different tradition, they might in time help others to appreciate what Catholics stood for.

Good Manners systematically spelt out what was required of the worshipper. Attending mass on Sundays and great festivals is the first precept of the Church; to miss without a justifiable cause is a mortal sin. Each home should possess a Bible, a Prayer Book and a hymn book. Also a crucifix and a picture or statue of the Holy Mother of God, blessed by a priest after they have been purchased. Some may find it helpful for their private devotions to have a small bottle of holy water and a rosary at home.

When they move into a new area, the faithful should introduce themselves to the local priest and not wait for him to call on them. They should give him their name and address, inform him if anyone in the house is unbaptized or unconfirmed, and tell him the name of their previous church. When they leave the parish they are to let him know where they are moving to so that he can give them an introduction to their new priest.

Lean was severe in his advice on the laity's relationships with the clergy. They are not to join in gossip or criticism about their vicar. Always greet the clergy in the street, men and boys by raising the hat and women and girls by bowing the head respectfully. If they see the priest when he is carrying the Blessed Sacrament to a sick person, they are not to speak to him. They should stand aside as he passes, raise the hat or bow, and say a silent prayer in adoration to their Lord in the Sacrament. They should not speak to a priest either when he is vesting for mass or immediately after mass, unless the matter is urgent. At these times the priest wishes to say his prayers undisturbed. They should avoid criticizing sermons, no matter how poor they may be, for God may use them to convey a message to someone. Clergy may have their faults, he added defensively, but they are only human like the rest of us.

In preparation for mass, communicants should spend some time the day before in prayer and self-examination. If they have committed a mortal sin they should go to confession. They should avoid late engagements such as going to the theatre or dances the night before, in order to be alert both spiritually and physically next morning, for they are to have an audience with their King. (There were similar expectations about preparing for Communion the night before in Evangelical churches where the monthly celebration was regarded as especially sacred.)

This is followed by detailed instructions on how worshippers should behave during the service – when to stand, sit, and kneel. When it is time to receive the sacrament, they should genuflect as they get out of their seat, walk to the sanctuary and kneel upright, not bending over the Communion rail. Extend the left hand forward with the palm upwards and place the right hand over it open flat. Hold the hands level with the chin so the priest does not have to stoop down (today's taller clergy and eucharistic ministers will say Amen to that!) In some churches it is customary to receive straight into the mouth. If leavened bread is used, take great care to consume any small particle or crumb that may remain on the palm of the hand. Ladies should avoid wearing large-brimmed hats at Communion, and no paint or rouge whatever should be put upon their lips (another Amen!).

The author notes with disapproval that in certain churches a custom has grown up of celebrating Holy Communion in the afternoon or evening. That was contrary to Catholic custom which forbids a celebration later than one hour after midday. Catholics should not attend evening Communion services, not because the service itself is wrong (it is after all still the mass), but because by their presence they are unintentionally encouraging others to receive Communion without fasting. On fasting Lean said the faithful should not take food or drink after midnight if they intend to receive Communion next day. Even having a cup of tea before going to Communion breaks the fast. If they want to receive Communion at a high mass, they should seek the priest's permission beforehand since Communion was not usually offered at this service. The fasting rule is, however, relaxed for the sick and elderly.

There are further instructions on church-going. The faithful should only wear working or holiday clothes if better ones are not available. Women and girls should dress in accordance with Christian modesty; they should wear a covering on their heads, though customs about this may vary. Everyone should get to church in good time and not stand in the porch talking. If there is a holy water stoop, they should dip a hand into it and make the sign of the cross; genuflect towards the reserved sacrament and quietly go to a seat. They shouldn't greet neighbours or shake hands with them. They should say quietly to themselves, 'This is the House of God and the Gate of Heaven', and kneel down and pray. If they have to wait for the service to begin, they shouldn't stare around but read the Bible or say the rosary and find the pages for the service in the Prayer Book and hymn book.

The author is equally meticulous in prescribing when to make the sign of the cross: on kneeling down to pray; on taking holy water; at grace before and after meals; when saying the *Angelus*; at the invocation of the Holy Trinity ('In the Name of the Father . . . '); when receiving an absolution or a blessing; at the end of the creed; at the end of the *Gloria in excelsis*; at the words 'Blessed is he that cometh in the Name of the Lord'; before the *Benedictus* at matins and the *Magnificat* at evensong; when benediction is given with the Blessed Sacrament; before and after receiving Communion; at the prayer for the faithful departed; on being sprinkled with holy water; and before the reading of the Gospel at mass ('make the sign of the cross with the right thumb, one the forehead, the lips, and the breast').[3] (Another manual prescribed even more occasions, spattering its pages with black maltese crosses, including four during the *Gloria in excelsis*.) The author warned readers that in some churches men sat in the pews on one side of the main aisle and women on the other.

There are sections on 'The Catholic Home' and the 'Training of Children'. A Christian upbringing is vital for the spiritual growth of a child to prepare him and her for the difficulties and temptations of later life. Responsibility for this rests with the parents, who should take their children to mass at as early an age as possible and to catechism or Sunday school. Children should be prepared for confirmation between the ages of 7 and 14, but the earlier the better. The author noted that John Wesley was confirmed and received his first Communion when he was 8. Boys and girls should be sent to the church school, if there was one.

Then there is advice about participating in the other sacraments. On baptism: choose a saint's name for a child rather than a 'fancy or pet' one; invite communicants to be godparents, not Roman Catholics or 'members of a Nonconformist sect'. On confirmation: it was instituted by the Apostolic Church acting under the guidance of the Holy Ghost. Lean wrote, 'The Apostles had probably received instructions from our Lord to institute such a sacrament during the great forty days.'[4] He was one of the clergy who had a pre-critical interpretation of the Scriptures.

On confession: go regularly to the same priest so that he can be your spiritual director; make a list of sins (but destroy it afterwards). Then a warning: 'If you omit a sin deliberately or tell a lie in confession, you have sinned against the Holy Ghost, and the absolution pronounced by the priest is null and void. You go away, not only unabsolved, but in greater sin than before.'[5]

On holy matrimony: Catholics should marry communicants, or one wishing to be confirmed; they should avoid mixed marriages; a nuptial mass (before noon) is highly desirable so that the first thing the newly wed do is to receive Communion together (but not during Advent or Lent); remarriage after divorce is adultery, and subsequent children are illegitimate.

On holy orders: Catholics should regard it as a privilege to have a priest in their family; parents should do all they can to foster vocations; a priest's first mass is a wonderful occasion at which all who can should be present; if they can't be present, they should ask the newly ordained to bless them when they first meet him. The grace of ordination comes through the laying on of the bishop's hands in the apostolic succession, so Nonconformist ministers should never be called 'clergy' or 'priests', though as a matter of courtesy they can be given the title of 'Reverend.' Boys and girls should also be made aware of the sanctity of the religious life. It is an honour to a family when one of its members becomes a monk or a nun.

On holy unction: 'The inward and spiritual grace is the forgiveness of sins and, if God wills, the restoration to bodily health.'[6] It is desirable that the sick should first make their confession. When the sacrament is administered at home, see that the sick person's face, hands and feet are clean (ready for anointing); have a small table covered with a white cloth at the side of the bed where the patient can see it; place a crucifix and two candles on it; have available a small basin of water, a plate with six small pieces of cotton-wool, another plate with a little salt and bread-crumbs (to cleanse the priest's fingers), and a small white napkin. Someone should stand by ready to assist the priest and uncover the person's feet. Those present should kneel during the administration of the sacrament.

Equally detailed instructions are given on how to prepare for and join in other services – matins and evensong, the litany, the churching of women, the Communion of the sick (celebrations in the house, or from the reserved sacrament), funerals, benediction, Holy Week, and so on. Nothing is left to chance. Much of Lean's liturgical material was taken from *Ritual Notes*. The directions for the administration of unction just listed, for example, are copied almost word for word from the relevant paragraphs of that book.[7]

Good Manners has notes on Catholic societies, religious orders and church papers, and explains the significance of the electoral roll and the system of government in the Church of England. There are pages of advice on how to address archbishops, bishops, archdeacons, abbots, priests, abbesses and priors, and explanations about the initials behind their names. For example, a letter to an abbess should be addressed 'The Right Reverend the Abbess of . . . ', or (if titled) 'The Lady Abbess of . . .', or 'The Mother Abbess', and the letter should begin, 'Dear Reverend Mother', and end, 'Yours respectfully'.

The book sold well because it was a simple do-it-yourself introduction both to the Catholic parish and to the Church of England. Those who read it could feel confident that if they joined a Catholic parish's worship and life they would not seem to be ignorant. But in practice only those individuals whose devotion to the Lord found a genuine expression in the detailed directions of *Good Manners* followed it closely. Others, for different reasons, regarded it as a guide to be adapted according to personal circumstances. Lean himself admitted that his directions might seem excessive to his readers, but he went on to argue that reverence and order in church help the congregation to enter more fully into the spirit of the worship. After all, he asked, are we not supposed to offer our bodies as a living sacrifice to God as well as our minds and souls?

It was the orderliness and outward signs of devotion in a Catholic congregation which impressed visitors. The ritual, combined with the obvious sincerity of those present, helped to make visitors aware of the numinous in worship, as N. P. Williams said in his talk to the 1932 Priests' Convention. As for the congregation, the standing, the sitting, the kneeling, the genuflecting – these actions done together created a deep sense of unity. The people in their pews and the priest at the altar all facing east were like an army spiritually marching together. Servers spoke of their role in the sanctuary as 'the drill' (another Anglo-Catholic military metaphor).

One unfortunate byproduct of things laid down in books like *Good Manners* was the rise of judgemental attitudes by some Catholics towards those who did not comply with its directions. They judged a stranger on how they saw him or her behave in church. 'He's not a Catholic because he doesn't make the sign of the cross,' they said; or, 'She's Evangelical because she didn't genuflect when she went up to Communion.' Conversely, if rigorist Catholics were in a less ritualistic church for a service, they tended to make the sign of the cross and genuflect in the 'right places' to show others what ought to be done. This attitude downgraded acts of reverence into recognition signals distinguishing 'us' from 'them'. It tended to make Catholics unpopular among other congregations. It was one of the reasons why Congress speakers complained that excessive fussiness in rituals put off many others. (Evangelicals had one major recognition signal: to be seen carrying a Bible to church.)

Another byproduct was for worshippers to be so fascinated by the ritual that it became more of an obsession than an act of worship. Clergy were as likely to be guilty of this as young members of sanctuary parties. Colin Stephenson told the story of a priest who swore audibly at poor servers who did something incorrectly at mass (though Stevenson's stories may have been embellished through a desire to entertain). W. J. Sparrow Simpson saw a more subtle problem with ritual:

'We must deliberately face the question whether, in the laudable desire to help their people to be devout, priests are not expecting ceremonial to do the work of dogmatic instruction. Are there not cases where the heart has been satisfied at the expense of the head; where devotional feeling has been cultivated without any corresponding guidance of the mind? We sometimes hear of what is called the magnetic power of the Eucharist as a great dramatic rite. It is, indeed, exceedingly impressive. But its meaning will not be properly apprehended without dogmatic instruction. It is possible to be attracted, interested, even fascinated by it, yet not to understand its principles. An indefinite sense of awe and mystery can exist without an intelligent grasp. And it maybe that this is more frequently the case than we sometimes are aware. The capacity for unintelligent participation in devotional acts is unlimited.'[8]

For the faithful Sunday was a busy day. Although the list of services at St Augustine, Kilburn, was typical of churches with a staff of curates and a community of sisters, parishes with just a vicar and a curate maintained a similar programme. People went to the early mass in order to receive Communion on a weekly or monthly basis according to their rule of life, and then to the sung or high mass later in the morning. There was catechism or Sunday school for their children either before the high mass (the children then going to church) or in the afternoon. Evensong was sung, perhaps concluding with devotions or benediction. Guilds for young adults often met after evensong. Some parishes had a children's mass in the morning as well.

Then there was a full programme of services and activities on weekdays. Mass was said at different times each morning to fit in with people's routines. Matins and evensong were said in church daily. In parishes where the priest was single-handed, a lay reader or another person said the offices on his day off. Devout Catholics attended at least one weekday mass if they could; a few were daily communicants.

Men and boys were enrolled as members of the choir or as servers. Women were not permitted in the sanctuary during a service but a few might be allowed to sit behind the choir stalls (discreetly hidden by an organ console or a pillar) to reinforce the singing. Only in chapels of public schools and convents with exclusively female worshippers were girls recruited as servers by more liberal-minded chaplains. Women were expected to care for the altar linen, arrange the flowers, and clean the brasses. This demarcation line between what women were allowed to do and not to do was followed in many other churches where the clergy (and the laity) could be as strict as the Catholics.

Devotional life was encouraged by various guilds. One of the most popular was the Confraternity of the Blessed Sacrament. It members attended the singing of its office once a month in the Lady chapel, during which the Blessed Sacrament was placed on the altar. The Guild of St Raphael had a smaller following, but the numbers of parish branches steadily increased as unction came to be understood as a sacrament of healing rather than as the last rites for the dying, especially after the Convocations authorized a rite for this ministry in the 1930s. The Guild of the Servants of the Sanctuary brought together sacristans, servers, acolytes and thurifers to keep a rule of life; it had monthly meetings which ended with the guild office, and an annual retreat. There were guilds and meetings for other groups in the congregation, including the elderly.

The Universities' Mission to Central Africa, the Society for the Propagation of the Gospel, the Melanesian Mission and other missionary bodies provided prayer material for parish groups and attracted those interested in supporting the overseas Church. Sales of work were held to raise funds, and parcels of educational and medical material dispatched to schools and hospitals in Africa and elsewhere, especially where a former curate or parishioner was working. Parishes also had links with religious communities. Men's communities could be relied on to provide a speaker or a missioner when invited. Women's groups had annual outings to the parish's linked convent. Communities' networks of friends and oblates supported many in keeping a rule of life.

The parochial year was marked by special occasions. The major festivals, the church's patronal festival, the bishop's visit for the annual confirmation service, the anniversaries (including those of the various Catholic societies and the national or provincial Congresses), and the teaching mission were all high points in the lives of the faithful. In these years it was still possible for well-staffed parishes (and not only Catholic ones) to offer a range of devotional, educational and social activities which could fill much of the leisure time people had in their working lives. Added to these were the welfare schemes for the sick, the housebound, the unemployed and others which were sponsored by parishes. Some parishes not staffed by nuns employed a district visitor or lady worker. The church and its buildings could still be the main focus of people's lives outside the home and workplace.

Sunday schools and catechism classes were slowly losing their numbers, but there were still a million children attending them in England at the end of our period. The Society of the Faith's material for Sunday schools, including its famous Sunday stamps, was widely used in Catholic parishes – and others. When he moved to the East End, H. A. Wilson produced his series of Haggerston Sunday school manuals, based on the Prayer Book and the Catechism, which were used for years afterwards. Children and young people provided the cast for tableaux, pageants and plays in church – a popular form of entertainment and instruction, and a means of enticing the lapsed or the uninstructed back into the church building.

In Catholic parishes the church school was regarded as a vital means of teaching children the faith. Every effort was made to ensure that Catholics were appointed to the staff. The English Church Union had for many years an education secretary, a Miss Chitty, whose brief was to supply church schools with teaching material and aids and to keep a register so that she could direct Christian teachers seeking jobs to vacancies. The parish priest or the curate came in to lead prayers and perhaps teach the catechism, and on Ash Wednesday, Ascension Day and one day in the autumn term each year the whole school went to church for mass, and had the rest of the day off, when trips to the seaside or countryside might be organized. The local state school was regarded as a second best for children from Catholic families unless it had an enviable reputation for preparing pupils to pass entrance examinations to the nearby grammar school. Better-off parents sent their children to Lancing or one of the other Woodward Schools, or to public schools where it was assumed the Christian faith would be taught. Girls went to schools run by women's religious orders.

Among national organizations the Church Lads' and the Church Girls' Brigade were favoured as these were Anglican foundations for those of 13 years and older. Some priests were suspicious of the Scouts and Guides because of their non-denominational character. Other clergy, however, saw the value of belonging to an international organization for youth, and they formed troops and companies attached to the church, the vicar or a curate acting as group scout master. Annual camps were an opportunity for priests and officers to live together with the members and experience a youthful form of Christian community. Putting up and furnishing a tent as a chapel was a priority when a party reached the camp site. Daily mass and evening prayers were accepted as a normal part of the programme. It was at such camps that the first intimation of being called to the priesthood came to some boys.

Parishes' days out by excursion trains or charabancs were arranged for the congregation, especially in places where many could not afford an annual holiday. In the summer whole families from poorer London parishes went for a fortnight or more to live in barns and church halls and gather hops in Kent or fruit in East Anglia. There were similar migrations to the countryside from Midland parishes. The priest lived with them, celebrated mass each day and acted as welfare and entertainment officer as well as chaplain. These camps did a great deal to strengthen the solidarity of congregations from the East End and other cities.

Catholics were urged to make a retreat each year. Obviously this was only possible for those who could afford the time and the cost, though parishes in poor areas arranged weekend retreats at a subsidized rate for their members. Quiet days were a substitute, though purists said they should never be called retreats.

It is, of course, misleading to suggest that every Catholic parish was organized along the lines outlined above. At already indicated, clergy at the Blue–Indigo–Violet end of the spectrum were less likely to be strict about everything laid down in *Good Manners,* assuming they'd read it. Where the English Use was adopted, the 'drill' was simpler for the congregation.

Another factor causing change was, as we have already noted, the increasing mobility of the population between the wars. On new estates or in other parts of the country where they went to find work, individuals and families found themselves in parishes of a different tradition to the one they had been brought up in. They felt awkward if they were the only ones who genuflected during the creed or before they went up to receive Communion. They usually dropped the more obvious gestures but tried to keep disciplines which they regarded as important – such as praying and fasting. Wise spiritual directors understood their situation and supported them. If they kept their rule of life, they were assured, it did not matter if they abandoned some of the externals at worship. They were still God's servants and – guided by the Holy Spirit – could help to spread the faith among others in their new congregation; and maybe in turn they would learn other things about following the Lord through the teaching and practices of the clergy and congregation in their new church.

However, being nurtured in a Catholic church did not always fulfil expectations. Joseph McCulloch was brought up in a Liverpool artisan parish where his family was the only one in the drab street that went to church, with the sole exception of a Roman Catholic household next door but one. He was taught by priests he admired and he joined the parochial guilds. In the early thirties he went up to Oxford as – in his own words – 'a champion of the Tractarians'. At the university, however, he gradually became disillusioned. 'Our parish priests at home had warned us from childhood of the grave and serious error of religious "spikery", that is, the mistaking of externals for the important things of religious. To be a "spike" was one of the chief crimes in the religious catalogue. We understood, or thought we understood, that the externals, the ceremonial and the ritual dance, were all for the sake of outward sense.'[9]

Many of the Catholics he met seemed to be more ambitious about getting tabernacles into their churches than following Bishop Weston's call to concern themselves about the plight of the poor. He also felt their teaching was so rigid that it lacked the charity which would draw 'Mr John Bull' to Christ. In fairness, it should be said that he was equally critical of Evangelicals and Modernists, and indeed of much else in the Church of England. He was ordained and became one of those angry young clergymen who irritate the hierarchy yet whose criticisms are sometimes justified. His model for the priesthood was Dick Sheppard. His reaction to the Catholic movement as he experienced it was not untypical. Some like him converted to Rome; others became increasingly Modernist; others lapsed. McCulloch remained a sacramentalist but allied that with openness to those of any faith or none. It was typical of him that, when in 1959 he became vicar of St Mary-le-Bow, in Cheapside, London, he instituted a series of weekday lunchtime public dialogues at which a stream of distinguished speakers (Christian and non-Christian) came to discuss issues of the moment. That church continues them today.

In contrast was the experience of Ivan Clutterbuck. He was taken by his parents to St George, Beckenham, where he was baptized in 1917 and as he grew up became deeply involved in its life and worship:

'From an early age I learnt the Via Crucis Via Lucis, or no-crown-without-a-cross approach to life, and this was certainly necessary if I was to carry out my church duties. For the first sixteen years of my life we lived at some distance from St George's and, since we had no car, I had to walk when buses were not available. Since daily Mass had to be at 6.30 or 7.00 a.m., it meant getting up early and a lonely journey. In time I was given a bike but even then the going could be hard in the winter. In Lent there were extra services but as I peddled through snow, rain and fog I knew I was earning a special place in heaven. After several years of this kind of philosophy I became uneasy if the going was not difficult and this outlook followed me for the rest of my life.'[10]

He was thankful that he was brought up in a strict regime of catechism teaching in Sunday school and spiritual direction in the confessional, though he admitted he was not as well grounded in the Scriptures as his contemporaries were who went to the Evangelical Christ Church down the road. Like McCulloch, he was shocked when he went to Cambridge and discovered that Anglo-Catholics were a small minority among the undergraduates and dons. But if anything that strengthened rather than weakened his own faith. After ordination and years in the ministry and a wartime chaplaincy in the Royal Navy, he learned to appreciate the truths which Evangelicals stood for and to be wary of the speculations of the radicals. In the 1960s he became secretary of the Church Union and organized the 1968 Anglo-Catholic Congress in the Royal Festival Hall.

20

Worship and the Arts

New Churches

The spread of new housing estates round the major cities after the first world war presented the Church of England with the task of planning, raising funds and building places of worship for their growing populations. Responsibility for this fell on the dioceses within which these estates appeared. The practice was for the bishop to launch an appeal for funds and to appoint someone, usually a clergyman, as the secretary responsible for promoting it. Little was done nationally to support these appeals, and there was not much inter-diocesan co-operation. The Hereford diocese raised part of the cost of St George and St Ethelbert in East Ham and the Mothers' Union provided funds for St Thomas, Dagenham, but these were rare examples. A few churches were paid for by wealthy individuals.

It took time to raise funds, so most building did not commence until the mid twenties. Usually a dual-purpose hall was erected which could be converted into a proper church when the money was forthcoming, or used as a parish hall afterwards when a church had been built beside it. Because financing was so spasmodic, many were not fully completed until years after they had been consecrated.

Winnington-Ingram launched a Forty-Five Churches Fund in the London diocese during these years, and by 1938 sixteen new churches had been consecrated and a further eight started. In other districts halls were being used. The Southwark diocese built twenty-five new churches on the south London estates. The Chelmsford diocese, which had only been created out of St Albans in 1914, was faced with the need for new churches in the estates to the east and north-east of London. It had inherited some money from the Bishop of St Albans' Fund (renamed the London-over-the-Border Fund), and before he died in 1923 Watts-Ditchfield supplemented this through a Crusade appeal. He consecrated nine new churches. His successor, Guy Warman, consecrated a further five. Barnes of Birmingham had two appeals, one in 1926 and the other in 1935, and built fifteen new churches.[1]

The churchmanship of a new church depended on circumstances – the diocesan policy, the source of the funding, or the kind of priests appointed to them. In the London diocese Winnington-Ingram's relaxed attitude allowed Catholicism to flourish in many of the new churches. On the Becontree-Dagenham London County Council estate the ritualist churches St Peter and St John the Divine were regarded by the Chelmsford diocese as allowable for Catholic families moving from parishes of a similar tradition in the East End.

Nearly all the new churches in London and elsewhere were built to the traditional plan: a nave with one or more aisles, a chancel with a choir, and a sanctuary with an altar at the east end. Distinctive features depended on the architect's personal style, the expectations of the congregation and its priest, and the opinions of diocesan boards. What Rawlinson referred to at the first Congress as 'the so-called liturgical movement' made no impact on the overall design of these churches, although modern materials and contemporary styles were incorporated into the construction and furnishings of many.

It was, however, a time when questions were being raised on how far it was appropriate to employ what is modern in churches and their worship. The mission church in which many of the new congregation began meeting – often a 'tin tabernacle' – was cared for by a curate from a neighbouring parish. In the case of Catholic missions it was usually found more appropriate to have a simple sung mass with Communion at around nine or ten o'clock as the main act of Sunday worship rather than a non-communicating mass at eleven. Frere is credited with one of the first when he was curate-in-charge of St Faith, Stepney, as early as 1890.

Some of these young priests found that, when they went on to become vicars of parish churches, they often inherited a non-communicating high or sung mass as the main act of worship on a Sunday morning. There were those, of course, who were glad to return to the kind of liturgy they were used to from earlier days; but others began to feel uneasy that there was no general Communion at these services. One said that he felt a non-communicating mass did not seem much different from benediction: all the congregation did was make an act of adoration to Christ in the sacrament instead of receiving him in Communion. None of them, however, questioned the rule of keeping the eucharistic fast. Curates of a few large churches with a staff, like All Saints, Margaret Street, were able to introduce a sung mass with Communion at nine or nine-thirty between the 8 o'clock and 11 o'clock celebrations, sometimes called 'the children's mass', at which parents received Communion with their newly confirmed youngsters. Elsewhere priests working alone in a parish who wanted to change had the delicate task of radically moving the 11 o'clock sung mass to an earlier hour at which Communion would be offered to all while they were fasting.

The experience of these younger clergy in mission churches was a factor in the spread of the parish communion which has often over been overlooked by historians. The daily high mass with Communion at the 1932 Priests' Convention was a sign of the changing times. A. G. Hebert's *Liturgy and Society* (1937) and *The Parish Communion* (1936) edited by him were successful publications because they were responses to a growing need. Donald Gray, in *Earth & Altar* (1986), linked the renewal of Anglican worship and the emergence of the parish communion with the aspirations of Christian socialists – the Lord's people gathered round the Lord's Table on the Lord's Day were then sent out to serve him in the society of which they were members. This vision of being 'gathered' was a factor in the emergence of the westward position for the celebrant and attempts to rearrange church buildings so that the congregation was more conscious of being together round the altar. Although this did not affect the plan of the churches built in the inter-war years, there were a few attempts to create greater space round the high altar and to bring the congregation nearer to it. This was done by shortening the chancel, sometimes setting the communion rail on three sides of the sanctuary and widening the space between the choir stalls. With this arrangement congregations had a sense of not being separated from the altar by the choir.

The John Keble church at Mill Hill was designed so that the choir was surrounded by the congregation. The vicar, O. H. Gibbs-Smith, an enthusiast for the parish communion, saw the church go through the stages of a wooden and a dual-purpose building to the present church, which was completed in 1936. Another church which broke from the traditional layout was St Michael and All Angels built in 1938 on the Wythenshawe estate south of Manchester. The architect, N. F. Cachemaille-Day, wanted to place the altar so that the congregation could be on three sides of it, but the Bishop of Manchester objected and the altar was moved back to the east wall to make room for choir stalls.

Ninian Comper, the most distinguished of contemporary church architects, began designing churches with spacious sanctuaries later in his career. He was much influenced by a fourth-century church complex at Treveste and other ancient churches in north Africa which he visited in the twenties. He wrote: 'The plans of the churches completed the lesson that it is from these examples of earlier times that we should draw for our parochially-used churches, rather than from the plans of the middle ages when the larger parish churches were influenced by the examples of the monastic choirs.'[2] It was an important step towards recognition that functional requirements should determine the liturgical layout of churches – a principle behind some church buildings planned later in the century, of which St Paul, Bow Common, is an outstanding example.

Comper was able to express this in his design for St Philip, Cosham, Hants. In plan the church is almost square: a nave and two aisles of four bays with the altar under a ciborium in the fourth bay, opposite a font in the first. The interior of the church was painted white, a Comper characteristic which was copied by Dearmer in Primrose Hill and by clergy in other churches. The organ and choir are in the west gallery. The congregation gathers on three sides of the altar. 'St Philip's realized all that Comper advocated in the planning of a modern church. It is his legacy to the future. It was the fulfilment of his quest for beauty and liturgical planning on rational principles; a church that was essentially modern yet indebted to the unfolding development of the Catholic tradition as it had evolved from Constantine to the twentieth century in which the heart and purpose of worship was the gathering of the baptized in the offering of the Mass.'[3]

Comper's former pupil, Martin Travers, became known in Catholic quarters through his friendship with Maurice Child, Ronald Knox, Samuel Gurney and the Society of SS Peter and Paul. He provided mini-baroque illustrations for the Congress reports and other publications. Although not a believer, he received many commissions from Catholic churches that could afford to use him. He redesigned the interior of St Mary, Bourne Street, and created a reredos for St Augustine, Queen's Gate, among other churches. His work became known as the 'Anglo-Catholic Congress style'. By the 1930s, however, enthusiasm for Baroque was declining. Travers remained a distinguished artist in Art Deco stained glass for years afterwards, but his association with the Catholic movement faded.

Music

By 1933 *The English Hymnal*, edited by Percy Dearmer and first published in 1903, had replaced *Hymns Ancient & Modern* in most Catholic parishes and communities and in some cathedrals as well. The book was intended to be, as Dearmer wrote in its preface, 'a collection of the best hymns in the English language, and is offered as a humble companion to the Book of Common Prayer for use in the Church'.[4] Papalists regarded it as too Anglican to be suitable for their congregations. They produced their own *English Catholic Hymn Book* as an alternative or supplement to it. A revision of the *English Hymnal* appeared in the same year as the Centenary Congress, and enticed parishes, as part of their celebrations, to bin the original book and purchase the revised edition.

The changes in the new edition were almost entirely musical. The only literary alterations were the introduction of Blake's 'Jerusalem' and 'in rare instances a few words have been altered at the request of the authors'.[5] A hundred new tunes were added by Vaughan Williams, the music editor, with the assistance of Martin Shaw. Shaw was a prolific composer with broadly Catholic sympathies. His experience as an organist in St Mary, Primrose Hill and St Martin-in-the-Fields led him to provide music which he knew the average choir and congregation could manage. Among his many works were *The Oxford Book of Carols* (1928) and an *Anglican Folk Mass*. The latter was popular because it was intended for unison singing with optional harmonies for the *Sanctus, Benedictus*, and *Agnus Dei*. It was also an alternative to Merbecke. But these books did more. They introduced English folk melody into hymnody and so into Anglican worship – in Catholic circles first, but then permeating throughout the Church of England and beyond. These indigenous tunes, their 'Englishness', were a welcome contrast to the kind of music which had dominated hymns up to that time.[6]

J. H. Arnold revised the plainsong chants in the new edition. He reminded those who used plainsong that originally it was performed unaccompanied, and that any organist who attempted to accompany it must master the elements of plainchant first. The accompaniment should be gentle and sensitive, he said, and there should be nothing discordant to interrupt the flow of the chant. His advice was a necessary corrective for priests who had introduced plainchant to usually unenthusiastic congregations in the belief that they were making the worship 'more Catholic'. And it was a warning to organists who were tempted to use plainchant accompaniment as a chance to show off their dexterity in daring improvisations.

Shaw and Arnold were among the group of clergy and musicians who in 1923 founded the English School of Church Music to train choirs and give advice through its publications on a wide range of relevant subjects. Particularly valuable for Catholics were reviews on new settings for the liturgy which were being published as more churches adopted the Eucharist as their main Sunday morning service. With the advent of the parish communion and its aim of full congregational participation, the classic settings of the mass were heard only in cathedrals and certain churches like St Bartholomew, Brighton, where the service was sung by a large choir accompanied on occasions by an orchestra.

The *English Hymnal* had a section headed 'For Mission Services' which included songs such as Sankey's 'Hold the fort, for I am coming,/ Jesus signals still' (570) and Duffield's 'Stand up! – Stand up for Jesus' (581). A note added that hymns in this section were 'not for ordinary use'. By that the compilers meant they did not envisage them being sung in liturgical worship. Their advice was ignored. Many of these songs entered the Sunday repertory. Brode's 'O Jesus, I have promised/ To serve thee to the end' (577) was sung at practically all confirmations.

Among Catholics the *Mirfield Mission Hymnbook* was popular for those who felt the *English Hymnal* was too highbrow. It was compiled in 1907 by a group of Mirfield fathers who were experienced in leading parish missions. Published by the Community of the Resurrection, it sold 700,000 copies before it was decided to revise it in 1922 after the first Congress.[7] By that year the book was being used not only for mission services but also as a supplement to the *EH* and the *A&M*. A few of the Evangelical revival songs which had become rather dated were dropped, and others added which were either more Anglo-Catholic or echoed the social claims of the Gospel. Thousands more copies were sold and a further revision was made in 1936, mostly to include new tunes. In the preface to this edition the Mirfield editors wrote:

> We have aimed not at compromise, but at comprehension; we hope to meet the needs of as many different types of persons as possible. In the present book we have striven to make provision for the fullest possible expression of devotion to our Blessed Lord and to His Church. Both subjective and objective types of hymns have their due place. The Evangelical assertion of the power of the Cross, and the cleansing of the Precious Blood, lead on to the gifts of grace which flow from the Risen Life of our Saviour in the fellowship of the Catholic Church.[8]

Drama

The children's pageants in the 1930 and 1933 Congresses were large-scale presentations of the kind of religious dramas which had been a feature of life in Catholic parishes for years. From the early days of the ritual revival, priests realized the value of plays and tableaux as teaching media. Dramas brought to life what was read in texts or heard in sermons. Illustrations in Bibles and paintings and drawings in books could, of course, stir people's imaginations; but plays based on scriptural stories and the lives of the saints made a deep impression on those who witnessed them – as well as on the performers themselves. The continuing popularity of Christmas and Passion plays in churches and elsewhere today shows that, even in our media-saturated age, such performances can still move people and instruct them. From the end of the nineteenth century there had been among Catholic clergy and laity a growing interest in the Oberammergau Passion Play – halted with the outbreak of war but revived with Congress pilgrimages afterwards.

Many Catholic clergy were theatre-buffs. They happily accepted invitations to become voluntary chaplains of local drama companies and theatres in London and other cities alongside their parochial responsibilities. At this time most Evangelicals and Protestants generally felt it was improper for Christians to frequent such places. Pinchard was chaplain of the Birmingham theatre until he left to become secretary of the ECU. It was concern for the welfare of actors and actresses which led to the formation of the Actors' Church Union in 1899. It had offices in 28 Soho Square and by 1931 there were 491 priest associates and 701 members, among them professional actors. Its supporters included celebrities of those days such as Lilian Baylis, Sybil Thorndike, Ellen Terry and Henry Irving. Among the practical work the Union sponsored were two hostels for the children of actors who were working in London.

Fr Hughson, Superior of the Holy Cross in America, visited the Union's office while he was in London for the 1930 Congress and was impressed. 'I arrived there at the stroke of noon,' he wrote afterwards, 'and I found the chaplain with his secretaries gathered round his desk with delightful informality for the Angelus and midday intercessions.'[9] Donald Hole, the Union's chaplain-secretary, was an enthusiastic supporter of the restoration of the Shrine of Our Lady at Walsingham and a friend of A. Hope Patten – another priest with a strong theatrical bent.

One common objection to these developments was that no actor was worthy of playing the part of Jesus Christ in any drama. The *Green Quarterly* invited Russell Thorndike to contribute an article answering it. He began by listing numerous medieval mystery plays in which actors performed the role not only of Christ but also of God the Father, and then tackled the question of the actor's physical appearance on the stage. No one knew what Jesus looked like, he wrote, but that did not prevent painters through the ages depicting him by using different male models. Where religious drama was concerned, what mattered was that the actor should be trained and experienced enough to be able to enter into the role of Christ with skill and sensitivity. To those who said no man lived who was worthy of portraying the incarnate Son of God, Russell replied by referring to a recent film about an English nurse who worked in Belgium in the opening weeks of the war and who was shot by the Germans on the charge of helping British soldiers to escape:

> Many people who raised a protest over the Nurse Cavell film were somewhat mollified when they heard the part was to be played by Sybil Thorndike because she has the reputation of being a good woman. 'Well, thank heaven she is,' say I, as a mere brother, but that does not concern Nurse Cavell, neither does it qualify Sybil for the part. If she can play Cavell well, she can still qualify for the part even if she were a Messilina. Art is only concerned with artistic results.[10]

It was argued that well-presented drama, especially Christian drama, can prepare the way for and lead into worship. Apologists pointed out that the Church has for centuries used pictures, statues, icons and stained glass windows to enlighten the worshipper, and an appropriate play or tableau can fulfil the same function. They argued that the liturgy inevitably involves the use of drama, reinforced by the traditional symbols which accompany its action. Those leading the liturgy are in one sense *personae dramatis* – especially the priest and the servers in the sanctuary and the preacher in the pulpit. This was strikingly demonstrated in Winchester during the Centenary celebrations when the performance of a play about St Swithin outside in the close concluded with a procession into the cathedral for a service.

Catholic priests and gifted individuals in congregations wrote and produced their own plays. While he was a curate at St Matthew, Westminster, Wilson was instructed by Atlay to revise the script of a nativity play which had been composed by a previous curate and produce it in church. When years later he went to Haggerston, Wilson took what became known as the Bethlehem play with him and it was performed each year in St Augustine on a temporary stage erected over the chancel. The same kind of thing went on in hundreds of parishes. Plays written by Bernard Walke were broadcast at Christmas for several years by the BBC from his church at St Hilary. Listeners were fascinated to hear the Gospel story related with Cornish voices. Walke got his diocesan bishop to preside over the play one year in full episcopal vestments on a throne above the stage and give the blessing at the end. Frere did this so well that strangers in the congregation thought he was one of the cast. The most hazardous part of the production was the cable which ran from the church over the fields to the house with the nearest telephone link. It had to be watched in case a cow tripped over it.

As a result of Catholic initiatives in religious drama, some dioceses set up bodies to advise in the production of plays. Bishops G. Bell of Chichester and J. H. Greig of Guildford appointed directors of religious drama for their dioceses, and in Chelmsford P. Widdrington was the first chairman of the diocesan Religious Drama Guild. Bell was an enthusiastic promoter of drama in cathedrals and broadcasts from them. He was a personal friend of John Reith of the BBC, and while Dean of Canterbury arranged several broadcasts from that cathedral. He persuaded John Masefield to write a play for performance there. *The Coming of Christ*, with music by Gustav Holst, was performed fives times to full houses during Whitsuntide 1928. The drama critic of the *Daily News* wrote: 'Since the murder of Thomas Becket Canterbury cathedral has not been the scene of a more startling event than the performance of John Masefield's *The Coming of Christ*.'[11] In 1929 Bell formed the Religious Drama Society which did much to sponsor this particular art. Other dramas based on Christian themes were produced by various writers with Anglo-Catholic convictions, the best-known being by T. S. Eliot and Dorothy L. Sayers.

Eliot came to faith between the years 1925 and 1930 and found in Catholicism a fulfilment of what he had been searching for. He was deeply influenced by his reading of Anglican classics from Richard Hooker and Jeremy Taylor to Newman and the Tractarians. Students of Eliot's poetry have detected his progress to faith from *The Waste Land*, published in 1922, reflecting his foreboding at seeing civilization threatened in the aftermath of war, to *Ash Wednesday*, published in 1930, which revealed he could be a believing Christian and remain a modern intellectual. He applied for British citizenship at about the time he was baptized and confirmed. For him the monarchy, Church and the democracy represented by Parliament were the bare bones of what might one day receive the breath of the Holy Spirit and become the hope of a Christian society. He was attracted to Anglo-Catholicism because it seemed to him to enshrine much of the truth as he had been searching for it. He appeared on the platform at later Congresses and Anglo-Catholic Schools of Sociology.

The most famous of his plays is *Murder in the Cathedral*, commissioned by Bishop Bell for the 1935 Canterbury festival. The play has various themes running through it – the spiritual and psychological struggle of Becket, the tragedy and glory of his martyrdom, the plight of the poor represented by the chorus of Canterbury women, the self-justification of the four knights for their crime – but the principal one is the conflict of power between Church and State. The liturgical custom of commemorating the saints and depicting their lives and martyrdom in drama gave him the model for applying his poetic gifts in scripting the play. In contrast to the rest of the text, Thomas' last sermon was written as Eliot himself might have preached it (or perhaps heard it preached in church). He followed tradition in linking the feast of St Stephen with that of the Nativity so that the audience would hear the archbishop saying he realized he himself would shortly become a martyr.

Dorothy L. Sayers was a member of a small group including Eliot, Charles Williams and C. S. Lewis who identified themselves with the Catholic wing of Anglicanism and whose work flourished from the 1930s onwards. Among her many writings – crime novels, popular theology, articles, culminating in translations of Dante – were religious dramas for production in church. She wrote *The Zeal of thy House* for the Canterbury festival of 1937, but her most famous was *The Man Born to be King*, scripted for broadcasting in children's hour at the request of the BBC in 1941. Her presentation of Christ's voice speaking modern English raised similar protests to those of years earlier. Sayers' initiative, however, revolutionized religious play-writing, and in future Christ was portrayed in the media in a variety of ways – some deeply moving, a few verging on the blasphemous.

Among those who were drawn to the Catholic movement by its association of Christian worship with the arts was John Betjeman. During holidays in Cornwell, the youthful Betjeman was befriended by Wilfred Johnson, the vicar of St Ervan, who instructed him in the role of the sacramental in Christian life. When he went up to Oxford, Betjeman attended high mass at Pusey House. He was taken by a friend to the 1927 Congress on the Thursday when he may have heard A. E. J. Rawlinson on the Eucharist, Sheila Kaye-Smith on the mass and art, and C. S. Gillett on the priesthood. The traditionalism and the Victorian legacy of Anglo-Catholicism attracted him, as did the ritual and its mystery. He remained a communicant (and an occasional penitent) for the rest of his life. After his marriage in 1933 he settled into the worship of whatever parish he happened to be living in. If he is now known to have doubts about the faith, it was probably because he was more honest in expressing them than many others. His poem on the Anglo-Catholic Congresses appears in collections of his works.

The Warham Guild and the Society of the Faith

The Warham Guild was founded in 1912 by Percy Dearmer to promote the production of vestments and furnishings for churches which adopted the English Use advocated in *The Parson's Handbook*. The Guild included Mr Francis Eeles who was largely responsible for the formation of the Central Council for the Care of Churches, and who took part in the conference on reservation at Farnham Castle in 1925 described earlier. Another member was the Revd Jocelyn Perkins, who was Sacrist of Westminster Abbey for nearly sixty years and, as a Sarum enthusiast, encouraged cathedrals to adopt that Use when they introduced vestments. The Guild aimed to do for the setting of the liturgy what Dearmer's *English Hymnal*, did for its musical setting.

The Guild published a number of pamphlets by Dearmer, Eeles, A. S. Duncan Jones and others on a variety of subjects – altar furnishings, the aumbry and the hanging pyx, episcopal vestments, and so on – and a *Handbook* in 1930 to advise how the Prayer Book's rubric about the 'ornaments of the Church and of the ministers thereof' could have artistic as well as functional merit in modern times. ('The word "ornaments" in the rubric is not confined, as in modern usage, to articles of a decorative character, but is used in a wider sense as including all articles whatsoever, used in the seemly performance of the services of the Church.'[12]) For many years the Guild was associated with Mowbrays and had quarters in the shop in Margaret Street.

The Society of the Faith was formed by two brothers, C. E. Douglas, vicar of St Luke's, Camberwell, and J. A. Douglas, and a group of friends as 'an Association of Christians in communion with the See of Canterbury for mutual assistance in the work of Christ's Church and for the furtherance of such charitable undertakings as may be from time to time decided upon, more especially for the popularization of the Catholic Faith'. They began by publishing material for Sunday schools, but rapidly developed in other directions so that in 1913 the Society founded the Faith Press Ltd in Leighton Buzzard and a sales outlet at 22 Buckingham Street, Charing Cross. It published church music, including masses by Charles Wood and Sydney Nicholson, carol services, Lent music, and settings in Anglican chant and plainsong for morning and evening prayer. After the war Faith Craft Works Ltd was set up to provide all kinds of ecclesiastical requisites such as woodcarving (roods, statues, panelling, stalls), plate and vestments, tabernacles and aumbries, paintings and stained glass. Another department hired out costumes for plays and pageants. Among other ecclesiastical firms it stood out as a champion of 'Congress' Anglo-Catholic liturgical belief and practice.[13]

Anglo-Catholics were largely responsible for the attempt to present the Gospel to modern men and women by employing the art forms which were becoming familiar to them. In one sense this was contrary to the strong tendency of Catholics to look to the past for teaching and inspiration, but it was individuals like Bell and Duncan Jones who pointed out the necessity of engaging with contemporary art forms in order to communicate what was traditional and unchangeable to the modern society. They argued that this was an aspect of the Church's mission which could not be neglected if the Congress movement was to be obedient to its evangelistic vision.

21

Preparations for the Centenary and the Second Priests' Convention 1932

Preparations for celebrating the Oxford Movement Centenary began soon after the 1930 Congress finished. At the beginning of 1931 the Congress executive and the English Church Union set up a joint Centenary committee and invited representatives from different parts of the country to Pusey House to draw up plans. The meeting agreed that the main objective of the Centenary should be the renewal of spiritual life in the Church, inspired by memories of the past and hopes for the future. Local conventions and retreats were to be arranged with the aim of encouraging the adoption of a simple rule of life: attending mass on Sundays and holy days; keeping Sunday as a day of worship, rest and recreation; receiving Communion at least three times a year including Easter; going to confession once a year; fasting in Lent and abstaining from meat on Fridays; upholding the Church's marriage law; and giving regularly to Church and overseas' missions.

The most important decision the committee made was to approach the Archbishops of Canterbury and York to ask if they would suggest to the bishops that special services should be held in their dioceses to celebrate the Centenary. They noted how successful a recent mission to Oxford University led by Temple had been and they believed that with his support the Centenary would be welcomed by most Anglicans. Although he disappointed them with his support for the South India scheme, they realized he was a key figure in the Church.

Temple had been chairman of the Doctrine Commission since it was inaugurated in 1923 and he had come to know a number of the Congress speakers among its membership: W. L. Knox, J. K. Mozley, A. E. J. Rawlinson, E. G. Selwyn, W. Spens, A. E. Taylor and L. S. Thornton. Temple's biographer, F. A. Iremonger, who worked with him in the Life and Liberty movement, called him a 'central churchman' and defined that as: '[one with] a firm hold on the articles of the historic creeds, a conviction that what is best in each school of thought within the Church is worth conserving, and a refusal to believe that any one group or party within the Church of England, or indeed in the whole Catholic Church, enjoys a monopoly of the truth. . . . If ever there was a full Church of England man, it was William Temple.'[1]

After the Pusey House meeting Pinchard got together a high-powered delegation representing a wide range of churchmanship to meet the Archbishops to discuss the Centenary. Included were the Bishops of Winchester, Oxford, St Albans, Truro, Salisbury and Croydon as well as the retired Bishops Chandler and Talbot; the Dean of Westminster; dons from Oxford and Cambridge; and Lords Sankey (the Lord Chancellor), Shaftesbury and Selborne. Even Inskip, one of the most vocal opponents of Anglo-Catholicism, was invited. He was unable to attend, but he sent a letter supporting the idea, saying he had no difficulty in celebrating John Keble, whose *Christian Year* he had long appreciated. But that did not deter him from continuing his attacks on Anglo-Catholicism at public meetings and in print.

Temple received the delegation in March 1931. Lang was abroad convalescing. The Bishops of Winchester and Croydon spoke on behalf of Evangelicals, acknowledging that the Tractarians had done much for the whole Church. Winchester said that Charles Simeon and John Keble had much in common in their devotion to God. Sir Walter Buchanan Riddell, the Master of Sidney Sussex College, said he was sure the proposal would be welcomed in Cambridge which had also benefited from the Movement. Archdeacon K. Gibbs of St Albans added that as a former Cambridge man he hoped there was some recognition of the Camden Society's contribution to the revival of the Church's worship and its setting. Temple said he had consulted Lang, who was 'most eager' that the Centenary should be observed throughout the Church of England. 'I suppose,' he said, 'there are very few churches in the country which are not in some degree influenced by the Oxford Movement. Very many of those, who trace their descent much more to other fathers than those of whom we are now thinking, would certainly find on reflection that much in the furnishing of their churches and the conduct of their services has, in fact, owed a great deal to the stimulus which the Oxford Movement introduced. The Church, thank God, is a fellowship in which we all learn from one another and that much more deeply.'[2]

As a result of this meeting the Archbishops appointed their own Oxford Movement Centenary committee, which included some of Pinchard's delegation and, as requested, wrote to the bishops inviting them to set up a Centenary committee to plan how the event was to be commemorated in their dioceses; 9 July 1933 was designated 'Centenary Sunday'. The ECU and the Congress executive contacted their local branches, urging them to co-operate with their dioceses in arranging joint celebrations. They pointed out it was a wonderful opportunity to show that Catholics stood for the whole Church. In dioceses where the bishop had taken part in local Congresses, this worked reasonably well, but in those where Catholics had memories of episcopal opposition there were initial objections. Why should they allow the diocese in on 'their' celebrations? Did the bishops want to dictate what could or could not be in the programme (e.g., no benediction)? In the end it was reported that all the dioceses had set up Centenary committees except one (probably Birmingham).

Parishes set targets for enrolling supporters for the Centenary celebrations: St Bartholomew, Brighton, and St Wilfrid, Harrogate, 1,000 each; Bristol, 500; St Agatha, Birmingham, 300, and so on. By October 1932 over 20,000 had registered. Local Catholic committees joined diocesan committees to arrange services with special preachers in cathedrals on Centenary Sunday. Other events were planned in deaneries and parishes for the following week. A reporter for the *Green Quarterly* wrote, 'The Archbishops' Committee has issued its programme which most happily coincides with the Congress programme.... We understand it is preparing a number of pamphlets for issue, and is arranging a course of lectures at Westminster Abbey.'[3] But the following year the same reporter noted sourly, 'In the midst of all this official activity there seems little or no indication of penitence for the harsh treatment often given to those whom all unite to honour.'[4]

Articles on the Oxford Movement began to appear in the religious press and in diocesan and parochial magazines. The ECU, at Charles Harris's suggestion, invited well-known authors to write books on the movement, which resulted in, among others, two substantial work published by SPCK: *Northern Catholicism*, edited by N. P. Williams and Harris, and *Liturgy and Worship*, edited by W. K. Lowther Clarke and Harris. Full length biographies on Pusey and other Tractarians appeared. The Church Literature Association published a penny pamphlet *What is the Oxford Movement?* which sold in tens of thousands. Cheap booklets were also published by the CLA on the *Heroes of the Revival* – Keble, Froud, Newman, Pusey, Lowder, Tooth, Mackonochie and Dolling. A set of slides showing pictures of persons and places connected with the Tractarians was prepared by K. Ingram. There was talk of a new Anglican missal being prepared.

In general most Anglican Evangelicals either tolerated the proposals for the Centenary or did little to express their opposition to it. But a few joined some Protestants in being more vocal. On 6 January 1933 *The*

Record quoted an article in *The Churchman*: 'To call on Evangelicals to celebrate that day [the anniversary of Keble's sermon] is like asking Roman Catholics to light fireworks on the Fifth of November ... The commemoration is designed by some to mark the unity of the Church, but it is singularly inappropriate to select the birthday of one of the parties in the Church, especially as the stated object of that party was the abolition of the others.' The Fellowship of Evangelical Churchmen passed a resolution urging the bishops to deny diocesan recognition of the celebration in which 'no loyal churchman can take part'. F. J. Chavasse, the principal of Wycliffe Hall, Oxford, son of a former Evangelical Bishop of Liverpool, and later Bishop of Rochester, went further than most by telling a meeting that in his opinion Anglo-Catholics should leave the Church of England and form themselves into a separate body like the Old Catholics. It is an indication of how far the Catholic movement had secured recognition in the Church's official circles that these objections were ignored.

But not all Evangelicals were opposed to the Centenary. They had been impressed by the work of priests in the slums and the evangelistic purpose of the first Congresses. The main speaker at the 1931 Islington Conference, E. A. Dunn of St Jude, Nottingham, said that while Anglo-Catholics' teaching 'left much to be desired, we are learning to understand them, to admire their self-sacrifice and devotion, and to work happily with them'.[5] What was called a 'Westminster Group' of Catholics and Evangelicals began meeting regularly to discuss their differences. F. Underhill at Liddon House joined because he said he had not realized how much Catholics and Evangelicals had in common until he got to know them better through the Life and Liberty movement.

In London the Centenary committee prepared an ambitious programme. The Albert Hall, the Queens Hall and the Caxton Hall were hired. The warden of Keble College gave permission for a high mass in the college quadrangle on condition that only the Prayer Book was used. St Mary, Oxford, was booked for midday on Friday, 14 July, the day and time of Keble's Assize Sermon one hundred years' previously. On Saturday there was to be a high mass in Winchester cathedral and a pilgrimage to Keble's grave. A visit to Hagleigh was also arranged. It was at that vicarage early in 1833 that a group of clergy promoted a petition from clergy and laity to Archbishop Howley of Canterbury defending the apostolic succession and the integrity of the Prayer Book.

The White City stadium was booked for the evening of 9 July for evensong, and for a high mass the following Sunday morning over which the Bishop of London agreed to preside. Some objected to the plan as they had done three years' previously, and Winnington-Ingram was criticized in the London press for giving permission for it. He replied by pointing out he had only agreed on condition that the Prayer Book Communion service was used, that there would be a certain number of communicants, that badges would be worn, and that there would be no procession outside the grounds. He could not see why any should object; he had often celebrated Communion out-of-doors for troops during the war. As a gesture of goodwill the White City authorities agreed to let the Congress use the stadium without charge. Those who were worried about the weather were told 40,000 seats would be under cover. Twelve hundred stewards were to be recruited.

The Centenary committee decided the occasion should be used as an opportunity to give a fresh voice to the Church's campaign for slum clearance. It would be particularly appropriate, they said, since the story of the slum priests was one of the most glorious in the history of the Movement. They also urged local committees to give publicity to parishes and societies which were sponsoring local housing schemes.

Preparations continued through the next two years. The Albert Hall was packed for a joint ECU and ACC anniversary meeting in July 1931 at which Pinchard launched an appeal for a special Centenary fund. All-in-one membership, accommodation and railway tickets were issued for those attending from other parts of Britain. In April 1933 a pageant depicting the story of the Evangelical and Catholic revivals was staged in the Albert Hall. It was under the direction of a professional producer and musicians and the cast was drawn from dramatic societies in London parishes.

The Centenary committee wrote to all the bishops in the Anglican Communion asking them to encourage their parishes to join in the celebrations, and they followed the letters up by sponsoring C. D. Russell, the Congress organizing secretary, and D. R. Rosenthal to visit North America in 1932. During the course of a four weeks' tour the two priests between them visited seventy cities and towns in Canada and the USA. In the USA Rosenthal, still in the midst of his struggle with Bishop Barnes of Birmingham, could hardly believe his eyes when he saw a diocesan bishop presiding at a service of benediction. He also wrote enthusiastically of the central heating and bathrooms with showers in clergy homes.

Other Catholics who were going abroad took the opportunity to speak about the Centenary, too. Fr Biggart CR went to South Africa to conduct a mission and afterwards gave talks using the Centenary slides. Fr Tribe SSM did the same during a world tour he was making on behalf of his community. In a letter to Kelham he described St James, Vancouver, as being exactly like St Alban, Holborn, thirty years' previously, with its staff of clergy doing similar work. The Archbishop of the West Indies asked for someone to visit them and the Revd Viscount Mountmorres, vicar of St Mark, South Farnborough, arranged to go out. H. J. C. Matthew, a priest popular among young Catholics, went to Ceylon. The results were encouraging. Applications for membership of the Centenary began to reach the London office as Anglicans booked to visit England for the celebrations. The committee suggested that all over the world on Friday 14 July 1933, there should be Eucharists and services with an address on the Oxford Movement, special prayers, Newman's hymn 'Lead kindly light', and an act of rededication. Notes for preachers were produced and copies of the slides dispatched with them.

The Second Anglo-Catholic Priests' Convention

As part of the preparations a second Priests' Convention was organized in Oxford for 11–15 July 1932. The arrangements were similar to those made for the one eleven years previously. A number of Oxford dons formed various committees: F. Hood was chairman of the organizing committee, and K. E. Kirk chairman of the subjects committee. One variation was in the worship. In 1921 members had been expected to receive Communion at early masses in college chapels or to say their own privately, and then go to a non-communicating high mass later in the morning. In 1932 the high mass was celebrated at 8 a.m. in different venues on successive days (Pusey House, St John, Cowley, St Barnabas and Keble College) and Communion administered to all. Arrangements were made for a few priests who wished to say their own mass. In his forward to the convention handbook Kirk wrote that in principle eucharistic worship is incomplete until the worshipper has received the Body and Blood of the Lord. Although he tactfully avoided expressing an opinion on the relative merits of a non-communicating high mass and what he called 'the beautiful and interesting "Parish Masses"', he obviously preferred the latter.[6] This view was echoed in two or three of the papers given at the convention. One thing which did not change was the weather. Anglo-Catholic gatherings seem to attract high temperatures. Those who had been at the previous convention said the heat-wave in 1932 was even greater than the one in 1921. (It was the hottest week of the year during the 150th celebrations which I went to in Oxford in 1983.)

The numbers attending were 481. The convention met in the Sheldonian Theatre. There were familiar names in the list of speakers – Kirk, Williams, Rosenthal, Briscoe, Mackay and Chandler. Newcomers were

H. de Candole of St John, Newcastle-on-Tyne, C. E. Tomkinson of St Stephen, Lewisham, J. A. R. Derham Marshall of St Margaret, Princes Road, Liverpool, T. G. Jalland of St Luke, Swindon, and A. H. Howe Browne of St John the Divine, Kennington. The only religious on the list was Fr Bede Frost OSB, to give an address on a priest's spiritual life. There was also one America priest, Edward Hardy of the General Theological Seminary, New York. The fact that the majority of the speakers were parish priests underlined the organizers' intention that the convention should be practical rather than academic. The overall title was 'Public Worship', with the subtitle 'Why People Do Not Go to Church'.

Williams gave the first paper. In a long address he explained how the decline in belief and the consequent decline in church attendance began with the scientific discoveries and philosophical developments in the centuries since the Renaissance. He compared the classic proofs for the existence of God – the ontological (the rationality of faith), the cosmological (the first cause of creation), the teleological (the design of creation), and the moral (the development of the concept of the good) – with the findings of modern science and the views of contemporary philosophers. The difficulty, he said, was that Natural Science was no longer an assured and stable truth ('the celestial mechanics of Newton have been upset by the discoveries of Einstein') and philosophers' views varied so much ('the world of modern thought is a chaos rather than a cosmos'). He felt that the moral argument for the existence of God was the most persuasive at the present time.

Many in the Sheridan that hot summer's morning must have felt lost as they listened to this brilliant and witty discourse. Williams was a polymath, equally at home in philosophy, science and history as well as theology. His paper fills seventeen pages of closely argued reasoning in the official report and is worth careful attention even now. But if these listeners were lost in the early parts of his talk, they may have felt more at home when he spoke of the role of the classic proofs for the existence of God is discussing the faith with unbelievers:[7]

> Though reason cannot create Faith, it has an all-important function to perform in clearing away preliminary difficulties and in coordinating the deliveries of Revelation with the rest of our knowledge. Reason is not the most important factor in the genesis of Faith; for, if it were, the possibility of Faith would not lie open to educated and uneducated alike, and 'the poor' would not have the Gospel preached to them. So far as any one of the constituents of Faith can be singled out as being of primary importance, it is the sense of the 'numinous', the sense of

the unseen, which is the most indispensable of all. It is this mysterious awareness of the Divine that can be either neglected and allowed to atrophy, or cultivated to the highest pitch of sensitiveness, like the ear which can be taught to distinguish between the fractions of a semitone, or the eye which can learn the subtle shades of colour, imperceptible to the untrained observer, within one band of the spectrum. It is this which can be acquired by association with those who possess it to a high degree – a fact which has been expressed by the Dean of St Paul's [W. R. Inge] in a vivid aphorism, 'Religion is caught, like measles, from those who already have it.'[8]

Holy lives, he went on, were more likely to convince sceptics than rational arguments. Next was the effect of attending worship with men and women of faith. The way worship was presented was important. 'Nothing but the best is good enough for God, or good enough to commend the idea of God to our fellow-men.'[9]

Before the Convention the organizers were conscious that two resolutions passed by a majority of the bishops at the recent Lambeth Conference had become highly controversial, particularly among Catholics. One was that 'where an innocent person has remarried under civil sanction and desires to receive the Holy Communion, it recommends that the case should be referred for consideration to the bishop, subject to provincial regulations' (no. 11). The other that where a married couple conscientiously wished to limit the number of their family and 'where there is a morally sound reason for avoiding complete abstinence, the Conference agrees that other methods may be used, provided that this is done in the light of the same Christian principles. The Conference records its strong condemnation of the use of any methods of conception control from motives of selfishness, luxury, or mere convenience' (no. 13).

Kirk addressed these questions in his talk. His Bampton lectures, *The Vision of God*, had been published the previous year and this, together with his other books on Christian ethics, made him a leading moral theologian in the Church of England. He began by saying he lamented that the teaching of Christian ethics was too weak in the Church to meet the challenge of the contemporary world. This weakness sprang from the fact that Christians were not sufficiently aware they were citizens of two kingdoms with divided loyalties. Consequently they tended to state what God's will is with one breath and then tone it down and modify it in the next, influenced by worldly values around them. Too often they judged what is right or wrong by how they feel about it rather than by the light of God's law. Or they fell into the error of saying, 'It's only the motive that counts', or, 'As long as you do what you honestly believe to be right, you are doing right.'

This led him to outline the distinction between an action which was wrong (even if committed by someone who was convinced it was right) and one which was blameworthy (committed by someone who knew it was wrong but persisted in doing it); and between things that are wrong in themselves (always sinful) and those that are wrong in certain circumstances (committed on occasions which might lead to sinfulness in oneself or in others). To assess each case it was necessary for the priest to be skilled in casuistry – the art of guiding each individual towards obedience to God's law, but with an understanding of how that individual can be helped to achieve this at that particular time.

He gave as an example of casuistry a situation in which a missionary, on going to a primitive people, discovered they practised complete promiscuity between men and women. 'He makes a few converts, and in their case insists on strict monogamy. At the same time, let us say, he becomes the trusted counsellor of the tribal headsman (not as yet a Christian), and then his problems begin. For the headsman and his council are seriously disturbed at the low sexual morality of the people. They are convinced, however, that monogamy is an impossible ideal to attempt to introduce, but believe that they could with good success promulgate and enforce a regulated and uniform polygamy. What does the wise missionary do in such circumstances? I have no doubt that he will associate himself with the official efforts to substitute ordered polygamy for promiscuity, whilst maintaining at the same time that monogamy is the only form of union consonant with the full purposes of God, and certainly that is the only custom allowable among Christians. And, although his actions will most certainly be misrepresented, I hold that beyond all question he has done the right thing. He has seen the inexpediency of pressing the Christian law before its time upon a non-Christian population, while at the same time he abates no jot of the high ideal of their calling for the members of his flock.'[10]

He dealt briefly with two other moral issues – murder and betting. Whether or not murder was wrong, he said, depended on the circumstances in which it was committed. (He did not mention the campaign for the abolition of the death penalty which increasing numbers were supporting, including Underhill and other priests.) Betting was not wrong if the sum of money involved was what would only be spent on personal leisure activities and affected no one else. Then he discussed at greater length the issues of the remarriage of divorced persons and birth control.

He pointed out that remarriage and birth control, although usually linked together as 'marriage problems', had a clear line of distinction between them. The remarriage of divorced persons was a matter of public discipline (canon law) whereas birth control was one of pastoral counselling (moral theology). The Church did not allow the remarriage of a divorced person, and so that settled the matter for those who were willing to obey. It was left to the bishop to decide whether or not an individual in such a marriage should be admitted to Communion. Birth control was one for the confessional or private discussion with the priest as a counsellor. Kirk did not prescribe what a priest should say to someone who sought absolution or advice, but he did suggest that in those circumstances the priest should remember the distinction he had made between actions which were wrong in themselves and those which were wrong in particular circumstances.

Kirk probably felt he could not be more dogmatic. He would be aware that some of those present welcomed the Lambeth propositions. But two or three years later, when he prepared his book *Conscience and Its Problems* for a second edition (1936) he revised what he had said on this subject. At Lambeth, he wrote, a majority of the bishops had taken a tentative step towards recognizing that birth control was acceptable when couples believed it was right to limit their number of children. But the wording of the propositions was vague and gave no guidance for the priest confessor and counsellor. In outline, his advice was as follows.

The priest who felt bound to uphold the traditional Catholic ban on contraception should realize that numerous Roman moral theologians had said that, if a penitent showed that he was trying to be obedient to God's law but was in error in one particular aspect of it, he might still be absolved provided he knew that what he was doing was sinful in the eyes of the Church. These theologians' justification for their opinion was that any of the faithful might be in error about some point of teaching and conduct during their lives, but there may be mitigating circumstances which need to be considered with pastoral care before an absolution was refused. It was very important that these mitigating circumstances should be taken into account and that contraceptive practices should not be condemned outright.

On the other hand, Kirk continued, the priest who agreed with the Lambeth proposition was in a more difficult position. Since the bishops of the Church of England had not offered their clergy any guidance on how to apply the proposition, it was left entirely to their own judgement. In these circumstances what they should try to do is to deal with individual cases in the light of the Lambeth resolutions as a means of mitigating the traditional ban, not as a means of replacing it.

What this amounted to was that Kirk was suggesting both kinds of priests should advise individuals in much the same way, but coming to a decision from two different angles. The first starts from the position of the traditional ban and looked for mitigating circumstances, while the second starts from the Lambeth proposition but ensures that the reasons for practising birth control are genuinely conscientious. It was a skilful exercise in the art of casuistry and an interesting example of how a Catholic moralist attempted to deal pastorally with the changing ethical standards of the time.

The third speaker at the convention was Candole on 'The Change in Social Habits and the Breakdown of the Parochial System'. He had been Davidson's chaplain before he went to St John as a curate in 1926. Five years later he was made incumbent when his vicar left, but he was ill during 1932 so his neighbour, C. J. Gardner of Christ Church, delivered his paper for him.

In it Candole described how the industrial revolution had resulted in the growth of the population in the cities and how the Church had lost touch with the majority of the working class. The parish was no longer an adequate structure; its boundaries meant nothing to those who lived in them. Greater mobility resulted in peoples' lives being dispersed between home and places of work and leisure. The Church could no longer assume that the parish was a community; it had to work to create a community from those who attended its services and turned to it for its ministries.

The Church of England, Candole continued, needed to reform its pastoral ministry to meet new needs. There should be teams of clergy working together, each with areas of pastoral care. While the parish was still adequate for those who lived in a district and could be members of the local congregation, many others could be reached more effectively beyond the parochial boundaries. The Church had to adapt to a situation in which people's outlook on life was influenced, not by religion, but by science, politics, art, literature, the cinema and the popular press. Even among practising Christians much Church teaching is disregarded because they are influenced by the secular character of contemporary society. 'The new religion of this-worldliness, harnessing to itself the mental and spiritual energies formerly given to religion, substituting in most subtle ways activities which absorb men's power of response to God, this remains the most powerful challenge to the Church.'[11] Yet he advised clergy to recognize that not everything in the modern world was evil. There were strong humanistic currents of thought and action which are Christian in the sense that they manifest the goodness of God, even though God himself is not acknowledged as their source. One way in which the Church could evangelize is for its members to identify themselves with these currents and – as Candole put it – 'sacramentalize them'.

The same theme was developed later in the convention by C. Tomlinson of St Stephen, Lewisham. One notable change in society, he said, was that as the result of education, free libraries and cheap newspapers, increasing numbers of ordinary people were no longer willing to accept what they were told unquestioningly. Sometimes intelligent questions can come in unexpected ways. Recently an insurance clerk from Catford had asked him about the connection between the mass and the mystery religions, and a mechanic on the train from Eastbourne to Victoria had enquired about the manuscripts of the New Testament. Priests needed to keep up to date with their reading if they were to teach such people with authority. The clergy were no longer looked up to as infallible guides, he said; it was the psychologists who enjoy that reputation.

Jalland put the case for encouraging families to come to the main Sunday mass together at a time when they could receive Communion. He thought special children's masses were a mistake because they separated children from their families and as they grew up the youngsters felt they had become too old for it and drifted away. He also criticized those who said they went to the eight o'clock mass to receive Communion and then to the eleven o'clock one to worship. The eleven o'clock tended to attract people from outside the parish who liked the ritual and the singing. That was not the kind of thing Catholics should encourage. He concluded by describing what he regarded as a model celebration of the Eucharist: four hymns and a sensible use of the proper; music ruthlessly subordinated to the rite; service books with the words of the service clearly laid out; a liturgical sermon; an orderly and efficient distribution of Communion; simple ritual. On the final point Jalland deplored the way clergy followed Fortesque with its 'many absurdities'. He quoted Frere, 'A large part of ceremonial began and still goes on upon purely utilitarian grounds.' 'Had this principle been more clearly grasped,' he concluded, 'fewer churches might have suffered from the fussy and faddy ritualism which too often mars the purity of liturgical worship.'[12]

Mackay was asked give a talk on the role of sermons in educating the laity. The vicar of All Saints, Margaret Street, was highly regarded as a preacher. Wilson said Mackay's style in the pulpit made him popular among those who liked their preachers to be cool and authoritative:

Of his [Mackay's] sermons he wrote, and read, every word, without giving much impression of reading. They were invariably as fresh, topical, and up-to-date, as they were devoid of clichés, platitudes, a word too many, a word too few. Always they were penetrating, packed with knowledge of contemporary and pristine human nature, flashing of phrase, impossible to ignore, difficult to forget. He ascended the pulpit, donned a stole, adjusted his pince-nez, and announced his text. You might, if you were a casual visitor to Butterfield's not particularly beautiful church of the tall spire in the street where stands that emporium of which it has been said that '*ibi Mowbray, ibi Ecclesia*', at first think him aloof, didactic, dictatorial. He would, perhaps, remind you of a bishop; or of your headmaster in the days when you were in juvenile trouble. But by the time he had delivered two or three sentences you would decide that he was a preacher who must be listened to; and he would not fail to hold your attention until the end of the last searching, incisive, and polished sentence.[13]

In his talk Mackay quoted W. B. Selbie, a Presbyterian scholar, who said all congregations need to be taught the elements of Christianity over and over again at appropriate intervals. Mackay then reminded his audience that since many learned much through the eye as well as the ear – newspapers, books, magazine, the cinema – the setting within which the sermon was presented mattered as much as what was spoken. That meant Catholics had to take care that their church interiors as well as the ritual did not distract but reinforced what was taught from the pulpit.

Mackay said he knew that religious services on the BBC ('the wireless') were causing concern since the idea was getting round that they could become a substitute for church-going. Letters appeared in the press about the comfort of worshipping at home rather than in a pew and about the superiority of the music and preaching to what was heard in many churches. One wag wrote that at home you didn't have to put anything in the collection. Mackay defended the broadcasts. Instead of complaining, he said, critics should admire the spirit in which the BBC does all it can to present the Christian faith to listeners. But he admitted such broadcasts had their limitations:

> We think of the sick and of such in health as the men in lighthouses and rejoice at the advantage that the BBC is to them. But our difficulty is that hundreds of thousands are now taking all their religious teaching through the BBC, and this can never be the whole of Christianity. The ethical message of St John the Baptist is all that the BBC can broadcast... The consequence is that in the face of an anti-God movement, which is very strong in England, although not yet as blatant as in Russia, a Christianity is in all innocence being defused which is a good as far as it goes, but cannot go down to the roots. For it must be remembered that a Christianity which is not Anglican, nor Roman Catholic, nor Orthodox,

nor Congregationalist, nor Wesleyan, not Baptist, nor Presbyterian is less Christian than any one of these denominations taken by itself. Father Martindale [a well-known Jesuit] can broadcast the most delightful little sketches of the saints, but they leave him a good deal more to say later on in the evening at Farm Street.[14]

Preachers should follow the first evangelists in proclaiming, not a new ethic, but the good news of a new power demonstrating God's love and holiness. No sermon should last more than twenty-five minutes. Sermons should be backed up by every opportunity to teach because so many were more ignorant of the essentials of the faith than they had been generations before. Confirmation classes, for example, should begin with the questions, What am I? What is God? What is sin? 'In view of the modern study of psychology there is no part of the Christian account of things which needs more careful explanation today than sin.'[15]

He described how in the previous year he had taken as the theme of a Lent course 'Religion – Why? Which? How? Where? When? What about it?' To his astonishment All Saints was filled for every session. In the present year he thought he would aim to help fewer people by offering simple instructions: how to say one's prayers, how to make one's confession, how to read the Bible, how to make one's communion, and how to assist at mass. 'The result was embarrassing. The church was filled every time from end to end . . . Courses of connected teaching put in the simplest way are what people want. Above all things, people need today to be taught how to read the Bible.'[16]

Perhaps the priests from small towns and villages who heard this talk afterwards reflected ruefully that they might be able to fill their churches if they had Mackay's reputation and the whole of London from which to attract a congregation.

Inevitably in such a gathering the liturgy attracted most discussion. There was general agreement among those present that their main aim should be to encourage people to attend mass on Sundays and Holy Days, but there was disagreement – sharp at times – on what rite was most appropriate. In the Church of England there had been a general assumption that the eucharistic rite of 1662 should be used. Only those Catholics who abandoned the Prayer Book and used the Roman missal disagreed. But the revision process had introduced the possibility of two authorized rites – the one in the Prayer Book and the other in the Revised Book. This opened the way for suggestions for a third rite which would bring Catholics together.

Chandler pressed for a return to the eucharistic rite of the first Prayer Book of 1549. He believed that, if a sufficient number of Catholics were united behind the proposal, a petition could be drawn up and presented to the bishops requesting permission to use it as an alternative to the rite in the Revised Book. Others favoured the interim rite. Some were content to continue using the Prayer Book service and interpolating silently parts of the Roman canon. So in the end nothing definite was decided, except that everyone agreed that the settings of the mass should be those that the congregation could join in: Merbecke's and Martin Shaw's were mentioned.

There were different ideas about what was suitable for Sunday evenings. A. H. Howe Browne said many were familiar with and appreciated the Prayer Book evensong and so it was wise to concentrate on presenting that service as attractively as possible with a good choir, a teaching sermon and a minimum of ceremonial. Its advantage was that it consisted largely of biblical material and therefore presented good opportunities for expounding the Scriptures.

Edward Hardy, on the other hand, said that in the Episcopal Church of the USA devotions to the Blessed Sacrament and benediction was a much more powerful draw than evensong. These offered congregations an opportunity to pray with their attention focused on the sacramental presence of the Lord and increased their appreciation for the meaning of the mass. He suggested that clergy should not be restricted to using only the traditional forms but should introduce more freedom and informality into the devotions: specific intercessions and popular songs of praise such as were used in mission services. That, he believed, would increase the relevance of the service for those who attended. He was also in favour of a greater flexibility in the celebration of the mass and experiments in the use of non-eucharistic services. He mentioned the use of visual aids, drama and dance in worship – which must have made many who heard him even more suspicious of 'Americanisms'.

Before and after the Prayer Book fiasco. the liturgy had been the subject of much bitter controversy, carried on at length in the correspondence columns of the church press and sometimes the secular papers. Rosenthal warned of the dangers of this:

> The distortion of Catholic perspective has been magnified immensely by the wide publicity that has been given to our controversies in the Press. The reporter – in his professional capacity – is only interested in his religion so far as it can provide him with a story. And controversy provides a story, while worship and devotion do not. The great British public is always interested in a fight, be it a cat-fight, or a prize-fight, or that most envenomed of all conflicts, a clergy-fight ... Not content with

washing our dirty linen at the parish pump, we send weekly bundles of it to Portugal Street [the *Church Times'* office] to be laundered in the presence of the whole Anglican Communion.[17]

He said that his preaching tour of North America had shown him that internal disputes among Catholics in England meant nothing to Anglicans over there, and he believed that the remedy to the controversies was to stop thinking of Catholicism in terms of the Church of England and to see themselves as members of the worldwide Anglican Communion.

The convention ended without any resolutions being passed but with exhortations to enrol their congregations as members of the Centenary Congress, and to support the work of their diocesan Centenary committees and local celebrations in parishes and deaneries.

There were noteworthy differences between the two conventions. The numbers in 1932 (491) were less than a half those in 1921. This may have been due to the effects of the economic depression of the early thirties. It could also have been a sign that there was less enthusiasm for the Congress movement. In 1921 the clergy who came to Oxford had great hopes that the pain and distraction of the war was over and that a nationwide mission based on Catholic teaching and worship would bring people back to the churches again. In the years that followed that hope had gradually faded. The subtitle of the 1932 convention – 'Why People do not go to Church?' – sounded a gloomy note, though the addresses were divided into two sections: 'Causes' and 'The Remedy.' There was a crisis of confidence among many clergy and they needed guidance and inspiration on how to minister in an age of change. The Bishop of Oxford, preaching at the opening service in St Mary's, pointed to the problem when he said, 'While we follow [the Tractarians'] devotion and whole-hearted spirit of service in their labour for our Church, we have to remember that we act in new circumstances and in a new age.'[18]

Consequently the focus was on the work of the Church and there was less attention to its response to the economic problems which were affecting the country. A notice was given out about the Anglo-Catholic Summer School's conference in Oxford the following month, but that was about all. Kirk foresaw the criticism that the conference should have focused more on the world's needs in the modern crisis – ethical, social, industrial, international – and roused those present to greater service. But, he said, the root of the world's crisis were men's untamed passions, and worship had its vital and powerful role in bringing those passions under the control of God. That alone justified the conference in seeking how to help more people to come to faith and worship in such times.

CENTENARY PREPARATIONS AND 1932 CONVENTION

So the priests left Oxford, puzzled or disturbed by some of the things they had heard, but having enjoyed the experience of being together. They had a renewed sense that hope, though deferred, was not lost. H. Beevor, the editor of the report, summed up their mood when he wrote afterwards: 'In the highways and hedges, the mines and factories, the shops and offices, the schools and universities, throughout the length and breadth of the land, the faith must be spread. Our unity is apostolic; for we are bound together by our seal to preach the glad tidings of Jesus Christ who, dwelling for ever on his throne of glory, reveals himself to man in the most holy Sacrament of the altar.'[19]

22

The Centenary Congress 1933

'To give thanks for the revival of Catholic faith and practice; to honour all those who have served the Movement; to humble ourselves in penitence for our own sins and negligences; and by renewing our consecration to the service of Christ in his Church to bring all men to the knowledge of God.'

According to the Congress handbook this was the aim of the Centenary celebrations. To pursue it, as we have seen, the executive committee prepared an ambitious programme which, centred on the Albert Hall, included visits to Oxford and other places connected with the Catholic revival. It was arranged that a daily newssheet, the *Centenary Chronicle*, should be published for participants. At the same time hundreds of other services, meetings and related events took place throughout England, Scotland, Wales and Ireland, and in parts of the Commonwealth and the USA. The administration involved was enormous and, in spite of minor hitches and unpredictable weather, the programme under the direction of Child, Russell and their staff was fulfilled according to plan.

The celebrations began on Sunday, 9 July, with special masses in hundreds of churches in London and in cities, towns and villages around the country. Archbishop Lang's sermon in Canterbury Cathedral that morning was broadcast by the BBC. He gave a brief, appreciative history of the Oxford Movement, quoting Gladstone's comment that it was 'a movement among the most remarkable in the Christendom of the last three and a half centuries'.[1] The establishment of the Church of England, he said, meant it was able to contain the interaction of Catholics, Evangelicals and Liberals on one another; they represented the three elements in religion which, von Hugel had claimed, are necessary for the fullness of the Body of Christ – the churchy or institutional, the mystical or personal, and the intellectual or speculative. It was an understanding of the Catholic revival – often put forward by Temple – which was becoming accepted by increasing numbers of the bishops and was filtering down to the parishes, even to the more tolerant Evangelical ones. It was not appreciated, however, by Catholics who believed all three elements were included in the revival.

Later that day fifteen thousand attended solemn evensong in the White City. Three processions from St John the Baptist, Holland Road, All Saints, Notting Hill, and St Catherine, Western Avenue, converged on the stadium. A high altar had been erected on a platform under a canopy in the middle of the football pitch. A long procession of servers, vested priests, choirs from several London churches, and members of the Church Lads' Brigade, Scouts and Guides led the Bishop of St Albans and his attendants to his seat. The Bishop of London was to have been present but he was ill with pneumonia.

The preacher, Fr Williams SSJE from New York, used the theme of service – the peace of the world – to say that Christian pacifism was the consequence of the Christian doctrine of man implicit in the Catholic faith. This was the first mention of the peace movement at one of the Congresses. Pacificism had grown among Christians and others after the war and in the thirties flourished as the international situation became more threatening. Dick Sheppard, a leading campaigner, in *The Impatience of a Parson* (1927) argued that the Church should be 'obliged to outlaw all war and to demand from its members that they should refuse to kill their brethren'. In 1934 he published a letter in the press inviting men to send him a postcard indicating that they renounced war. It evoked so many replies that he founded the Peace Pledge Union (PPU) with its membership drawn from the 'religious, rational, or broadly humanitarian in conviction'.[2] They included many Catholics, though some were wary of an organization which had among its followers atheists such as C. E. M. Joad (as he was until later in life) and Bertrand Russell. The PPU grew to over a hundred thousand but faded away during the second world war.

On Monday morning seven motor coaches waited in the rain outside the Albert Hall to take Congress members on visits to convents at Woking, Clewer and Thames Ditton. A priest in cotta and stole said the Lord's Prayer, the Hail Mary, and a collect for protection with the coach parties, and then hurried up and down sprinkling the vehicles – and some of the drivers – with holy water. Mass was celebrated in the chapel at Woking and prayers were said in the chapels of the other convents. The coaches arrived back just in time for their passengers to join the evening meeting at the Albert Hall. A similar outing took place to Ascot Priory, founded by Pusey, on Wednesday.

The daily timetable in the Albert Hall was different from previous congresses. The main teaching sessions were at 2.00, 6.00 and 8.00 p.m., the latter being a repeat of the 6.00 session to accommodate larger numbers. An altar was set up on the stage where a high mass was celebrated each morning. Evensong was sung there each afternoon, led by choirs from different London churches each day. Many Catholics were initially uneasy at the prospect of celebrating mass in a hall associated with secular activities such as boxing, but they were deeply impressed – as was everyone else in the packed congregation – by the solemn high mass of requiem for the departed heroes of the Oxford Movement sung there on Tuesday morning. The altar was vested in a black frontal with panels containing emblems of the Passion and six unbleached candles. Over it was a huge crucifix with a bronze figure on wood hanging against a back cloth of emerald green. At the bottom of the steps leading up to the altar was a catafalque covered with a black and gold pall and surrounded by six towering candlesticks.

The preacher was Eric Milner-White, Dean of King's College, Cambridge. Requiem masses, he said, were one of the Catholic practices restored to the Church through the movement. He avoided any reference to purgatory: he described the dead as being 'beyond the veil'. In this he was following the provisions of the Revised Prayer Book which provided a collect and readings for All Souls' Day (2 November) and three occasional prayers in commemoration of the faithful departed. Milner-White also said he was glad some religious houses and college chapels had begun the practice of commemorating individual Tractarians at mass. Such commemorations were allocated particular days in the official calendar of at least one province overseas (the West Indies) and he hoped the custom would spread throughout the Anglican Communion. Then his delivered a rhetorical eulogy for the past heroes of the revival:

> On our debt to them we need not enlarge, except to say that the graces and truths which under God they have restored to the Church in this land could only have been restored by souls who showed them forth shiningly. Penitence has been given back to us by great penitents; the wide world of prayer by those whose first work of their days and years was to kneel; the love of God, and the love of God's poor little ones, by mighty lovers and shepherds; the Holy Sacrifice by priests who trod close upon the great High Priest; fearless and profound theology by great doctors, to whom truth, in an age of new thought, was as dear as love; beauty and reverence in worship by souls steeped in holy fear; and that best victory, which comes only through suffering, by those who suffered – suffered secretly, openly, patiently, invincibly. But over all these

our fathers, examples and heroes, each with his or her special grace and task, stood, the single life of them all, One full of grace and truth, Jesus, the incarnate, the crucified, their Lord and their God.[3]

On Thursday the singing at a sung mass of the Blessed Sacrament was led by Desmond Morse Boycott's St Mary-of-the-Angels Song School. The *Church Times* reporter noted: 'Their rendering of the Plainsong of the Mass showed what can be done by a choir from a working class district of London, against all the contention of pessimists, who proclaim that neither the boys or the men of such districts will sing Plainsong, or, if they do, their voices can never be disciplined to pure and impersonal tones. It is clear that the choir of St Mary's has been so trained, it could give the people at the Mass at the Albert Hall a devotional and very beautiful rendering of the liturgical singing and the hymns.'[4]

Contributors at the main sessions were briefed to speak on the past history of the Catholic revival, the contemporary situation, and their hopes for the future.

In describing the past, speakers tended to repeat the views of historians like R. W. Church and S. L. Ollard who interpreted the Oxford Movement as a divine summons recalling the Church of England to the Catholic faith. They portrayed the Church in the years before 1833 as a moribund institution of class privilege subject to the State. This interpretation was echoed in dozens of talks and sermons during the Congress years and after. Rosenthal declared: '[The purpose of the Oxford Movement] was to preach Christ as he had not been preached in England for centuries – Christ Incarnate, Crucified, Risen and Ascended, not a dead but living Saviour whose present help is given through the Church which he founded and the sacraments which are the covenanted channels of his grace.'[5] Another speaker described the Church of England as fallen into Erastian slumbers, lethargy and worldliness.

In recent times this view has been questioned. Modern writers have demonstrated that these earlier historians underestimated the strength of the High Church tradition in the eighteenth and nineteenth centuries, and that the Oxford Movement owned more to that tradition than they recognized. R. W. Church in particular seems to have so reverenced the memory of the Tractarians, some of whom he knew in his youth, that he instinctively downplayed the role of their High Church contemporaries.

Peter B. Nockles has pointed out that Newman and his followers failed to appreciate the role of the High Churchmen in reviving Church life from 1820 onwards.[6] In his inaugural lecture to the Anglo-Catholic History Society Geoffrey Rowell referred to researches which showed how 'notable patrons of churches and institutions which were bastions of the High Church tradition' contributed to the revival in diocesan and parochial life, outside the influence of the Oxford Movement.[7] Indeed, one commentator, Richard Sharp, ended a lecture he gave in Oxford during the 150th celebrations in 1983 by wondering whether the Church of England might have been better off if its reform had been left for the High Churchmen to accomplish without the Tractarians: 'The Church gained many blessings by "the movement of 1833" but we should also pause briefly to consider whether the losses may not have been greater than we often suppose.'[8] Such a brave dash of historical revisionism would not have been welcomed in the Albert Hall in 1933.[9]

A different perspective was presented by Sir Raymond Beazley of Birmingham University. As a professional historian, he suggested that the Tractarians represented a reaction to the social and political movements at the time – the 1830 revolution in France which dethroned the Bourbons, the 1832 Reform Bill in England, the rise of socialism and workers' unions in industrial cities, and the anti-clericalism which led to physical assaults on bishops and to journalists' attacks on the Church's privilege and wealth. This caused the Tractarians, he said, to go back to the past to seek historical and theological justification for reaffirming the spiritual authority of the Church and its ministry and to clash with those who saw the Church's role differently.

Two outstanding Anglican leaders, Beazley went on, stood out to change this situation. One was Thomas Arnold of Rugby, who wanted to open the Church of England to all Nonconformists without any requirements of confirmation or episcopal ordination so that Christians could unite to evangelize the nation. The other was J. H. Newman, who believed his fellow Anglicans needed to be taught that the Church of England was part of the Catholic Church and that, whether they appreciated it or not, they were all members of it. Both believed that they knew best how to restore the Church for its mission in the country. The main thrust of Keble's famous 1833 assize sermon, he pointed out, was not the abolition of the Irish bishoprics but a warning of 'national apostasy'. Growing numbers in the population were either ignorant of what the Church stood for or were turning their backs on it. Not since the time of the Non-Jurors had the State's power over the Church been challenged as it was by the Oxford Movement. He regretted the Tractarians had been as antagonistic to liberalism (he meant in the political sense) as their successors were to science; but in the circumstances of their age, he added, it was understandable.

C. Tomkinson spoke of the sufferings followers of the Tractarians had to endure after Newman's submission to Rome. With few exceptions the

Church's hierarchy were hostile to them. Pusey was suspended and misrepresented. Anglo-Catholic clergy were harassed and summoned before the courts. He challenged the commonly held view that the Tractarians were an off-shoot of the Romantic Movement. That, he said, was not sufficient to explain the personal sacrifices of those men and women who devoted themselves to the service of the poor. Anyone who joined a newly founded religious order just to fulfil an artistic dream was soon disillusioned when confronted with the community's real work. 'It was one thing to build a Gothic church,' he said, 'but quite another thing to plant it in the evil slums of Pimlico or Leeds. It needed more than the romantic temperament to carry the banner of the Church to cholera stricken hovels of Devonport, or the jungles of Melanesia.'[10]

Marcus Atlay took the chair for Beazley's and Tomlinson's addresses. It was the first time he had appeared at a Congress since he had resigned from the executive ten years before. He was greeted with cheers by those who remembered he was responsible for initiating the first Congress in 1920. In a brief speech he urged Catholics to be faithful in attending mass. He died the following year while on holiday in France.

A. Pinchard recalled the struggles of priests who sought to beautify worship and reserve the sacrament in spite of the opposition of bishops and the rioting of mobs. Did younger clergy realize, he asked, that five of their predecessors had been sent to gaol for introducing rituals and customs which they now took for granted? Had they heard what the English Church Union had done to defend those earlier priests? Behind his remarks was his anxiety that the Union was failing to attract new members from the generation of men who had been ordained since the war.

Several speakers referred to the work of priests and religious orders in the slums. Mr J. G. Lockhart, chairman of the English Church Union's committee on the slums, said that it was the social concern of Anglo-Catholics, especially in their attempts at relieving slum clearance, for which they would be remembered in the future. The Prince of Wales sent a message of greeting to the Centenary committee saying how much he admired Basil Jellicoe's work in Somers Town. A short film of the St Pancras House Improvement Society was shown at the Imperial Institute during the week. Walter Monckton, who was Attorney-General to the Duchy of Cornwall (and who acted as adviser to Edward VIII during the abdication crisis of 1936), said he spoke as an ordinary member of the Church of England who did not belong to any 'combative organization or body within the Church'. Nevertheless he praised the Oxford Movement for its struggle for social justice, commending the teachings of Bishop Gore and Canon Scott Holland and the example of priests like Fr Lowder and Fr Dolling.

He listed work done by the Church and other voluntary societies among the unemployed and their families. He thought that up to 300,000 of the unemployed throughout the country had benefited from these activities. He noted that Jellicoe's society had built 170 new flats and reconditioned 10 old houses; 47 new flats were under construction. He urged churches everywhere to co-operate with local governments in launching similar schemes: at least a million new homes were urgently needed. A letter to the executive from the prime minister, Ramsay MacDonald, was read out saying something similar.

As the executive hoped, the scandal of the slums and Jellicoe's initiatives were mentioned by several speakers. But in other parts of the country Catholics felt financial support for the Church's efforts was being soaked up by London. A Mr Hall of Manchester wrote to the Congress saying he hoped the London housing associations would not neglect the needs of slums in the northern cities. 'We lack the support of the rich and distinguished persons who lend patronage to your schemes,' he said.[11]

The Congress went on to assess the contemporary situation in the light of what had been achieved. Kirk, now Regius Professor of Moral and Pastoral Theology at Oxford, was as usual logical and lucid. He listed the five truths which, he thought, the Oxford Movement had revived or recovered for the Church of England.

First, the truth of the Church's sacramental character. 'It seems incredible that any body of Churchmen should have let so obvious a principle die of inanition.'[12] He admitted that truth had not died out completely among certain groups in the Church, but many Anglicans before 1833 had not sought the grace of the sacraments as even the Reformers had expected.

Second, the truth of the social mission of the Church. But, Kirk added, they must not forget that Evangelicals, with others, had been equally concerned about the state of the poor and that the former had been largely responsible for the campaign which had led Parliament to make the slave trade illegal. What was distinctive about the Oxford Movement's contribution was the formation of religious communities, both for men and women, and the establishment of missions and settlements in the slums. The Tractarians' incarnational theology led them to see that no sphere of human affairs was without the possibility of being sanctified by the Holy Spirit, and they taught that God's grace – especially his sacramental grace – was essential for those working for human equality and dignity. 'When every allowance has been made for the share played by others in developing the modern sense of corporate social responsibility,' Kirk commented, 'it may still be said that the Tractarians contributed elements of vital importance which would have been lacking apart from them.'[13]

Third, the truth of personal holiness. Unlike some other Catholics with a Nonconformist upbringing, he appreciated his earlier Methodist upbringing. He said that, in their quest for personal holiness, the Tractarians were following the example of the Methodists. Although there were examples of personal holiness in the Church of England at the beginning of the nineteenth century, as in all ages, nevertheless among many of the clergy and laity the ideals of Christian sanctity had become sadly tarnished.

'If there was one thing in which the poetic vision of Keble, the burning zeal of Newman, and the grave earnestness of Pusey were unanimous, it was this conviction – that no one is incapable of sanctity, and that the Church which is not calling every man and woman to enter into this their true inheritance is a Church which is betraying one of its most sacred tasks. To this conviction we owe more reforms than we can say: the revival of sacramental confession and frequent Communion; of self-examination and self-discipline, upon prayer and intercession and meditation; the institution of theological colleges; the organization of missions and retreats and quiet days; and much else that is now so completely bound up with our entire Church life that we scarcely stop to consider it.'[14]

Fourth, the truth of the pastoral authority of the Church. Kirk followed the theme of his talk at the Priests' Convention the previous year. He carefully distanced himself from Roman Catholic concepts by explaining he was referring to pastoral not penal authority. 'There was no inquisitorial element about the Oxford Movement; there never has been in English Catholicism.' But the Body of Christ has an authority to lead God's children in the ways of truth and righteousness, and loyalty to that authority is second only to the voice of God speaking through the enlightened conscience. It was not sufficient to say, as many did dogmatically, 'This is what the Church teaches', and suppose that there is nothing further to be said. Such people need 'to draw out the full savour of true Catholicism and apply it to the needs and necessities of their own time'.[15]

Fifth, the truth of the Church's spiritual independence. Opponents of the Tractarians consistently appealed to the secular arm to enforce their demands, and this highlighted for many – and not just the Tractarians – that the Church has an authority which is not dependent on the State. The Church must always assert this or she will cease to be the Catholic Church. 'The right of the Church to live her own life, to proclaim her own truths, to guide her own members, is a right which the great Leviathan has always denied; but a Church which does not assert it in season and out of season is a Church which carried the seeds of death within itself.'[16]

Kirk said he realized that there were other truths that were important, and that other churchmen had proclaimed some of these truths, but the five he had listed were the dominant characteristic of Catholicism. Reviewing the five, Kirk said he thought the first three had survived and developed. The truth of sacramentalism was more widely taught and practised, the truth of social mission was being pursued more conscientiously, and the truth of personal holiness was still being sought in spite of the modern Sunday making formal churchmanship a phenomenon of the past.

But the last two, he thought, had not been realized. The inability of the Church of England to make up her mind on moral and doctrinal issues meant that she spoke with a confusion of tongues and weakened in her members any sense of her spiritual authority. 'The only authority which men will respect, whether in Church or State, is an authority which, however firmly it bases itself upon the proved truths of the past, is vivacious enough to bring them into vital contact with the ever-changing moods of the present.' The blame, he believed, was the lack of a truly Catholic theology which, under the guidance of the Holy Spirit, tested contemporary thought with the eternal truth of the Gospel. 'Something of this spirit, I believe – the spirit which made *Lux Mundi* the great book it was – is missing in Anglican scholarship at the moment; and that is why we do not treat the authority of the Church with the same respect as it commanded, both from its adherents and from its opponents, in the heyday of the Oxford Movement.'[17] This depended as much on the spirit of educated Church people as on bishops, clergy and scholars.

The fifth truth was in grave danger while the State had so much control over the Church. He was thinking not only of the Prayer Book fiasco but also of trends in society which flouted Christian morality, such as the abandonment in the Act then being promoted in Parliament of the idea of marriage as a life-long commitment. The Church had to face that challenge – but were her members strong enough to do that?

Several speakers paid tributes to John and Charles Wesley as Anglicans seeking spiritual revival for the Church. In a sermon in John Wesley's old college, Lincoln, Fr Frere described the Evangelical revival of the eighteenth century as one of those 'divine movements' which carry forward the Kingdom of God. Methodism, he noted, began almost exactly a hundred years before the 'divine moment' they were celebrating. The Wesley brothers began their devotional and charitable activities in Oxford in 1729, and they were called 'Methodists' for the first time in 1733. Their group was predominantly a movement of personal piety whereas the Tractarians were primarily concerned that the Church should recover an understanding of itself as the Divine Society. The first Methodists did not doubt the truth about the Church – after all, they were eighteenth-century High Churchmen – but they saw their calling as one of encouraging its members in holiness. It was after his meeting with the Moravians that John Wesley changed from working within the Church to working beyond it. He never regarded himself as anything but an Anglican, yet in the end against his brother Charles' advice he was forced to take actions which eventually led to the Methodists' breakaway from the Church of England. But still Catholics should honour them, Frere concluded. 'The Methodists wished for freedom of the individual soul; the Tractarians, without neglecting that, were urgent to secure the autonomy of the Church and its rights and duties and privileges.' He wished more Anglicans had the Methodists' 'tremendous zeal and enthusiasm for evangelization'.[18]

Criticism of certain aspects of the movement came from speakers from other parts of the Anglican Communion. Bishop Mark Carpenter-Garnier of Colombo spoke in a quiet and clear voice which, wrote the *Church Times* reporter, made his stern reproof of Anglo-Catholic party spirit and their need to be contrite about it all the more effective. Speaking as one who lived far away from Britain, Carpentier-Garnier said that the bitterness and antagonism expressed in the letters published in the ecclesiastical press greatly damaged the Church's witness. A published letter may at the time of writing seem an effective repartee to an opponent, but weeks later, when the passage is read overseas, it suggests nothing but a travesty of the Christian spirit. Expatriates could not understand why there was so much fuss over trivialities. In India they were discussing the scheme for reunion which was causing so much controversy in England. He wished those Catholics who debated this matter so angrily in the press in this country could listen to the charitable way in which his brother bishops in India were discussing differences with the other Churches. Also, he said, terminology was misleading. The term 'Anglo-Catholic' was regarded by English people living abroad as something foreign being foisted on the Church of England. 'My fear is that we are in danger of losing sight of our true vocation and of becoming content to be a self-contained and self-satisfied group, instead of making our contribution to the whole Anglican Communion, and so to the Catholic Church.'[19]

Another speaker from outside England criticized Anglo-Catholics for their insularity. K. D. Mackenzie, later elected Bishop of Brechin, said that terms like 'Anglo-Catholic' and 'Anglican Communion' could be misleading to Scotsmen like himself. They could be misinterpreted as being essentially English and therefore contradictory to what the word Catholic really meant. 'How absurd is that tendency, not yet completely eradicated,' he commented, 'to treat all Anglican life as though it were an export from this country! There is a completely autonomous Church which is compelled to call itself (alas!), "The Church of England in Canada". There is an institution which did once quite seriously style itself, "The United Church of England and Ireland in Australia and Tasmania". And do not our hackles arise when in Scotland we sometimes hear the shrine of our predilection referred to as "the English Church"?'[20]

He thought it was a mistake to regard Anglo-Catholicism as the fruit only of the Oxford Movement. He probably enjoyed reminding his largely English audience that in 1784 Samuel Seabury was consecrated as Bishop in America by Scottish bishops, so the Catholic faith of the Episcopal Church of Scotland spread across the Atlantic fifty years before the *Tracts for the Times*. New England was Catholic in mind and spiritual outlook, he said, while Old England was still Hanoverian. What Anglicans needed was the Catholic spirit which released them from crude John Bull nationalism, individualism, parochialism, provincialism, insularity and the snobbishness of the establishment. 'Internationalism is our birthright,' he went on. 'We will not be deprived of it either by the hallucination of papal absolutism or by the nightmare of an omnicompetent civil power . . . Let us think internationally. Let us think as members of a worldwide Movement, determined to preach the whole faith of the whole Church as the only thing which makes sense of the universe and brings order to life.'[21]

The Bishop of Algoma said the Church of England lacked much which other provinces had gained. 'The Mother Church may well learn something from her daughters. They have freedom. Their Bishops are not overruled by ecclesiastical lawyers. They have real and absolute synodical government with power to enact canons. For them the Revised Prayer Book was not impeded by a few Protestant MPs. This freedom gives us a strong psychological advantage.'[22]

Fr Biggart CR warned that departure from the Catholic faith led to false worship. Bolshevism could only be understood as a new religion attempting to replace that of the persecuted Orthodox Church. 'Today in Russia the tomb of Lenin takes the place of the tombs of the Holy Apostles Peter and Paul in the veneration of the Catholic world. Leningrad is their Rome, and Lenin's grave their central shrine.' Since worship was a key factor in maintaining unity, he wanted an international committee of Anglican liturgists who would suggest that when separate provinces reformed their prayer books, they would make sure that their revision of the Eucharist emphasized 'its sacrificial character, which would make plain to all people the primary purpose for which the Blessed Eucharist was ordained, which is, in the splendid words of our catechism, for "a continual remembrance of the sacrifice of the death of Christ and the benefits which we receive thereby". Once granted this main objective, then varieties of language or ceremonial use are of secondary consideration and may well be left to adjust themselves to local requirements.'[23]

Little was said at this Congress about the international situation. Perhaps that was inevitable as the event had been planned as a celebration and a review of the Anglo-Catholic movement. It was two laymen who touched on these wider concerns, Lord Justice Slesser (to give him his title by now) and T. S. Eliot in their introductory remarks as chairmen of two meetings. Slesser said that democracy depended on the Christian understanding of God's purposes for society, and that he was disturbed that it was being crushed in different parts of the world. Besides Russia, Mexico and Spain, he could think of two European countries in which the Church was tolerated but not allowed to influence state policy. Presumably he meant Italy and Germany. By 1933 Mussolini was building up an Italian army, navy and air force to further his imperialist ambitions, and the first reports were appearing in the press of violence against the Jews under Hitler, the newly elected German Chancellor. It was news of this which prompted the committee to request that at Centenary services prayers should be offered not only for Christian unity but also for world peace. T. S. Eliot was due to take the chair for a session but was prevented by what he called 'a trifling accident'. In a letter to the chairman which was read out he said he had come to believe in a European as distinct from an insular or imperialist culture. He seems to have envisaged the countries of Europe being brought together in a reunited western Christendom which would be an insurance against any future war.

Two speakers, N. P. Williams and D. Rosenthal, were asked to share their vision of 'The Next Hundred Years'. Williams wanted people to remember the word 'Catholic' was used in the primitive Church as meaning 'orthodox' in distinction from Arians and other heretics who denied the incarnation. In future years, he said, Catholics must never cease to insist on the orthodox faith in God becoming man in Jesus Christ. That was the bedrock of the Gospel on which the Church was founded. He described the Church as 'an extension of the incarnation'. (This used to be a favourite dictum among Catholic preachers who wanted to emphasize the unity of Christ and his people. It gradually fell into disuse as scriptural descriptions of the Church as 'the Body of Christ' and 'the fellowship of the Holy Spirit' gained prominence.) The greatest challenge to the Church in the next century, Williams reckoned, would be to maintain that incarnational faith in defense of attack from different quarters.

As for the state of the Christian world in 2033, Williams thought that would depend on the extent to which the Church had become united. He dared to hope that by then there would be 'the complete reunion of Christendom, by a sweeping advance of the Gospel all over the world, and by a brilliant efflorescence of Christian civilization such as history has never hitherto known'. Then he added, 'But we have to prepare for Armageddon first.'[24] By this he meant an assault on the Christian faith by a God-denying, secular and materialistic society. He foresaw this in terms of an attack on the Church's doctrine and morals rather than a physical persecution of Christians. The whole Church was entering a dark age ('a Night of Power') when the forces of secularization would emerge in strength. The climax of this attack, he thought, would be about the year 1960, when Christian apologists would be tempted to water down the doctrine of the incarnation in an attempt to make the faith more acceptable to questioning minds.[25]

However, he thought this assault on the Church might well be a factor in speeding up the process of reunion. Christians would be drawn together to present a united front against the attack. To prepare for it they must be well instructed in the essentials of the Catholic faith. Remember, he said, that Evangelicals in the Church of England were also Catholic in the true sense of that word – orthodox believers in the Gospel of the incarnation. The Tractarians did not think of their task as making the Church of England Catholic; they believed it was already Catholic. Anglo-Catholics should stand firm on this faith and not attempt 'to trick out an Anglican jackdaw with feathers borrowed from the Roman or any other peacock'. They should pray and work for the conversion of the human race and the establishment of a Christian civilization based on a universal recognition of God's sovereignty. This would 'banish the Palaeolithic irrationality of war from the face of the earth, and will guarantee to every law-abiding citizen justice, equality of opportunity, healthy conditions of existence, and a fair share of the good and delightful things of life'.[26]

Rosenthal saw the Centenary celebrations as a prologue to a spiritual drama which would unfold, scene by scene, in the next hundred years. Inspired by the Christ-like devotion of the Tractarian heroes of the past, present-day Catholics must aspire to greater holiness and to closer unity with Christians of other traditions. Then they must look beyond their petty controversies and see themselves as God's agents for the transformation of society. 'If we can make the Church in our different parishes a society of men and women who are not only faithful to their own ecclesiastical traditions, but who are also foremost in all common effort for the enrichment and uplifting of human life, then good men everywhere will not be repelled by its narrowness as so often they are today; they will be attracted by the largeness of its visions and the width and beauty of its sympathy.' What he looked for in the next hundred years was 'a Catholicism in touch with the progressive forces of social and political thought not only to England but to the world'.²⁷

C. B. Mortlock saw dangers ahead. Like Williams and Rosenthal he believed a crisis of apostasy was coming: 'A negative Protestantism has prepared the way and Modernism has provided the route maps for the advance of the Godless.' The devil often takes the guise of the good churchman counselling commonsense and even moderation to deceive even the elect. Referring to a tale which a few years later C. S. Lewis was to use in *Screwtape Letters*, he said, 'You remember the story of the council in hell when the various ministers plenipotentiary were giving advice about the campaign against mankind. Many proposals were advanced, but none seemed really satisfactory until one diabolical counsellor said, "Why not tell them there is no hurry?" That was the most successful diplomatic stroke made in hell for many aeons.'²⁸

The chairmen for the Thursday and Friday sessions were Lord Irwin, Halifax's son, who had just returned from being Viceroy of India, and Lord Lloyd. The editor of the *Chronicle* noted that although they took opposite sides on the Indian question – Irwin wanting India to have commonwealth status, Lloyd being against it – they nevertheless were united in the Catholic faith.

On Friday, as planned, high mass was celebrated in the quadrangle of Pusey House. The congregation of 4,000 travelled from different parts of the country by train, coach and car. Members of one south coast church flew in two aeroplanes to an airfield near Oxford. In the thirties numerous private flying clubs were established and small planes buzzed about the skies unhindered in those pre-radar days. The congregation then went from Pusey House to St Mary's for the commemorative sermon at midday by Fr E. K. Talbot CR.²⁹

Talbot said that the Oxford Movement had enabled the Church of England to recover its conscious of being a divine society, and because of this it was enabled to meet two challenge at the present time which the early Tractarians could not have dreamed of. The first was the vindication of the faith in the face of new knowledge. With the Scriptures as the paramount authority, the Church's experience in adapting to change throughout the centuries had equipped her to discern what was of God in contemporary thought and see how it related to the faith she has received. The freedom to speculate was one of the glories of the English Church. But he added a warning: 'An ideal of comprehension which means the inclusion of every point of view, however mutually contradictory, is a false one. Truth and error are for ever opposite. But often error conceals a single truth, obscured or forgotten, pleading for its place in the whole proportion of faith. Let us not hanker after a system which can peremptorily smother the protesting truth along with the error: but rather trust the deep consciousness of the Church, guided by the Holy Spirit, to extricate and appropriate the truth, and to destroy error in the only way in which, in the end, it can be destroyed, by exposing it as error – as contrary to the deepest and most living experience.'[30]

The second challenge which resulted from the Church's consciousness being awakened by the Oxford Movement, he said, concerned her mission to human society. That did not mean setting forward Christianity as a means of saving civilization. It may not be God's purpose to save a particular civilization. Rather, the Church's task was to disclose the Kingdom of God as the order that had been brought from heaven by the incarnation of God himself within human nature, and in the fellowship of the Holy Spirit to be the embodiment of that Kingdom on earth. In the end it was a matter of relationships – with God and with each other. 'The Eternal God – the supremely real – transcendent over all his creation – offers to each and all of his children the citizenship of a universal spiritual order, brought within the courses of history by the Incarnate Word and controlling the life of man by the life-giving Spirit, cleansing, unifying, sustaining and enlightening his whole nature. That citizenship is free and universal. It lies within the awful prerogative of man to accept or refuse. But for judgement or salvation it remains the abiding truth of human life. It claims to subordinate to itself all the powers of man in their several functions and to draw into its service every activity of which he is capable. The Church by the very meaning of its faith and the purpose of its sacraments is in the world to declare and effect the incorporation of human life into the universal society – the City of God, whose existence stands not in ideal of human construction, but in the consequence of God's self-giving in creation.'[31]

On Saturday afternoon between four and five thousand children crowded into and around St Augustine's, Queens Gate, for prayers before processing to the Albert Hall to present a Pageant of Youth similar to the one at the 1930 Congress. The demand for tickets was so great that a second presentation was made in the evening.

News of the plans to have a high mass in the White City stadium on the last Sunday of the Congress had been widely publicized by the press, so the Protestant Alliance had time to plan their counter demonstrations. Their members paraded the streets of London early on that Sunday morning with a loud speaker van inviting protesters to go to the White City. They flew kites over the stadium announcing that 'The Protestant Alliance declares this High Mass illegal', but took them down when told to by the police. The congregation in the stadium heard a loud speaker blaring, 'The Bishop of Rome hath no jurisdiction in this Realm of England', before it was silenced as the service began. Noticing that the mass was being held on St Swithin's day, the *Centenary Chronicle* reported, 'There appeared recently in a religious weekly a letter from an irate Protestant gentleman calling upon the Deity to indicate his disapproval of Anglo-Catholics by visiting their open-air services with thunder and hail and tempest. Mr Porcelli was promptly, and properly, rebuked by his more charitably minded co-religionists; and Dr Barnes, if he saw the letter, must have been distressed to find one with whom he has so much in common echoing so closely the technique of the African rain-making magician.'

The organizers estimated that there were between 45,000 and 50,000 present in the stadium. Many Catholic parishes in and around London cancelled their late morning masses so that their congregations could attend. At twelve o'clock various processions entered the arena. The Bishop of St Albans was escorted by a number of notables, including the Admiral of the Fleet, the Air Marshall of the Royal Air Force and several high-ranking Army officers – indicating that the occasion was officially regarded as being of national importance. Archbishop Germanos was accompanied by the Greek ambassador. The Prayer Book service was followed. The mass was a votive of the Holy Spirit. A brass band and large choir under Captain Palmer led the singing of Merbecke's setting and the hymns.

There was no sermon, which was fortunate for, in contrast to the blazing summer weather which had usually accompanied Congress events, squalls of wind and rain lashed across the field at intervals during the service. 'The weather took on a real John Knox mood,' somebody said afterwards. The bishops and their assistants were sheltered under the canopy, as were those who had seats in the stands. The rest stood stoically where they were. The sun came out in time for the prayer of consecration, when a fanfare of trumpets greeted the elevation, and six men received Communion. But then the rain set in again and many went home wet. No doubt for years afterwards Mr Porcelli gleefully told his friends how the Almighty had heard his prayers and sent his rain upon the unjust, drenching those who were betraying the Protestant Church of England.

A number of Roman Catholic priests and laity attended some of the sessions. One wrote to the *Chronicle* saying that, while he was unable to recognize the validity of Anglican orders, he was full of admiration for 'the sincerity of your motives and the saintliness of many of your members'. The summer issue of the *Blackfriars* magazine included an article signed 'Jacobin' regretting that the Malines Conversations had not been followed up by 'some semi-official conference . . . where approaches may be attempted with courage, patience, humility, even hope'. The writer then went on to suggest that 'when an Anglo-Catholic devoutly makes use of his sacraments, some sort of sacramental experience is not to be unexpected . . . There are elements in the situation which make his perception far from being only hallucination.' He added, 'We see real holiness in many lives influenced by the Oxford Movement, and the theory sketched above at least does something to explain a sacramental quality which makes it so different from the holiness of the Evangelical or the Moslem [sic].' This was pounced on by the *Universe* which coldly remarked that the Dominicans are 'at home in the remotest recesses of the speculative in theological science'. Ronald Knox, from the Roman Catholic chaplaincy in Oxford, was reported to have said that the Centenary celebrations were 'pathetic'. If that is true, it is out of character, for Knox was usually courteous in his relationships with his former Anglican colleagues.

The editor of the *Chronicle* invited a leading Evangelical, A. J. MacDonald, Rector of St Dunstan's in the West, Fleet Street, to contribute an article. MacDonald said Evangelicals admired much in Anglo-Catholic devotion to holiness and piety of life, and they recognized the widespread influence of Tractarian methods of order, regularity and beauty in worship. They appreciated the zeal for sound learning and the demand for social righteousness which were characteristic of the great leaders of the Oxford Movement and many of their followers. But he criticized Anglo-Catholics for not recognizing 'the great gulf created by those who turned their backs on what the Reformation had done in this country to secure support for a Reformed and Protestant Church'. He regretted their attempts to 'Latinize' the Church's ceremonial. Most English people are offended by vestments and incense. Why abandon the simple traditional vesture they were all used to? He ended by saying the main division was doctrinal: 'Evangelicals cannot give assent to certain interpretations of the Eucharist put forth by Anglo-Catholics, nor to the practice of confession, the use of incenses, Reservation and Benediction.'

The following is a round-up of Centenary events in London and elsewhere.

One day Congress members filled St Sophia Cathedral in Bayswater for an Orthodox Eucharist. They heard Archbishop Germanos of Thyateira preach an appreciative sermon on the Oxford Movement and they were delighted to receive the Blessed Bread afterwards.

At a Centenary Exhibition at the Imperial Institute in South Kennsington, arranged by Sir Eric Maclagan, Director of the Victoria and Albert Museum, vestments designed by Martin Travers and others were displayed. Alongside them was a high mass set from St Augustine, Kilburn, first used in 1870. There were also personal items which formerly belonged to Dr Pusey, including the chair on which he sat to hear confessions, and the plain wooden cross with which Marian Hughes was invested when she was professed by Pusey as the first woman religious in the Church of England. Also in the exhibition were Newman's surplice and a letter dated 3 October 1845, written a few days before he resigned his fellowship at Oxford (loaned by the Birmingham Oratory); the prayer desk used in Lancaster gaol by Fr Green when he was imprisoned for his ritual practices; Bishop E. King of Lincoln's pastoral staff, and pages from *Punch* deriding the ritual movement.[32]

Through the Pageant of Youth the committee had attempted to inspire the younger generation with all that the Centenary stood for, and in different parts of the country children and adolescents were included in local services and events. Street processions of Sunday schools and youth organizations with banners and bands marked the Centenary in many places. There were special services at summer holiday camps. The London Rover Scamp Camp held an open air mass at their camp in Hatfield Park when 109 received Communion.

During the celebrations a Seven Years' Association was launched in which young Catholics undertook a simple rule of life which included a pledge to be faithful witnesses in their places of employment and leisure. Membership was to be reviewed and renewed in seven years' time during what was expected to be the next Congress in 1940. In the event it continued for some years after the second world war until it faded away as its members grew into middle age.

Catholic parishes in Coventry city cancelled their Sunday services so that their congregations could go to the cathedral where Bishop Mervyn Haigh presided at a sung mass. Eighteen priests assisted in distributing the sacrament to 753 persons. In Cornwall a Centenary mass was sung in the ancient church of St Madryn near Tintagel with 50 communicants – twice the number usually there for Easter.

A sung mass for children was held in York Minister in the presence of Archbishop Temple. Temple took a leading role in various Centenary events in his diocese, telling congregations that his father, Frederick Temple, as a junior fellow of Balliol, had known Newman and Pusey personally.

Liverpool Catholics kept to their agreement with members of the Orange order (made years previously during a local congress) and did not arrange an outdoor procession; but masses and services were held throughout the diocese to refute – as the *Church Times* triumphantly observed – the claim by the former Bishop F. J. Chavasse that Liverpool was 'England's premier Protestant diocese'. A thanksgiving service was held in Manchester Cathedral for both the Evangelical and the Oxford movements.

The Evangelical rector of Birmingham, Canon Guy Rogers, preached at a Centenary service in Leamington saying how much he learned from reading about the Tractarians and from hearing Gore preach. 'If ever the day should come,' he said, 'when your tinder shall kindle at our spark, or our spark kindle your tinder, the Church of England will suddenly glow with a Catholicity as yet undreamed of.'

Three thousand, including some from London and Oxford, attended a sung mass in Winchester Cathedral. Many later went on to Hursley and placed a wreath on Keble's grave. At a service in St Hilda, Leeds, the vicar read aloud one of Pusey's sermons, saying it was appropriate in the church Pusey himself had built. The Bishop and the choir of Gloucester cathedral went to Fairford to celebrated mass in the village where Keble was born.

In several cathedrals and churches sermons were delivered at noon on the same Friday as the one in Oxford. In St Ann, Manchester, the preacher was Frank Bennett, the Dean of Chester. St Michael, Rotherham, Christ Church, Doncaster, Goldthorpe parish church and many others had midday sermons. In most dioceses the bishop took part in the services. One exception was Birmingham, though that did not prevent the occasion being celebrated in Anglo-Catholic churches and public meetings. A wreath bearing the inscription 'In grateful and affectionate remembrance from the Oxford Movement Centenary Committee' was placed on the grave of Cardinal Newman in the Birmingham Oratory, and another at the statue of Bishop Gore in the churchyard of the cathedral.

The ECU arranged an outdoor mass in the grounds of Halifax's home in Hickleton. Halifax spoke briefly how his love of the Eucharist had grown since his confirmation eighty years previously. A hundred and thirty robed Guild of the Servants of the Sanctuary and twenty priests sang their office in the cathedral of Newcastle-on-Tyne.

On the Friday of the Centenary week three thousand attended an evening service in the Albert Hall in Nottingham, led by three hundred from local church choirs. The preacher was Fr Talbot who had been driven from Oxford after delivering his sermon in St Mary's that morning. On the same evening Dewsbury town hall was crowded to hear a lecture on the Tractarians by Hamilton Thompson, Professor of History at Leeds University. In Norwich a procession of eighteen hundred, headed by a crucifer and acolytes, choirs and vested clergy, walked from St Peter Mancroft to the cathedral for evensong and a sermon by H. L. Goudge.

In Wales there was a sung mass at St David's and prayers at various stations round the cathedral. In Llangorwen, where Isaac Williams was born, a commemorative tablet to the Tractarian was dedicated at a special service. The Episcopal Church of Scotland had special masses and meetings in various places.

At St John, Sandymount, Dublin, the one church which maintained Catholic ritual in defiance of the Church of Ireland's canon law on ceremonial, there was a sung mass of thanksgiving. The Centenary was celebrated more modestly elsewhere in Ulster and the Irish Republic; although they were restricted in their rituals, many Church of Ireland clergy were Catholic in conviction. The Archbishop of Dublin preached at All Saints', Grangegorman, where Fr Dolling once sang in the choir and George Tyrrell worshipped.

It was announced that in the USA the Catholic revival would be celebrated in Philadelphia from 22–26 October – the sixth congress in the States since the first in 1923. Ten thousand had already applied for tickets.

In the last number of the *Chronicle* the editor – perhaps inspired by the knowledge that the Pope had declared 1933 to be a Holy Year – indulged in a dream of what the Church would be like for the bicentenary in 2033:

> This week – with the electrical amplification of speeches, the broadcasting of Centenary sermons, the aeroplanes in which one enterprising congregation flew to Mass at Oxford – we have been able to apply some of the astonishing machinery of modern science to sacred uses. Even Mr H. G. Wells could hardly give an adequate forecast of what the Centenary of 2033 will be like. Bishops, certainly, will pilot their own flying machines across the Atlantic. Our speech, our clothes, our social and political systems will be different. Perhaps the Congress will be advertised by electric sky-signs at night. Perhaps the Roman Catholic hierarchy – nay, even the Pope himself – will take an official part in the celebrations of a Movement which has done so much to revive Catholic worship and discipline in Britain and overseas. Certainly the Archbishop of Canterbury will sing the Pontifical High Mass at whatever arena can be found vast enough to accommodate the million or so people who will want to be there. The timid and the conservative need not be alarmed. Material circumstances change, the spiritual verities remain the same. 'What God hath cleansed . . .' We must not look askance at modern developments in secular life, at electric appliances or sports stadiums. We must rather adapt them to the service of our Holy Mother the Church, secure in the

knowledge that the gates of hell cannot prevail against us and that Jesus Christ is the same yesterday, today and for ever.[33]

The same edition of the paper also carried a more down-to-earth notice. It announced that the Women's Auxiliary of the Anglo-Catholic Congress had made all the vestments for the high mass at the White City stadium and they were donating them to missions. They offered to make further vestments – a high mass set for £7.7s., copes for £2 and dalmatics for 17/6 – provided the purchasers were willing to give them to priests working overseas.

Postscript

The experience of working together in preparation for the Centenary led the leaders of the Anglo-Catholic Congress and the English Church Union to consider proposals they had received from many of their members that the two organizations should merge. In London joint ACC–ECU anniversary rallies had been arranged at the Albert Hall for some years, and local committees had held similar united rallies after the provincial Congresses. By the 1930s both organizations were in debt as financial support waned during the great depression. Since Pinchard was retiring as secretary of the Union at the end of 1933, it seemed an opportune time to consider the proposals seriously.

A joint committee was set up with Slesser in the chair to draft a scheme. This was circulated to all local committees, who voted overwhelmingly in support of it. The only opposition came from some older members on the Union's council, who were still suspicious of Maurice Child and felt the Anglo-Catholic ethos of the Congresses was too papalist for the ECU. Halifax was incensed when he heard this. He wrote to the council warning that the Catholic witness in the Church would be weakened if the scheme was rejected, and threatened to resign. His letter had the desired effect. The opposition collapsed. Halifax died a few weeks later having accomplished his final task for the Catholic cause. Slesser's committee completed their assignment in a few weeks and the Church Union was launched in January 1934.

Besides continuing the activities of the ECU, the new Union took over the work associated with the ACC – the fiery cross campaign, the ordination fund, the summer schools, the pilgrimages, the publications, the Seven Years Association, and the preliminary plans for the proposed 1940 Congress. When the local committees of the ACC and ECU had joined together, the new body found itself with about 9,000 members and 85,000 associates.

Plans for the 1940 Congress had to be abandoned as war became inevitable, but in the early forties the spirit of Congress Anglo-Catholicism was kept alive by the publication of 12 popular paperbacks called the *Signpost* series. The authors were a young generation of Catholic scholars, all born in the first decade or so of the twentieth century. They included Julian Casserley, Donald MacKinnon, Eric Mascall and Tom Parker. In their books they discussed various aspects of the faith, arguing that Catholic Christianity was the answer to the problems of the age, and that only by a return to that tradition could disaster be avoided.

Another manifestation of the same spirit was *Catholicity: a Study in the Conflict of Christian Traditions in the West* published in 1947. Soon after he became Archbishop of Canterbury, Geoffrey Fisher invited three groups – Anglo-Catholics, Evangelicals and Free Churchmen – to produce reports on what they saw as their differences and points of convergence with the others as a means of increasing mutual understanding. Dom Gregory Dix wrote much of *Catholicity* with Fr Gabriel Hebert. It revealed the same openness to the ecumenical movement which Bishop Weston had shown in commending the Lambeth Appeal. So on reunion the group declared: 'The true way of synthesis is not to take our contemporary systems or "isms" or Church traditions and try to pierce them together, either as a whole or in selected items, but rather to go behind our contemporary systems and strive for the recovery of the fulness of Tradition within the thought and worship and order and life of each of the sundered portions of Christendom.'[1] It is the position maintained by Catholics in the Church of England during ecumenical discussions ever since.

The Church Union organized a sixth Anglo-Catholic Congress in 1948. Considering the difficulties of such a venture in post-war England, it was a notable achievement. Thirteen thousand registered for it. The sessions were repeated in the Central Hall and the Kingsway Hall, since the Albert Hall was not available. The most memorable of them was a demonstration of a primitive Eucharist performed by members of the Seven Years Association with a commentary by Dix, now well known through the publication of his *The Shape of the Liturgy*. The CU organized other congresses and conventions at intervals in the following years but – with the exception of the 150th anniversary celebrations of the Oxford Movement in 1983 – numbers steadily declined.

The five interwar Congresses have been described as 'the high noon of Anglo-Catholicism'. It is an appropriate title if we compare the numbers attending with those of later years, but it needs some qualification. Anglo-Catholicism as a movement in the Church of England did not reach a twelve o'clock high and then fade like the sun sinking over the horizon. Rather, its light became more diffuse as increasing numbers in the Church began – in varying degrees – to accept what Catholics stood for.

In his letter to the *Church Times* in 1920 Marcus Atlay had written, 'We desire above all things to publish plainly and distinctly the good things of the Catholic Faith and the Christian religion. The Congress is designed to be evangelical, but we also have to make clear to the world where we stand and where we are meant to stand, that we are not going in any direction save in the direction of our Lord through His grace given to us in the Sacraments of the Catholic Church in England.'

If we bring together not just the gatherings in London and the provinces but also the activities which Congress supporters initiated – among others, those listed above which the Church Union took over – then we can see that a fair amount of what Atlay hoped for was realized. The Congresses were a massive public relations exercise to commend to the rest of the Church of England the Catholic faith and practice as lived in hundreds if not thousands of Anglo-Catholic parishes. And in this they were remarkably successful. In the decades after 1920 many in the Church, including most bishops, modified their attitudes. They may not have embraced all that Catholics taught about the sacraments and the ordained ministry, but many gradually moved into a broadly Prayer Book Catholicism with a willingness to consider – if not always to embrace – changes in worship and in pastoral care. They also learned from Catholics' ideals of mission within society.

In his address to the Centenary Congress Kirk said he believed three of five Catholic truths which the movement proclaimed were more widely accepted in the Church – the truth of the sacraments, that of social mission, and that of personal holiness. It was a discerning summary of the situation as it was then and as it developed later. That is why in the years after 1945 Evangelicals were heard to complain that the Church of England had too much of an Anglo-Catholic face. Kirk's other two truths – the ability of the Church to make doctrinal and moral decisions and to obtain complete freedom from the State – remain unfulfilled today.

Had Atlay and those who organized the first Congress lived longer, they would have been gratified that at the 1948 Congress Bishop William Wand of London was its president, and one of its principal speakers was Michael Ramsey, then Professor of Divinity at Durham University and later to become the Primate of All England. They would have seen it as a vindication of their contention that Catholics, far from being a party within the Church, *were* the Church of England, itself part of the one universal Catholic and Orthodox Church. If we apply these development to the spectrum which I introduced in Chapter 3, we could say that during and after the Congresses more and more Church of England clergy and laity entered the Indigo and Blue zones – a few of them venturing into the Green and Yellow ones.

That was true of many Evangelicals. When, in 1967, the National Anglican Evangelical Congress at Keele agreed that the parish communion should be the main act of Sunday worship in their churches, it signified they were beginning to respond to Catholic sacramental theology. Years later the charismatic movement and a common interest in contemporary liturgy helped Evangelicals and Catholics to draw closer together. They also found a common cause in evangelism, social concern and world development, and in challenging the varieties of radical Christianity which emerged (as N. P. Williams had prophesied) in later generations. Evangelicals were represented on the Anglican–Roman Catholic International Commission when it began meeting in 1969. That would have astonished old Bishop Knox of Manchester!

However, we should recognize that from the twenties onwards the Congresses were not the only facilitators of these developments. The inauguration of the Church Assembly in the same year as the first Congress brought Catholics, Evangelicals, Modernists and the rest into face-to-face encounters in which they were obliged to listen to one another, to worship and to make decisions together. Indeed, on certain matters Anglo-Catholics and Evangelicals found themselves supporting each other against the rest of the Assembly. Through the new constitution this process continued locally in deanery and diocesan conferences. Although such meetings could sometimes expose divisions among Catholics – over whether or not to accept the Revised Prayer Book, for example, or the South India scheme – yet they promoted mutual understanding.

Other things also helped. There was increasing respect throughout the Church for the various religious communities and their work. There were joint parochial, deanery and diocesan initiatives in mission and social action. There was a growing appreciation of the giftedness of Catholic scholars, not least in biblical and liturgical studies. There was a new awareness of the Anglican Communion as a worldwide Church rather than a collection of overseas' missions. All these contributed to a developing sense of the Church of England's inherent Catholicity. And undergirding it was the continuing High Church tradition linking the present with the past.

But these reflections take us beyond the scope of this book. Our story ends with the Centenary Congress. That era is now part of our history. The generations of Anglican priests and laity who were on the committees which organized the Congresses have long since been – in Salvation Army terms – promoted to Glory.

I met some of them in my early years. I was confirmed in 1936 at the age of nine by Bishop A. E. J. Rawlinson of Derby. At Mirfield I attended lectures by Fr Lionel Thornton. As a parish priest in London-over-the-Border I met older clergy who had taken groups to the Congress meetings in the Albert Hall. At the Oxford conferences organized by the Chelmsford Diocesan Worship and the Arts Association in the fifties I had conversations with the elderly Percy Widdrington, with his well-worn soutane,

POSTSCRIPT

a biretta on the back of his head, and a drooping pipe which scattered ashes about his person. At St Augustine, Rush Green, Romford, where I was priest-in-charge, Mr Sidney Haskell, the lay reader, told me how he, as a young man in the congregation at the Ascension, Lavender Hill, had been at the Centenary Congress. He gave me a cutting from the *Church Times* with a picture of the high mass in the White City stadium, which stirred my interest in the subject and ultimately led to the writing of this book. They all looked back with a sense of wonder and gratitude to God for those great gatherings.

Reading the literature which the Congresses produced, I recognize how much I owe in my Christian pilgrimage to the Faith which these speakers and writers expounded and handed on. I believe that, in spite of mistakes by some, through them the Holy Spirit was enlightening and equipping Anglicans to be more faithful to the Gospel of Jesus Christ and the Catholic Church in a changing world. So I can appreciate the nostalgia with which those I met looked back on the Congress years as days when, they said (perhaps with understandable exaggeration), Catholics really were Catholics and everybody kept the fasts, made their confessions, and went to mass. For them, the Congresses were truly the high noon of the Catholic movement.

That nostalgia is beautifully echoed by John Betjeman in his poem, 'Anglo-Catholic Congresses'. It was written years after he had attended one of the Congresses, and it makes a fitting finale to this story.

> We, who remember the Faith, the grey-headed ones,
> Of those Anglo-Catholic Congresses swinging along.
> Who heard the South Coast salvo of incense-guns
> And surged to the Albert Hall in our thousands strong
> With 'extreme' colonial bishops leading in song;
>
> We, who remember, look back to the blossoming May-time
> On ghosts of servers and thurifers after Mass,
> The slapping of backs, the flapping of cassocks, the play-time,
> A game of Grandmother's Steps on the vicarage grass –
> 'Father, a little more sherry. I'll fill your glass.'
>
> We recall with triumph, that Sunday after Ascension,
> When our Protestant suffragan suffered himself to be coped –
> The SYA and the Scheme for Church Extension –
> The new diocesan's not as 'sound' as we'd hoped,
> And Kensit threatens and has Sam Gurney poped?

LIFT HIGH THE CROSS

Yet, under the Travers baroque, in a limewashed whiteness,
The fiddle-back vestments a-glitter with morning rays,
Our Lady's image, in multiple-candled brightness,
The bells and banners – those were the waking days
When the Faith was taught and fanned in a golden blaze.[2]

Notes

Page vii

1 'Lift High the Cross', G. W. Kitchen and M. R. Newbolt, *Hymns Ancient & Modern*, New Standard Edition, 1983, No 72.

Chapter 1

1 Wilson, *Received with Thanks*, 1940, p. 53.
2 *Ibid.*, p. 43.
3 *Report of the First Anglo-Catholic Congress*, SPCK, 1920, p. 10.

Chapter 3

1 Copy in Wilkinson, *The Church of England and the First World War*, 1996, illustration no. 2.

2 McLeod, *Class and Religion in the Late Victorian City*, p. 27; quoted in Hastings, *A History of English Christianity 1920–2000*, 2001 edn, p. 66.

3 The *Green Quarterly*, Winter 1931–32, vol. ix, no. 1. Bulmer Thomas was probably referring to St Saviour, Hoxton, a parish for years under an episcopal ban. It was a bold prophecy, but off-target by a few miles in geography as well as in churchmanship. It was fulfilled sixty years later in a way he would never have imagined when George Carey, converted as a young man in the conservative Evangelical parish of St Mary, Dagenham, was installed in the Canterbury *cathedra*.

4 Wilkinson, *Church of England*, p. 274.
5 Vidler, *The Modernist Movement in the Roman Catholic Church*, 1934, p. 266. For Tyrrell's influence on Anglo-Catholics see Leonard, *George Tyrrell and The Catholic Tradition*, 1982, p. 136.
6 Yelton, *Anglican Papalism: An Illustrated History 1900–1960*, 2005.

Chapter 4

1 *The Report of the First Anglo-Catholic Congress London 1920*, pp. 44–5.
2 *Ibid.*, p. 51.
3 *Ibid.*, p. 35.
4 *Ibid.*, p. 38.
5 *Ibid.*, p. 39.
6 *Ibid.*, p 42.
7 *Ibid.*, p. 57.
8 *Ibid.*, p. 60.
9 *Ibid.*, p. 153.
10 *Ibid.*, pp. 92–9.
11 *Ibid.*, p. 96.
12 *Ibid.*, p. 102.
13 *Ibid.*, p. 180. Milner-White made the novel (but, as many of his hearers must have thought, impractical) suggestion that in any scheme of reunion, both

his fellow priests and Nonconformist ministers should submit to reordination at the hands of Orthodox bishops, not because he doubted the validity of Anglican orders but because he wanted to show that the Nonconformists were not being asked to do anything Anglicans were not willing to do as well.

14 *Report*, p. 99.
15 *Ibid.*, p. 101.
16 *Ibid.*, pp. 83–4.
17 *Ibid.*, p. 198.
18 *Ibid.*, p. 195.
19 *Ibid.*, p. 197.
20 *Ibid.*, p. 194.
21 *Ibid.*, p. 199.
22 *Ibid.*, p. 200.

Chapter 5

1 Dark, *Archbishop Davidson and the English Church*, 1929, p. 135.
2 Maynard Smith, *Frank Bishop of Zanzibar*, 1926, p. 171.
3 Herbert Hensley Henson, *Retrospect of an Unimportant Life*, vol. ii, 1943, p. 5.
4 Maynard-Smith, *op. cit.*, p. 227.
5 Lockhart, *Cosmo Gordon Lang*, 1949, p. 267.
6 *Ibid.*, p. 234.
7 *Ibid.*, p. 235.
8 *Ibid.*, pp. 338–9.
9 Bettensen, *Documents of the Christian Church*, 1946, pp. 441–5.
10 Knox, *Reminiscences of an Octogenarian*, 1934, pp. 319–20.
11 Maynard-Smith, *op. cit.*, p. 236.
12 Palmer, *Gadfly for God*, 1991, p. 136.
13 *The Times*, 20 November 1918.
14 Henson, *op. cit.*, p. 233.
15 Bell, *Randall Davidson*, 1935, p. 1012.
16 Barlow, '*A brother knocking at the door*': *The Malines Conversations 1921–1925*, 1996, pp. 187–93.

Chapter 6

1 Bell, *Randall Davidson*, 1935, p. 959.
2 *Ibid.*, p. 957.
3 *Church Times*, 9 January 1920.
4 *Ibid.*, 8 April 1920.
5 Harrison, *The Centenary History of St Matthew's Church and Parish, Northampton*, 1995, p. 57.
6 *Report of Proceedings* 1920–21, p. 59.
7 *Ibid.*, p. 64.
8 From the thirteenth century the Houses of Convocation were part of the realm and therefore their sessions coincided with those of Parliament. This practice was abolished with the establishment of the General Synod in 1970.

NOTES

9 Merritt, *Catholic Representation in the House of Laity*, ECU 1929, p. 6.
10 Hastings, *History of English Christianity 1920–2000*, 2001 edn, p. 64.

Chapter 7

1 Bell, *Randall Davidson*, 1935, pp. 1154–5.
2 *Report of the First Anglo-Catholic Priests' Convention 1921*, p. XV.
3 Anglo-Catholic Congress Executive Committee Minutes, 4 July 1921.
4 *Ibid.*
5 All Saints, Margaret Street parish magazine, August 1921, p. 136.
6 *Report*, p. 11. The German school-master must have visited Winchester before the war when Britain was involved in a naval race with Germany in building battleships, which were regarded as essential for the defence of the country against any invasion (the plot of Erskine Childer's famous novel, *The Riddle of the Sands*).
7 *Ibid.*, p. 18.
8 *Ibid.*, p. 22.
9 *Ibid.*, p. 27.
10 *Ibid.*, p. 1.
11 *Ibid.*, pp. 34–5.
12 *Ibid.*, p. 46.
13 *Ibid.*, p. 48.
14 *Ibid.*, p. 63.
15 *Ibid.*, p. 42.
16 *Ibid.*, p. 45.
17 In the *Dictionary of English Church History*, 1948 edn, p. 369.
18 *Report*, p. 127.
19 Fitzgerald, *The Knox Brothers*, 1977, p. 119.
20 Jones, *A Life Simply Offered: Father Wilson of Haggerston*, ACHS, nd, p. 7.
21 *Report*, p. 115.
22 *Ibid.*, pp. 118–19.
23 *Ibid.*, p. 78.
24 *Ibid.*, p. 80. There is a memoir by Sparrow Simpson in a posthumous collection of Rawlinson's sermons and writings in *An Anglo-Catholic's Thoughts on Religion*, 1924, pp. xiv–xlviii.
25 *Report*, p. 83.
26 *Ibid.*, p. 98.
27 *Ibid.*, p. 100.
28 *Ibid.*, p. 102.
29 *Ibid.*, pp. 102–3.
30 *Ibid.*, p. 109.
31 *Ibid.*, p. 185.
32 *Church Times*, 29 July 1921.

Chapter 8

1 Minutes of the Anglo-Catholic Congress Executive Committee, 3 and 29 November and 15 December 1921.
2 There is a copy of this handbook in the Manchester Central Library.

3 *Church Times*, 6 October 1922.
4 *Ibid.*, p. 325.
5 *CT*, 23 June 1922, p. 653.
6 *CT*, 30 June 1922, p. 700.
7 Wilkinson, *Christian Socialism: Scott Holland to Tony Blair: The 1998 Scott Holland Lectures*, 1998, p. 93.
8 *CT*, 30 June 1922.
9 Taken from cuttings from the *Yorkshire Post* collected in a scrapbook in Leeds Central Library entitled *The Anglo-Catholic Congress in Leeds 1922*.
10 *CT*, 23 June 1922.
11 Quoted in Peart Binns, *Blunt*, 1969, p. 116.
12 Woods and MacNutt, *Theodore, Bishop of Winchester*, 1933, p. 190.
13 *CT*, 3 July 1925.

Chapter 9

1 Anglo-Catholic Congress Executive Committee Minutes, 11 May 1922.
2 Quoted in the *Church Times*, 13 July 1923.
3 My copy has 'Alan H Rowe – Newfoundland' written in the cover; perhaps he was one of the group which came from Canada.
4 Copy of the correspondence in the ACC Minutes, 22 March – 1 May 1923.
5 Minutes, 11 May 1923.
6 *The Report of the Anglo-Catholic Congress, July 1923*, pp. 72–9.
7 *Church Times*, 1 June 1923.
8 *CT*, 13 July 1923.
9 *Report*, p. 3.
10 *Ibid.*, p. 13.
11 *Ibid.*, p. x.
12 *Ibid.*, pp. 56–7.
13 *Ibid.*, p. 61.
14 *Ibid.*, p. 71.
15 *Ibid.*, p. 33.
16 *Ibid.*, p. 141.
17 *Ibid.*, p. 146.
18 *Ibid.*, p. 149.
19 *Ibid.*, p. 150.
20 Henson, *Retrospect of an Unimportant Life*, vol. iii, p. 277.
21 *Report*, p. 161.
22 *Ibid.*, p. 163.
23 *Ibid.*, p. 24.
24 *Ibid.*, pp. 27–8.
25 *Ibid.*, p. 106.
26 *Ibid.*, pp. 108–109.
27 *Ibid.*, pp. 115–116.
28 *Ibid.*, p. 117.
29 *Ibid.*, p. 122.
30 *Ibid.*, p. 186.
31 *Ibid.*, pp. 191–192.

NOTES

Chapter 10

1 Wilkinson, *The Community of the Resurrection*, 1992, p. 186.
2 Mason, *SSM: History of the Society of the Sacred Mission*, 1993, p. 164.
3 Fitzgerald, *The Knox Brothers*, 1977, p. 159.
4 *Northern Catholicism*, eds Williams and Harris, 1933, p. 60; Pigott, *Sir Will Spens and Liberal Anglo-Catholicism*, ACHS, 2006, pp. 8–10.
5 Minute Book of the Confraternity of the Blessed Sacrament, 25 June 1924.
6 *Ibid.*, 17 June 1927.
7 Palmer, *Gadfly for God*, 1991, pp. 137–138.

Chapter 11

1 *Green Quarterly*, Spring 1929.
2 Michael Yelton gives an account of Maurice Chandler's life and the origins of the Society of SS Peter and Paul in Chapter 5 of his *Outposts of the Faith: Ten Anglo-Catholic Portraits*, 2009.
3 Clarke, *Bishop Chandler: A Memoir*, 1940, pp. 105–6.
4 *Green Quarterly*, April 1924.
5 *Ibid.*, October 1927.
6 *Report of the First Anglo-Catholic Congress*, p. 181.

Chapter 12

1 'This is the Catholick Faith: which except a man believe faithfully, he cannot be saved.'
2 English Church Union Report of the Committee on Prayer Book Revision, 1922, quoted in Gray, *The 1927–28 Prayer Book Crisis*, the Alcuin Club and the Group for Renewal of Worship, no. 61, 2006, p. 6.
3 ECU, *A Suggested Prayer Book*, p. 350.
4 Copy in the *Church Times*, 25 March 1927.
5 In Parliamentary terms, a document attached to a Church Assembly measure was 'deposited' on the table of the House. If it remained there for a certain number of weeks without an MP calling for a debate on it, it was then sent for royal assent. This is how most of the measures submitted by the Assembly to Parliament were passed.
6 Offical Report Fifth Series Parliamentary Debates Commons 1927, vol. 211, 28 November–16 December, p. 2598.
7 *Ibid.*, p. 2617.
8 Henson, *Retrospect of an Unimportant Life*, 1950, vol. 3, p. 225.
9 Temple to Lang, 22 February 1930, Lang Papers, vol. 7, p. 20, quoted in Robert Beaken, *Their Proper Place: Archbishop Lang and Anglo-Catholicism, 1928–1942*, ACHS, 2007, p. 6.
10 *Green Quarterly*, Sept 1928.

Chapter 13

1 *Church Times*, 8 July 1927.
2 *Report of the Anglo-Catholic Congress*, 1927, p. 47.

3 *Ibid.*, p. 51.
4 *Ibid.*, p. 56.
5 *Ibid.*
6 *Ibid.*, p. 122.
7 *Ibid.*, p. 123.
8 *Ibid.*, p. 124.
9 *Ibid.*, p. 125.
10 *Ibid.*, p. 127.

11 *Ibid.*, p. 129. The rubric in the 1662 Prayer Book referred to by Rawlinson reads: 'If the consecrated Bread or Wine be all spent before all have communicated, the Priest is to consecrate more according to the Form before prescribed: Beginning at [Our Saviour Christ in the same night, &c.] for the blessing of the Bread: and at [Likewise after Supper, &c.] for the blessing of the Cup.'

12 *Ibid.*, p. 209.

13 *Ibid.*, p. 208. Eric Mascall nominated Hutchinson as one of the four most outstanding priests he had known (the others were Gregory Dix, Lionel Thornton and Gabriel Hebert). Mascall, as a young tutor at Lincoln Theological College, sometimes stayed with Hutchinson during vacations to assist in his work. He described how Hutchinson – who apparently looked just like, and was sometimes mistaken for, Mussolini – went on to be chaplain of the British Embassy in Istanbul during the second world war, and afterwards vicar of St Bartholomew, Brighton (E L Mascall, *Saraband*, 1992, pp. 176–180).

14 *Report*, p. 210.
15 *Ibid.*, p. 216.
16 *Ibid.*, p. 215.
17 15 July 1927, p. 90.
18 *Kettering Church Chronicle* 1927, in the town's public library.
19 CT, p. 35.
20 CT, p. 35.

21 I became very familiar with these prayers when, as a small boy, I had to memorize them when I began serving at an early weekday mass in St Laurence, Long Easton, before going to school. I led the priest into the sanctuary carrying the heavy *English Missal* to its stand on the right-hand ('epistle') side of the altar, returned to the altar step and knelt down. After arranging the vessels on the altar, the priest came and stood by me and we recited in a low voice alternate verses of Psalm 43. Then he said a short form of confession and I repeated it. At the phrase '... and I confess to you, father ...' I had to turn my head and shoulders briefly towards him as he had done to me – a gesture which acted unintentionally as a sign to the congregation, who may have been following the half-heard murmur of the prayers in their manuals, where we had got to. After a few more verses and responses, the priest moved up to the altar saying the Lord's Prayer (the first part of the Prayer Book Communion Service) aloud. These prayers of preparation were taken from the Roman Missal and had been borrowed by Anglican ritualists along with much else from that book.

22 Westerners insisted on 'tarp-ing' (*T*aking the *A*blutions in the *R*ight *P*lace), because otherwise the consecrated Bread and Wine remained on the altar until the end of the service. Gaselee commented on the practice of scrupulous souls who, as they were leaving at the end of the service, genuflected towards the altar

NOTES

if they suspected the Elements had not been consumed: 'The conclusion of the Liturgy', Gaselee said, 'should not be converted towards its close into a Mass of Exposition. If the Elements are retained on the altar from the Communion until after the Blessing, they should *literally* be regarded as covered with the fair linen cloth, and not treated with outward acts of worship. If there are some who find this, from a sense of reverence, a difficult course, the place of the ablutions soon after Communion will probably commend itself.' *Report*, p. 202.

23 *Report*, p. 201.

Chapter 14

1 Jasper, *The Development of the Anglican Liturgy 1662–1980*, 1989, p. 104.

2 Prestige, *The Life of Charles Gore*, 1935, p. 342.

3 Stone was a leading authority on the subject. Even today his two-volume *A History of the Doctrine of the Holy Eucharist* (1908) remains a valuable resource for scholars.

4 Woods, ed., *Reservation: Report of a Conference held at Farnham Castle on October 24–27 1925*, 1926, p. 87.

5 *Report of the Anglo-Catholic Congress*, 1927, p. 169.

6 The correspondence was published by the ECU in 1920. It can be found on the Project Canterbury website, together with other useful resources.

7 The Report of the Royal Commission on Ecclesiastical Discipline 1906 enumerated practices connected with reservation which its members regarded as grave breaches of the law: services of adoration, Corpus Christi processions, benediction and mass of the presanctified. These practices, it declared, 'should be promptly made to cease', if necessary by proceedings in the Ecclesiastical Courts. But the number of churches in which reservation was used in this way was relatively small in those days as only a few cases were recorded.

8 Frere, 'The Authority for Reservation', *Truro Diocesan Gazette*, August 1928.

9 Stone, *Word and Sacraments: The Anglo-Catholic Congress Book*, no. 23, 1923, p. 11.

10 Woods, *Reservation*, p. 18.

11 *Ibid.*, p. 55.

12 *Ibid.*, p. 89.

13 *Ibid.*, p. 111.

14 *Ibid.*, pp. v–vi.

15 Slater, *A Century of Celebrating Christ: The Diocese of Birmingham, 1905–2005*, 2005, p. 60.

16 Barnes, *Ahead of His Age*, 1979, p. 163.

17 *Ibid.*, pp. 167–8.

18 *Ibid.*, p. 166.

19 Rosenthal and Belton, *The So-Called Rebels*, 1930, p. 73.

20 Barnes, *op cit*, p. 267.

21 *Ibid.*, p. 269.

22 Woods, *Reservation*, p. 18.

23 There is an account of this episode with biographical notes and photos of the clergy and churches involved in Michael Yelton, *The Twenty-One: An Anglo-Catholic Rebellion in London, 1929*, ACHS, 2009.

24 Rosenthal and Belton, *op cit*, p. 89.
25 *Ibid.*, p. 140.

Chapter 15

1 Prestige, *The Life of Charles Gore*, 1935, p. 429.
2 Reckitt, *Religion and Social Purpose*, 1935, p. 53, quoted in Mascall, *Saraband*, 1992, p. 196. Mascall thought highly of Reckett and the Christendom Group.
3 *The Return of Christendom*, p. 113, quoted in Bryant, *Possible Dreams*, 1996, p. 149.
4 Quoted in Hastings, *A History of English Christianity 1920–2000*, 2001, p. 191.
5 *Catholicism and Property*, SSPP, p. 3.
6 *Ibid.*, p. 24.
7 *Green Quarterly*, June 1929.
8 *Crockford Prefaces*, 1947, p. 174.
9 Peart Binns, *Blunt*, 1969, p. 171.
10 *Ibid.*, p. 173.
11 *The Church Times*, 7 March 1924.
12 Morse-Boycott, *Ten years in a London Slum*, nd, p. 59.
13 There is an account of Jellicoe's work in Farrer, *One Part of London: Aspects of Anglo-Catholicism in Camden*, ACHS, 2009, pp. 117–23.

Chapter 16

1 *A Spiritual Aeneid*, 1919, p. 4.
2 Knox, *Reminiscences of an Octogenarian*, 1935, p. 153.
3 Fitzgerald, *op cit*, p. 153.
4 Knox's other major work was *Enthusiasm* (1950), a study of the tension between the institutional and the charismatic in the Church based on the history of the sectarian movements of the seventeenth and eighteenth centuries.
5 Finch, *G. K. Chesterton: A Biography*, 1986, p. 277.
6 Chesterton, *The Catholic Church and Conversion*, 1926, p. 27.
7 Finch, *op cit*, p. 239.
8 Republished by Virago in 1983.
9 Kaye-Smith, *Three Ways Home*, 1937, p. 116.
10 Kaye-Smith, *Anglo-Catholicism*, 1925, p. 116.
11 Kaye-Smith, *Three Ways Home*, p. 195.
12 Johnson, *One Lord, One Faith*, 1928, p. 20.
13 *Ibid.*, p. 25.
14 *Ibid.*, p. 195.
15 *Ibid.*, p. 208.
16 Milner White, *One God and Father of All: A Reply to Father Vernon*, 1927, p. 4.
17 *Report of the Anglo-Catholic Congress 1927*, p. 31.
18 Pickering, *Anglo-Catholicism: A Study in Religious Ambiguity*, 1989.
19 Chesterton, *The Catholic Church and Conversion*, p. 6.

Chapter 17

1 *The Times*, 1930, 19 June.
2 *Church Times*, 4 July 1930.
3 *Report of the Anglo-Catholic Congress: London 1930*, p. xvii.
4 *Church Times*, 4 July 1930.
5 *Report*, p. 14.
6 *Ibid.*, p. 9.
7 *Ibid.*, p. 19.
8 *Ibid.*, p. 27.
9 *Ibid.*, p. 28.
10 *Church Times*, 4 July 1930.
11 *Report*, p. 36.
12 *Ibid.*, p. 53.
13 *Ibid.*, p. 58.
14 *Ibid.*, p. 59.
15 *Ibid.*, pp. 63–4.
16 *Ibid.*, pp. 66–7.
17 *Ibid.*, p. 69.
18 Nowadays we are familiar with the word 'Church' as meaning 'the People of God' and 'Apostolic' as 'being sent'. But among most of the laity and many of the clergy in the Albert Hall that summer 'Church' conjured up a picture of bishops, priests and perhaps synods, and 'Apostolic' the apostolic succession. It was only as the revival of biblical studies among Catholic theologians spread into the teaching of parish priests that the scriptural meaning of the two words became common knowledge.
19 *Report*, p. 90.
20 Hoskyns spoke not only as a New Testament scholar but also as the son of a diocesan bishop (also named Edwyn Hoskyns, Bishop of Southwell 1904-1925).
21 Hoskyns' influence on Ramsey is discussed in Chadwick, *Michael Ramsey: A Life*, 1990, pp. 27ff.
22 *Report*, p. 95.
23 *Ibid.*, p. 176.
24 *Ibid.*, p. 187.
25 *Church Times*, 13 July 1930. Since the ECU meeting was not part of the Congress programme, Henson's talk was not printed in the report though it was extensively quoted in *The Times*, the *Church Times* and elsewhere.
26 *Ibid.*
27 Henson, *Retrospect of an Unimportant Life*, vol. 2, pp. 258–9.
28 *Report*, p. xviii.

Chapter 18

1 *Green Quarterly*, September 1922.
2 Harrison, *The Centenary History of St Matthew's Church and Parish, Northampton*, 1993, p. 64.
3 *Report of the First Priest's Convention 1921*, p. 180.
4 *Ibid.*, p. 181.

5 His *Annus Eucharisticu*, 1930, was republished by the Canterbury Press in 2002 as *The Eucharistic Year: Seasonal Devotions for the Sacrament* with an introduction by Julian Litten.

Chapter 19

1 Shortly after its publication Lean became rector of Wroughton, Bletchley. According to his entry in Crockford he wrote *The Drama of the Holy Mass* (1932) and *The Voice of Undivided Christendom* (1933) but did not include *Good Manners* in his list.
2 Lean, *Good Manners in Church and Out*, 1932, p. 49.
3 *Ibid.*, p. 108.
4 *Ibid.*, p. 46.
5 *Ibid.*, p. 42.
6 *Ibid.*, p. 60.
7 *Ritual Notes*, nos 277–8.
8 Simpson, *Christ and the Church*, 1936, p. 6.
9 McCullock, *We Have Our Orders*, 1943, p. 31.
10 Clutterbuck, *Marginal Catholics*, 1993, p. 100.

Chapter 20

1 Yelton and Salmon, *Anglican Church-Building in London 1915–1945*, 2007, p. 11; Hewitt, *A History of the Diocese of Chelmsford*, 1984, pp. 76, 94; Slater, *A Century of Celebrating Christ: The Diocese of Birmingham, 1905–2005*, 2005, pp. 124–32.
2 Symondson and Bucknall, *Sir Ninian Comper*, 2006, p. 152.
3 *Ibid.*, pp. 167–8.
4 *The English Hymnal*, p.12.
5 Williams' Note to the 1933 Edition, p. xx, quoted by Luff (ed.), 'The Birth and Background of the English Hymnal' in *Strengthened for Service: 100 Years of the English Hymnal 1906–2006*, 2005, pp. 1–30.
6 This theme is developed in Webster, *Anglo-Catholicism, Theology and the Arts 1918–1970*, ACHS, 2008.
7 Wilkinson, *The Community of the Resurrection: A Centenary History*, 1992, p. 94.
8 *The Mirfield Mission Hymn-Book: New Edition (Revised) with Supplement*, 1936, p. iii.
9 Hole, *The Church and the Stage: Early History of the Actors' Church Union*, 1934, p. 130.
10 *The Green Quarterly*, Winter 1928–29.
11 *Daily News*, 29 May 1928, quoted in Jasper, *George Bell Bishop of Chichester 1967*, p. 42.
12 Warham Guild, *Handbook*, 1963 edn, p. 19. In the 1960s Mowbrays underwent their own reorganization. In 1969 their church furnishings interests were combined with those of Wippell and the Guild was included in the relocation to Exeter as part of the Wippell Mowbray Church Furnishing Ltd. By 1980, when

Wippell took over the firm in its entirety, the Warham Guild name was all that remained.

13 Both Faith Press and Faith Craft closed down in 1973.

Chapter 21

1 Iremonger, *William Temple*, 1948, p. 494.
2 *Church Times*, 20 March 1931.
3 *The Green Quarterly*, July 1932.
4 *Ibid.*, July 1933.
5 *Church Times*, 10 January 1931.
6 *Report of the Second Anglo-Catholic Priests' Convention*, 1932, p. xv.
7 In the *Report* the editors said that some of the papers had been 'slightly developed and enlarged', p. x.
8 *Report*, pp. 22–3.
9 *Ibid.*, p. 24.
10 *Ibid.*, pp. 26–7.
11 *Ibid.*, p. 46.
12 *Ibid.*, p. 108.
13 Wilson, *Received with Thanks*, 1940, pp. 150–1.
14 *Report*, p. 69.
15 *Ibid.*, p. 71.
16 *Ibid.*, p. 71.
17 *Ibid.*, pp. 50–1.
18 *Ibid.*, p. 7.
19 *Ibid.*, p. 172.

Chapter 22

1 *Church Times*, 14 July 1933, p. 57.
2 Wilkinson, *Dissent or Conform?* 1986, p. 120.
3 *Report of the Oxford Movement Centenary Congress, July 1933*, p. 191.
4 *Church Times*, 21 July 1933.
5 *Report*, p. 107.
6 Nockles, *The Oxford Movement in Context: Anglican High churchmanship, 1760–1857*, 1994.
7 Rowell, *Prejudices & Perspectives: Anglo-Catholic History Reconsidered*, Anglo-Catholic History Society, 2000, p. 7.
8 Sharp, *New Perspectives on the High Church Tradition: historical background, 1730–1780*, in *Tradition Renewed: The Oxford Movement Conference Papers*, Geoffrey Rowell (ed.), 1986, p. 18.
9 I made a minor contribution to this revisionism in an essay on Alexander Knox (1757–1831), an Irish lay theologian who lived in Dublin and who, because of his belief in the Catholicity of the Church of England and the Prayer Book, is regarded as one of the High Church forerunners of the Oxford Movement. His views were widely respected in England as well as in Ireland during his lifetime. See the *Church Quarterly Review*, October–December 1956, no. 325, vol. CLVII, pp. 463–4.

10 *Report*, p. 12.
11 *Centenary Chronicle*, Thursday 13 July 1933.
12 *Report*, p. 29.
13 *Ibid.*, p. 30.
14 *Ibid.*, p. 31.
15 *Ibid.*, p. 32.
16 *Ibid.*, p. 32.
17 *Ibid.*, pp. 34–5.
18 *Ibid.*, p. 173.
19 *Ibid.*, p. 63.
20 *Ibid.*, p. 63.
21 *Ibid.*, p. 119.
22 *Church Times*, 21 July 1933.
23 *Report*, pp. 122–3.
24 *Ibid.*, p. 96.
25 Robinson's *Honest to God* was published in 1962 and van Buren's *Secular Meaning of the Gospel* in 1963.
26 *Report*, p. 101.
27 *Ibid.*, p. 112.
28 *Ibid.*, p. 186.
29 In 1985 the preacher on this occasion was another Mirfield father, Trevor Huddleston.
30 *Ibid.*, p. 154.
31 *Ibid.*, p. 155–6.
32 Some of these memorabilia were exhibited at the 150th celebrations in Oxford in 1985.
33 *Centenary Chronicle*, Saturday 15 July 1933, p. 4.

Postscript

1 *Catholicity: A Study in the Conflict of Christian Traditions in the West*, 1947, p. 47.
2 Poem: 'Anglo-Catholic Congress', from *Collected Poems*, by John Betjeman © 1955, 1958, 1962, 1964, 1968, 1970, 1979, 1981, 1982, 2001, p. 265. Reproduced by permission of John Murray (Publishers.) Grandmother's Steps was a game in which one person faced a wall and the rest of the group crept up silently on him/her. From time to time the person facing the wall suddenly turned round and anyone caught moving was sent back to the starting point. The first of the group to touch that person without being caught was the winner. Michael Yelton tells me that Gurney did not in fact 'pope': the suggestion that he should do so may have been a joke among his friends. At one time I thought of calling this book, 'The Waking Days'.

Brief Biographies

ATLEY, Marcus Ethelbert: Curate of St Matthew, Westminster, 1904; Vicar, 1914; Chairman of the Anglo-Catholic Congress 1919–22; Canon of Gloucester, 1923; d. 1934.

BAVERSTOCK, Alban Henry: Curate of St Michael, Walthamstow, 1897; Vicar of St John the Evangelist, Hinton Martell, Dorset, 1899; retired 1930; d. 1950.

BLUNT, Alfred Walter Frank: Curate of St John the Baptist, Carrington, Nottingham, 1907, Vicar, 1909; Vicar of St Werburgh, Derby, 1927; Bishop of Bradford, 1931; retired 1955; d. 1957.

CHANDLER, Arthur: Fellow of Brasenose College, Oxford, 1883; Vicar of All Saints, Poplar, London, 1891; Bishop of Bloemfontein, 1902; Vicar of St Mary, Bentley, Hants, 1921; President of the Anglo-Catholic Congress, 1924–33; retired 1936; d. 1939.

CHILD, Maurice: Curate of St Andrew, Haverstock Hill, London, 1909; Curate of St James the Less, Plymouth, 1912; of Holy Trinity, Sloane Street, London 1914; of St Mary, Bourne Street, London 1917; Librarian of Pusey House, Oxford, 1922; General Secretary of the Anglo-Catholic Congress, 1925; Joint Secretary of the Church Union, 1934; Rector of St Dunstan, Cranford, Middlesex, 1935; d. 1950.

DUNCAN-JONES, Arthur Stuart: Curate of St Paul, Newington, 1904; Junior Dean of Gonville and Caius College, Cambridge, 1904; Dean, 1910; Rector of Blofield, Norfolk, 1912; Rector of Louth, Lincolnshire, 1915; Vicar of St Mary, Primrose Hill, London, 1916; St Paul, Knightsbridge, 1928; Dean of Chichester, 1929; d. 1955.

FRERE, Walter: Curate-in-charge, St Dunstans, Stepney 1887; Community of the Resurrection 1895; Superior 1902–13, 1916–22; Bishop of Truro 1922; retired 1935; d. 1938.

GORE, Charles: Fellow of Trinity College, Oxford, 1875; Principal of Pusey House, Oxford 1884; Vicar of Radley 1893; Canon of Westminster, London 1894; Bishop of Worcester 1902; Bishop of Birmingham 1905; Bishop of Oxford 1911; retired 1919; d. 1932.

HOOD, Archibald Frederick: Vice Principal of St Stephen's House, Oxford 1920; Librarian of Pusey House, 1922, Principal 1934; Vicar of St Mary Aldermary, London 1954; Canon of St Paul's Cathedral 1961; retired 1970; d. 1975.

HOSKYNS, Edwyn Clement: Curate of St Ignatius, Sunderland, 1908; Army Chaplain 1914; Fellow and Dean of the Chapel of Corpus Christi College, Cambridge 1919; d. 1937

JOHNSON, Vernon Cecil (Father Vernon SDC): Curate of St Martin, Brighton 1910; Society of the Divine Compassion 1913; became a Roman Catholic 1929; d. 1969.

KIRK, Kenneth Escott: Curate of Denaby Main, South Yorkshire 1912; Army Chaplain 1914; Tutor at Keble College, Oxford, 1919; Fellow of Trinity College, Oxford 1922; Chair of Pastoral and Moral Theology, Oxford 1933; Bishop of Oxford 1937; d. 1954.

LACEY, Thomas Alexandra: Curate of St Michael, Wakefield 1876; of St Benedict, Ardwick, Manchester 1879; Fellow of the College of St Mark and St John, Lichfield, 1876; Vicar of St Edmund, Northampton 1892; Vicar of Madingley, Cambridge 1894; Chaplain of the House of Mercy, Highgate, London 1903, Warden 1910; Canon of Worcester 1918; d. 1931.

MACKAY, Henry Falconer Barclay: Curate of All Saints, Margaret Street, London 1888; of All Saints, Clifton, Bristol 1891; Librarian of Pusey House 1895; Vicar of All Saints, Margaret Street 1908; Canon of Gloucester 1934; d. 1936.

MONTFORD, John Arthur Mannering: Curate of St John, Taunton 1896; Assistant Missioner in St Albans diocese 1902; Rector of St John, Loughton, Essex 1910; Vicar of the Ascension, Lavender Hill, London 1915; resigned because of ill-health 1923; licensed to officiate from 1923; d. 1956.

PINCHARD, Arnold Theophilus Biddulph: Curate of Holy Trinity, Bordesley, Birmingham 1885; of Dartford 1987; Vicar of Holy Trinity, Lomas de Zamora and Priest in charge of Christ Church, Barracas, Argentine 1889; Vicar St Jude, Birmingham 1896; Secretary of the English Church Union 1920; resigned 1933; d. 1934.

RAWLINSON, Alfred Edward John: Priest-in-Charge of St John, Wilton Road, London; Army Chaplain 1914; Tutor of Keble College, Oxford 1918; Student (Fellow) of Christ Church, Oxford 1922; Archdeacon of Auckland 1929; Bishop of Derby 1936; retired 1959; d. 1960.

ROSENTHAL, George David ('Rosie'): Curate of St Alban, Birmingham 1906; Curate-in-charge of St Gregory, Small Heath, Birmingham, 1913; Vicar of St Agatha, Sparkbrook, Birmingham, 1918; d. 1938.

RUSSELL, Cecil Edward: Curate of St Saviour, Ealing 1913; Vicar of St Catherine, Manston, Kent 1919; Secretary of the Fiery Cross Association and of the Anglo-Catholic Ordination Fund 1925; Organizing Secretary of the Anglo-

Catholic Centenary 1930; Assistant General Secretary of the Church Union 1934; Vicar of St Leonard, Flamstead, Hertfordshire 1937; d. 1959.

SLESSER, Henry Herman: Counsel to the Labour Party 1912; Barrister 1923; Attorney General 1924; MP Leeds South East 1924; Lord Justice in the Court of Appeal 1929; retired 1940; d. 1979.

STONE, Darwell: Curate of Ashbourne 1883; Vice Principal of Dorchester Missionary College 1885; Principal 1888; Principal of Pusey House, Oxford 1909; retired 1934; d. 1941.

UNDERHILL, Francis: Curate of St Paul, Swindon 1901; Curate of St Thomas the Martyr, Oxford 1903; Vicar of St Alban, Bordesley, Birmingham 1911; Vicar of St Mary Magdalene and St John, Cowley, Oxford 1923; Warden of Liddon Hall and Curate-in-Charge of the Grosvenor Chapel, London 1929; Dean of Rochester 1932; Bishop of Bath and Wells 1937; d. 1942.

WILLIAMS, Norman Powell: Chaplain and Fellow of Exeter College, Oxford 1909; Lady Margaret Professor of Divinity, and Canon of Christ Church, Oxford 1927; d. 1943.

WILSON, Herbert Arthur: Curate of St Mary, Ashford 1913; of St Matthew, Westminster, London 1915; Secretary of the Anglo-Catholic Congress 1919–1923; Vicar of St Augustine of Canterbury, Haggerston 1925; d. 1954.

Bibliography

The Papers of the English Church Union in the Lambeth Palace Library (C U Dep 1–99) include the minutes and documents of the Anglo-Catholic Congress and of other organizations linked to the movement.
Reports of the Anglo-Catholic Congress, SPCK 1920; Society of SS Peter and Paul, 1923, 1927, 1930, 1933.
Reports of the Anglo-Catholic Priests' Conventions, SSPP 1922 and 1931.
Prestige, L. (ed.), *The Congress Books*, 3 vols, SSPP 1923.

Abbot, E. et al., *Catholicity*, Dacre Press, 1947.
Anson, P. F., *Fashions in Church Furnishings 1840–1940*, Faith Press, 1960.

Barker, D., *G. K. Chesterton: A Biography*, Constable, 1973.
Barnes, J., *Ahead of His Age: Bishop Barnes of Birmingham*, Collins, 1979.
Barlow, B., 'A brother knocking at the door': The Malines Conversations 1921–1925, Canterbury Press, 1996.
Bell, G. K. A., *Randall Davidson: Archbishop of Canterbury*, Oxford University Press, 1935.
Bettenson, H., *Documents of the Christian Church*, Oxford University Press, 1946.
Bryant, C., *Possible Dreams: A Personal History of the British Christian Socialists*, Hodder & Stoughton, 1996.

Cammeron, A. T., *The Religious Communities of the Church of England*, Faith Press, 1918.
Carpenter, S. C., *Winnington-Ingram*, Hodder & Stoughton, 1949.
Cecil, Lord H. et al., *Anglo-Catholicism Today*, Philip Allen, 1934.
Chadwick, O., *Hensley Henson*, Canterbury Press, 1983.
Chadwick, O., *Michael Ramsey: A Life*, Clarendon Press, 1990.
Chesterton, G. K., *Autobiography*, Sheed & Ward, 1936.
Chesterton, G. K., *Catholic Church and Conversion*, Weidenfeld and Nicholson, 1986.
Church Guide for Tourists and Others, Mowbray, 1936.
Clarke, C. P. S., *The Oxford Movement and Afterwards*, Mowbray, 1932.
Clarke, C. P. S., *Bishop Chandler*, Oxford University Press, 1940.
Clutterbuck, I., *Marginal Catholics*, Gracewing, 1993.
Cross, F. L., *Darwell Stone*, Dacre Press, 1943.

Dark, S., *Archbishop Davidson and the English Church*, Philip Allen, 1929.
Dark, S., *Mackay of All Saints*, Centenary Press, 1937.
Dictionary of English Church History, Mowbray, 1948.
Donovan, M., *After the Tractarians*, Philip Allen, 1933.

Finch, M. F., *G. K. Chesterton: A Biography*, Macmillan, 1926 (Ignacius Press, 2006).

BIBLIOGRAPHY

Fitzgerald, P., *The Knox Brothers*, Coward, McCann & Geoghegan, New York, 1977.

Gray, D., *The 1927–28 Prayer Book Crisis*, 2 vols, The Alcuin Club and the Group for Renewal of Worship, 2005 and 2006.

Gunstone, J., 'Catholics in the Church of England' in Wilkinson (ed.), *Catholic Anglicans Today*, Darton, Longman & Todd, 1968.

Harrison, M. C., *The Centenary History of St Matthew's Church and Parish, Northamption*, Pentland Press, 1993.

Hastings, A., *A History of English Christianity 1920–2000*, SCM Press, 2001.

Headlam, A. C., *The Doctrine of the Church and Christian Reunion*, John Murray, 1920.

Henson, H., *Retrospect of an Unimportant Life*, Oxford University Press, 1943.

Herbert, A. G., Dix, G., et al., *Catholicity: A Study in the Conflict of Christian Traditions in the West*, Dacre Press, 1947.

Hewitt, G., *A History of the Diocese of Chelmsford*, Chelmsford Diocesan Board of Finance, 1984.

Higgs, O., et al., *In This Sign Conquer: A History of the Society of the Holy Cross 1855–2005*, Continuum, 2006.

Hole D., *The Church and the Stage: Early History of the Actors' Church Union*, Faith Press, 1934.

Hughes, Dom Anselm, *Rivers of the Flood*, Faith Press, 1961.

Ingram, K., *Basil Jellicoe*, Centenary Press, 1936.

Iremonger, F. A., *William Temple*, Oxford University Press, 1948.

Irvine, C., *Worship, Church and Society; Arthur Gabriel Hebert*, Canterbury Press, 1993.

Jagger, P. J., *Bishop Hendry de Candole: His Life and Times 1895–1971*, Faith Press, 1975.

Jasper, R. C. D., *Arthur Cayley Headlam*, Faith Press, 1960.

Jasper, R. C. D., *George Bell Bishop of Chichester*, Oxford University Press, 1967.

Jasper, R. C. D., *Development of Angelican Liturgy*, SPCK, 1989.

Johnson, V., *One Lord One Faith*, Sheed and Ward, 1929.

Kaye-Smith, S., *Anglo-Catholicism*, Chapman & Hall 1925.

Kaye-Smith, S., *Three Ways Home*, Cassell, 1937.

Kemp, E. W., *N. P. Williams*, SPCK, 1954.

Kemp, E. W., *Kenneth Escott Kirk*, Hodder & Stoughton, 1959.

Knox, E. A., *Reminiscenses of an Octogenarian*, Hutchingson & Co, 1918.

Knox, R. A., *A Spiritual Aeneid*, Burns Oates, 1918.

Knox, W. L., *The Catholic Movement in the Church of England*, Philip Allen, 1923.

Kojecky, R., *T. S. Eliot's Social Criticism*, Farrar, Straus & Giroux, 1972.

Lacey, T. A., *The Anglo-Catholic Faith*, Methuen, 1926.

Lean, L., *Good Manners in Church and Out: A Guide to Church Customs for the Laity*, Catholic Literature Society, 1932.

Leonard, E. M., *George Tyrell and the Catholic Tradition*, Darton Longman & Todd, 1982.
Lockhart, J. G., *Cosmo Gordon Lang*, Hodder & Stoughton, 1949.
Luff, A., *Strengthened for Service: 100 Years of the English Hymnal 1906–2006*, English Hymnal Company, 2005.

Mackenzie, K., *The Liturgy: Papers read at the Priests' Convention, Tewkesbury, May 1938*, SPCK, 1938.
Mascall, E., *Saraband*, Gracewing, 1992.
Mason, A., *SSM: History of the Society of the Sacred Mission*, Canterbury Press, 1993.
Mayard-Smith, H., *Frank Bishop of Zanzibar*, SPCK, 1926.
McCulloch, J., *We Have Our Orders*, Michael Joseph, 1943.
Merritt, E. D., *Catholic Representation in the House of Laity*, ECU, 1929.
Milner White, E., *One God and Father of All: A Reply to Father Vernon*, SPCK, 1927.
Morse-Boycott, D., *A Tapestry of Toil*, Faith Press, 1970.
Morse-Boycott, D., *Ten Years in a London Slum*, Skettington, 1929.

Nockles, P., *The Oxford Movement in Context*, Cambridge University Press, 1994.
Noel, Conrad, *Autobiography*, Dent, 1945.

Orford, A. and Davage, W. (eds), *Piety and Learning: The Principals of Pusey House 1884–2002*, Pusey House, 2002.

Palmer, B., *Gadfly for God: A History of the Church Times*, Hodder & Stoughton, 1991.
Peart Binns, J. S., *Blunt*, Mountain Press, 1969.
Penhale, F., *Catholics in Crisis*, Mowbray, 1986.
Pickering, W. S. F., *Anglo-Catholicism: A Study in Religious Ambiguity*, SPCK, 1991.
Prestige, G. L., *The Life of Charles Gore*, Heinemann, 1935.

Rawlinson, G. C., *An Anglo-Catholic's Thoughts on Religion*, Longmans Green, 1924.
Reckitt, M. B., *P. E. T. Widdrington*, SPCK, 1961.
Reckitt, M. B., *The Return of Christendom*, Allen & Unwin, 1922.
Reckitt, M. B., *As It Happened: An Autobiography*, Dent, 1941.
Rosenthal, G. D. and Belton, F. G., *The So-Called Rebels*, Mowbray, 1930.
Rowell, G., *The Vision Glorious*, Oxford University Press, 1983.
Rowell, G. (ed.), *Tradition Renewed: the Oxford Movement Conference Papers*, Darton Longman & Todd, 1986.
Russell, C. E., *Rosenthal*, Centenary Press, 1939.

Scott, C., *Dick Sheppard: A Biography*, Hodder & Stoughton, 1977.
Selwyn, E. G. (ed.), *Essays Catholic and Critical*, SPCK, 1926.
Selwyn, E. G. (ed.), *Reservation: Report of a Conference held at Farnham Castle on October 24-2 1925*, SPCK, 1926.

BIBLIOGRAPHY

Sheppard, H. R. L., *The Impatience of a Parson*, Hodder & Stoughton, 1928.
Simpson, W. J. S., *Christ and the Church*, SPCK, 1936.
Simpson, W. J. S., *The History of the Anglo-Catholic Revival from 1845*, Allen & Unwin, 1932.
Slater, T., *A Century of Celebrating Christ: The Diocese of Birmingham, 1905–2005*, Phillimore, 2005.
Smout, M., et al., *Four Bishops of Liverpool 1880–1965*, Liverpool Diocesan Centenary Committee, 1985.
Stone, D., *A History of the Doctrine of the Holy Eucharist*, (London) 1908.

Temple, W., *Thoughts on Some Problems of the Day*, Macmillan, 1931.

Vidler, A., *The Modernists Movement in the Roman Catholic Church*, Cambridge University Press, 1934.
Vidler, A., *Scenes from Clerical Life*, Collins, 1977.

Walke, B., *Twenty Years at St Hilary*, Methuen, 1935.
Waugh, E., *The Life of Ronald Knox*, Chapman & Hall, 1959.
Wilkinson, A., *The Church of England in the First World War*, SPCK, 1978.
Wilkinson, A., *Christian Socialism: Scott Holland to Tony Blair: The 1998 Scott Holland Lectures*, 1998, p. 93.
Wilkinson, A., *Dissent or Conform?* SCM Press, 1986.
Wilkinson, A., *The Community of the Resurrection*, SCM Press, 1992.
Williams, B., *The Franciscan Revival in the Anglican Communion*, Darton, Longman & Todd, 1982.
Williams, N. P. and Harris, C. (eds), *Northern Catholicism*, SPCK, 1933.
Wilson, H. A., *Received with Thanks*, Mowbray, 1940.
Woods, E. S. and MacNutt, F. B., *Theodore Bishop of Winchester*, SPCK, 1933.
Woods, T. (ed.) *Reservation Report of a Conference Held at Farnham Castle on October 24–27, 1925*, SPCK, 1926.

Yelton, M., *Anglican Papalism: An Illustrated History 1900–1960*, Canterbury Press, 2005.
Yelton, M., *Outposts of the Faith: Ten Anglo-Catholic Portraits*, Canterbury Press, 2009.
Yelton, M. and Salmon, J., *Angelican Church-Building in London*, Spire Books, 2007.

Anglo-Catholic History Society (ACHS) Publications

Beaken, R., *Their Proper Place: Archbishop Lang and Anglo-Catholicism 1928–1942*, 2008.
Farrer, M., *One Part of London: Aspects of Anglo-Catholicism in Camden*, 2009.
Gunstone, J., *Anglo-Catholic Congresses in the Provinces*, 2004.
Gunstone, J., *'Father Atlay's Congress': The Organisation of the First Anglo-Catholic Congress*, 2006.
Jones, T. E., *A Life Simply Offered: Father Wilson of Haggerston*, 2004.

Maiden, J., *Church and Party: Anglo-Catholicism and Prayer Book Revision 1927–1928*, 2006.
Pigott, A., *Donnish, Unrealistic, or even Insincere: Sir Will Spens and Liberal Anglo-Catholicism 1900–1940*, 2004.
Rowell, G., *Prejudices & Perspectives: Anglo-Catholic History Reconsidered*, 2000.
Webster, P., *Anglo-Catholic Theology and the Arts 1918–1970*, 2008.
Yelton, M., *The Twenty One: An Anglo-Catholic Rebellion in London 1929*, 2009.

Index of People

Armitage Robinson, J., 71, 73
Arnold, J.H., 279
Atlay, M., 2–10, 38, 40, 52, 53, 66, 86, 89, 107, 114, 117, 122, 141, 144, 147, 165, 300, 327, 344, 345

Bacon, P.G., 174
Baldwin, S., 19, 20, 23, 118, 225, 252
Barnes, E.W., 12, 30, 171, 203, 206–15, 262, 293, 309, 337
Baverstock, A.H., 103, 110, 147, 270, 278, 361
Beazley, R., 326, 327
Beevor, H., 259, 321
Bell, G.K.A., 60, 69, 115, 301, 304
Belloc, H., 217, 237, 249
Belton, F.G., 95, 158, 206, 207
Betjeman, J., 302, 347
Biggart, F., 142, 143, 263, 309, 332
Blunt, A.W.F., 36, 119, 225, 226, 227
Boggas, R.J.E., 80
Brancker, T., 274, 275
Briscoe, J.K., 97, 173, 174, 270, 277, 278, 310
Brockman, R.T., 117, 274
Browning, P.T., 113, 123
Buchan, J., 181, 183
Bull, H.P., 118, 122, 142, 217
Bulmer Thomas, I., 27
Burge, H.M., 86–90, 146, 269
Butler, B.E., 186, 233, 245–50

Candole, H. de, 311, 315
Chamberlain, N., 6, 19, 20, 229
Chandler, A., 55, 136, 137, 139, 162, 306, 310, 322
Cheetham, E.S., 267
Chesterton, G.K., 50, 217, 233, 236, 239, 240, 248, 249
Child, M., 162, 163, 165, 170, 195, 234, 296, 322, 343, 361
Churchill, W., 19, 20, 71
Clayton, G.H., 4, 47, 145, 191, 192
Clutterbuck, I., 292
Colville, C., 165, 229

Comper, N., 278, 295, 265
Cornibeer, A.E., 155
Crouch, W.J.B., 83

Dark, S., 54, 157, 208, 227
David, A.A., 274, 275
Davidson, R., 28, 29, 54–60, 65, 67, 70, 72, 74, 86, 175, 176, 182, 212, 225, 227
Deakin, C.R., 1, 123
Dearmer, P., 12, 127, 151, 179, 277, 296, 302, 303
Dix, G., 142, 344, 354
Dixon, W.D., 88, 89, 155
Donaldson, St Claire G.H., 135
Douglas, J.A., 156, 303
Duncan-Jones, A.S., 179
Dwelly, F.W., 179

Eeles, F.C., 206, 303
Eliot, T.S., 221, 301, 302, 333

Frere, W.H., 36, 48, 51, 69, 71, 80, 81, 130, 136, 137, 139, 142, 163, 176, 179–82, 185, 190, 202, 203, 212, 217, 254, 294, 300, 316, 330, 331
Furse, M.B., 10, 52, 57, 80, 86
Fynes-Clinton, H., 156, 157, 279

Garnier, M.C. Carpenter, 113, 118, 193, 201, 331
Gibbs-Smith, O.H., 295
Gillett, C.S., 87, 221, 263, 303
Gore, C., 14, 22, 30, 51, 66, 69, 71, 75, 76, 114, 115, 118, 120, 132, 149, 163, 179, 180, 200, 203, 204, 208, 216–20, 254, 261, 266, 327, 340
Goudge, H.L., 92, 93, 110, 113, 187, 203–5, 276, 341
Gurney, S., 162, 234, 296, 347

Halifax, Viscount (C.L. Wood), 4, 6, 22, 34, 56, 67, 71, 72, 74, 116, 130, 147, 148, 162, 265, 277, 279, 335, 340, 343

369

Hardy, K., 217
Hardy, E., 311, 319
Harris, C., 148, 149, 156, 180, 307
Headlam, A.C., 25, 46, 47, 57, 59, 60, 65, 151, 203, 209, 217, 254, 257, 262
Heald, G., 79
Hebert, A.G., 142, 295, 343
Henson, H.H., 24, 30, 56–60, 65, 70, 71, 86, 135, 151, 182, 212, 213, 220, 265, 266, 269
Hood, A.F., 259, 310
How, J.C.H., 41, 98, 99, 145
Howe, J., 136, 138, 139
Hudson, N.B., 258
Hugel, Baron F. von, 31, 186, 322
Huntington, J.O.S., 135, 136, 142
Hussey, J.R., 79, 275, 276

Inge, W.R., 6, 9, 123, 128, 312
Ingram, K., 164, 166, 167, 183, 217, 252, 307
Inskip, T., 32, 306

Jalland, T.G., 311, 316
Jellicoe, J.B.L., 229–31
Jenkinson, C., 230, 231
Johnson, V.C., 142, 233, 242–5
Joynson-Hicks, W., 32

Kaye-Smith, S., 98, 197, 233, 239–41, 302
Kelly, H.H., 142
Kensit, J., 252, 347
Kenyon, R., 119, 219, 221, 224, 264, 265
Kidd, B.J., 71, 87, 180, 182, 246
Kirk, K.E., 59, 95, 118, 131, 187, 198, 308, 310, 312, 314, 320, 328–30, 345
Knox, E.A., 65, 109, 132, 149, 177, 181, 235, 236, 346
Knox, R., 98, 162, 233–7, 242, 245, 246, 248, 249, 296, 338
Knox, W., 145, 146, 245, 254–6, 305

Lacey, T.A., 72, 98, 106, 125, 151, 152, 160, 179, 180
Lang, C.G., 28, 57, 59, 60, 65, 69, 182, 212–4, 252, 306, 322

Langford-Jones, R., 106, 107
Lean, L., 282–6
Leary, T.H., 1, 117, 151, 272, 273
Lee, J., 132, 133
Lewis, C.S., 302, 335
Lockhart, J.G., 327
Long, C.N., 89, 97, 100, 211, 212, 215
Lowther Clarke, W., 162, 307

MacDonald, Ramsey, 19, 20, 23, 207, 328
Mackay, H.F.B., 1, 2, 18, 40, 53, 89, 101, 125, 131, 171, 193, 201, 225, 244, 255, 272, 310, 316–18
Mackenzie, K.D., 331
Major, H., 25, 30
McCulloch, J., 291, 292
Mercier, D.J., 71, 72
Merritt, E.D., 83, 84
Milner, W.F., 279
Milner-White, E.M., 45, 46, 145, 245, 324
Montford, J.A., 4, 9, 105, 106, 122
Morse Boycott, D., 27, 158, 229
Moss, C.B., 156, 157
Moulsdale, S.R.P., 100, 118
Mozley, J.K., 113, 131, 146, 305

Nickson, G., 67, 68, 118
Noel, C., 217, 218, 279

Oliver, C., 6, 165

Paget, H.L., 109, 110, 112
Patten, H., 119, 279, 299
Peck, W.G., 222, 254, 255
Phillips, L.A., 94, 110
Pinchard, A.T.B., 4, 44, 45, 81–3, 148, 150, 163, 211, 275, 299, 306, 327, 343
Portal, J.B., 71
Priestley, J.B., 16

Ramsey, A.M., 221, 262, 345
Rawlinson, A.E.J., 115, 146, 187, 188, 190, 198, 234, 294, 302, 305, 346
Rawlinson, G.G., 102, 103, 113

INDEX

Ridgeway, F.E., 10, 57, 86, 134
Riley, A., 75, 80, 156, 157
Rogers, C.F., 95, 96, 101, 105
Rogers, G., 340
Rosenthal, G.D., 120, 194, 206–11, 215, 219, 254, 256, 257, 263, 264, 309, 319, 325, 333–5
Royden, M., 17, 76, 98
Russell, C.E., 162, 215, 309, 322

Sayers, D.L., 17, 221, 301, 302
Selwyn, E.G., 131, 145, 146, 187, 203, 205, 257, 305
Seymour, V., 24, 153, 155, 202
Shaw, G.S., 174
Shaw, M., 297, 319
Shedden, R., 38, 42, 66, 185
Sheppard, H.R.L. (Dick), 18, 75, 79, 179, 292, 323
Simpson, W.J. Sparrow, 93, 146, 193, 287
Slesser, H.H., 19, 116, 118, 133, 181, 194, 218, 233, 247, 249, 333, 343
Spens, W., 146, 205, 305
Stockley, J.J.G., 104, 105, 116
Stone, D., 4, 5, 7, 8, 34, 45, 49, 66, 146, 148, 155, 177, 179, 181, 185, 187, 200, 202, 203, 205
Studdert-Kennedy, G.A., 133, 134, 225

Talbot, E.K., 51, 145, 335, 340
Talbot, E.S., 57, 137, 306
Taylor, A.E., 39–43, 49, 56, 146, 187, 305
Temple, W., 25, 28, 75, 79, 109, 111, 115, 135, 146, 151, 179, 182, 203, 216, 219–21, 224, 252, 254, 269, 270, 305, 306, 322, 339
Thorndike, S., 299, 300

Thornton, L.S., 42, 43, 56, 142, 146, 195, 221, 255, 259, 260, 305, 346
Tomkinson, C.E., 311, 326
Travers, M., 125, 296, 339, 348
Turner, C.H., 39, 56
Tyrrell, G., 31, 341

Underhill, E., 98, 104, 173, 186
Underhill, F., 4, 48, 49, 67, 76–8, 86–8, 104, 110, 155, 164, 214, 219, 308, 313

Vidler, A., 31, 213
Vyvyan, W.L., 39

Waggett, P.N., 142
Walke, B., 279, 300
Watts Ditchfield, J.E., 24, 32, 57, 86, 129, 293
Weston, F., 3, 11, 19, 22, 30, 38–40, 44, 53–71, 120, 123, 129–31, 134, 136, 139, 143, 147, 150, 158, 161, 186, 291
Widdrington, P., 118, 217–21, 279, 301, 346
Williams, C., 302
Williams, N.P., 56, 66, 77–9, 91, 92, 105, 149, 162, 177, 186, 198, 287, 307, 310, 311, 333–5, 346
Williams, V., 297
Wilson, H.A., 3–6, 8, 10, 15, 22, 50, 53, 86, 87, 98, 104, 107, 108, 122–4, 126, 158, 161, 165, 252, 289, 300, 316
Winnington-Ingram, A., 2, 51, 57, 129, 139, 151, 200, 214, 252, 269, 293, 308
Woods, F.T., 57, 65, 67, 69, 86, 120, 179, 203, 206, 276

Outposts of the faith
Anglo-Catholicism in some rural parishes
Michael Yelton

| 978 1 85311 985 9 | 234 x 156mm | 256pp | £22.99 |

The Anglo-Catholic movement which flourished in the early and mid twentieth century is famed for its dedicated and heroic work in inner-city slum areas, yet little is recorded about its impact in rural areas, nor have the stories of its more flamboyant rural priests been told.

Outposts of the Faith tells the entertaining stories of ten parishes where the Anglo-Catholic movement made a particular impact, or took a significant turn that affected the wider church and the subsequent direction of the movement.

Included are the stories of a number of well known names – Athelstan Riley, Samuel Gurney, Maurice Child and Clive Beresford among others, about whom very little has previously been written.

Available from all good bookshops
or direct from Canterbury Press
Tel: + 44 (0)1603 612914   www.canterburypress.co.uk

The Labour of Obedience
The Benedictines of Pershore, Nashdom and Elmore - A history
Petà Dunstan

978 1 85311 974 3   234 x 156mm   288pp   £21.99

This important study of key Anglican Benedictine communities in the first half of the 20th century provides a vital record of how the Anglican Communion dealt with an issue that was as divisive then as today's disputes over sexuality and women bishops.

It was the heyday of Anglo-Catholicism in the Church of England. Religious life was flourishing for the first time since the Reformation. The first shock came when the Abbot of Caldey, a flamboyant character noted for luxurious tastes, and his monks went over to Rome.

Nashdom - the great Benedictine community to which Gregory Dix belonged and, in many ways, the ultimate expression of Anglo-Catholicism -   threatened to do likewise over the crisis of the Church of South India where the very idea of priestly ordination and identity was being challenged. Thanks to Archbishop William Temple the crisis was averted, the monks of Nashdom stayed and the scene was set for Anglican Papalism to enter the stage.

Available from all good bookshops
or direct from Canterbury Press
Tel: + 44 (0)1603 612914   www.canterburypress.co.uk

Heaven and Earth in Little Space
The re-enchantment of liturgy
Andrew Burnham

978 1 84825 005 5   216 x 135mm   224pp   £16.99

This timely and significant book asks whether the widespread falling away of the appeal of religious worship is connected with the simplification of liturgical practice over recent decades. Has a well-meant policy of making the language and style of worship more accessible resulted in a loss of the sense of mystery - and has this accelerated the decline?

The author, who was involved with the development of Common Worship, explores the wider Catholic and Orthodox traditions where nothing like the reforms that have happened within Anglicanism have taken place.

Five centuries of change in the Anglican tradition are surveyed, the altered rhythm of the liturgical year, the decline in singing, the rise of the modern worship song – and much more in an attempt to define what renewal of the liturgy for today's church might look like and how re-enchantment would work in practice.

Available from all good bookshops
or direct from Canterbury Press
Tel: + 44 (0)1603 612914   www.canterburypress.co.uk

www.ingramcontent.com/pod-product-compliance
Lightning Source LLC
Chambersburg PA
CBHW071330080526
44587CB00017B/2782